CW01085973

The Lancashire and Yorkshire Railway; Being a Full Account of the Rise and Progress of This Railway, Together With Numerous Interesting Reminiscences and Incidents on the Line

THIS BOOK

OF OBSERVATIONS AND RECOLLECTIONS DURING

MY RAILWAY CAREER IS

Dedicated to my dear Wife,

WHO,

BY HER ZEAL AND INDOMITABLE ENERGY,

HAS ADDED ANOTHER JOY TO MY LIFE

BY WRITING THIS BOOK AT THE DICTATION OF

THE AUTHOR

PREFACE.

AFTER serving the Lancashire and Yorkshire Railway Company for close upon forty-nine years, I retired from their service at the end of June, 1895 The Company not complying with my moderate conditions, though they had done so in the cases of other officers who had retired before me, I have, in order to maintain and uphold the position I have so long held with the public and the Company, determined to write this book concerning my observations and recollections, with incidents connected with the Company, during my services, confining them principally to the Yorkshire Division, from January, 1847, to the end of June, 1895, and commencing with an abridged history of my early life.

It contains facts and incidents which have occurred on the railway under my immediate observation, and also deals with the policy of managing and working railways to the best advantage of the proprietors and of the public.

ERRATA

Page 44, line 5, for ' December," read "August."

Page 46, line 5, for "November, 1850," read "February 5th, 1852",
line 27, for "folk," read "people'

Page 49, line 6. for "1850," read ' 1849 "

Page 58, line 4, for "Leeds to Low Moor," read "Leeds to Wakefield"
line 5, for "to Leeds   The Lancashire," read "when the Lancashire'
line 12, for "September," read "August, 1854 "

Page 60, line 1, for "June 13," read "June 17."

Page 65, line 10, for "January, 1859,' read " April, 1863 "

LANCASHIRE AND YORKSHIRE RAILWAY.

I WAS born on March 5th, 1824, in the parish of Dewsbury, Yorkshire, where schools were few and far between.
I can just remember the first school I went to, which was
a dame's school in the village. I soon became too much
for the old lady, who often tied one end of a cord round
one of my legs and the other end to the stair foot. I
heard her say to my mother one day, when she happened
to see me in that position, that it was the only way by
which she could keep me under control

My father's means being too small to allow him to send
me to what was called a boarding school, I became, in
1831, one of the first scholars at the National Schools,
Dewsbury, and paid one penny per week. I had to walk
to school five days a week, carrying my dinner in a basket,
a distance of four miles to and from my home, in all sorts
of weather. The schoolmaster's name was Joseph Peace,
and the boys thought him a most cruel master. However,
we served him well out occasionally.

I was about nine years of age when I left school, and
was put to work to learn the fine woollen cloth finishing
business. I had to work from six o'clock in the morning
to seven o'clock at night, except Saturdays, when I ceased
work at five o'clock, and was paid two and sixpence per
week. As I grew older I gradually earned more money,

and then my dear old mother gave me a few coppers
a week for spending money Boy-like, I went in for
keeping rabbits and all kinds of birds, poultry, &c.
This amusement I soon tired of, sold off my stock,
and invested my money in a lot of pigeons I made
a cote for them on the house top. After keeping them
in a few weeks, some of my boy companions came to
see me let them out for the first time. I opened the door,
and out they came upon the roof of the building, gave a
good look round, and away they flew, and never returned.
This proved a worse business than the first, as all my
money had flown away. After a while I got a dog, made
up my mind to be a sportsman, and commenced saving
my money to buy a gun. Eventually I heard of one for
sale, and went to look at it. I found it was an old flint-
lock gun, with a barrel forty inches long, and the price
was fifteen shillings. Not being possessed of so much, I
looked out for a partner, and got one, and together we
bought it. The gun being joint property, we arranged
to have it on alternate weeks. This arrangement often
proved very inconvenient to me, so I continued saving up
my money, and at last bought him out. I then had the
gun altered. About ten inches were cut off the end of
the barrel, and it was re-constructed into what was called
a cap gun I thought then I was making my way towards
being a sportsman. When I was approaching my
eighteenth birthday, I had a tendency for athletics, and
became a prominent member of clubs—such as cricket,
football, knur and spell, foot-racing, hurdle jumping, and
other sports. During the winter evenings I attended a
night school, and improved my education. In 1842 the
Mechanics' Institution was reinstated at Dewsbury. I
was one of the committee, and we rented a room in the
Old Cloth Hall, situated on Batley Carr Road. Afterwards we removed to the schoolroom in connection with

the New Connexion Chapel, situated in Batley Road. I attended two or three times a week, up to the time of my obtaining an appointment on the Lancashire and Yorkshire Railway, in the latter part of the year 1846.

I remember going to Manchester to see my grandfather in 1845. I left Thornhill Station, which at that time was the only railway station for Dewsbury. I travelled in a passenger wagon train in a stand-up carriage. This carriage was simply a square wood box or wagon, without seats or roof, exposed to all sorts of weather, and the passengers all wedged in, like cattle in a truck. Of course, going to see my grandfather, I must go in my Sunday clothes, and had on a new top hat. To my surprise and sorrow, on emerging out of Summit Tunnel, I found my new hat entirely spoilt, the down being frizzled up by the small hot cinders emitted from the funnel of the engine. I arrived at Manchester about noon, immediately made my way to my grandfather's, and gave a loud rap at the door, which was opened by a girl, who showed me into a side room. My grandfather soon made his appearance, expressed his surprise at seeing me there, and said, "Tom, my boy, whatever has brought you here, without writing to tell us you were coming?" After a little conversation, I told him I had come to have my head shaved and to buy a wig. He then burst out in loud laughter, which had the effect of bringing my grandmother into the room, who also had a good laugh, and said she thought I was going to do a very foolish thing, in spite of my explanation that I was under the impression I should benefit by it. My grandfather took me to a place next day, where I had my head shaved and got a wig, which cost me £3 10s. On the day I returned home he called me into his room to have a quiet talk together, and gave me some very good advice. In one of his remarks he said, "If ever you become fortunate in business, and desire to possess property, never build, but buy"

On my return home I again travelled by train in a stand-up box from Manchester to Thornhill, in a downpour of rain the whole of the journey. This and the previous fizzle completely put an end to my brand new hat In those days people were not so well educated in extortionate habits, otherwise a claim would have been made for a new hat upon the railway company. Since then the railway companies have progressed marvellously in providing comfort and facilities for the travelling public, particularly in third-class accommodation. When the line was first opened the third class were called wagon passengers, and porters were not allowed to assist them in any way with their luggage. If they were not at the booking-office window ten minutes before the train was due, the clerk had instructions not to book them. The only accommodation provided as a carriage was a simple square wood deep-sided box wagon, with a door in the centre. Passengers had to stand, jammed together like so many cattle The guard travelled in this box, with the brake fixed in one corner. Afterwards an Act of Parliament compelled railway companies to run certain trains each day, at 1d. per mile. These were called "Parliamentary" trains, and left Manchester for Leeds at 7 a m, 1-10 and 6-30 p m ; and Leeds to Manchester at 7-40 a m, 1-20 and 5-45 p m The guard's van was attached in the rear In those days the permanent-way iron rails were pegged on to huge blocks of stone, 3 ft. to 4 ft square Imagine the noise and oscillation when trains passed over them.

The first improvement made for this class of passengers was by fixing plain wooden seats in the box wagon to sit upon. Some time after this a top was put on the wagon,

Type of First Third-class Railway Carriage (1841).

but the sides were still left open. Again, after a while the open sides were made up with wooden slides for windows, and the woodwork was painted dark brown, which made it look something like a carriage. The public gave them the name of "Daw Green Reds." These were soon superseded by an entirely new make of carriage, consisting of four seated compartments, fitted up with glass windows and roof lights in the carriage top; and eventually they had further concessions given to them; in the winter months they had hot-water tins supplied in the compartments, and additional third-class trains were run daily for their convenience. The Company had discovered that third-class travelling was remunerative, and with the view of cultivating this traffic they provided still more comfortable accommodation by upholstering the backs and seats of each compartment, and booked third class by all trains. They then built third-class saloon carriages, beautifully fitted up with settees and tables. Some of the railway companies even went so far as to build third-class dining cars, most elaborately fitted with all necessary conveniences.

In 1845 the fine woollen cloth trade declined. Trade generally was at a very low ebb, and I determined to try some other business. In December, 1846, I made application for a position on the railway to Mr. George Anderton, of Cleckheaton, who was then a director on the Manchester and Leeds Railway, now called the Lancashire and Yorkshire Railway. I succeeded in getting an appointment, and commenced my railway career in January, 1847, at Brighouse Station, under Mr. William Cawkwell, who was then station master. He afterwards rose to the high position of general manager for the London and North-Western Railway Company, and became their managing director. After my appointment, I gave up the gun, but kept the dog, and made up my mind to devote the whole of my time to railway work on the Manchester and Leeds Railway.

Before entering upon the subject more immediately in view, it may not be out of place to insert a copy of the first time table of the Manchester and Leeds Railway, issued in March, 1841.

TIMES OF THE DOWN TRAINS STARTING.

DISTANCES FROM MANCHESTER.	MANCHESTER TO LEEDS. The Trains depart from	1st. Sowerby Bridge to Leeds, meeting trains for Sheffield, Derby, Birmingham, London, York, Selby, and Hull.	2nd. Man. to Leeds, meeting trains for Sheffield, Chesterfield, Derby, Birmingham, Nottingham, Leicester, London, York, Selby, Hull, and Darlington.	3rd. Manchester to Leeds.
Miles		h. m.	h. m.	h. m.
	MANCHESTER, at	....	7 0 m.	9 0 m.
5½	MILLS HILL, for Oldham......	....	7 20 m.	9 20 m.
7¾	*Blue Pitts*, for Heywood, &c.	....	7 30 m.	....
10½	ROCHDALE	....	7 37 m.	9 34 m.
13¼	*Littleborough*.................	....	7 45 m.	....
19¼	TODMORDEN, for Burnley......	....	8 0 m.	9 54 m.
21	*Eastwood*	....	8 4 m.	....
23½	*Hebden Bridge*	....	8 16 m.	....
26	*Luddenden Foot*	....	8 22 m.	....
28	SOWERBY BR., for Halifax	6 20 m.	8 30 m.	10 20 m.
31	*Elland*	6 26 m.	8 39 m.	....
34	BRIGHOUSE, for Bradford......	6 36 m.	8 48 m.	10 36 m.
36	COOPER B., for Huddersfield..	6 44 m.	8 54 m.	10 45 m.
40½	*Dewsbury*	7 0 m.	9 4 m.	....
43½	*Horbury*	7 8 m.	9 12 m.	....
47½	WAKEFIELD	7 18 m.	9 22 m.	11 8 m.
50½	NORMANTON	7 30 m.	9 39 m.	11 25 m.
60	LEEDS, arrivals in	7 55 m.	10 0 m.	11 45 m. ..

FARES : First Class Passengers, 3d. per mile ; Second Class, 2d. per mile. Ch
Infants in arms not charged.

Gentlemen's Carriage, with 4 wheels, 6d. per mile : and parties riding in their ow
larger number of Horses, if one property, 3d. per mile each. Any distance under 6 :

Passengers, &c.

LONDON, 1st Class, 6s. by day, and 7s. by night, less ; 2nd Class, 5s. by day, 6s.
and are protected from the Weather.

		£ s. d.		£ s.
DERBY	First Class Fare	1 2 0	Second Class	0 16
YORK		1 0 0		0 13
SELBY		0 18 0		0 12

Gentlemen's Carriages to London, by 7h. 0m. Morning Train, £5 5 0. Horses
Morning and 9h. 0m. Evening Trains, by way of Derby to Manchester, or to any Sta
Particular Trains are met by Stage Coaches and Omnibuses, at certain Station
Down Trains on Sundays. Furbisher's at Oldham for Mills Hill meet the first and t
Wednesdays, Thursdays, Fridays, and Saturdays, the 7th only. Chaffer's at Burnle:
1st only. Ellison's at Hebden Bridge for Keighley and Skipton meets the 7th Dow:
Mallinson & Co.'s at Brighouse for Bradford meet the 2nd, 3rd, 5th, 6th, and 7th, W<
and 1st and 3rd, Sundays, Up Trains. Elam's at Cooper Bridge for Huddersfield m<
Class and Inside, 17s. ; and Second Class and Outside, 10s. 6d.), Bawtry (at 19s. 6d.
every Week-day, except on Saturdays, when it departs from Wakefield at half-past :

TIMES OF THE DOWN TRAINS STARTING.

DISTANCES FROM MANCHESTER.	MANCHESTER TO LEEDS. The Trains depart from	WEEK DAYS. 1st. Sowerby Bridge to Leeds, meeting trains for Sheffield, Derby, Birmingham, London, York, Selby, and Hull.	2nd. Man. to Leeds, meeting trains for Sheffield, Chesterfield, Derby, Birmingham, Nottingham, Leicester, London, York, Selby, Hull, and Darlington.	3rd. Manchester to Leeds.	4th. Manchester to Leeds, meeting trains for Sheffield, Derby, Birmingham, Nottingham, Leicester, London, York, Hull, and Darlington.	5th. **Mail.** Manchester to Leeds, meeting trains for York, Selby, Hull, Darlington, and Newcastle.	6th. Manchester to Leeds, meeting trains for Sheffield, Chesterfield, Leicester, Nottingham, Derby, York, Hull, Darlington, and Newcastle.	7th. Manchester to Leeds, meeting trains for Sheffield, Derby, Birmingham, Nottingham, Leicester, London, York, Selby, Hull, and Darlington.	8th. Manchester to Leeds.	9th. **Mail.** Manchester to Normanton.	SUNDAYS. 1st. Manchester to Leeds.	2nd. **Mail.** Man. to Leeds, meeting trains for Sheffield, Chesterfield, Derby, Birmingham, Nottingham, Leicester, York, Hull, and Edinburgh.	3rd. Manchester to Leeds.	4th. **Mail.** Manchester to Normanton, for York, Darlington, and Edinburgh.
Miles		h. m.	h. m.	h. m.	h. m.	h. m.	h. m.	h. m.	h. m.	h. m.	h. m.	h. m.	h. m.	h. m.
	MANCHESTER, at	......	7 0 m.	9 0 m.	10 30 m.	11 30 m.	1 10 e.	4 45 e.	6 30 e.	10 0 e.	8 0 m.	11 30 m.	6 30 e.	10 0 e.
5¼	MILLS HILL, for Oldham	......	7 20 m.	9 20 m.	10 56 m.	11 50 m.	1 36 e.	5 5 e.	6 56 e.	10 20 e.	8 26 m.	11 50 m.	6 56 e.	10 20 e.
7¾	*Blue Pitts*, for Heywood, &c.	......	7 30 m.	......	11 5 m.	......	1 48 e.	......	7 8 e.	......	8 38 m.	......	7 8 e.	......
10½	ROCHDALE	......	7 37 m.	9 34 m.	11 18 m.	12 4 e.	1 58 e.	5 19 e.	7 18 e.	10 34 e.	8 48 m.	12 4 e.	7 18 e.	10 34 e.
13½	*Littleborough*	......	7 45 m.	......	11 26 m.	......	2 6 e.	......	7 26 e.	......	8 56 m.	......	7 26 e.	......
19¼	TODMORDEN, for Burnley	......	8 0 m.	9 54 m.	11 42 m.	12 24 e.	2 22 e.	5 39 e.	7 43 e.	10 54 e.	9 13 m.	12 24 e.	7 43 e.	10 54 e.
21	*Eastwood*	......	8 4 m.	......	11 46 m.	......	2 25 e.	......	7 47 e.	......	9 17 m.	......	7 47 e.	......
23½	*Hebden Bridge*	......	8 10 m.	......	11 58 m.	......	2 38 e.	5 52 e.	8 3 e.	......	9 33 m.	......	8 3 e.	......
26	*Luddenden Foot*	......	8 22 m.	......	12 4 e.	......	2 44 e.	......	8 9 e.	......	9 39 m.	......	8 9 e.	......
28	SOWERBY BR., for Halifax	6 20 m.	8 30 m.	10 20 m.	12 12 e.	12 50 e.	2 52 e.	6 5 e.	8 17 e.	11 20 e.	9 47 m.	12 50 e.	8 17 e.	11 20 e.
31	*Elland*	6 26 m.	8 39 m.	......	12 21 e.	......	3 1 e.	......	8 27 e.	......	9 57 m.	......	8 27 e.	......
34	BRIGHOUSE, for Bradford	6 38 m.	8 48 m.	10 28 m.	12 29 e.	1 6 e.	3 9 e.	6 21 e.	8 35 e.	11 36 e.	10 5 m.	1 6 e.	8 35 e.	11 36 e.
36	COOPER B., for Huddersfield	6 44 m.	8 54 m.	10 45 m.	12 37 e.	1 15 e.	3 17 e.	6 30 e.	8 43 e.	11 45 e.	10 13 m.	1 15 e.	8 43 e.	11 45 e.
40½	*Dewsbury*	7 0 m.	9 4 m.	......	12 47 e.	......	3 27 e.	6 40 e.	8 55 e.	......	10 25 m.	......	8 55 e.	......
43½	*Horbury*	7 8 m.	9 12 m.	......	12 57 e.	......	3 37 e.	......	9 6 e.	......	10 36 m.	......	9 6 e.	......
47¾	WAKEFIELD	7 18 m.	9 22 m.	11 8 m.	1 9 e.	1 38 e.	3 49 e.	6 53 e.	9 20 e.	12 8 e.	10 50 m.	1 38 e.	9 20 e.	12 8 e.
50¾	NORMANTON	7 30 m.	9 39 m.	11 25 m.	1 24 e.	1 55 e.	4 5 e.	7 10 e.	9 38 e.	12 25 e.	11 8 m.	1 55 e.	9 38 e.	12 25 e.
60	LEEDS, arrivals in	7 56 m.	10 0 m.	11 45 m.	1 45 e.	2 15 e.	4 25 e.	7 30 e.	10 0 e.	......	11 30 m.	2 15 e.	10 0 e.	......

FARES: First Class Passengers, 3d. per mile; Second Class, 2d. per mile. Children under 7 years of age, in First Class Carriage, charged Second Class Fare; and in Second Class, Waggon Fare; and in Waggon, without any deduction. Infants in arms not charged.

Gentlemen's Carriage, with 4 wheels, 6d. per mile; and parties riding in their own Carriage, 2d. per mile each; Servants riding outside, and Children, Waggon Fare. A single Horse, two-wheel Carriage, or Pony Phaeton, 4½d. per mile. Any larger number of Horses, if one property, 3d. per mile each. Any distance under 6 miles, charged as 6 miles, in all cases. The Manchester 7h. 0m. Morning Train is the only one by which Passengers can go through to London in Waggons.

Passengers, &c., may be booked through at the Manchester Station to the following places:—

LONDON. 1st Class, 6s. by day, and 7s. by night, less; 2nd Class, 5s. by day, 6s. by night, less; and 3rd Class 4s. less than by any other route. The 2nd Class are sent by Special Trains, and are less time on the road than by any other route; and are protected from the Weather.

		£ s. d.		£ s. d.		£ s. d.
DERBY	First Class Fare	1 3 0	Second Class	0 16 0	Third Class	0 9 0
YORK		1 0 0		0 13 0		0 9 6
SELBY		0 15 0		0 12 0		0 8 6
SHEFFIELD	First Class Fare	0 12 0	Second Class	0 7 9	Third Class	0 5 0
HULL		1 3 0		0 15 6		0 11 0

Passengers may be also booked through from every STATION.

Gentlemen's Carriages to London, by 7h. 0m. Morning Train, £5 5 0. Horses are sent to London by the 7h. 0m. Train at considerably less than by any other route. Passengers wishing to come from London by the 6h. 0m., 9h. 15m. Morning and 9h. 0m. Evening Trains, by way of Derby to Manchester, or to any Station on the Manchester and Leeds Railway, must book for Rugby.

Particular Trains are met by Stage Coaches and Omnibuses, at certain Stations along the line, as follows:—Furbisher's at Mills Hill for Oldham meets the 3rd, 4th, 6th, 7th, and 8th Down Trains on Week-days; and the 1st, 2nd, and 3rd Down Trains on Sundays. Furbisher's at Oldham for Mills Hill meet the first and the extra Rochdale Train only. Chaffer's at Todmorden for Burnley, &c., meets the 6th and 7th Down Trains on Mondays; the 7th and 8th on Tuesdays; and on Wednesdays, Thursdays, Fridays, and Saturdays, the 7th only. Chaffer's at Burnley, &c., for Todmorden meets the 2nd and 5th Up Trains on Mondays; the 1st and 2nd on Wednesdays; and on Tuesdays, Thursdays, Fridays, and Saturdays, the 1st only. Ellison's at Hebden Bridge for Keighley and Skipton meets the 7th Down Train on Tuesdays and Saturdays. Ellison's at Keighley, &c., for Hebden Bridge meets the 2nd Up Train on Tuesdays and Saturdays. Bradford and Co.'s and Mallinson & Co.'s at Brighouse for Bradford meet the 2nd, 3rd, 5th, 6th, and 7th, Week-days; and 1st and 3rd, Sundays, Down Trains. Bradford & Co.'s and Mallinson & Co.'s at Bradford to Brighouse meet the 2nd, 3rd, 6th, and 7th, Week-days; and 1st and 3rd, Sundays, Up Trains. Elam's at Cooper Bridge for Huddersfield meets every Down Train; and those from Huddersfield to Cooper Bridge meets every Up Train. The Express Coach at Wakefield Station for Doncaster (for First Class and Inside, 17s.; and Second Class and Outside, 10s. 6d.), Bawtry (at 19s. 6d. and 12s.), Gainsborough (at 22s. and 15s. 6d.), and Lincoln (at 27s. and 16s. 6d.), meets the 1st and 2nd Down Trains, and departs on the arrival of the 2nd Train every Week-day, except on Saturdays, when it departs from Wakefield at half-past 7 o'clock, A.M.

TIMES OF THE UP TRAINS STARTING, OR TRAINS FROM LEEDS TO MANCHESTER, &c.

		WEEK DAYS.										SUNDAYS.			
LEEDS to MANCHESTER The Trains depart from	1st.	2nd.	3rd.	4th. Mail	5th.	6th.	7th.	8th. Mail	9th. Mail	1st.	2nd. Mail	3rd.	4th. Mail
LEEDS, at		h. m.	h. m.	h. m.	h. m.	h. m.	h. m.	h. m.	h. m.	h. m.	h. m.	h. m.	h. m.	h. m.
NORMANTON	8 0 m.	7 40 m.	8 40 m.	10 16 m.	1 20 e.	3 0 e.	4 3 e.	5 45 a.	7 15 e.	8 0 m.	9 0 m.	10 16 m.	6 0 e.	7 13 e.
WAKEFIELD	8 0 m.	8 0 m.	9 5 m.	10 41 m.	1 40 e.	3 20 e.	4 15 e.	4 5 e.	7 40 e.	8 25 m.	10 41 m.	6 29 e.	7 40 e.
HORBURY	6 9 m.	8 16 m.	9 23 m.	10 50 m.	1 56 e.	3 36 e.	4 45 e.	6 17 e.	7 55 e.	8 34 m.	10 52 m.	6 44 e.	7 55 e.
DEWSBURY	6 16 m.	8 20 m.			2 10 e.	3 50 e.		6 23 e.		8 39 m.		6 59 e.	
COOPER B., for Huddersfield	6 27 m.	8 42 m.			2 22 e.	4 2 e.		4 33 e.		8 11 m.		7 11 e.	
Batley, for Bradford	6 42 m.	8 26 m.	9 44 m.	11 18 m.	2 30 e.	4 16 e.	3 5 e.	6 51 e.	8 18 e.	9 26 m.	11 19 m.	7 26 e.	9 38 e.
ELLAND	6 54 m.	9 8 m.	9 55 m.	11 31 m.	2 48 e.	4 38 e.	5 15 e.	7 1 e.	8 30 e.	9 56 m.	11 31 m.	7 38 e.	9 39 e.
SOWERBY Br., for Halifax	7 3 m.	9 17 m.			2 57 e.	4 47 e.		7 8 e.		9 47 m.		7 47 e.	
LUDDENDEN FOOT	7 18 m.	9 27 m.	10 4 m.	11 46 m.	3 7 e.	4 57 e.	5 39 e.	7 17 e.	8 45 e.	9 57 m.	11 46 m.	7 57 e.	9 45 e.
HEBDEN BRIDGE	7 20 m.	9 34 m.			3 14 e.	4 54 e.				10 4 m.		8 4 e.	
EASTWOOD	7 36 m.	9 42 m.			3 22 e.	5 2 e.		7 23 e.		10 12 m.		8 12 e.	
TODMORDEN, for Burnley	7 42 m.	9 56 m.			3 36 e.	5 19 e.				10 26 m.		8 23 e.	
LITTLEBOROUGH	7 47 m.	10 2 m.	10 34 m.	12 16 e.	3 42 e.	5 32 e.	6 0 e.	7 47 e.	9 15 e.	10 32 m.	12 16 e.	8 32 e.	9 15 e.
ROCHDALE	8 2 m.	10 18 m.			3 56 e.	5 58 e.				10 48 m.		8 48 e.	
BLUE PITS, for Heywood	8 11 m.	10 28 m.	11 6 m.	12 38 e.	4 8 e.	6 19 e.	6 22 e.	8 4 e.	9 37 e.	10 58 m.	12 38 e.	8 58 e.	9 37 e.
MILES PLATTING, for Oldham	8 18 m.	10 36 m.			4 16 e.	6 50 e.				11 6 m.		9 4 e.	
MILES HILL, for Oldham	8 27 m.	10 46 m.	11 12 m.	12 50 e.	4 29 e.	6 6 e.	6 54 e.	8 32 e.	9 49 e.	11 16 m.	12 50 e.	9 13 e.	9 49 e.
MANCHESTER, arrival in	8 40 m.	11 0 m.	11 25 m.	1 1 e.	4 40 e.	6 29 e.	6 48 e.	8 36 e.	10 0 e.	11 30 m.	1 1 e.	9 30 e.	10 0 e.

N.B.—AN EXTRA TRAIN FROM ROCHDALE TO MANCHESTER EVERY MORNING AT 8 O'CLOCK.

Luggage to the following extent may be taken, at their own risk, free of charge:—First class passengers, 112 lbs.; Second class, 60 lbs.; Wagon, 40 lbs. Any excess charged, for any distance under 30 miles, ½d. per lb., and over 30 miles, ¾d. per lb. extra. The Company's Servants are not allowed to porter for Waggon passengers.

Waggon passengers must be at the booking office 10 minutes before the time of departure, or they cannot be booked for that description of vehicle. Gentlemen's carriages and horses must be at the Station a quarter of an hour before the departure of the Train; and if horses are to be sent from the intermediate Stations, it is advisable to give previous notice.

The Company do not hold themselves responsible for any luggage, matter, or thing, unless booked, and paid for accordingly.

Passengers are particularly requested to see their luggage in and out of the Carriages; and their attention is directed to an extract from 1st William IV, Cap. 68, exhibited at every Station.

Gratuities are not allowed to be taken by any of the Company's servants. Smoking is strictly prohibited on any of the Company's Premises.

The Trains by which Waggon passengers may be booked are those which depart from the Manchester Station at 7h. 0m. Morning, 2h. 30m. Noon, and 6h. 30m. Evening; also from Leeds to Manchester at 7h. 40m. Morning, 1h. 20m. Noon, and 6h. 46m. Evening; and by all the Sunday Trains.

The Train which departs from Manchester 10h. 30m. A.M. meets Road Coaches at Eckington, for Worksop, Newark, Lincoln, Boston, and Lynn at very reduced fares and great saving of time.

TIMES OF THE UP TRAINS

DISTANCES FROM LEEDS.	LEEDS TO MANCHESTER. The Trains depart from	1st. Normanton to Manchester, meeting London Mail train at that station from London, Birmingham, Sheffield, &c.; also for Liverpool, Bolton, Preston, &c.	2nd. Leeds to Manchester, meeting trains from Sheffield and York; also for Liverpool, Bolton, and Lancaster.	3rd. Leeds to Manchester, meeting trains from York, Hull; also for Liverpool, and Bolton.
Miles		h. m.	h. m.	h. m.
	LEEDS, at	....	7 40 m.	8 40 re.
9¼	NORMANTON	6 0 m.	8 0 m.	9 5 re.
12¾	WAKEFIELD	6 8 m.	8 16 m.	9 20 re.
16¼	*Horbury*	6 16 m.	8 30 m.	....
19¼	*Dewsbury*	6 27 m.	8 42 m.	....
24	COOPER B., for Huddersfield..	6 42 m.	8 56 m.	9 43 re.
26	BRIGHOUSE, for Bradford	6 54 m.	9 8 m.	9 55 re.
29	*Elland*	7 3 m.	9 17 m.	....
32	SOWERBY BR., for Halifax ..	7 13 m.	9 27 m.	10 8 re.
34	*Luddenden Foot*	7 20 m.	9 34 m.	....
36¼	*Hebden Bridge*	7 28 m.	9 42 m.	....
39	*Eastwood*	7 42 m.	9 56 m.	....
40¾	TODMORDEN, for Burnley	7 47 m.	10 2 m.	10 38 re.
46½	*Littleborough*........	8 2 m.	10 18 m.	....
49¼	ROCHDALE	8 11 m.	10 28 m.	11 0 re.
52¼	*Blue Pits*, for Heywood	8 18 m.	10 36 m.	....
54½	MILLS HILL, for Oldham......	8 27 m.	10 46 m.	11 12 re.
60	MANCHESTER, arrival in...	8 40 m.	11 0 m.	11 25 re.

N.B.—AN EXTRA TRAIN

Luggage to the following extent may be taken, at their own risk, lbs. ½d. per lb., and over 30 miles, ½d. per lb. extra. The Company's Servan

Waggon passengers must be at the booking office 10 minutes before a quarter of an hour before the departure of the Train ; and if horses an

The Company do not hold themselves responsible for any luggage, n

Passengers are particularly requested to see their luggage in and out

Gratuities are not allowed to be taken by any of the Company's ser

The Trains by which Waggon passengers may be booked are those Wm. Morning, 1h. 20m. Noon, and 5h. 45m. Evening ; and by all the Sunday

The Train which departs from Manchester 10h. 30m. A.M. meets Ro

A

COMPANION

TO THE

MANCHESTER & LEEDS

RAILWAY.

WITH A PLAN OF THE LINE, TIMES OF THE TRAINS
STARTING, FARES, &c.

———————————

HALIFAX
NICHOLSON AND WILSON, PRINTERS, CHEAPSIDE
1841

MANCHESTER AND LEEDS RAILWAY.

CAPITAL £1,950,000.

RAISED IN

13,000 £100 Shares,

AND

13,000 £50 Ditto.

Chairman—Henry Houldsworth, Esq.

Deputy Chairman—William Entwistle, Esq.

Directors.

Richard Barrow, Esq.
Hon. Captain Best, R.N.
Thomas Broadbent, Esq.
Samuel Brooks, Esq.
Leo Schuster, Esq.

Robert Gill, Esq.
James Hargreaves, Esq
James Hatton, Esq.
James Simpson, Esq.
John Smith, Esq.

Managing Director—Robert Gill, Esq.

Engineers { George Stephenson, Esq.
T. L. Gooch, Esq.

Solicitor—J. B. Brackenbury, Esq., Manchester.

Secretary—J. Jellicorse, Esq

Secretary's Office—Clowes Buildings, Hunts Bank, Manchester.

A COMPANION

MANCHESTER & LEEDS RAILWAY.

———————

Before entering upon the object more immediately in view, it may not be improper to make a few preliminary remarks on the 3 Railways, which in conjunction with the Manchester and Leeds line, form a direct communication with the Eastern and Western Seas.—namely, the Manchester and Liverpool, the Leeds and Selby, and the Hull and Selby Railways

The first of these, the Manchester and Liverpool Railway, originated in the year 1824, when a prospectus of the undertaking was issued, and a Company formed. In 1826, the necessary Act of Parliament was obtained, and in the month of June of that year the work was commenced. The line, in length 31 miles, was opened throughout on the 15th September, 1830. The Manchester Station is situate in Liverpool Road.

An Act for the formation of the Leeds and Selby Railway obtained the Royal Assent on the 1st June, 1830 The work was commenced in the early part of 1831. The line was opened for the conveyance of passengers on the 22nd September, 1834, and for the transit of merchandise on the 15th December following The whole length is 19 miles and 7 furlongs, including the Tunnel at the Leeds end. The Leeds station is situate at the East end of the town, near to the upper end of Marsh Lane

An Act authorizing the making of the Hull and Selby Railway, in length 30¾ miles, was obtained in 1836 ; and operations were commenced in the following year The line was opened throughout on the 1st July last

About the commencement of the year 1831, it was considered that the traffic between the important towns of MANCHESTER and LEEDS was such as to call for a more speedy mode of communication and transit between the two places, than was afforded by the ordinary conveyances. A number of gentlemen influenced by this and other considerations, formed themselves into a Company, and decided upon the construction of a *Railway*, as the best means of supplying the desideratum. The first step was to obtain the services of *George Stephenson* and *James Walker, Esqrs*, Civil Engineers, to survey the country, and decide upon the easiest and most advantageous route and from the report of those gentlemen it was determined that powers should be applied for in the approaching Session of Parliament, to commence the undertaking near St George's Road in Manchester, and carry it on to Brighouse, a distance of 34½ miles; where the Directors, for the present deemed it prudent to stop—the most advantageous route from thence to Leeds not having been then decided upon Subsequently, however, the terminus was fixed at Sowerby Bridge, and on the 28th February, 1831, the Bill for the formation of a Railway between Manchester and that place, was introduced into the House of Commons by Lord Morpeth, and read a first time. On the 11th March following it was read a second time and committed. The opposition to the Bill by the Rochdale Navigation Company, and the dissolution of Parliament in the month of April following, however, put an end to its further progress

At a meeting of the Board of Directors held at Manchester on the 8th June following, it was determined that the application for an Act of Parliament should be renewed in the approaching Session, and at the same meeting Mr. Walker presented his report on the proposed line between Sowerby Bridge and Leeds The total expense of completing the line between Manchester and Leeds was estimated at from £700,000 to £800,000.

The Bill was accordingly re-introduced into the House of Commons in the subsequent Session, and having been read a first and second time, was committed on the 28th June, 1831. Its further consideration was entered upon by the Committee on the 4th July; and on the 12th, after 7 days investigation, it was determined by a majority of 18 to 15, that the preamble of the Bill had not been proved, and it was accordingly thrown out

From this time down to the year 1835, no further measures for the completion of the undertaking appear to have been adopted However, in the month of October in that year the project was revived; and at a Meeting held at Manchester on the 21st of that month, it was resolved, that subscriptions be immediately entered into for raising the Capital of the Company, which was fixed at £800,000, giving a preference, however, in the application for shares, to the original subscribers A Bill was accordingly introduced into the House of Commons in the month of February, 1836, and after passing through the various stages in both Houses of Parliament, notwithstanding the opposition received from Canal Companies and the proprietors of land, the Act of 6 and 7 William IV. Chapter iii, enabling the Company to form a Railway between Manchester and Leeds, received the Royal Assent on the 4th July, 1836 By section 290 of this Act it is declared, that as the line of this Company and that of the North Midland Railway follow the same course between Normanton and Leeds, it had been agreed that this Company should suspend the making of its line between those two places, for eighteen calendar months after the passing of that Act; and if the North Midland Company should, within the said time, commence and proceed with the formation of the line between the said places, then the powers of this Company for the formation of that part of their line should cease

Several alterations in the projected route having been found necessary, a special general meeting of the Company was held at Manchester, on the 9th of November, 1836, when it was determined to apply to Parliament in the ensuing Session for powers to vary the line: of which application notice was given, and the Act of 7 William IV. Chapter 24, received the Royal Assent on the 5th May, 1837. By Section 80 of this Act it is declared, that all and every the provisions in the former Act having relation to the arrangement with the North Midland Company shall be in full force, although the points of junction of such Railway with this line and that of the York and North Midland, may be altered.

A meeting of the Inhabitants of Halifax, was held on the 21st October, 1836, when it was unanimously resolved that application should be made to the Railway Company, requesting that powers be applied for to make a Branch from their line to that town, for the convenience of its neighbourhood This power was subsequently obtained in the Act of 2nd and 3rd Victoria, Chapter 55, which received the Royal Assent on the 1st July, 1839 By this Act also the Company are empowered to make a Branch line to Oldham, as well as other specified diversions Also, an extension of the main line at the Manchester end to Hunt's Bank, being their proportion of the proposed junction line of the Liverpool, Bolton, and Bury, and Leeds Railways; but the Liverpool Company have for the present declined making their proportion. The Branch lines to be made within three years from the passing of the Act. The Company have since determined on a Branch line to Heywood.

Robert Gill, Esq. is the Managing Director, who has devoted his whole time and attention to the work. *Mr Gooch*, a pupil of Mr. Stephenson, has been the resident Engineer on the line

Ground was first broken on the 18th August, 1837 The portion of the line between Manchester and Littleborough, (length 13½ miles,) was opened on the 3rd July, 1839, and the further portion between Hebden Bridge and Normanton, (27½ miles) on the 5th October last. This latter opening took place rather earlier than was at first intended, in consequence of a recent Act of Parliament coming into operation on the 9th of that month, which requires that a month's notice shall be given to Government prior to the opening of a Railway, in order to its being surveyed by an engineer appointed for the purpose, whose favourable report is necessary before travelling can be permitted thereon. The residue of the line, with the exception of the Summit Tunnel, having been surveyed by Sir Frederick Smith, the Government Inspector, it was opened to the public on the 4th January, 1841.

The completion of the Tunnel was considerably delayed, it having given way in several places, owing to the insufficiency of the materials employed in its construction; but having been favourably reported by Sir F. Smith, it was opened on the 1st March last, on which day the Directors with their friends traversed the line as far as Normanton, the carriages being decorated with flags, and accompanied by a band of music.

MANCHESTER is a town of great antiquity, situated upon the navigable river Irwell, which joins the Mersey 7 miles below the Town. It was a principal Roman Station, under the name of Mancunium, the site of which is still known as the Castle-field. The Woollen manufacture was established here as early as the reign of Edward the 2nd, under the name of " Manchester Cottons."

The Cotton manufacture, properly so called, is supposed to have been introduced towards the close of the 16th century, by Flemish Protestant emigrants * since which time, by the aid of machinery, and the inventions of Watt, Hargreaves, Arkwright, and others, in the last century, it has been very greatly extended Manchester may now be considered as the metropolis of the Cotton manufacturing district , and in point of wealth and population, is second only to London Every part of the trade, from the importation of the raw material to its completion, is here carried on , but the branch for which the town is more particularly famed, is Spinning According to the Return of R. Rickards, Esq Factory Inspector, there were in Manchester in 1835, 101 Cotton Mills, driven by steam and water power equivalent to 5231 horses, and employing 32,689 persons * The linen, woollen, and silk manufactures are not neglected.

There are in Manchester about 20 churches, the chief of which, the *Collegiate Church*, situate at Hunts Bank, was founded A D. 1422, by Thomas West, Lord de la Warre ; it is considered to be one of the finest in the kingdom The College was originally founded under Royal license, dated 22nd May, 9th Henry 5th, with an establishment consisting of a Warden, 8 Fellows, 4 Clerks, and 6 Choristers, and was

---

* Baines's History of the Cotton Manufacture

endowed with the glebes and tythes of the parsonage It was dissolved in the first year of Edward the 6th, and the lands demised to the Earl of Derby, but re-established on the accession of Queen Mary, and renewed by a Charter of Queen Elizabeth. The present Charter was granted by Charles the 1st, on the 30th September, 1635. The establishment consists of a Warden, appointed by the Crown, and 4 Fellows, chosen by the Warden and Fellows, or a majority of them. The Hon. and Rev. Dr. Herbert is the present Warden

The principal PUBLIC BUILDINGS are—The *Exchange*, situate at the junction of the Market Place, Exchange Street, St Mary's Gate, and Market Street, erected by subscription at an expense of £20,000, and opened 2nd January, 1809, forming the public resort for the Merchants, Manufacturers, and principal traders of the town and neighbourhood. The *Town Hall*, in King Street, erected in 1824, at an expense of £28,000 The *Corn Exchange*, in Hanging Ditch The *Athenæum* in Cooper Street. The *Royal Institution* in Mosley Street. The *Cloth Hall* in York Buildings, for the sale of Yorkshire Cloths The *General Infirmary* and *Dispensary*, situate at Picadilly, erected in 1755, and since greatly enlarged The *Portico* in Mosley Street The *Museum* in St Peter's Street. The *Blind Asylum*, and *School for the Deaf and Dumb*, in Stretford Road The *Mechanic's Institution* in Cooper Street. The *Blue Coat School*, near the Collegiate Church, the *New Grammar School*, at the back of Do The *Post Office* in Brown Street The *Carpenters' Hall* in Garrett Road, the *Barracks* in New Regent Road and in Hulme

The *Places* of PUBLIC AMUSEMENT consist of the *Theatres* in Fountain Street and Spring Gardens, the *Assembly Rooms* in Mosley Street the *Music Hall* in Lower Mosley Street, the *Billiard Rooms* in Mosley Street and Cross Street the *Botanic Gardens*, Stretford Road, and the *Zoological Gardens* in Broughton Road The *Races* are held on Kersal Moor, on Wednesday and two following days in Whitsun-week.

The annual income of the *Town Charities* amounts to £2392 18s 1d

The *Market days* are Tuesday, Thursday, and Saturday. On the Tuesday the business between merchants and manufacturers, is chiefly transacted, and the principal provision Market is held on the Saturday. The *Fair* is held on the eve, day, and morrow of St Matthew, 20th, 21st, and 22nd September.

In 1654, by command from Oliver Cromwell, Charles Worsley was returned member for the Borough of Manchester, and in 1656, Richard Radcliffe, Esq. took his seat as its representative The elective Franchise ceased on the Restoration, until the passing of the Reform Act, under which it was empowered to send two representatives to Parliament, and in December, 1835, Mark Philips, Esq and the Right Hon. C. P.

Thomson, (now Lord Sydenham) were elected. The present members are Mr. Philips and R. H Greg, Esq

Manchester was formerly governed by a Boroughreeve, but since the passing of the Municipal Reform Bill, it has been raised to the dignity of a Corporate town The Corporation consists of a Mayor, Recorder, 15 Aldermen (of whom the Mayor is one) and 48 Common Councilmen — 8 of the Aldermen are changed triennially, and 16 Councillors yearly. William Nield, Esq. is the present Mayor. The validity of its Charter has been disputed, but confirmed

Manchester bestows the titles of Duke and Earl on the Montague family. The first Earl was Sir Edward Montague, who received the title in 1625 from Charles 1st. His great grandson, the 4th Earl, was created Duke of Manchester on the 30th April, 1719

The Population of Manchester amounted in 1831 to 142,026, and of the Parish, to 279,398 souls. It has since greatly increased

This important town is now connected by Railway with London, Liverpool, Birmingham, Preston, Bolton, Bury, Stockport, Leeds, Hull, and intermediate towns. The Station of the Liverpool Railway, as before observed, is in Liverpool Road, that of the Birmingham Railway, (open to Stockport,) in Store Street, London Road, and the Bolton and Bury Station in New Chapel Street, Salford

---

Leaving the Station, which is situate at the East end of the town, in Lees Street, Oldham Road, by a brick-built viaduct of 72 arches, we immediately pass on our left the Engine and Carriage Repository, and *St. George's Church*, and proceeded by embankment and cutting to MILLS HILL, 5½ miles from Manchester This is the Station for *Oldham*, which lies about two miles to our right, and *Middleton*, about a mile and a half to our left A Branch line will eventually be made to the former place. Omnibuses meet and await the arrival of the various trains.

Proceeding forwards, we cross the Rochdale Canal twice, once by an iron bridge, and again by a skew bridge at a very unusual angle, and continue on an embankment up the valley. Crossing the Heywood branch of the same canal by an iron bridge, we arrive at the HEYWOOD and BLUE PITTS Station, 7¾ miles from Manchester Heywood, which is a large manufacturing village, with a population of about 10,000, lies about a mile and a half to our left A Branch Railway is in course of formation, and will be completed in April next. At present a Canal Packet is the only conveyance to the town

Advancing up the valley, we shortly pass on our left *Castleton Hall*, and afterwards crossing the Rochdale and Oldham Road, &c by a viaduct of 25 arches, and the canal by an iron bridge, we arrive at the

ROCHDALE Station, 10½ miles from Manchester. The Station is situate about half a mile from the town.

Rochdale is a large manufacturing town, built on the river Roach, from which it takes its name. It is well situated for trade, having Canal navigation connecting it with the river Calder to the East, and the Duke of Bridgewater's canal to the West. The Woollen manufacture, consisting of Flannels, Baizes, Coatings, and Broad Cloth, forms the staple trade of the town and neighbourhood. Calicos and strong cotton goods are also made here, in the manufacture of which there were employed in 1835, 38 mills of 1176 horse power, and employing 4,296 hands * It was famed for its manufactures as early as the reign of Queen Elizabeth

The Market days are Monday and Saturday. The first is a great Corn market, and is attended by the principal growers and dealers in this and the adjoining counties The three annual Fairs are held on the 14th May, on Whit-Tuesday, and the 7th November.

The *Parish Church*, dedicated to St Chad, was founded about the close of the 11th century The value of the vicarage exceeds £2000 per annum, and is enjoyed by the Rev Dr. Molesworth, under the patronage of the Archbishop of Canterbury There are also two other Churches, several Dissenting Chapels; many Public Schools for the instruction of youth, together with numerous Charities for the poor of the town

The *Places of Amusement* are a Theatre, with two Assembly Rooms, and two Billiard Rooms.

On leaving the Station we have a good view of the town Proceeding towards Littleborough, about a mile and a half from Rochdale, we pass on our right BELFIELD HALL, an ancient mansion, which formed part of the inheritance of the Knights of St. John of Jerusalem, till the dissolution of that order It is now the property of the Townley family Half a mile beyond Belfield Hall is CLEGG HALL, also on our right, formerly the possession of the family of that name, but now enjoyed by Joseph Fenton, Esq of Bamford Hall It was erected about the year 1620, on the site of a more ancient mansion, celebrated for the freaks and visitations of a supernatural guest called "Clegg Hall Boggart." The cause which gave rise to the stories still existing respecting the "Boggart," is said to have been the murder of the lawful heirs of the property by an unnatural uncle, who seized on their inheritance. The annoying pranks of the ghostly visitor were not got rid of, until all the existing parts of the old mansion, which had not been destroyed when it was first rebuilt, were demolished † The Hall is now divided into several dwellings, and is in part used as an alehouse.

---

* Baines's History of the Cotton Manufacture
† Roby's Traditions of Lancashire, 2nd Series, vol 2

In this neighbourhood, too, was the family mansion of the Byron family, which was the subject of the following tradition.

In the reign of Edward the 4th, Sir Nicholas Byron, its then owner, had a neice named Eleanor, who was betrothed to her cousin Oliver Chadwyck of Healey Hall The time for the celebration of the nuptials was at hand, and Eleanor retired to rest the night before the bridal, but sleep was denied.

Connected with the family was an old superstition, that if on a bridal eve a taper was burnt, made from the fat of a young sow, anointed with the blood of the inquirer, and sundry diabolical and cabalistical rites performed at midnight, a spirit would appear, and pronounce the good or evil destiny of the betrothed.

Eleanor had scrupulously attended to all the prescribed forms of the incantation, and as the fated hour approached, lay anxiously expecting the issue, when suddenly there came a rushing wind, the door flapped to and fro, the curtains shook, the pictures glared horribly from the wall, and, starting from one of the panels, stalked down the portrait of a maiden aunt of the house of Byron Advancing to the foot of the bed, she opened out a fiery scroll, on which the appalled maiden read these ominous words—

"Maid, wife, and widow in one day!
"This shall be thy destiny"

Eleanor struggled hard, but could neither move nor speak. At length a loud cry escaped her, and the vision disappeared.

On the following morning the wedding procession set out; and as it drew nigh to Healey Hall, a messenger rode forward in great haste, and whispered to Byron, who immediately called out to Oliver, that the Traffords, who had an old and bloody feud with the Byron family, had taken advantage of their absence at the feast, and invaded their threshold. Saying which, he rode off with his attendants, followed by Oliver, after he had first placed his wife under suitable protection. The enemy were quicky routed, but the prediction was complete, for Eleanor became

"Maid, wife, and widow, in one day"

her husband being slain during the battle *

We now arrive at LITTLEBOROUGH Station, 13½ miles from Manchester. This village, pleasantly situated at the foot of Blackstone Edge, was a small Roman station, on the road from Manchester to York, and several antiquities have been found in the neighbourhood. The *Church*, founded in the 15th century, was rebuilt in the year 1815.

Continuing our course from Littleborough along an embankment, we pass on our left the mansion and print-works of Mr Hudson. Thence

* Roby's Traditions of Lancashire. 1st Series, vol 1

diverging to the west side of the valley, by a deep excavation through the rock, which carries us under the turnpike road, we immediately enter the SUMMIT TUNNEL, one of the greatest triumphs of modern skill, by a fine massive arch of masonry. The Contractor for this stupendous undertaking was *Mr. John Stephenson*, *Barnard Dickenson*, *Esq* being the resident Engineer. It was commenced in the latter part of the year 1837. The number of hands employed varied from 800 to 1200 the average may be taken at 1000. There were 15 shafts sunk for the excavation of the works, 2 of which were worked with gins, the others by stationary engines with a power of 202 horses. Besides which, an average of 150 horses have been employed. 23,000,000 of bricks have been disposed of in the works, exclusive of Ashlar-stones and pierre-pointing. Roman cement was used instead of mortar, of which 8000 tons were consumed.

The dimensions of this immense work are as follow —Length, 2869 yards. Height from the rails to the crown of the arch, 21 feet 6 inches. Width at the level of the rails, 22 feet. The greatest width, (about 6 feet from the ground) 24 feet.

There is a slight curve at each end of the Tunnel of about 4 chains in length. It has a gradient falling from the north or Yorkshire end to the south or Lancashire end, of 1 in 330 (16 feet per mile) or about 26 feet 1 inch in the whole length. The rails are laid on wooden sleepers, by means of strong cast-iron chairs.

The entire cost of this mighty undertaking amounted to the sum of £251,000, being after the rate of £87 per lineal yard.

The northern mouth terminates in a spacious sort of rotunda, or elliptical open shaft, of about 60 feet by 30, inside measure, built of brick, and about 35 feet in height.

After emerging from the tunnel into this shaft, we immediately plunge into another of about 70 yards in length, which was necessary owing to the depth of the excavation, and its proximity to the canal, which burst in upon the works during their progress, and rendered an open cutting impracticable.

Proceeding a short distance, and passing under the turnpike road, we enter the *Winterbutt Lee Tunnel*, in length about 420 yards, and afterwards skirt down the north-west side of the valley, through cuttings and along embankments. Crossing the canal by an iron bridge, we enter upon the Gauxholme viaduct, consisting of 17 arches of 35 feet span, with a centre one of 60 feet, having on our left the warehouses of the Rochdale Canal Company, and the Bacup Road. We now enter the *Vale of Calder*, which is here but a very diminutive stream. Proceeding along the north-west side of the valley, on an embankment, and crossing the canal by a fine cast-iron skew-bridge of 101 feet span, (believed to be the finest specimen of the skew-bridge in the world,) we shortly pass on our right the extensive establishment of Messrs. Fielden, for the manufacture of Cotton, Calicos, and Sheetings, in which about 900 hands are at present employed The works have recently been considerably extended by the erection of weaving sheds There are also other mills in the neighbourhood, belonging to this well-known and opulent firm

We now arrive at the town of TODMORDEN, 19¼ miles from Manchester, and 40¾ from Leeds, situate partly in the County of Lancaster, and partly in the West Riding of Yorkshire. It is a thriving place, the principal manufacture of which is Cotton. The *Old Church*, situate on an eminence in the centre of the town, on our right, is dedicated to St. Mary, and is supposed to be of the date of the Reformation. It is at present disused, except for sepultural purposes.

Thursday is the Market day for corn and provisions A Cattle Market is held on the first Thursday in every month.

Proceeding through the town, we pass on our right *Todmorden Hall*, the residence of James Taylor, Esq a member of the family so celebrated as the Whitworth Doctors Afterwards crossing the Burnley Turnpike Road, (which town lies about 9 miles to our left, and through which a projected branch from Preston to this place will pass,) and the adjoining property by a stone viaduct of 7 arches of 60 feet span, one of which is fitted up as a temporary Station-house, we pass on our left *Christ Church*, built by Government, and opened in 1832 The Rev. Joseph Cowell is the Incumbent, under the patronage of the Vicar of Rochdale.

We now enter the *West Riding of Yorkshire* Skirting along the north-west side of the valley, we pass on our left *Stansfield Hall*, late the residence of William Sutcliffe, Esq. and shortly afterwards enter the *Milwood Tunnel*, in length 225 yards. On the eminence to our left is *Cross-stone Church*, rebuilt by Government in 1834. The Vicar of Halifax is patron, and the Rev. John Fennell, Incumbent. We then pass through the *Castle Hill Tunnel*, 192 yards in length, and, crossing an angle of the valley by a viaduct of 5 arches and 45 feet span, arrive at the *Horsfall Tunnel*, which is 424 yards in length. Emerging thence we proceed on an embankment along the north side of the valley, close by the Myrtle Grove Independent Chapel. Here, side by side, the 3 rival lines of communication, the railway, canal, and turnpike road, pursue their course. A little further, on the right, is *Stoodley Bridge*, and on the hill above may be seen the PIKE, a lofty column, erected by subscription in 1814, in honour of the Duke of Wellington's unparalleled military achievements. We afterwards pass on our right *Wood Mill*, occupied by Messrs. Oliver, and immediately after, on our left, *Underbank*, late the residence of Christopher Rawdon, Esq but now occupied by Mr. George Ashworth, one of the proprietors of the Calais or Underbank

Woollen mill, on our right. Further on is *Charlestown*, where was originally intended to have been a tunnel 250 yards in length, at a depth of 50 feet below the surface of a projecting piece of ground. but owing to the loose nature of the soil, which continually fell in as the works progressed, the Company have been compelled to abandon their original line for the present, and to carry the works *round* the projection, by curves of 12 chains radius, along which the trains are conducted at a decreased speed. In consequence of such deviation of the line, a considerable diversion of the turnpike road, at this part has been made. Crossing the turnpike road and river by a skew-bridge of 3 arches, and the canal by an iron bridge, close to the cotton manufactory of Mr Whiteley, and proceeding down the south side of the valley, on our left is the village of MYTHOLM, beautifully situated amidst romantic mountain scenery. The *Church*, dedicated to St. James, was erected by Government in 1835, on land given by the Rev. J A Rhodes, who also furnished the stone of which the fabric is composed. The Rev Frederick Tollar is the Incumbent. The Rev. Mr. Rhodes has a neat mansion near the Church. There are several mills here, chiefly employed in the Cotton manufacture. After passing through a short tunnel of 124 yards in length, we come in sight of the village of HEBDEN BRIDGE, remarkable for its extensive Cotton mills. Gas Works were erected here in 1838, by Messrs Crossley and Son. This is the Station for *Keighley* and its neighbourhood, distant about 11 miles. The distance from Manchester is 23¾, and from Leeds 36½ miles.

Proceeding down the right bank of the Calder, which has been diverted in several places, to save the expense of crossing it by a number of bridges, about a mile and a half from Hebden Bridge, on our left, is EWOOD HALL, celebrated as the birth place of *Robert Farrar*, Bishop of St David's, who suffered as a protestant martyr at Caermarthen, on the 30th March, 1555. It is now occupied by S Fawcett and W. Buckley, Esqrs. Further down on the same side is *Brearley Hall*, and beyond is *Mytholmroyd*, where is a large manufactory, the property of Messrs. Fielden. A little lower is *Luddenden-foot*, and close to the line is a Worsted mill, the property of the Company, and occupied by Jonathan Ackroyd, Esq. On the hill to our right is seen *Sowerby Church*, erected in 1762. The Rev. W. H Bull, M. A. is the Incumbent, under the patronage of the Vicar of Halifax. *Haugh-end*, in this township, is memorable as the birth place of that learned and excellent prelate, *Archbishop Tillotson*, in memory of whom a handsome monumental statue was erected in Sowerby Church about 50 years ago. After traversing a deep cutting, and passing through a tunnel 640 yards in length, we immediately arrive at the SOWERBY BRIDGE Station, 28 miles from Manchester, and 32 from Leeds. This is one of the Stations for

Halifax, distant 3 miles, whither omnibuses ply on the arrival of the trains. Immediately opposite to the Station, on our left, is *Hollins*, formerly the residence of James Crossley, Esq and now the property of Samuel Wood, Esq

Leaving the Station, we pass on our right, *St. Georges Church*, consecrated on the 27th of October last, and crossing the Blackstone-edge road, and the Ripponden stream, which flows down the valley to our right, by a viaduct of 5 arches of 43 feet span, we proceed down the meadows on the right bank of the Calder, past Sowerby Bridge This is a rapidly improving village, containing several corn, scribbling, and worsted mills, chemical works, &c also Gas Works for the lighting of the mills, streets, &c. The population is about 10,000. The *Church*, situate in the centre of the village, was erected by subscription in 1820, in lieu of a more ancient edifice The curacy, valued at £160, is in the patronage of the Vicar of Halifax. The Rev. Charles Rogers, M A is the present Incumbent There are also places of worship for the Independent and Wesleyan denominations.

We now enter one of the deepest and most extensive excavations on the line, the greatest depth being 80 feet below the surface. Three lofty bridges, one of them having 3 arches, carry the roads across the excavation to places on the hill to our right. Crossing into the valley, we proceed down the meadows on a low embankment, with *Norland* on the hill to our right, and Stern Corn mill immediately on our left. A little further up the hill, on the same side, is *Woodhouse*, the residence of Mr Howarth. Crossing the river by a stone viaduct of 3 arches, on our right we pass Copley Mill, the property of R. K. Dawson, Esq. at present unoccupied Again crossing the river by a stone viaduct of 3 arches, we skirt along the north-west corner of *North Dean Wood*, where the Branch line to HALIFAX, which will be about 2 miles in length, is expected to join the main line. On the hill to our left is Skircoat Green, and in the valley below is Salterhebble Proceeding to the north side of the valley on an embankment, with the rich woods of Elland in front, we cross the Salterhebble and Stainland roads by a bridge of one arch, and a little further, the river and canal by a viaduct of 4 skew arches of 64 feet span Passing under the Halifax and Huddersfield road, we immediately enter the *Elland Tunnel*, in length 424 yards. Emerging from which, on our right is *Elland Hall*, formerly the seat of the family of that name, which became extinct in the reign of Edward the 3rd, in consequence of a deadly family feud, the particulars of which are briefly as follow Sir John Elland, from some unexplained cause of hostility, had murdered in the presence of their families, Hugh of Quarmby, Lockwood of Lockwood, and Sir Robert Beaumont of Crossland Hall When the eldest sons of these families came of age, they resolved to avenge their parents' death for this purpose they lay in wait for Sir John as he returned from holding the Court leet at Brighouse, and slew him on a hill near Brookfoot, about half a mile from that place Not satisfied with this act of revenge, they determined to extirpate the very name of Elland, and to this end they concealed themselves in Elland mill, and on the approach of the family across the dam, on their way to church, they slew the young knight with an arrow, and wounded his son so desperately, that he soon afterwards died The estates descended to the daughter of Sir John, who married one of the Savile's, and carried the property into that family. The Earl of Scarborough is the present owner The house, with the exception of the "Hall," now used as the kitchen is quite modern. It is at present occupied by Mr T F Lambert

Crossing the Elland and Obelisk road, canal, and river, by 2 viaducts of 3 arches each, we proceed to the south-east side of the valley, past the town of ELLAND It formerly possessed a charter for a Market, which has been discontinued for ages. The principal trade of the town and neighbourhood consists of puddings and coarse woollen goods, chiefly for the American market Gas-works have been established here within the last few years The population is about 4000

The *Church*, dedicated to St Mary, is supposed to be of the date of the 13th century The Vicar of Halifax is patron, and the Rev C. Atkinson, M A is the Incumbent There are also Chapels for the Independent, Wesleyan, and Unitarian denominations

We now skirt down the south-east side of the valley, having on our left *Ash Grove*, the residence of Edward Rawson, Esq Here the river is seen winding gracefully down the valley A little lower is *Cromwell Bottom*, with its immense stone quarries, above which may be seen *Southowram Church*, in the incumbency of the Rev John Hope, under the patronage of the Vicar of Halifax We then enter a deep cutting, whence a large quantity of excellent stone blocks or sleepers, for laying the rails upon, were obtained It may be observed, *en passant*, that stone blocks or sleepers are mostly used where the line runs upon, or below, the surface of the ground , and wooden sleepers, where there is an embankment, as they are more easily raised, should occasion require.

Leaving the cutting, we immediately pass on our left *Lillands*, the residence of Miss Helm, and proceeding down the right bank of the Calder, from which the line is protected by a strong stone wall, arrive in sight of the village of *Brighouse*. On the hill to the left is the *Church*, dedicated to St Martin, consecrated in the year 1831 The Vicar of Halifax is patron, and the Rev. John Boyle, Incumbent To the west of the Church is the newly erected parsonage, commanding fine and extensive views of the surrounding neighbourhood, the scenery of which is highly picturesque and beautiful Crossing the Leeds and Elland turnpike road by a stone viaduct of 6 arches of 45 feet span, with Rastrick on our right, and passing under the Bradford and Huddersfield road, we arrive at the BRIGHOUSE Station, 34 miles from Manchester, and 26 from Leeds

Brighouse is a large, well-built, and flourishing village, possessing facilities for trade rarely to be met with. The river Calder skirts the south side of the village, by means of which, and the canal of the Calder and Hebble Navigation Company, a direct communication is kept up with London, Liverpool, Hull, and other important places Excellent turnpike roads connect the village with the towns of Halifax, Bradford, Leeds, Wakefield, Huddersfield, and intermediate localities Its principal trade consists in corn, malt, and cards; besides which a great proportion of the working classes are employed in the adjoining stone quarries of Hipperholme and Rastrick, whence a great quantity of stone is brought to Brighouse, and shipped to all parts of the kingdom. The population is about 3,500.

Omnibuses from Huddersfield, 4 miles, Halifax, 6 miles, and Bradford, 7 miles, meet and await the arrival of most of the trains

Continuing our course down the south-east side of the valley, on the hill to our left is the village of *Clifton*, abounding in excellent coal Here may be seen a number of furnaces, for the conversion of the coal into coke Passing on our right *Woodhouse*, formerly the residence of John Armitage, Esq but now of John Archbell, Esq we soon enter a deep excavation through Bradley Wood, whence several portions of fossil trees, and also large quantities of shells, were obtained. Afterwards crossing the river by a stone viaduct of 2 arches of 76 feet span, we proceed down the valley on an embankment, with the rich woods of *Kirklees* on our left. *Kirklees Park* is celebrated as containing the burial place of the renowned freebooter *Robin Hood*, and also the site of a Benedictine Nunnery, founded in the reign of Henry the 2nd, by one of the Reyners The Hall, the seat of Sir George Armytage, Bart, is of the date of James the 1st. and commands fine views of the southern vale of Calder

We now arrive at the COOPER BRIDGE Station, 36 miles from Manchester, and 24 from Leeds, the nearest Station for *Huddersfield*, distant about 4 miles up the valley to our right, whither a Branch line is likely to be formed, for which there is every facility. Immediately on our left is *Obelisk Grove*, the residence of Mrs Fairburn

Crossing the Bristal and Huddersfield turnpike road, and continuing down the valley on an embankment, on our right is *Heaton Lodge*, the seat of Joseph Starkey, Esq, and on the left are the *West Mills*, occupied by Messrs Tyas for the grinding of Corn, near to the hamlet of *Batty-*

ford, in Mirfield, where is a new *Church*, consecrated on the 28th October last, and in the incumbency of the Rev Thomas Nevin, M A Crossing the river again by a viaduct of 2 arches of 76 feet span, and passing through a short cutting, on the hill side to the left is *Bank House*, the residence of Benjamin Wilson, Esq A little beyond, near the line, is the Woollen manufactory of Messrs Wheatley Mirfield abounds in gentlemen's seats, but a special reference to each would take up too much time and space. It is a favourite seat of the Woollen manufacture, the business of malting is also carried on to a very considerable extent

Crossing the river, and the Mirfield and Hopton road, by a stone viaduct of 13 arches of 45 feet span each, on our left is the Corn mill of Mr. Charles Wooler A little further, on our right, is the Hopton Independent Chapel, and on our left *Canal Lodge*, the residence of Joseph Stancliffe, Esq and *Blake Hall*, the seat of Joshua Ingham, Esq the birthplace of *John Hopton* the persecuting Roman Catholic Bishop of Norwich in the days of Queen Mary On the hill above Blake Hall is the *Parish Church* of Mirfield, rebuilt in 1826 Sir George Armytage, Bart. is patron, and the Rev. Ralph Maude, M A. is Vicar *Mirfield* formed part of the Saxon Parish of Dewsbury up to the year 1261, when it was erected by the Pope into a Rectory, through the intercession of Sir John Heaton, then lord of the manor, whose lady had been waylaid and robbed, and her attendant murdered, on their way to Dewsbury Church on the morning of Christmas day. At the east end of the Church is a conical mount, surrounded by a moat, said to have been erected by the Saxons, and in after times to have formed a place of defence to the manor-house of the lords, which immediately adjoined it. This antique mansion was taken down in 1827, and a commodious inn erected on its site, still popularly called *Castle Hall* Owing to its proximity to the Church, it is an ancient proverb in Mirfield, that

> " ——when by death one gets a fall,
> ' He's neighbour then to Castle Hall. '

Crossing over to the Hopton side of the river by a skew-bridge of 6 arches, we skirt down the south-east side of the valley, and shortly pass through the grounds and in front of the mansions of Thomas and Charles Wheatley, Esqrs. Lower down, on our left, are the Cloth mills of Messrs Nussey and Sykes, and the Corn mill of Mr. Pilling. On the hill is *St John's Church*, Dewsbury Moor, consecrated 24th September, 1827, and in the incumbency of the Rev John Payne After passing through a deep cutting, where the coal strata may be distinctly observed, we proceed on an embankment to the DEWSBURY Station, passing on our right the Thornhill-lees Iron Works, and on our left, near the Station, the Blanket and Woollen manufactory of Messrs Hagues and Cook. The

Station is situate at *Thornhill-lees*, about three quarters of a mile from Dewsbury, 40½ miles from Manchester, and 19½ from Leeds

Dewsbury is a place of great antiquity It was the common centre whence Christianity spread itself over the vale of Calder, through the preaching of *Paulinus*, the Roman missionary, who erected a cross here, of which the wheel-cross bearing his name, that stands on the outside of the church, is supposed to be a fac-simile It afterwards formed the head of a Saxon parish, containing an area of 400 square miles

The principal trade of the town and neighbourhood consists in blankets and carpets The finer descriptions of goods are also made here The population is about 12,000 Wednesday is the market day

Thornhill lees, where the station is situate, was formerly an extensive park, containing the residence of the Thornhill family, (of which little more than the site remains,) from whom the estates passed to the Savile's They are now enjoyed by the Earl of Scarborough

Leaving the Dewsbury station, and traversing a deep excavation, we continue down the valley on an embankment. with *Thornhill* on our right, where are a number of collieries belonging to Joshua Ingham, Esq. The *Church*, dedicated to St Michael, is a venerable structure, and contains many monuments of the Savile family The rectory valued at £988, is in the gift of the Earl of Scarborough, and enjoyed by the Rev Henry Torre. A little further, we pass on our left the village of *Ossett*, where is a neat *Church*, in the patronage of the Vicar of Dewsbury, and incumbency of the Rev. O L Collins We then cross the river by a wooden bridge, which is thrown over only as a temporary work, in consequence of a suit pending in Chancery, between the Company and the proprietors of Healey Low Mill, the latter being supported, it is supposed, by the Calder and Hebble Navigation Company We shortly afterwards arrive at the HORBURY BRIDGE Station, 43½ miles from Manchester, and 16½ from Leeds The station house is formed of one of the arches by which the Wakefield road crosses the line On our left is *Jenkin House*, the residence of Mr George Knowles

Proceeding towards Wakefield, we pass on our right the worsted mills of Messrs Foster, and shortly enter a tunnel about 150 yards long, from which we emerge into a deep rock excavation, three quarters of a mile in length. The greatest depth is 70 feet This was one of the first works commenced, but from its magnitude was one of the last completed. Proceeding, we have on the hill to our left, *Horbury*, a large clothing village, with a population of about 4000. The *Church*, which has a small spire, was rebuilt in 1791, by and at the expense of the late *John Carr, Esq*, the eminent architect, who was a native of the village, and afterwards resided at York The Rev. John Sharp, M A is the Incumbent.

Shortly afterwards we are carried through the richly wooded grounds and in front of *Lupset Hall*, the mansion of Daniel Gaskell Esq   About three quarters of a mile further, on the left, is *Thornes House*, the residence of Benjamin Gaskell, Esq , and beyond the mansion is a neat *Church*, consecrated in 1831, of which the Rev W. H Brandreth is Incumbent   We now come in view of the town of WAKEFIELD, Crossing the Pontefract road by a viaduct of 16 arches, we arrive at the Station, situate at the bottom of Kirkgate, near its junction with Thornes Lane   The distance from Manchester is 47½, and from Leeds 12½ miles.

Wakefield, a large, opulent, and handsome town, may be considered in many respects as the capital of the West Riding   It contains an office for the registration of wills and deeds, and is the place where the Sheriff holds the Court for the election of members for the Riding   It is one of the towns in which Quarter Sessions are held in rotation , and has a large House of Correction.

The market day is Friday, when much business is done in Corn and Wool.   A handsome *Corn Exchange*, with a Saloon over, was erected in Westgate in 1838   A Cattle Fair is held here every other Wednesday.

The *Parish Church*, dedicated to All Saints, with its elegant tower and spire 237 feet high, situate in Kirkgate, was erected in 1329, and rebuilt, with the exception of the latter, in 1409   The vicarage, worth about £600 per annum, is enjoyed by the Rev Samuel Sharp, M A , under the patronage of the Queen   There are also 3 other Churches, with Chapels for various Dissenting persuasions

The principal *Public Edifices* are—The *Chapel* on the *Bridge*, which was re-edified and endowed by Edward the 4th, as a sanctuary for prayer for the souls of the slain at the *Battle of Wakefield*, fought on the 24th December, 1460, between the Yorkists under their Duke, and the Lancasterians under *Margaret*, Queen of Henry the 6th, and her generals the Dukes of Somerset and Leicester, when the Duke of York was slain   It is now occupied as a cottage   The *Grammar School* of Queen Elizabeth, founded A D 1592, by the Saville's, ancestors of the Earl of Mexborough   The *Court House* in Wood Street   The *House of Correction*, bottom of Westgate   The *Register Office* in Kirkgate   The *Lunatic Asylum*, about 2 miles from the town, capable of accommodating nearly 700 patients   The *Theatre* in Drury Lane, Westgate.   The *West Riding Proprietary School*, built in 1833, by a Company of Proprietors, with a capital of £15,000, in £100 shares, and attended by about 200 students.   The population of Wakefield is about 16,000

Pursuing our course down the Vale of Calder, we shortly enter a deep cutting, where the coal strata may be distinctly traced   We then pass under the rich woods of *Heath*, with the mansion of George Smyth, Esq overlooking the valley, on our right.   Here the river has been considerably diverted A little further we pass on our right *Kirkthorpe*, with its pretty *Church*, in the incumbency of the Rev. John Pullein, B A. In the distance to the left is the village of Stanley In the township of Stanley-cum-Wrenthorpe is the field of action celebrated in an ancient song, where the battle was fought between Robin Hood, Will Scarlet, and Little John, with the Pindar of Wakefield, "All on the green " it is called the "Pindar's field" to this day

Continuing down the valley by embankment and cuttings, we leave on our left *Newland Hall*, the seat of Sir Edward Dodsworth, Bart., situated in a beautiful part of the vale of Calder Here also the course of the river has been changed, to save the expense of bridges We shortly afterwards arrive at the terminus of the Manchester line, and its junction with that of the NORTH MIDLAND COMPANY, on which the rest of our journey is performed. A little further is the NORMANTON Station, 50½ miles from Manchester, and 9½ from Leeds Here the passengers and goods for *Derby* and the *South*, and those for *Hull*, *York*, and the *North*, proceed by the *North Midland*, *York*, and *Selby* trains Large station and warehouses for the convenience of the Companies, are in course of erection

Proceeding forwards, about a mile and a half from Normanton, the *York Railway* joins the line of the North Midland Company, and about 2 miles and a half beyond, that is 4 miles from Normanton, a branch from the same railway joins the North Midland line. We shortly pass on our left *Methley Church*, which is dedicated to St Oswald, and contains many monuments of the Waterton and Savile families Over the south door is a statue of *King Oswald*, the patron saint, supposed to be contemporary with the original edifice, which existed prior to the Domesday survey The Rectory, in the patronage of the Duchy of Lancaster, is enjoyed by the Hon and Rev A. H Cathcart Beyond the Church is seen *Methley Hall*, the stately mansion of the Earl of Mexborough, delightfully situated in one of the most beautiful parks in the country. Ilbert de Lacy, the great Norman Baron, became possessed of this property by grant from William the Conqueror After passing through the Waterton and Dymoke families, it came, in the reign of Elizabeth, to Sir John Savile the Judge, who rebuilt the Hall Sir John Savile, a descendant of the above, was created *Baron Pollington* in 1753, and *Viscount Pollington* and *Earl of Mexborough* in 1768. The present mansion was built by the late Earl

About a mile beyond Methley, in the distance to the right is *Swillington Hall*, the residence of Sir John Lowther, Bart , and about two miles and a half further, on the same side, is *Temple Newsham*, the beautiful seat of Lady William Gordon Its ancient name was Newhusum, corrupted into Newsam, to which an establishment here of the

Knights Templars in 1181, gave the additional name of Temple. On the dissolution of that order about 1311, the estates were granted by Edward the 3rd to Sir John Darcy, from whom they passed to Thomas Lord Darcy, who was beheaded in the reign of Henry the 8th, and his estates confiscated to the Crown. They were subsequently granted by Henry to Matthew, Earl of Lennox, the father of Lord Darnley, the husband of *Mary Queen of Scots*, and on his death descended to James the 1st, who granted them to the Duke of Richmond. They were sold by the Duke to Sir Arthur Ingram, the founder of the Irwin peerage, who erected the present princely mansion. They afterwards became the property of the Marquis of Hertford, through his marriage with the daughter of the 10th Viscount Irwin, from whom they passed to Lady Gordon, the present possessor.

After leaving Temple Newsam, we shortly enter an excavation, which brings us to the LEEDS Station, a handsome and commodious brick building, in Hunslet Lane, about half a mile from Briggate, the principal street in Leeds.

Leeds, situated on the river Aire, is the most populous market town in Yorkshire, and the metropolis or principal seat of the Woollen manufacture. It is mentioned in Domesday Survey as a farming village, with a population of about 300. It had formerly a *Castle*, supposed to have stood upon Mill Hill, and which was for a short time the place of confinement of *Richard* the 2nd, prior to his murder in Pontefract Castle; but when or how it was destroyed is unknown.

Besides the Woollen manufacture, the wholesale Tobacco trade is extensively carried on in Leeds, a number of mills having been erected here for the cutting of this American produce.

The *Borough* was first incorporated by a Charter of Charles the 1st, A.D. 1626, under which it was governed till 1661, when Charles the 2nd granted the burgesses a new Charter, with additional powers and privileges. A third Charter was granted by James the 2nd in 1684. The Corporation, since the Municipal Reform Act, consists of a Mayor, Recorder, 15 Aldermen, (of whom the Mayor is one,) and 48 Common Councilmen. 8 of the Aldermen are changed triennially, 16 Councillors yearly. *William Smith, Esq* is the present Mayor.

The Market days are Tuesday and Saturday. A Cattle Fair is held every alternate Wednesday. There are also 2 Annual Fairs, one held on the 10th and 11th of July, for horses, and the other on the 8th and 9th of November, for horned Cattle.

Quarter Sessions for the Riding are held here in rotation.

The principal *Public Buildings* are—The *Court House* in Park Row. The *Commercial Buildings* in Boar Lane. The *Mixed Cloth Hall*, bottom of Park Row. The *White Cloth Hall* in Duncan Street. The *Philo-*

sophical Hall, in Park Row. The *Corn Exchange,* at the top of Briggate. The *Infirmary,* in Infirmary Street. The *Library,* in Commercial Street. The *Post-office* is in Mill Hill. The *Barracks* are situate about a mile from Briggate, on the Harrogate Road. The *Public Cemetery* adjoins upon Woodhouse Moor. The places of *Public Amusement* are the *Theatre,* in Hunslet Lane; the *Assembly Rooms,* over the north side of the White Cloth Hall, and the *Concert Rooms,* in Albion Street The *Charitable Institutions* in Leeds are numerous, and well supported.

The population of Leeds at the census in 1831 amounted to 123,393.

The *Parish Church,* dedicated to St. Peter, situate at the bottom of Kirkgate, of reign of Edward III., has just been rebuilt, and is expected to be opened at Whitsuntide next The vicarage, worth £1,300 per annum, is in the gift of the parishioners, and enjoyed by the Rev. W. F. Hook, D.D. There are six other churches in Leeds, together with two Roman Catholic chapels, and about thirty belonging to other denominations of Dissenters.

In the year 1654 Leeds was invested by Oliver Cromwell with the elective franchise, but the first and only member previous to the Reform Act was Adam Baynes, Esq., of Knostrop. The borough now returns two members, at present they are Edward Baines, Esq., and Sir William Molesworth.

3

ADDITIONAL INFORMATION.

WE deem ourselves fortunate in the circumstance, that while our little work was going through the press, the ninth half-yearly meeting of the Company was held at Manchester, on the 3rd of March last, whereby we are enabled to correct some inaccuracies which might otherwise have found a place in these pages, as well as to supply additional information respecting the expenses incurred in the construction of the line

	£	s.	d.
It appears that the total receipts of the Company on account of Calls up to 31st December, 1840, after deducting those in arrear, and also such parts thereof paid in advance as have become due, was	1,081,427	13	7
On account of Money in advance of Calls	185,322	15	1
On account of Mortgages and Bonds	1,211,882	0	0
On account of Interest on Calls not paid up, and Interest from Bankers, after deducting interest on sums paid in advance of Calls	8,368	12	4
On account of surplus receipts from traffic	31,481	8	4
On account of premium on unappropriated shares which have been sold, after payment of £200 to the Funds of the Benevolent Institution	335	0	0
TOTAL RECEIPTS	£2,518,817	9	4

EXPENDITURE

UP TO 31st DECEMBER, 1840

	£	s.	d.
On account of forming the Line and Stations	2,290,057	10	10
On account of working the line	93,151	7	7
On account of Loans	64,441	14	0
On account of Junction line to Hunt's Bank	46,120	17	5
On account of Surplus land &c. available for re-sale	30,737	9	8
TOTAL EXPENDITURE	£2,523,508	19	6
Deduct from this sum the total Receipts	2,518,817	9	4
Leaves a balance due to the Bankers of	£4,691	10	2

REVENUE ACCOUNT.

	£	s.	d.
Total Receipts on account of Passengers up to 30th June, 1840	35,080	2	8
From 30th June to 31st December, 1840	24,898	9	3
On account of Goods, Parcels, Carriages, and Live Stock	12,787	5	9
	£72,765	17	8

EXPENDITURE.

	£	s.	d.
On account of Locomotive Power to 31st December, 1840	12,892	19	1
Expenses in the Coaching and Merchandise departments, including duty on Passengers (£4232 12 0)	19,752	18	1
Police and other expenses	3,707	9	5
Miscellaneous Expenses	4,931	2	9
Total Expenses up to 31st December, 1840.	41,284	9	4
Deduct this from the foregoing receipts, leaves a balance in hand up to 31st December, 1840, of	£31,481	8	4

It appears that the original Contracts for the completion of the works on the main line amounted to £1,153,166; which, together with the expense of extra works and contingencies, estimated at £230,633, amount in the whole to £1,383,799. The actual expenditure, exclusive of rails, chairs, &c up to December, 1840, amounted to £1,580,951 13 1; and the estimates for the completion of the works amount to £146 000, making a total of £1,726,951 13 1, being an excess of £343,152 13 1. The aggregate length of the Tunnels was estimated at 4,567 lineal yards, but the actual length is 5,432 yards; and the expenses thereof have amounted to nearly £80 per lineal yard, The excess in the Summit Tunnel alone has been £108,000, the original taker having abandoned his contract soon after the commencement of the works, on payment of the penalty of £3000. The additional expense in the Winterbutt Lee Tunnel, owing to the softness of the ground, which required to be upheld by solid masonry, amounted to £30,000. £4,000 has been laid out in securing the embankment at Slack's valley, and £3,000 upon the bridge at Healey Low Mill, owing to the delay in the works incurred by a Chancery suit, which was eventually decided in favour of the Company, with costs besides some small sums expended on other parts of the line. With regard to Parliamentary and Law Expenses, including Engineering, management, salaries, and interest, up to the time of opening the line, estimated at £150,000, there will be an excess of about £78,000. The estimate for iron rails, chairs, sleepers, and fittings amounted to £150,000, the actual expenditure is expected to exceed this sum by upwards of £40,000. The stations, locomotive and other stock, engine sheds, and buildings required for conducting business as General Carriers, estimated at £350,000, will amount to about £388,000. These excesses, together with £30,000 paid for surplus stock, chiefly for land and buildings, which may ultimately be resold, amount in the whole to the sum of £579,000.

The total estimates for the above purposes given in March, 1839, amounted to £2,283,799. To this add the excess of £579,000, as stated above, and £310,000 for the formation of the Extension line, and the branches to Oldham, Heywood, and Halifax, making the total Capital £3,172,000. The Company are applying for a new Act of Parliament, enabling them to raise an additional sum of £487,500, by the creation of 19,500 £25 shares, which, with the sum they are empowered to raise upon security of the tolls, to the extent of one-third more, will amount to £650,000.

The traffic on the line as far as Littleborough from 30th June up to 5th October, 1840, when the portion between Hebden Bridge and Normanton was opened, amounted to £15,002 12s. 6d, and on both parts of the line up to 31st December last, when the remainder of the line, excepting the Summit Tunnel, was opened, amounted to £17,463 11s. 9d. The number of passengers conveyed during the 6 months ending 31st December, 1840, was 401,833, over an average distance of 8½ miles each, being equivalent to 3,415,580 travelling one mile each, or about 7,000,000 per annum

The best estimate the Directors could form of the expense of completing the main line, including engines, locomotive, and other stock, amounted to £2,864,000

OMNIBUSES from *Oldham* to the *Mills Hill* Station, from *Halifax* to the *Sowerby Bridge* Station, and also from *Huddersfield* to the *Cooper Bridge* Station, to meet every train

COACHES leave Chaffer's Office, *Burnley*, for the *Todmorden* Station, on the following days, namely —

On Monday, at 8 A M	On Friday, at 6 A M
— Tuesday, at 6 A M	— Saturday, at 6 A M
— Wednesday, at 6 A M	— Sunday, at 9½ A M
— Thursday, at 6 A M	

The following TRAINS from *Manchester* meet *Burnley* Coaches at Todmorden, VIZ —

On Monday, at 5 P M	On Friday, at 5 P M
— Tuesday, at 5 and 6½ P M	— Saturday, at 5 P M
— Wednesday, at 5 P M	— Sunday, at 1½ P M
— Thursday, at 5 P M	

The distance from *Burnley* to Manchester will be performed in 2 hours

To Liverpool	in 3½ hours	To York	in 3½ hours
— Leeds	in 3 —	— Hull	in 4½ —

OMNIBUSES leave the Railway Office, opposite the *Bowling Green Inn, Bradford*, for the Brighouse Station at 15 minutes past 7, and 8 o'Clock in the morning, and 30 minutes past 12, and 4 o'Clock in the afternoon, *on Week Days*. Also, *on Thursdays* at 7 in the evening. *On Sundays* at 30 minutes past 8 in the morning and 30 minutes past 6 in the evening

And return from *Brighouse* to Bradford at 49 minutes past 9 o'Clock in the morning, 19 minutes past 12, 49 minutes past 5, and 50 minutes past 8 in the afternoon, *on Week Days*. Also, *on Thursdays* at 45 minutes past 8 in the morning. *On Sundays* at 20 minutes past 10 in the morning, and 50 minutes past 8 in the evening

A TABLE OF CROSS DISTANCES ON THE MANCHESTER AND LEEDS RAILWAY.

FROM THE MANCHESTER STATION	miles		miles
		To Wigan	19½
		Broughton	2¾
		Cheetham Hill	2¼
	miles	Droylsden	3½
To Ashton	7¾	Fairfield	4¾
Bolton	11	Harpurhey	2
Bury	10½	Kersal Moor	3¾
Leigh	14½	Openshaw	3½
Liverpool	32½	Rushulme	2½
Stockport	6		

A TABLE OF CROSS DISTANCES ON THE MANCHESTER AND LEEDS RAILWAY.

FROM THE
MILL HILL Station

	miles
To Oldham	2
Middleton	1½
Bury	7½
Heap	6½

FROM THE
HEYWOOD & BLUE PITTS Station

To Heywood	1½
Bury	4¾

FROM THE
ROCHDALE Station

To Rochdale Town	¾
Bacup	7¾
Bury	7
Haslingden	10¼
Butterworth	2
Castleton	1½
Spotland Bridge	1¼
Thurnham	2½
Wardleworth	3¼

FROM THE
LITTLEBOROUGH Station

To Butterworth	1½
Stubley	¼

FROM THE
TODMORDEN Station

To Bacup	5
Burnley	9

FROM THE
HEBDEN BRIDGE Station

To Keighley	11½
Mytholm	½
Mytholmroyd	1

FROM THE
SOWERBY BRIDGE Station,

	miles.
To Halifax	3
Bradford	11
Ripponden	3
To Elland	3
Sowerby	1
Stainland	5

FROM THE
BRIGHOUSE Station

To Bradford	7
Halifax	6
Huddersfield	4
Clifton	1¼
Low Moor	4¼
Northowram	4¼
Rastrick	¾
Southowram	3

FROM THE
COOPER BRIDGE Station

To Huddersfield	3¾
Batley	4½
Birstal	4½
Cleckheaton	4
Gomersal	4½
Heckmondwike	2¾
Hightown	2
Hopton	2
Kirkheaton	3
Mill Bridge	2¼
Mirfield Town	2½

FROM THE
DEWSBURY Station

To Dewsbury Town	¾
Batley	3
Gawthorpe	2⅜
Gomersal	5¾
Heckmondwike	2¾
Kirkheaton	3¼
Ossett	3¾
Thornhill	1¼

FROM THE
HORBURY BRIDGE Station

To Horbury	1
Crigglestone	4
Lupset Park	2
Thornes	2¾
Ossett	2
Walton	3

I may say here at this time the rule and practice for signalling away all passenger trains leaving Manchester Station was done by an inspector blowing a bugle.

The branch line from North Dean to Halifax was opened in July, 1844 ; gradient, 1 in 45

During the time I was at Brighouse I observed it was not unusual for special goods and mineral trains to be despatched fifteen or twenty wagons long, with simply a man placed on the last wagon, and supplied with a hand lamp and a red flag for the purpose of protecting his train. Brake vans were seldom attached to the rear of such trains.

I remember an incident when the station master called my attention to a batch of important documents which had just arrived by train from Manchester, and required to be delivered immediately to Mr. George Anderton, one of the directors, who resided at Cleckheaton. Instructions were sent to the stable for a horse to be saddled and sent up to the station for me. When it came I observed it was a 'bus horse, and not accustomed to the saddle ; nevertheless, I took up the documents and mounted, and away we went to Cleckheaton, a distance of over four miles. On going over Clifton Common, and passing some boys playing at cricket, the ball came whizzing past the horse's head. The animal took fright and bolted After running a short distance he performed a somersault, but was quickly on his legs again, leaving me sprawling in the mud, with my hat crushed over my face I got up, pulled myself together, and found my horse standing some twenty or thirty yards away When I got to him I found he had burst both his knees ; fortunately, there was a highway water trough close by. After washing the horse's knees and grooming myself down, I again mounted and trotted off to Cleckheaton—I with my crushed hat, and the horse with his burst knees. All went well up to a few hundred yards of the end of my journey. A strong north wind was blowing at the time, and on passing the market place, near to Mr. Williamson's oil warehouse, a gust of wind caught me and away went my hat and wig flying in the air. I dropped off the horse, and after a good chase, assisted by some young fellows who happened to be standing at the corner of the street, I caught my wig, and they bringing my hat, I put myself in order, mounted for the third time, and made another start with my crushed hat and dirty wig, the horse with his crushed knees, and the fellows shouting "John Gilpin." At last I arrived at Mr. Anderton's residence, and gave him the documents. He looked very hard both at me and the horse, and said, " I think you have had a rough journey, Normington." I replied, " I have, sir," and explained to him what had happened. He then gave a good hearty laugh, and said, " I hope you will arrive safe at Brighouse." I said " Thank you, sir," bid him good day, and trotted back to Brighouse. On arriving there the stable manager was waiting to take the horse to the stable. He soon observed something was wrong, and made a similar remark to that made by Mr. Anderton about my having had a rough journey, and said the man who saddled the 'bus horse for me deserved horse-whipping, and that I ought to think myself lucky in having arrived back without some broken bones.

At this time passengers for Bradford by trains were changed at Brighouse and conveyed from there by omnibus, there being no railway through

In October, 1847, I was appointed to the position of station master at Mumps Station, Oldham. This was an extension of a branch line connected with the main line at Mills Hill Station, afterwards called Middleton Junction. I made the necessary arrangements at the station, which was opened on the 1st of November. A very dense fog prevailed all the day The working arrangements passed off satisfactorily, although there was some difficulty in dealing with the trains, as they had to stop at the arrival end of the platform. The engine was then uncoupled, afterwards coupled together with a drag chain, and was then turned up a siding, and dragged the train along the platform line into the station, this being the only way for the engine to get round the train for the return journey. I remember a few days after the station was opened the general manager, accompanied by the passenger superintendent, paid a visit to the station. The general manager, who was a comical-looking little man, was blind of one eye, and wore a large eyeglass for the other. On looking round the station he had to pass along the top of a high embankment—some forty feet slope—when he had the misfortune to slip, and came sliding down the soft clay and dirt to the bottom. He seemed to be no worse for the mishap, further than the spoiling of his white waistcoat and his clothing being well besmeared with mud clay.

The branch line from Heaton Lodge to Huddersfield, in connection with the Manchester and Leeds main line of railway, was opened in 1847. Prior to this Huddersfield passengers were conveyed to and from Cooper Bridge Station by omnibuses.

On Easter Monday, 1848, I was somewhat amused by seeing an Oldham wedding. The parties arrived by train from Manchester, and nineteen persons left the carriage. They formed themselves into couples, and walked in procession from the station, one man taking the lead and playing the fiddle, whilst two walked, one on either side, each carrying an earthenware vessel with two handles, containing beer, which was frequently passed to those walking in the procession. These two vessels were intended for presentation to the bride and bridegroom later on in the day In those days it was said they married people at the Manchester Cathedral in lots, or several couples at the same time, who were told to pair themselves when they got outside

In the year 1848 the line to Blackpool was opened for passenger traffic, and during the summer season cheap excursions were run on Sundays from Mumps (Oldham) Station to Blackpool. Day tickets were issued at one shilling to ladies and one and sixpence to gentlemen, averaging four trains of twenty-five coaches each during the season

I remember receiving a private letter from the passenger superintendent, desiring me to keep all excursionists outside the station until he arrived from Manchester. I did so on the following Sunday morning. He arrived by special engine, accompanied by four inspectors At that time there would not be less than two thousand passengers who had previously booked and were impatiently waiting to come into the station for their trains. The superintendent explained to me the reason he had come with his inspectors. He had received some private information to the effect that half the people who bought shilling tickets were men dressed in female attire. I laughed, and said, "If any man would do that to save sixpence, let him go." He replied, sharply, "You are encouraging the fraud," and said he would examine all the passengers himself. The mode he adopted was this He partly opened the passenger entrance door, so as to admit only one person at a time ; he then placed one of his inspectors upon a chair, at the entrance, holding up a long pole with a notice board fixed at the top, lettered in large type, "All ladies first, to hold up their tickets in their hands above their heads," he himself standing partly behind the chair, peeping

at the passengers as they passed through When
some two hundred ladies had passed the gazing
point some dissatisfaction arose amongst the crowd
waiting anxiously to pass to the platform. Husbands
were not inclined to allow their wives to go alone, and
sweethearts were determined not to be separated. A
great rush was made for the entrance, the people bursting
open the passage door, knocking over the chain, the
inspector with his pole, and the superintendent, who was
peeping from behind, sending them all sprawling on the
floor in the passage. I just came on the scene in time
to see the crowd rushing through the passage, and
trampling over the superintendent. I made a rush, got
hold of his coat collar, and, assisted by another man,
dragged him away into the waiting room, where he lay
for some time unconscious I was only just in time to
save his life. When he regained consciousness he asked
me what I had done with the passengers. I told him they
were half way on their way to Blackpool, and said it
would have been much better had he taken my view upon
the private information he told me he had received. It
was very well known on the line that the superintendent was a most eccentric man.

There is a steep gradient in this branch of 1 in 27,
a mile in length, situated between Middleton Junction
and Werneth, Oldham, and a stationary engine was fixed
at the top of the incline, with a rope attached to it, for
the purpose of pulling up and letting down trains to the
bottom of the incline. The first passenger train in the
morning from Oldham, Werneth Station, was run to
Middleton Junction, without an engine or rope attached,
to meet the main line train from Manchester to Yorkshire.
The train consisted of one brake van and two coaches. I
well remember one day travelling by the last passenger
train from Manchester to Oldham. It consisted of five

coaches and brake van, engine No. 131, I think, which was a new one, the driver being William Bates. The engine being attached to the rope at the bottom of the incline in the usual way, the train travelled about half way up the incline, when the rope broke, and the train came to a stand. I went to the driver and asked him what he intended doing under the circumstances. He replied, " It's all up, lad ; we shall have to stop here all neet." I said, " Nonsense"; but he said the engine could not get up the incline itself without the rope. Seeing that it was a strong new engine, I suggested to the driver and guard that we should set the train back to the bottom of the incline, and test the question The train was set back, we got the passengers into two carriages, and shunted the other portion off into a siding. The engine was then coupled to the two coaches The driver repeatedly declared that it was not possible to get up the incline, not even the engine alone, without the rope. However, I prevailed upon the driver to try, and after my explanation he agreed to try. The two coaches and brake van were then set back on the level some four hundred yards towards Middleton Junction The driver gave a good start, and ran well up to within some three hundred yards of the top of the incline, when the train came to a stand. I told the driver he had not done his best, having no steam to start with. After some sharp words had passed between us, he agreed to make another trial. The train was again set back, a further distance on the level this time, and, steam being well up, we started again, and arrived safely on the top of the incline. The passengers gave a good hearty cheer for accomplishing what was considered to be an impossibility. This test resulted in more powerful engines being built, and the dispensing with ropes for assisting trains on all steep inclines. Mr. William Hirst, then locomotive superintendent, accompanied by some of the directors, took charge of the first engine, No. 151, which took the first passenger train of six coaches up the Oldham incline without the assistance of a rope, in June, 1851

In December, 1848, the Dewsbury, Batley, and Leeds Branch was opened, and the Lancashire and Yorkshire Railway Company commenced to run passenger trains from Mirfield to Leeds and Leeds to Mirfield, over this branch, in connection at Mirfield with main line trains to and from Manchester, and discontinued in August, 1850. After this date the passenger traffic to and from Manchester to Leeds was conveyed by the London and North-Western Company

Cleckheaton branch line, from Mirfield to Low Moor, was opened for traffic in July, 1848, and passengers for Bradford were conveyed by omnibus from Low Moor in place of Brighouse   The new line from Sowerby Bridge and Halifax to Low Moor was opened on August 7th, 1850. The Wakefield, Knottingley to Goole, and Knottingley to Askern lines were opened on March 29th, 1848.   A special train of fifty carriages left Pontefract, full of people, joined by some of the directors, to Goole   The towns and villages along the line made the day a general holiday   The branch line between Pontefract and Methley Junction, in connection with the Midland Railway, for Leeds, was opened for traffic in April, 1848.

In 1849 the receipts of the Company were gradually decreasing, in consequence of bad trade all over the country.   With the view of reducing the working expenses, the directors decided on a reduction of staff, salaries, and wages throughout the line.   I received instructions in August to proceed to Mirfield and take up the position of station inspector, at a reduction of five shillings per week.   This was very awkward and discouraging to me, as I had just taken to myself a wife.   I went to Mirfield in September, and rather than take a station inspector's position I preferred to become a guard, with the view of gaining experience on the line, and I continued acting in that capacity to the end of January, 1854.

The Huddersfield to Penistone line was opened July 1st, 1850, for traffic in connection at Penistone with the Manchester, Sheffield, and Lincolnshire Railway to and from Sheffield and London The branch line from Brockholes to Holmfirth was also opened for traffic July 1st, 1850. I commenced guard's duties and took charge of trains which run between Low Moor, Mirfield, and Huddersfield, in September, 1849. At that time the train arrangements were to run between Low Moor, Mirfield, and Huddersfield, in connection there with trains to and from Penistone. A service of trains were run between Holmfirth and Brockholes, in connection with trains to and from Huddersfield The engine working this train was stabled at Holmfirth. I had the honour and pleasure of taking charge of the first passenger train which arrived and departed from Holmfirth, on July 1st, 1850. The superintendent of the line was responsible for making the time table for the working of those branches. But the one he issued to the public did not work well, nor give satisfaction to them, and continual alterations in the times of running were made, with no better results. I happened to be in the booking office at Huddersfield Station when I heard the superintendent and the clerk in charge there talking over this unsatisfactory state of things. The superintendent said it was not possible on such a complicated line to make a time table to please the public, and that he would give a five-pound note to anyone who could produce one. In a few days after this I submitted one, which was adopted. It not only met the public requirements, but reduced the working expenses by dispensing with the engine stabled at Holmfirth. I made the working arrangements for all trains from Bradford to Huddersfield to run through to Holmfirth, but I never received the promised five pounds.

In November, 1850, the memorable flood at Holmfirth took place I remember walking through the village on the evening of that day on my way to the railway station, and passing through the groups of inhabitants, who were frantic with fear, they having had some intimation that the water in the Billbury reservoir was likely to burst the embankment. I left in charge of the last train at nine p m On arriving at Mirfield about midnight; the sky was beautiful and clear, and the full moon, shining in all its brilliancy, showed the great flood which was running down the river Calder, carrying along with it pigs, cattle, and furniture of all descriptions, proving that the disaster had happened, and that their worst fears were realised. I left Mirfield the next morning in charge of the first train, arriving at Holmfirth about seven o'clock, when I beheld a most heartrending sight. The village was a complete wreck, mills, shops, and houses, with their families, and even graveyards, were swept away by the tremendous flood. The roads and fields in the valley were knee deep in mud, and dead bodies could be seen everywhere. The whole valley echoed with the people's lamentations, while thousands upon thousands of folk flocked daily to see the havoc the flood had made.

The Wakefield and Barnsley branch was opened on January 1st, 1850. It was then only a single line. The Lancashire and Yorkshire Railway Company undertook to work it, and, if necessary, make it into a double line. The traffic increased, and the line was doubled (with the exception of Woolley Tunnel), and opened on Saturday, April 21st, 1855. There being only a single line through the tunnel, it was worked by pilot engine, which was arranged to pilot all trains through.

The Leeds, Dewsbury, and Batley Railway was made by an independent company, and opened in August, 1848. The Lancashire and Yorkshire Railway Company worked it, and prior to discontinuing to run their trains to Leeds over this line they had an offer to take up the line at a guarantee of six per cent dividend, but unfortunately for the Company they declined the offer. The Dewsbury and Batley Company then offered the line to the London and North-Western Company. They wisely accepted the offer, and commenced to run their trains over it in 1849.

In 1842-43 the inhabitants of the town of Huddersfield memorialised the Manchester and Leeds Railway Company, now the Lancashire and Yorkshire Railway Company, to make them a branch line from Heaton Lodge to Huddersfield in connection with their main line. The Company surveyed a valley line, but the memorialists demurred to this, they desiring the line to be on the higher level. This led to a meeting at Huddersfield of the two parties for the purpose of deciding the question. The meeting proved to be rather a stormy one, and in the excitement, it was said, unfortunately the general manager made the remark that the Huddersfield traffic was not worth stopping an engine for. He was hooted, and the meeting was broken up. The memorialists afterwards made the branch line for themselves on the higher level, and when it was opened, in 1847, the London and North-Western Company worked it. In the meantime the memorialists had desired the London and North-Western Company to make them a line from Huddersfield to Stalybridge in connection there with their line to Manchester. Fortunately, the Company complied with their request, and opened it in 1849, and having secured the Dewsbury, Batley, and Leeds branch, gave the London and North-Western Railway Company a competitive through line from Manchester to Huddersfield, Dewsbury, and Leeds.

I remember, on Thursday, May 9th, 1850, being in charge of a train from Huddersfield to Low Moor. Being market day at Bradford, this train conveyed the Manchester merchants, who had arrived by main line trains from Mirfield to Low Moor, and were afterwards taken on by omnibus to Bradford. However, on arriving at Low Moor, about 10-45 a.m., one of the directors, who was travelling by the same train from Cleckheaton, came to me, and said the train was very full, and many of the merchants were anxious to go through to Bradford by train. I replied that the Government inspector had been over the line, but I did not know whether he had given the necessary certificate to the Company. He then asked, "Do you think it would be safe to run the train on to Bradford?" I replied, "If you say go, I will take the train and arrive there safely." He said, "Then we will go." I, knowing that no staff had been definitely arranged for Bradford new station, picked out four porters from Low Moor platform, and took them along with me on the engine. On approaching the new station I dropped them off at the several points necessary to turn the engine and train on to the line for the platform. At the time the masons were busy laying down the flags. They all looked up, and were astonished at seeing a train coming into the station, having had no notice. On arrival a crowd of passengers surrounded me, and gave me three good hearty cheers, which were worthy of remembrance. After this the director came to me, and said, "Seeing that the train has arrived safely, why should not all other trains come in, and dispense with the omnibuses at Low Moor?" I replied that there was nothing to prevent this, pro-

viding proper arrangements were made. He said, " Make
the arrangements," and I made the temporary arrangements accordingly. The line from Low Moor to Bradford
was opened permanently for passenger traffic on Friday,
May 10th, 1850.

In 1850 there was some alteration made in the
management amongst the officers Captain John M.
Laws was made general manager. The divisional
passenger superintendents were Mr. George Hall, for
Manchester ; Captain Brinstead, for Yorkshire ; and Mr.
Henry Blackmore, for Lancashire

I remember being guard in charge of an excursion train
from Holmfirth to Hull, in August, 1852. The train
consisted of twenty-five carriages, full of passengers On
the return journey, the engine and train came to a stand
on the sharp curve of a rising gradient, situated about
half way between Thongs Bridge and Holmfirth Stations.
It was midnight, and very dark, and in those days
carriages were not lighted. I left my van, walked up to
the engine, and asked the driver what was wrong. He
replied that the train was too heavy, and the engine
could not possibly take it further. I asked him if he
could take half the train, and he said he would try. I
then gave the assistant guard a hand lamp, told him to
go back towards Thongs Bridge Station, show his red
light, and stop any engine or train which might be
coming to Holmfirth. I then divided the train into two
portions, and sent the driver on to Holmfirth with the
first. We had proceeded towards the station some two
hundred yards, when I heard the echo of an engine
running at a great speed up the valley. I felt sure it
was coming towards Holmfirth. I immediately jumped
off the first portion of the train and ran back to the rear
part, which I had left standing on the line. To my
amazement I found the assistant guard standing by the

4

brake van; he had not gone back as I had previously instructed him to do. I still heard the echo of the engine coming at a great speed. I continued running back in great fear, and almost breathless with the thought of what I feared would happen It turned out to be an empty engine coming to Holmfirth, and, fortunately, the engine driver was well on the look out. He caught sight of my red light just as he entered the sharp curve, and brought his engine to a stand within twelve inches of the train which was standing on the main line full of passengers. After the engine had passed me I turned back to the train, and on finding that the engine had just stopped clear of smashing into it, I said to the driver, "Ah, Jim, thou'rt worth thy weight in gold for being on the look out," and, pointing to the assistant guard, said, "As for thee, I could hang thee on that tree, and never think I had done wrong." His neglect and carelessness might have led to death and injury to a large number of passengers.

In December of the same year I was guard in charge of the last passenger train which left Mirfield at eleven p.m. for Huddersfield. It was a very dark, wet night. On passing what was called Brookes' Brick and Tile Works the engine became defective, began to run slow on rounding the sharp curve up to Hill House, and gradually got worse. When I heard the Bangor mail, from Normanton, approaching, I jumped off my train, and ran back to meet the mail, showing a red light to the engine driver, just in time for him to stop the train, and prevent what might have been a very serious collision.

In January, 1851, Bradley Wood Branch, which was made by the London and North-Western Company, was opened for goods traffic. In 1852 they ran goods trains between Huddersfield and Halifax and Halifax to Huddersfield, up to about 1859. It was then closed for

a time, and re-opened by the Lancashire and Yorkshire
Railway Company, who commenced to run over it a
service of passenger trains, at my suggestion, in January,
1860, between Halifax and Huddersfield.

I remember one Saturday in July, 1853, when I was in
charge of the last passenger train from Huddersfield, due
at Bradford at 11-10 p.m. On arriving at Low Moor the
engine broke down, and the driver said it could not be
moved from the main line. In those days all engines
were stabled at Mirfield, and there was no telegraphic
communication. The station master said there would be
no engine available until nine o'clock on Sunday morning.
The passengers, numbering about thirty, would have to
walk to Bradford, a distance of over four miles. Seeing
it was midnight, I said that it was too bad to have to
walk. "Have you no shunt horses about?" He replied
they had been turned into the field hours ago, not being
wanted until Monday. I then asked him to send one of
the platform porters for one, and told him to bring it to
the station harnessed, which he did. We then put all
the passengers into a third-class carriage, which was fitted
up with a good outside brake. The horse was yoked in
front of the carriage, with a man in charge of it. I took
charge of the carriage brake, and off we went to Bradford
about midnight. The horse pulled the carriage on the
line through the dark Low Moor Tunnel, which is over
1,000 yards long, and brought the carriage to a stand at
the top of the incline going into Bradford, a distance of
over two miles. He was then detached from the carriage
and taken back through the tunnel to Low Moor I then
took the carriage down the descending gradient of 1 in
50 over a mile long into the station at Bradford, arriving
there safely about one o'clock on Sunday morning. The
passengers assembled on the platform and gave me three
good hearty cheers. This was the second time I had been

honoured with cheers by the passengers on arriving at Bradford Station

A little incident occurred whilst we were descending the gradient into Bradford. A timid passenger kept putting his head out of the window, and called out to me, "Are you sure you can stop the carriage?" I, knowing that a brake applied to a single carriage brings it to a stand almost immediately, replied, "Yes; look out," at the same time applying the brake sharply, which brought the carriage suddenly to a full stop, knocking the passengers together. They shouted, "That's too sudden a stop, you have burst some of our noses"; especially the timid passenger, who was a doctor, and happened to be looking out of the window

All engine drivers, firemen, and guards working on this section of the line resided at Mirfield; therefore, after finishing with the last train either at Huddersfield or Bradford, we returned home to Mirfield with the empty engine. On this night a passenger who resided at Mirfield happened to be too late for the last train from Bradford, and was told by the staff that if he waited at the station he could get to Mirfield by the empty engine. On seeing me arrive at the station with one carriage and no engine, he came up to me in astonishment, and asked me where was the engine. I said, "It's broken down, and left at Low Moor." He then asked, "How are you going to get home?" I said, "Oh, walk it." He said, "Then I'll join you"; and off we went together about 1-30 in the morning, arriving at Mirfield about five o'clock, having walked a distance of over 12 miles, not forgetting to call our friends up on the way for refreshment

I acted as guard three years and four months, a post which entailed very rough and hard work in those days. The guard's van had then an elevated portion fixed on the top to sit in, usually called "Jack-in-the-box." The brake handle was fixed outside on the top of the van, and every time a train had to stop, the guard attending to his brake was exposed to all weathers. Three of us worked the service of trains which ran between Bradford, Mirfield, Huddersfield, and Holmfirth. We changed workings every alternate day : First day, 7 a.m. to 11 p.m ; second day, 11 a.m. to 12 p.m.; third day, 4-30 a.m. to 1 p.m.; and each was on duty every alternate Sunday, from 7 a.m. to 10 p m. During the three years and four months I travelled in charge of trains 221,400 miles.

In May, 1853, Mr. George Hall, passenger superintendent at Manchester, resigned. It was then arranged by the directors for the line to be worked in two divisions. They appointed Mr. Henry Blackmore superintendent over the Western Division, with Mr. George Aylesbury for his assistant ; Captain Binstead, R.N , superintendent for the Eastern Division, and Mr. Alexander Barber as his assistant. This was the commencement of working the line upon the principle of divisional management. At this time the Company paid a dividend for the first half year of $3\frac{1}{4}$ per cent, and for the second half $3\frac{1}{2}$ per cent. When divisional management was discontinued, in June, 1871, the Company paid a dividend for the first half-year of $7\frac{3}{4}$ per cent, second half 8 per cent. In 1872 the Company paid a dividend for the first half-year of $7\frac{5}{8}$ per cent, for the second half $9\frac{1}{4}$ per cent.

It will be observed that this change of management only took eighteen months to destroy the foundation laid for cultivating traffic by the divisional officers. After 1872 the Company's dividends gradually dwindled down in face of an increasing population and improved trade throughout the whole line. Up to the time of the changed management the directors were very sanguine, and I often heard them say that the line would eventually pay a 10 per cent dividend. I was of the same opinion, and I am sure it would have done had divisional management been adhered to similar to that of the London and North-Western Railway Company. When divisional management was first adopted, in 1853, dividends gradually went up to the time of centralisation, and since then the shareholders know best how they have had to suffer, which misfortune has led to so many stormy half-yearly meetings, all being eager for an explanation of the cause of the depreciation suffered by their stock. The meetings generally ended with a reply from the chairman that the directors had done the best they could. But in reality the dwindling of the dividends was caused by loss of traffic for want of cultivation. In February, 1854, I was appointed as outside station master at Sowerby Bridge, and was there up to the end of April, 1859. I found this station very rough and difficult to work, because of the want of accommodation to deal with the busy exchange traffic, there only being one up and down short platforms, and the up platform being situated within thirty yards of the end of a long tunnel. The system of dealing with the passenger trains was as follows. On the arrival of the Bradford and Leeds portion of trains on the up platform they were set back into a bay siding clear of the main line. Then came the Normanton and Wakefield portion. The passengers were then placed in their respective trains, and the two portions joined together and made up into one train, varying from seventeen to twenty-five vehicles. A pilot engine often had to assist up to Summit Tunnel. On the arrival of the train at Rochdale it was divided, the Normanton and Wakefield portion despatched to Liverpool, and the Bradford and Leeds portion despatched to Manchester. The down trains arrived on the down platform in two portions, having been coupled together at Rochdale I had the trains divided, the passengers rectified and placed in their respective trains, then despatched the portion of the train from Liverpool to Wakefield and Normanton, and the portion of the train from Manchester to Bradford and Leeds.

In those days a branch train ran between Halifax, North Dean, and Elland, in connection there with the up and down main line trains. This branch train service did not serve all requirements, as Halifax and Huddersfield passengers often had to travel in this way : From Huddersfield to Mirfield, change there for the up main line train, and on arriving at Sowerby Bridge change there for a branch train to Halifax. Passengers from Halifax travelled to Sowerby Bridge, changed there for the down main line train to Mirfield, and changed there for the branch train to Huddersfield.

In February, 1854, the Manchester, Sheffield. and Lincolnshire Railway Company commenced to run trains from Penistone and Huddersfield In January, 1854, the Great Northern Railway Company commenced running passenger trains from Doncaster, over Askern Branch, to Knottingley, and then over the Methley Branch and the Midland Railway Company's line to Leeds, and from Leeds the same way to Knottingley and Doncaster for London In January, 1854, the Lancashire and Yorkshire Railway Company established their Railway Servants Insurance Society, for the purpose of insuring an allowance to them in the event of accidents. The Railway Company subscribed £400 per annum, and every servant, on becoming a member, subscribed a penny per week. I was one of the first members to join. Although the Company established this society for the benefit of their servants, many of them objected to become members. However, in November, 1857, the directors passed a resolution that all the servants employed in their workshops, goods, or passenger departments, or employed in any way on the

line in connection with trains, be required forthwith
either to become members of that society, or to leave the
Company's service.

During the time I was at Sowerby Bridge Station
many slight accidents occurred whilst shunting operations were going on on the down main line, which arose
through the station being situated at the east end of a
long tunnel, the trains only being protected whilst at the
station by what was called an auxiliary signal. This
was a disc or spectacle signal fixed at the west end of the
tunnel, and worked by a pointsman at the station. There
was no system of working tunnels by telegraph then as at
present. It often occurred when the tunnel was full of
smoke that goods trains had entered at the west end
unknown to the pointsman, and he was not aware one
was approaching until he saw it emerge from the tunnel.
He then put on "danger" to the auxiliary signal. In
the meantime a second goods train had passed the
auxiliary signal before being put to danger, thus
occasioning slight collisions. So many of this kind of
accidents occurring led me to invent a method which
would ensure the auxiliary signal being put to danger by
the engine when passing it in the first instance before
entering the tunnel, thus protecting its own train.

The invention was this I had an independent wire
laid down from the station to the auxiliary signal post, a
distance of 1,750 yards One end was attached to a wheel
at the station in charge of the pointsman, the other end
being attached to a latch, which was connected by a
chain on the quadrant at the bottom of the auxiliary
signal post. It was also connected to an iron treadle
which was fixed inside the rail of the four-foot. When
an engine passed over it the flange of the engine wheels
pressed down the treadle, which released the latch, and
the auxiliary disc signal went on to danger. Some time

after this our permanent way inspector brought a gentleman to look at it, who afterwards patented the invention, with the addition of a bell being attached to the pointsman's wheel at the station. This bell was an improvement, having the effect of calling the attention of the pointsman that an engine or train had passed the auxiliary signal. It was unfortunate for the gentleman who patented the principle, as in a short time afterwards the Company adopted the system of having all long tunnels worked by telegraph Nevertheless, this invention prevented many accidents.

In June, 1855, the London and North-Western Railway Company commenced to run what is called the Bangor mail, leaving Normanton at 10-25 p m. for Huddersfield, and the 1-57 a.m. train from Huddersfield to Normanton, in connection at the latter place with the mails to and from the North.

In June, 1855, Mr. Newall's patent continuous brake was first applied to the Lancashire and Yorkshire passenger trains.

In November, 1856, a general order was issued to all stations, giving notice to station masters that no train should follow another at a less interval than five minutes, and that goods trains must be shunted into a siding clear of the main line ten minutes before a passenger train was due. This order created no little confusion at many of the stations not having sufficient siding accommodation ; consequently, goods trains had to be shunted from one main line to another, which resulted in serious delays to traffic on the opposite line

In the latter part of this year the directors decided to arrange with the British Telegraph Company to establish one uniform system of telegraph communication over the whole of the Company's lines. When this system came into operation it gave great assistance in working the traffic over the line with more punctuality and safety.

The West Yorkshire branch line from Wakefield to Leeds, and Leeds to Low Moor, was made by an independent company, and opened October, 1857, to Leeds. The Lancashire and Yorkshire Railway Company commenced to run passenger trains from Wakefield to Leeds, in connection at Wakefield with trains to and from Goole branches; also through trains were run from Barnsley to Leeds and Leeds to Barnsley. The branch line from Leeds to Low Moor was opened for passenger traffic in the middle of September, when the Lancashire and Yorkshire Railway Company commenced to run passenger trains from Low Moor to and from Leeds, in connection at Low Moor with main line trains to and from Manchester

On the 6th of September, 1858, Her Majesty the Queen travelled from Gosport by special train, which was despatched at 9-45 a.m., to London, and from London to Leeds: over the Great Northern Railway from London to Doncaster; afterwards over the Lancashire and Yorkshire Railway from Doncaster via Knottingley to Wakefield; thence from Wakefield, over the new line, called the Wakefield, Leeds, and Bradford Company. The royal train left London at 12-55 p.m., Doncaster at 5-10 p.m., arriving at Leeds at 6-15 p m, and accomplishing the journey in five hours and twenty minutes, the distance being one hundred and ninety-two and a half miles. Now, in 1895, the distance is run in three hours and fifty minutes. The next day Her Majesty opened the new Town Hall, at Leeds, afterwards went by coach to York, there to join the royal family, who had left London by special train at 8-20 a m, arriving at York at 1-25 p m. Her Majesty joined the royal train, which was despatched at 1-55 p m. for the North.

The following letter appeared in the *Manchester*

Examiner and Times, in 1858. I insert it here to show the inconveniences the public had to contend with at that time. Now, in 1895, the journey is accomplished in three hours and thirty minutes —

IMPORTANT TO TRAVELLERS.

To the Editor of the Examiner and Times.

SIR,—A friend of mine, who applied a short time ago for medical aid, was ordered at once by her medical adviser to Harrogate. She, determined to take advantage of the extraordinary offers of the East Lancashire Railway Company, started from Rawtenstall about ten in the morning, and arrived a little before ten in the evening. This was rather tedious, yet not very unreasonable when we consider that it was in the daytime, and, moreover, when they had travelled 40 miles they were only about eight miles from home—*i.e*, at Todmorden. In returning, however, yesterday, it was not so pleasant and agreeable, at least for an invalid. They started from Harrogate a little before three o'clock in the afternoon, and proceeded to Church Fenton, and stayed there about two hours From Church Fenton they proceeded to Normanton, and waited there about two hours more. From Normanton they came on to Todmorden, slowly and safely, where they arrived a little before nine o'clock At Todmorden all those who were destined for Colne, Accrington, Preston, Rawtenstall, Newchurch, Stacksteads, and Bacup (and there were passengers for all these places) were left, and after some delay they were forwarded along with luggage wagons to Rose Grove. Here a porter " kindled a fire," boiled some water in a large kettle, and hunted out some crockery, fortunately one of the company had a little tea, and another sugar, &c, &c., and they thus managed to assist each other in a friendly way. What a pity the company does not provide beds as well as kettles ! From Rose Grove they proceeded by luggage train between twelve and one, and arrived at Accrington about one o'clock. From Accrington those destined for Rossendale proceeded by luggage train about three o'clock. At Ramsbottom they fortunately met with another luggage train for Bacup, and arrived at Rawtenstall about twenty minutes past four in the morning

By inserting this simple statement of facts it may be the means of contributing, in some degree at least, to better regulations in connection with extraordinary cheap trips At all events, it will throw some little light upon the literal darkness in which excursionists generally have to travel.   A PARTY CONCERNED

Rawtenstall, August 17, 1858
P.S. I enclose my card

On Thursday, June 13, 1858, a serious collision occurred at Spring Wood Junction, at the west end of the short tunnel, about three hundred yards from Huddersfield Station. It was caused by five loaded coal wagons escaping from the goods sidings at Honley Station, which was on a falling gradient of one in one hundred to Huddersfield. The 1-30 p.m. London and North-Western passenger train from Huddersfield to Manchester was passing the junction at the time, when the runaway wagons ran completely through it, resulting in three passengers being killed and eleven seriously injured. The sidings at Honley were considered to be secure, by the use of what was called a Scotch block That was a thick piece of wood placed across the siding rail. This accident proved that the Scotch block was not a surety, and led to what are now called throw-off or safety points being fixed at all sidings leading on to the main line; and the Board of Trade inspectors recommended all railway companies to adopt the principle, and dispense with the wood Scotch blocks.

I remember a rather amusing incident, which occurred at Sowerby Bridge Station on the arrival of a passenger train from Liverpool. The porters commenced changing the passengers and placing them in their respective trains. The platform being rather low caused some difficulty in getting ladies into the carriages, as, at that time, enormous crinolines were worn I noticed a porter very busy attending to a lady. He was carrying a bag and other parcels along the platform to the carriage for Leeds. After putting the children and the parcels into the compartment, he stepped back to allow the lady to get in. She was wearing a very large steel-hooped crinoline, and had got one foot on the step, when this ridiculous article flew upwards. The porter was just about giving her a helping hand, when she stepped back, completely extinguishing him, and he was so entangled in the steel hoops that both were brought down sprawling on the platform, to the merriment of the passengers, who quickly assisted in extricating the man from his unpleasant position.

Another little incident occurred which I remember. Some changes in the staff took place, and a new porter, selected from the country, was appointed to fill up the vacancy. I gave him instructions what his duties would be on the arrival of trains. On the arrival of the train from Liverpool, soon after, I heard him calling out in a loud voice, "All *swop* here for Bradford and Leeds." I went up to him and told him to call out "Change here for Bradford and Leeds." He turned and said, "You can can call it what you like, but its *swopping*." It took me a few weeks to get him educated to his duties. Nevertheless, eventually he made a very good porter.

The Lancashire and Yorkshire Railway Company commenced to run passenger trains in and out of Doncaster on the 1st of September, 1858, arranged for by Mr. Cawkwell.

During the time I was at Sowerby Bridge Station, the Temperance Society ran their annual excursion trip to Liverpool. I often thought what a flourishing society it must be, as we had generally to make up two or three special trains to convey the members. It was considered to be the best patronised excursion that left the Yorkshire district, and was commonly called Sowerby Bridge teetotal trip. This term was somewhat amusing, as always on their return, on the arrival of the trains at the station, a large number of the passengers were found laid in the bottom of the carriages helplessly drunk, and had to be taken away from the station on platform trucks. In the year 1858 we despatched for Liverpool four very heavily loaded trains, and knowing, by experience from previous years, what to expect on their return, I arranged for an extra staff to be on duty, with additional platform trucks, in readiness when the trains arrived. My expectations were more than verified; we had more than four truck loads of drunken passengers to wheel off the platform into the station yard in the small hours of the morning, for their friends to get home as best they could

In 1858 working arrangements were made between Manchester and Leeds Railway and the East Lancashire Railway Companies, when Mr. James Smithells was appointed traffic manager for both companies pending the amalgamation.

The magnetic telegraph came into operation between the principal stations on the line in December, 1858. This rendered great assistance in working the traffic with more punctuality and safety.

On February 6th, 1859, the Manchester, Sheffield, and Lincolnshire Railway Company commenced to run passenger trains between Sheffield, Penistone, and Huddersfield, and Huddersfield to Penistone

In April, 1859, I was appointed by the directors assistant passenger superintendent to Captain Binstead, R N., for Yorkshire Division.

During the five years I was in charge at Sowerby Bridge Station the staff, along with myself, had very difficult and heavy work to contend with, in addition to long hours on duty. One half the staff commenced duty at 5-30 a.m and left off at 8 p.m. ; the other half commenced duty at 7 a m. and left off at 10 p m., or after the last passenger train had gone, which in the summer season was very often near midnight. I myself commenced at 8 a.m., and worked until 10 p m., and very often much later. On Sundays we all came on duty every alternate Sunday, commencing at 7-30 a.m , and remaining until 7-45 p m.

Mr. W. Cawkwell, goods manager, resigned in May, 1859, and was appointed general manager for the London and North-Western Railway Company, and Mr. James Smithells was then appointed, and took the whole charge of both lines (the Lancashire and Yorkshire and East Lancashire) as general traffic manager, in August, 1859. In September, 1859, the amalgamation of the Lancashire and Yorkshire Railway Company and the East Lancashire Railway Company took effect. The two lines were afterwards known as the Lancashire and Yorkshire Railway.

On Sunday, May 1st, 1859, I proceeded to Wakefield, and took charge as divisional passenger assistant superintendent, which comprised the whole of the line from Rochdale to Goole and Normanton, with its branches, including Todmorden to Burnley Branch. On my appointment as assistant superintendent it was verbally intimated to me by the directors that they would look to me for improved working arrangements being made, as the system had become somewhat disorganised. I soon found that it was so, and set to work with a determination to place the working machinery on a more satisfactory basis. Knowing the continuous complaints made by the travelling public between Huddersfield and Halifax, when changing at Sowerby Bridge, about being so long on the journey, and having to change twice in such a short distance (a little over ten miles, the time occupied being over an hour), I determined that the first step in my new capacity should be to devise a new time table over this section of the line which would give better travelling facilities. I submitted one, coupled with the re-arrangement of working the branch trains, which was for through trains to run from Halifax over Bradley Wood Branch to Huddersfield, and from Huddersfield over Bradley Wood Branch to Halifax, accomplishing the journey in twenty-five minutes, without change. The

64

new service was agreed to, and commenced to run in January, 1860. It dispensed with the old circuitous route by Sowerby Bridge and Mirfield, and abolished the branch trains which ran between North Dean and Elland. After this the Huddersfield passengers to and from the main lines were changed at Brighouse, and to and from Halifax at North Dean.

In August, 1859, Thurstonland Tunnel and others on the line were provided with telegraph instruments, and a man was placed at each end to work the same, with instructions. When the train entered the tunnel the signalman gave notice to the signalman at the other end by a tick on the telegraph needle, which was acknowledged, then pegged over the telegraphic needle No other train was then allowed to follow until the signalman at the other end released the telegraphic needle. This was the first attempt at working tunnels under the block system, which had the effect of working them with safety. In September of the same year I suggested, with the view of increasing the receipts, that we should adopt the principle of booking third-class passengers by local trains, which stopped at all stations, but this was not agreed to. I also recommended that the times of the running of passenger trains should be telegraphed to and from all the principal stations. This was agreed to, and instructions issued in the Yorkshire Division to commence on the 27th October Afterwards, to my surprise, the directors ordered the instructions to be withdrawn until it was ascertained what the London and North-Western and other companies were doing. I often wondered what other companies had to do with our schemes of working the line with more punctuality and safety. However, the directors again agreed to the principle, and commenced on March 1st, 1860.

On Sunday, the 16th of October, 1859, I was in charge

of a special train which conveyed Lord Brougham from Halifax to Preston. I arrived at Halifax about 2 p.m., when his lordship made his appearance a little after 3 p.m. The special train conveying his lordship left at 3-10 p.m., arriving at Preston at 4-55 p.m , in good time for his train to the North, which was due to leave at 5-10 p.m.

The London and North-Western Railway Company commenced to run passenger trains from Mirfield to Normanton, and Normanton to Mirfield, in January, 1859, and discontinued them in 1865 ; also to and from Bradford and Huddersfield to Halifax, and Halifax to Huddersfield.

On January 1st, 1860, the following gentlemen were in office as directors and managers :—

Directors.

Chairman, F. W. Wickham, M P.
Deputy-Chairman, George Wilson, Esq.

George Anderton, Esq.	John Hargreaves, Esq
James Andus, Esq	James Hatton, Esq
Thomas Barnes, Esq.	James Holme, Esq.
W J Blacklock, Esq.	W. H. Hornby, Esq
Jos Craven, Esq	John R Kay, Esq
Thomas Dugdale, Esq	James Pilkington, Esq.
Samuel Fielden, Esq.	Joshua Radcliffe, Esq

Officers.

James Smithells, General Traffic Manager, ⎫
Hy Blackmore, Passenger Superintendent, ⎬ *Western Division.*
George Aylesbury, Assistant, ⎭
Captain Binstead, R N , Passenger Superin- ⎫
tendent, ⎬ *Eastern Division.*
Thomas Normington, Assistant, ⎭
James Shaw, Passenger Superintendent, ⎱ *East Lancashire*
Henry Goodier, Assistant, ⎰ *Division.*

The new time table between Halifax and Huddersfield was commenced January 1st, 1860 In consequence of there being only a single line of rails between Dry Clough

5

Junction and North Dean Station, it was necessary for safe working that a man should be appointed to take sole charge of all trains passing over this section of the line, and he was called a pilot guard.

On the 16th of January, 1860, the Lancashire and Yorkshire Company commenced to run a service of three trains per day from Pontefract to Leeds, and Leeds to Pontefract, over Methley Branch. This was done with a view to give facilities to the business people of Leeds who were desirous of residing in the country; but not booking third class by all trains, it had not the desired effect.

In March, 1860, an alteration of the superintendents' divisions took effect. The Western Division was extended to Walsden, and the Eastern Division terminated at Todmorden.

I was very pleased to note that after the amalgamation with the East Lancashire Railway Company, in September, 1859, the gentry and manufacturers of Accrington, Blackburn, Darwen, Colne, Harwood, Church, Padiham, and Haslingden, made a presentation to Mr. James Shaw, their much-respected superintendent of the East Lancashire Railway. The present consisted of a magnificent timepiece, and a purse containing £170. The presentation was made on Monday, April 16th, 1860.

In August, 1860, a very serious accident happened to an excursion train full of passengers, whilst travelling over a steep gradient between Accrington and Helmshore The train broke loose, and the rear portion of ten coaches ran back. The guard, not having sufficient brake power, was unable to stop its retrograde movement before coming into collision with a goods train which was travelling on the same line. This led to all passenger trains being fitted up with Mr. C. Fay's and Mr. J. Newall's patent continuous brakes in October, 1860.

In November, 1849, the branch single line from Todmorden to Burnley was opened. Afterwards it was constructed into a double line, and opened in July, 1860.

In June, 1860, a quick train service was established, to run between Belfast, Fleetwood, Blackpool, and Yorkshire Stations. The boat left Belfast at 7 p.m. The train left Fleetwood and Blackpool at 7-30 a.m., arriving at Leeds at 10-30 a.m. On the return journey the train left Leeds at 4-15 p.m., arriving at Blackpool and Fleetwood at 7-15 p.m., and at Belfast, by boat, at 7 a.m. This was the first attempt to cultivate the Belfast and Blackpool traffic from Yorkshire, which proved a success to the Company; and since then these facilities have been extended.

Since the directors decided, on March 1st, 1860, to carry out my suggestion, submitted in October, 1859, to adopt the principle of telegraphing the running of passenger trains to and from the principal stations, it proved so advantageous to the Company that it led to the directors appointing Mr. R. Dodwell to be superintendent over that department, in April, 1860.

With a view of economising the working expenses, I suggested, in March, 1860, that excursion agents should be dispensed with, and that the whole of these arrangements should be dealt with by the divisional management, when the directors decided that in future all guaranteed excursions, such as millhands, schools, institutions, and day trips to Belle Vue, should be managed by the district officers, and the agents should only deal with advertised excursions, and commission of 4 per cent upon net earnings of £9,580, all earnings above that $7\frac{1}{2}$ per cent. The arrangement created some rivalry between the district officers as to which could realise the largest amount of money with the least cost. The excursion agent for Yorkshire Division, not having acted up to expectation, I again, in 1861, urged that agencies should be dispensed with, and the directors decided to give notice to the agent for Yorkshire that his services would not be required. However, the agent for Yorkshire Division prevailed upon his friends to memorialise the chairman and the directors to the effect that it was upon political grounds that I urged that excursion agencies should be dispensed with. I was very much surprised to find this diplomacy had its effect, and the agent for Yorkshire Division was reinstated for the season of 1861, and was paid for commission close upon £900 for less than five months' agency.

After the close of this season the directors found out that they had been misled by the agent's diplomacy, and dispensed with his services. I then, in addition to my ordinary duties, undertook to do the excursion agents' business, and did so from 1862 to the end of 1866. For the five years the receipts liable for the agents' commission amounted to over £95,000. This, after deducting printing and advertising expenses, left a clear saving to the Company of over £3,000.

After the amalgamation in 1859 the board of directors was modified, and the following gentlemen constituted the board.—

Directors.

Chairman, H. W. Wickham, Esq., M P
Deputy-Chairman, George Wilson, Esq

George Anderton, Esq	James Holme, Esq.
Richard Atkinson, Esq.	Wm. Hy. Hornby, Esq.
James Andus, Esq.	James R Kay, Esq
Thomas Barnes, Esq	William Leaf, Esq
W M T. Blacklock, Esq	William Marshall, Esq
Jos Craven, Esq	James Pilkington, Esq
Thomas Dugdale, Esq.	Joshua Radcliffe, Esq
Samuel Fielden, Esq	John R. Ralph, Esq.
John Hargreaves, Esq.	James Riley, Esq
James Hatton, Esq.	William Stuart, Esq

Officers.

James Smithells, Traffic Manager

Hy. Blackmore, Passenger Superintendent, }
George Aylesbury, Assistant, } *Western Division.*

Captain Binstead, R.N., Passenger Superin- }
tendent, } *Eastern Division*
Thomas Normington, Assistant, }

James Shaw, Passenger Superintendent, } *East Lancashire*
Henry Goodier, Assistant, } *Division.*

On the night of the 7th January, 1861, a serious
accident occurred to the Bangor mail train, due to leave
Normanton at 10-30 p.m. for Huddersfield, Crewe, and
Bangor. On passing Cleckheaton Branch junction at
Mirfield the engine driver of a goods train from the branch
overran the junction stop signal, and failed to bring his
train to a stand before his engine fouled the up main
line. At the time snow was falling very heavily, and
covered the ground to the depth of some eight or ten
inches. My reason for recording this accident is in consequence of a most remarkable incident occurring. I received
a telegram at Wakefield at 11-20 p m., and I at once
got an engine to take me to Mirfield. On approaching
Thornhill Station the signalman stopped the engine at his
cabin, and told me the engine could go no further in consequence of two long goods trains standing upon the
main line between there and Mirfield. I then left the
engine and walked through the deep snow up the line, a
distance of over three miles, to the scene of the accident.
I had got about half way when I observed a black object
lying in the snow on the embankment. I crossed the
line to see what it was, and found it was one of my
inspectors who had left Mirfield, and was making his way
to Thornhill Station to make arrangements necessary for
working the traffic over the single line. The man was
completely exhausted, and said he was " almost starved

to death." I took out my flask and gave him some
brandy. After a while I got him on to his feet and
walked him about a short time, when he said he thought
he could manage to walk on to Thornhill, and I proceeded towards Mirfield. On arriving there I saw a
very melancholy sight. The station staff were busy
extricating the injured passengers from the wreck and
taking them to the station. They were principally
German emigrants for Liverpool on their way to America.
On my inquiries as to the cause of the accident, I found
the engine of the Bangor mail had come into collision
with what was called a copper-knobbed goods engine,
which stood foul upon the up main line. Both were
forced off the rails; the Bangor engine. running at a quick
speed, broke loose from the train, and, after running a
considerable distance, got on to the goods line loop with
all wheels, and came into collision with a break van
attached to the rear of a goods train standing in the
loop. The engine was embedded in the break van, with
its front wheels reared up. This was considered to be
a most remarkable incident, of which I made a note

The Great Northern Railway Company discontinued
running passenger trains between Doncaster, Pontefract,
and over the Methley Branch to Leeds, and Leeds to
Doncaster, the same route, at the end of May, 1861.

In July, 1861, I suggested that we should commence
to run cheap half-day excursions from and to the various
local stations in the district, and those which were
adopted to run to Littleborough proved a great success.
During the summer season we conveyed from four to five
thousand passengers a week, and continued up to the
change of management in 1871. After this the fares were
increased, which destroyed the traffic The public then
turned to other places of recreation which were offered to
them by other railway companies, at less fares for much
longer distances, which succeeded in diverting the traffic.

In October, 1861, some slight alteration was made in the superintendents' divisions. Burnley Branch was taken from Yorkshire Division and added to East Lancashire Division. This was for the purpose of the managers for the three divisions to meet at Todmorden.

In 1861 the Company adopted the principle of semaphore signalling at all stations and junctions, and dispensed with the old disc spectacle signal. This was a great improvement, and resulted in the line being worked with fewer accidents.

In May, 1862, with a view of curtailing working expenses by reducing carriage mileage, I suggested that first and third class passengers only should be booked by Parliamentary trains, but the suggestion was not agreed to. Had this suggestion been adopted, it would have saved at least three second-class carriages per train having to be hauled about the line comparatively empty.

In March, 1862, a traffic agreement was entered into between the London and North-Western and the Lancashire and Yorkshire Railway Companies for the division of traffic at all competitive stations. This agreement took effect from the 1st day of January, 1862, and was to remain in force for fourteen years. I never liked this agreement, and I remember saying at the time, to one of our directors, that I feared the London and North-Western Company would in future reap the greatest advantage. The divisional arrangements led to an agreement between the two companies that their officers should hold periodical meetings together for the purpose of adjusting any discrepancies that might exist or occur in the workings at any of the competitive stations. I do not know the conditions of dividing the traffic in the re-agreement made in 1877; at anyrate the London and North-Western Company's dividend kept going up, and Lancashire and Yorkshire down.

After the excursion agency was transferred to the district officers, I revised the working arrangements in connection with the season's excursions to Scarborough and back, which gave greater facilities to the public, made more money, and reduced the working expenses by saving 3,420 miles empty running, 40 days' working time, and 26 engines for the season; and the season's excursions to Blackpool by the re-arrangement saved 36 engines empty running during the season.

The Company not printing a sheet time table for the main line showing connections with the branches and other companies' lines made it very inconvenient for the public, compelling them to look over half a dozen sheet time tables in tracing the end of their intended journey. I devised a new one for the main line, for Yorkshire Division, showing all the connections to and from the branches with the principal stations on other companies' lines, thus making one sheet do instead of six. The directors considered it a great improvement, and that the information it contained with respect to showing the through communication with other lines would be of great service, not only to the public, but also to the Company's servants. They resolved to adopt it, and it was carried into effect in February, 1863, and is in use at the present day in the Yorkshire District. This new sheet time table gave such satisfaction to the public that the directors ordered a similar one to be devised and issued to the public for the Lancashire Division

In 1862 tank engines were introduced, and it was recommended that a number of them should be built for the purpose of running passenger trains on branches with steep gradients, and for goods and coalyard shunting purposes. Since then the improvements made in engine building have been marvellous, especially on the Lancashire and Yorkshire line.

In January, 1862, a question was raised by all railway companies as to the best method of warming first and second class compartments in railway carriages. Some of the companies tried Peter Salmon's system of warming with the exhaust steam from the engine. Afterwards the method was disapproved by all railway company's officers. Not only was the cost considerable, but great inconvenience was caused in severe frosty weather by having to fix and couple up piping in connection with the engine and carriages of the train, and the warming was not effective for the whole length of trains. Another scheme was brought forward for warming compartments in carriages by means of charcoal and hot water, which was also not approved. Our Company then adopted hot-water foot warmers, and ordered boilers to be fitted up for the purpose of heating water at the various principal stations. The cost of these tin foot warmers varied from ten to twenty shillings each. There is the additional cost to be added to this of boilers and fitting up, repairs, coal, and water, and extra staff to attend to the same. Nevertheless the principle has continued, with increasing cost yearly, up to this (1892). I may add that eventually third-class passengers, through constant agitation, shared in this pleasant luxury. It is surprising to observe that, after more than thirty years have elapsed since the heating of railway carriages with steam from the engine was introduced, and so unanimously denounced as being impracticable by the officers of all railway companies, that there should again be an attempt made to bring forward the same idea.

In 1891 the first attempt was made in warming compartments in railway carriages on the hot-air principle. This was done by placing a cast-iron cavity in the smoke box of the engine. The cold air was admitted into the cavity by means of a bell mouth in front of the engine, with an outlet for the hot air on the top of the smoke box near the bottom of the chimney, the air being heated on passing through the cavity. The hot air was conveyed in a pipe on the top of the engine and over the centre of the carriages outside. On passing over the top of the carriages the hot air was admitted into the respective compartments by means of small grids, which could be opened and closed as required by a valve placed inside the compartment. The railway companies' engineers demurred to this principle, alleging that it was objectionable having to fix pipes to be coupled up with the engine and the carriages of the train, and because there would not be sufficient force to drive the hot air the whole length of the train. Notwithstanding these objections, I observed in 1893 that the Companies were about adopting with steam, at a much greater cost, the very principle of laying pipes coupling up the engine with the carriages on the train, which principle—with hot air—they so strongly denounced in 1891.

In 1895 another hot-air principle for warming compartments in railway carriages appeared. The method consists in utilising the waste heat from the roof lamps, which is now discharged through the ventilator into the atmosphere; thus each compartment makes it own heat. For this purpose an apparatus, containing a number of tubes, is placed in the case of the roof lamp, to which the reflector now in use can be attached. On the side of the lid is a cold-air collector, consisting of two bell-shaped openings, and between them is a swinging valve, which works automatically, for the purpose of collecting pure fresh air from the outside atmosphere. These collectors work equally well whichever way a train is moving, and require no attention whatever. There is an outlet from the apparatus into the compartment of the carriage, to which a pipe is attached and placed along the ceiling behind the rack and upholstering, and down under the seat. The cold air enters the collector, and in passing through the apparatus becomes heated, and is then conveyed through the pipe and discharged into the compartment under the seat at a temperature of more than one hundred degrees of heat. A valve is placed in a convenient position in the compartment, so that the temperature can be easily regulated or the hot air turned off completely at the will of the passenger. This scheme dispenses with the inconveniences and great cost in working expenses of which the railway companies complain. What this insignificant-looking apparatus can do time alone will show.

Since that time (1862) the engineering and other departments, through the pressure of the travelling public, have tried many other methods to supersede the inadequate hot-water tins, but hitherto have not attained the object required. The schemes which they have brought forth have been both inadequate and expensive.

In 1893 I suggested to a gentleman that the waste heat from the roof lamp, which is discharged through the ventilator into the atmosphere out of the carriage top, might be utilised. Some months after this we had a long conversation upon the subject, when he suggested that if I would get him a roof lamp he would test the question. I bought an oil roof lamp in October, 1894, and the test showed that the apparatus provided could generate 100 degrees of heat from the pure cold air, as it passed through the apparatus into the compartments of the carriage. At this time railway companies were dispensing with oil and adopting Pope's patent gas, which gives a more brilliant light. I then bought one of Pope's carriage roof lamps, and a test was made with this lamp with gas, when it was found to be a greater success. The apparatus generated and poured into the carriage compartment over

150 degrees of heat. We, therefore, concluded this would be considered by all railway companies' managers to give more than sufficient warmth in compartments of railway carriages. The principle was secured by patent, which covers all waste heat escaping from railway carriage roof lamps, and all other descriptions of lamp. In October, 1895, a circular giving a description of the apparatus and its workings was sent out to all the managers of railway companies in England, Ireland, and Scotland.

We were surprised to find that most of the railway companies' engineers condemned the principle before they had even seen the apparatus This led to the general managers being undecided what to do in the matter. However, in October, 1896, I again ventured to call the attention of all managers of railway companies to the inexpensive hot-air heating and ventilating apparatus, pointing out its advantages.

Apparatus for Heating Railway Carriages, Tram Cars, &c., with Pure Hot Air.

The patentees of the above invention beg respectfully to introduce to the notice of railway managers some details of their apparatus for warming railway carriages with pure hot atmospheric air.

I.—DESCRIPTION.

The method consists in utilising the waste heat from the roof lamp, which is now discharged through the ventilator into the atmosphere. For this purpose a cavity containing a number of tubes is placed in the case of the roof lamp, to which the reflector now in use can be attached On the outside of the lid is a cold-air collector, consisting of two bell-shaped openings, and between them is a swing valve, which works automatically for the purpose of collecting pure fresh air from the outside atmosphere. This collector works equally well whichever way a train is moving, and requires no attention whatever. There is an outlet from the cavity into the compartment of the carriage. The cold air enters the collector, and in passing through the apparatus becomes heated, and is then conveyed through the pipe and discharged into the compartment at a temperature of over 100 degrees.

A grid or valve is placed in a convenient position, so that the temperature can be easily regulated, or the hot air turned off completely, at the will of the passengers.

II.—ADVANTAGES.

The following are some of the advantages of this mode of heating railway carriages :—

1. Although the waste heat from the roof light is utilised for warming the compartment, the light is not in the least degree interfered with for illuminating purposes, while all disagreeable effluvia from the gas is discharged outside, through the ventilator, as at present.

2. The apparatus being self-contained, the light in each compartment creates its own heat—no coupling being required, and therefore causes no inconvenience. Vehicles can be attached to or detached from any part of the train, as can now be done by all trains, while in summer it will serve as a ventilator, especially in smoking compartments and guards' vans.

3 The carriages will be well ventilated with pure dry warm air, all damp and musty smells destroyed, and the upholstering always well aired and preserved. This will be a great advantage early in the morning, as the foul air will be replaced with pure fresh air.

4. No risk of any danger whatever to the passengers.

5 It can be adapted to any size or shape of lamp, and where double burners, or flames similar to the Coligna lamp, are used, one apparatus will heat two compartments efficiently.

6. Its cheapness. The first is the only cost, because when a compartment is once fitted up it will be permanent, while the original cost will be most reasonable.

7. No additional duty imposed on the engine drivers, guards, or the staff at the stations.

All the lamps now in use can be utilised without being disturbed, the only alterations required being—

1 A hole in the lid to receive the collector pipe, which is fastened to the lid.

2. A cast rim is placed where the glass is at present, and which is made to again receive the glass, only lowered about two inches, so as to couple the outlet to the pipe that goes under the seat.

His Royal Highness the Prince of Wales visited Halifax on Monday, August 3rd, 1863, on the occasion of his opening the new Town Hall, on Tuesday, the 4th, when special accommodation was provided at the station. The radius of the station workings on the north side were situated about one hundred yards from the mouth of a long tunnel. There were only two narrow, short platforms. The up platform would hold a train of fourteen coaches and the down platform twelve. Telegraphic communication was then in its infancy. This limited accommodation created no little difficulty in making out the working arrangements for dealing with the enormous numbers we anticipated would visit the town of Halifax on Tuesday. I was requested by the directors to make the necessary working arrangements for the occasion. I did so, and have pleasure in inserting a copy of them showing the whole arrangements, from which it will be observed that the workings of the special trains were alphabetically arranged. We arrived and despatched at the station 226 ordinary and special trains. We had 510 coaches marshalled up into special trains. The arrangements made for the Tuesday were calculated to convey at least 150,000 passengers in 24 hours; but a continuous downpour of rain from Monday afternoon to mid-day on Tuesday, no doubt, had its effect upon the number of people visiting the town. However, the approximate number of passengers conveyed in and out of the station was 125,000.

His Royal Highness the Prince of Wales, attended by Lieutenant-General Knollys, Major Teesdale, and suite, left London at 10 a.m. by special train, which travelled over the Great Northern Railway, and arrived at Doncaster at 1-25 p.m. The royal train then travelled over the Lancashire and Yorkshire Railway, and arrived at Wakefield at 2-15 p.m., where an address was presented to the Prince by the Mayor and Corporation. The train was then handed over to the Lancashire and Yorkshire Railway officials, who took charge of it to Halifax The Great Northern engine was detached from the train, and one of the Lancashire and Yorkshire engines named Wickham, with a gondola carriage conveying the chairman and directors, was attached in front of the royal train. Instructions had been given to the station masters and inspectors at all stations on the line to Halifax that they would be held responsible for keeping the main line clear of obstruction thirty minutes before the royal train was due to pass, and for ten minutes after the pilot engine that followed the train had also passed. One platelayer, with proper signals, was placed on the line every half mile between Wakefield and Halifax. The royal train was also telegraphed from station to station from Wakefield to Halifax. The royal train was despatched from Wakefield at 2-25 p.m. An engine named Anderton acted as pilot, which followed ten minutes after. The royal train arrived at Halifax Station at 3-1 p m., but was not due until 3-10 p.m. Instantly the Prince was recognised a loud burst of cheering greeted him, and the royal standard was hoisted on the principal façade of the building. A raised platform, two seats deep, was erected inside the station, in the centre of the arrival platform, for the accommodation of the Mayor and Corporation and friends. This was covered, along with the platform, with crimson cloth. This raised platform was intended to be quite opposite the royal carriage when the train came to a stand in the station. The royal train consisted of six vehicles—brake van and two ordinary saloons, the royal carriage, and behind these were another saloon and brake van in the rear. The composition of this train was my guide in placing a man with a red flag for a signal to the engine-driver with the royal train to bring his engine to a stand at this place. The royal carriage would then have been directly opposite the raised platform, where the Mayor and Corporation, magistrates, and their friends had assembled to be in readiness to receive his royal highness on his alighting from the railway carriage. This being the first time the Mayor and Corporation had appeared in their new robes of office, they became the observed of all observers The Mayor wore his gold chain of office and cocked hat: his robe was black, trimmed with rich silk velvet, bordered with ermine, and he looked very dignified The town clerk's robe was of black stuff; he also wore a cocked hat. The robes of the aldermen were bright scarlet, and those of the councillors light purple. The old beadle (Jesse Radcliffe), in his drab coat and bright buttons, knee breeches, scarlet waiscoat, trimmed with gold lace, and cocked hat, carrying the mace, led them to the raised platform. Two incidents occurred. The first was in consequence of the railway directors attaching their gondola carriage in front of the royal train at Wakefield unknown to me, which lengthened the train some twelve yards. This resulted in the royal carriage being brought to a stand twelve yards short of the raised platform. This led to some confusion, and his royal highness had to step out of the railway carriage on to the bare platform, and wait until the Mayor and Corporation walked up to the place where he had alighted, to receive him. It was also a great disappointment to the ladies and friends assembled on the raised platform, because they were unable to witness the reception by the Corporation. The second incident was this : A grand carpet had been specially manufactured by Messrs. Crossley, carpet manufacturers, Dean Clough Mills, to be laid down along the station entrance for his royal highness to walk over to the Mayor's carriage waiting for him outside the station, but it was not there when wanted. Some ten minutes after the Mayor's carriage, containing his royal highness and escort, had driven away, one of Messrs Crossley's men came to the station carrying the missing carpet on his back

The escort, consisting of the Heckmondwike Artillery, with two guns, Captain Firth in command ; and the 2nd West York Yeomanry Cavalry, under the command of Colonel Edwards, M.P., with their respective bands, were waiting. outside the station. After Sir Charles Wood, M P., had accompanied his royal highness to the carriage in waiting, and taken his seat, and the usual military salute had been given, the royal cortége moved off in the direction of Manor Heath, the residence of John Crossley, Esq., whose guest the Prince was during his visit to Halifax. Shortly afterwards it commenced to rain, which caused the passengers in thousands to rush to the station. The arranged special service of trains was then set in motion, at 5-30 p.m , and continued running until all were cleared out, about 11-30 p m , after despatching about 35,000 passengers. For the morning part of the day we brought into the town, by ordinary and special trains, some 25,000 passengers—total, in and out, 65,000. All passed off without any casualty either to passengers or to rolling stock. On the following day, Tuesday, the 4th, I had 510 coaches working to cover the ground of special arrangements. in addition to the ordinary stock. The special train service was set in motion

6

eaily in the morning, the first arriving about 6 a.m., and continued running up to midnight. We calculated the special and ordinary trains to have brought into the town 60,000 passengers, and we despatched, by ordinary and special trains, 65,000 The trains departed from the up platform direct to four sections of the line, and from the down platform to three sections. All passed off with the greatest regularity and satisfaction, without any casualty to passengers or rolling stock

Before the directors left the station I was called into the station master's office, when the chairman said they had been analysing my working arrangements, and were very much pleased with them, and they highly complimented me on the way in which I had devised them for such an important occasion The chairman expressed his view that the whole scheme of arrangements was most admirable. The scheme not only ensured safety, but was calculated to deal with any number of passengers ; and they passed a vote of thanks to me in the room.

ON TUESDAY, AUGUST 4TH, 1863.

SPECIALS—GOOLE AND BARNSLEY TO HALIFAX.

	A1	B1	C1	A2	D1	B2	A3	C2
	am	am	am	am	am	am	am	am
GOOLE ....dep.	...	...	6 20	...	...	...	...	...
Rawcliffe	6 30	...	6 30	...	...	...	...	...
Snaith	6 40	...	6 37	...	...	...	...	...
Hensall	6 45	...	6 43	...	...	...	...	...
Whitley Bridge	6 50	...	6 53	...	...	...	...	...
Knottingley	6 55	...	7 5	...	...	...	...	...
Pontefract	...	...	7 10	...	...	...	...	...
Featherstone	...	...	7 20	...	...	...	...	...
Crofton	...	...	7 30	...	...	...	...	...
WAKEFIELD	...	6 50	7 40	...	8 20	...	...	...
BARNSLEY	...	...	7 25	8 0	...	...	9 0	...
Darton	...	...	7 33	8 10	...	...	8 45	...
Haigh	...	...	7 37	8 15	...	...	8 53	...
Crigglestone	...	...	7 42	8 20	...	...	8 57	...
Horbury Junction	...	6 55	7 48	8 25	8 25	...	9 7	...
Horbury	...	7 0	7 52	...	8 31	...	9 11	...
Thornhill (for Dewsbury)	...	7 10	8 0	...	8 40	...	9 20	...
Mirfield	...	7 20	8 10	...	8 50	9 0	9 30	...
Halifax............arr.	...	7 50	8 40	...	9 20	9 10	10 0	...
Low Moor	...	8 10	9 0	...	9 40	9 40	...	9 50
Bradford	...	...	...	...	9 50	...	...	10 0
Thornhill	...	8 45	9 40	...	...	...	...	10 30
	a	c	c	b	d			

Train marked *a* returns empty to Barnsley, and train marked *b* runs empty to Wakefield.

Trains marked *c* run empty to Thornhill via Low Moor, and the train marked *d* runs empty to Bradford.

SPECIALS—HALIFAX TO GOOLE AND BARNSLEY.

		D2	D3	A1	A5	C3	A6	D1	B3	A7
		am	pm	pm	pm	pm	pm	pm	pm	pm
Bradford	.	10 0								
Low Moor		10 10								
Halifax	dep	10 20								
HALIFAX	dep		5 0	6 30		7 55		7 45	8 45	
Mirfield			5 30	7 0		8 30		8 15	9 15	
Thornhill			5 40	7 10		8 10		8 45	9 25	
Horbury			5 50	7 20		8 50		8 55	9 35	
Horbury Junction			6 0		7 10	8 55		9 5	9 40	
Crigglestone			6 22		7 15		9 5			9 50
Haugh			6 28		7 50		9 10			10 5
Darton			6 32		7 55		9 15			10 10
BARNSLEY			6 40		8 5		9 25			10 20
WAKEFIELD			6 5	7 30		9 5		9 15	9 50	
Crofton									10 0	
Featherstone									10 10	
Pontefract									10 20	
Knottingley									10 25	
Whitley Bridge									10 35	
Hensall									10 40	
Snaith									10 45	
Rawcliffe									10 55	
GOOLE	arr								11 0	

D3 train returns empty from Wakefield to Halifax via Low Moor

A4 train returns from Wakefield to Barnsley, and works the Barnsley Branch as per time table. A6 and A7

The 7.25 and 8.45 a.m. trains from Barnsley are by ordinary train to Horbury Junction, and the passengers leaving Halifax
at 5.0 p.m. proceed by ordinary train from Horbury Junction. Passengers for Goole, &c., by the 6.30 p.m. train from Halifax,
proceed by the 7.40 p.m. ordinary train from Wakefield

Two guards commence with A1 train Barnsley to Horbury Junction, and work all trains marked A

Two guards commence with B1 train Wakefield to Halifax, and work all trains marked B

Two guards commence with C1 train Goole to Halifax, and work all trains marked C

Two guards commence with D1 train Wakefield to Halifax, and work all trains marked D

SPECIALS—TODMORDEN, &c., TO HALIFAX.

	E 1	F 1	G 1	H 2	I 2	J 2	F 3	E 3	G 3	H 4	I 4
	am	am	am	am	am	am	am	am	am	am	am
Todmorden.....dep	5 30	6 0	6 30	7 10	7 45	8 15	8 55	9 30	9 50	10 45	11 30
Eastwood	5 37	6 7	6 37	7 20	7 53	8 23	9 3	9 37	9 57	10 53	11 37
Hebden Bridge	5 45	6 15	6 45	7 30	8 0	8 35	9 10	9 45	10 5	11 0	11 45
Mytholmroyd	5 50	6 20	6 50	7 37	8 5	8 40	9 15	9 50	10 10	11 5	11 50
Luddenden Foot .	5 55	6 25	6 55	7 42	8 10	8 45	9 20	9 55	10 15	11 10	11 55
Sowerby Bridge .	6 5	6 35	7 5	7 50	8 20	9 0	9 30	10 5	10 30	11 20	12 5
HALIFAX . . . ...arr.	6 15	6 50	7 20	8 5	8 35	9 10	9 45	10 20	10 40	11 35	12 20
Low Moor	6 35	7 10	7 40	8 30	9 0	9 40	10 5	11 15	.		
Leeds .. .	7 0	..	..	8 55	9 30	...	10 35	...	.	...	.
Bradford		7 20	8 0	.	..	10 10		11 30	..		..
	a	a	a	a	a	a	a	a	a		

Trains marked *a* run empty from Halifax to Low Moor, Bradford, or Leeds

Two guards commence with E 1 train, Todmorden to Halifax, and work all trains marked E

Two guards commence with F 1 train, Todmorden to Halifax, and work all trains marked F.

Two guards commence with G 1 train, and work all trains marked G.

SPECIALS—LEEDS, &c., TO HALIFAX.

	H 1	I 1	J 1	F 2	E 2	G 2	H 3	I 3	J 3	F 4	E 4
	am	am	am	am	am	am	am	am	am	am	am
Bradford ... dep	...	.		7 30		8 10			10 30		11 45
LEEDS	5 30	5 50	6 20	..	7 45	...	9 6	9 40	.	10 45	
Holbeck	5 34	5 54	6 24	..	7 50	.	9 10	9 45		10 50	
Armley	5 40	6 0	6 30	..	7 55	.	9 15	9 50		10 55	
Bramley	5 45	6 5	6 35	.	8 0		9 20	9 55		11 0	
Stanningley	5 50	6 10	6 40		8 5		9 25	10 0		11 5	
Laister Dyke	6 0	6 16	6 46		8 10		9 30	10 5	.	11 10	.
Low Moor	6 10	6 30	6 56	7 45	8 20	8 30	9 46	10 20	10 45	11 25	12 0
Halifax arr.	6 30	6 50	7 20	8 10	8 45	8 55	10 6	10 40	11 10	11 45	12 20
Todmorden	7 5	7 25	8 0	8 45	9 20	9 40	10 40	11 10			
	b	b	b	b	b	b	b	b			

Trains marked b run empty from Halifax to Todmorden

Two guards commence with H 1 train, Leeds to Halifax, and work all trains marked H

Two guards commence with I 1 train, Leeds to Halifax, and work all trains marked I

Two guards commence with J 1 train, Leeds to Halifax, and work all trains marked J

SPECIALS—HALIFAX TO TODMORDEN.

	E5	F5	G4	H6	I6	J5	E7	F7	G6	H8	I8	J7	E9
	pm	pm	pm	pm	pm	pm	pm	pm	pm	pm	pm	pm	pm
Bradford .... dep				4 30	5 0						8 15	9 15	9 50
Leeds						5 35	6 10	6 45	7 15	8 5			
Low Moor				5 0	5 30						8 30	9 45	10 30
HALIFAX dep	3 40	4 10	4 40	5 30	6 10	6 40	7 10	7 30	8 15	9 0	9 30	10 20	11 0
Sowerby Bridge arr	3 55	4 25	4 55	5 40	6 15	6 50	7 20	7 40	8 25	9 10	9 40	10 30	11 10
Luddenden Foot	4 5	4 35	5 5	5 50	6 25	7 0	7 30	7 50	8 35	9 20	9 50	10 40	11 20
Mytholmroyd ..	4 10	4 40	5 10	5 55	6 30	7 5	7 35	7 55	8 40	9 25	9 55	10 45	11 25
Hebden Bridge	4 15	4 45	5 15	6 0	6 35	7 10	7 40	8 0	8 45	9 30	10 0	10 50	11 30
Eastwood	4 22	4 52	5 22	6 10	6 43	7 20	7 48	8 10	8 55	9 40	10 10	11 0	11 40
TODMORDEN .	4 30	5 0	5 30	6 20	6 50	7 30	8 0	8 20	9 5	9 50	10 20	11 10	11 50
	a	a	a	a	a	a	a	a	a	a	a	a	a

Trains marked a run empty from Bradford or Leeds to Halifax

SPECIALS—HALIFAX TO LOW MOOR AND LEEDS.

		H5	I5	J4	E6	F6	G5	H7	I7	J6	I8	F8	G7	H9
		pm	pm	pm	pm	pm	pm	pm	pm	pm	pm	pm	pm	pm
Todmorden	dep	3 30	4 0	4 30	4 40	5 5	5 40	6 25	7 0	7 35	8 5	8 30	9 10	9 55
Halifax		3 50	4 20	4 50	5 25	5 15	6 15	7 0	7 20	8 15	8 45	9 15	9 45	10 40
Low Moor		4 0	4 30	5 0	5 45	6 5	6 35	7 25	7 50	8 35	9 5	9 25	10 5	11 0
Laister Dyke		4 5	4 35	5 5		6 15	6 45	7 35		8 45	9 15	9 45	10 15	11 10
Stanningley		4 5	4 35	5 5		6 20	6 50	7 40		8 50	9 20	9 50	10 20	11 15
Bramley		4 10	4 40	5 10		6 25	6 55	7 45		8 55	9 25	9 55	10 25	11 20
Armley		4 15	4 45	5 15		6 30	7 0	7 50		9 0	9 30	10 0	10 30	11 25
Holbeck		4 20	4 50	5 20		6 35	7 5	7 55		9 5	9 35	10 5	10 35	11 30
LEEDS	arr.	4 25	4 55	5 25		6 40	7 10	8 0		9 10	9 40	10 10	10 40	11 35
Bradford					6 0				8 5					
					b	b	b	b	b	b	b	b	b	b

Trains marked b run empty from Todmorden to Halifax.

	K1	L1	S1	M1	N1	P2	S2	O2	Q2	R2	S3	K3	M3	L3	N3	P4	O4
	am	am	am	am	am	am	am	am	am	am	am	am	am	am	am	am	am
PENISTONE dep			5 30				7 15				8 30						
Denby Dale			5 40				7 30				8 40						
Shepley			5 45				7 35				8 45						
Stocksmoor			5 50				7 40				8 50						
Brockholes			6 0				7 45				8 55						
Holmfirth		5 30		6 0	6 30			7 40				9 20		10 0			
Thongs Bridge		5 33		6 5	6 35			7 45				9 25		10 5			
Brockholes		5 37		6 10	6 40			7 50				9 30		1010			
Honley		5 42		6 15	6 45			7 55			9 0	9 35		1015			
Berry Brow		5 46		6 20	6 50			8 0			9 5	9 40		1020			
Lockwood		5 50		6 25	6 55			8 5			9 10	9 45		1025			
Huddersfield	5 30	6 0		6 30	7 0	7 45		8 15	8 40	9 0	9 25	10 0	1020	1035	11 0	1120	1150
Brighouse	5 40	6 10		6 40	7 10	7 55		8 25	8 50	9 10	9 35	1010	1030	1045	1110	1130	12 0
Elland	5 50	6 20		6 50	7 20	8 5		8 35	9 0	9 20	9 45	1020	1040	1055	1120	1140	1210
North Dean	6 0	6 30		7 0	7 30	8 15		8 45	9 10	9 30	9 55	1030	1050	11 5	1130	1150	1215
HALIFAX	6 10	6 40		7 10	7 40	8 25		8 55	9 20	9 40	10 5	1040	11 0	1115	1140	12 0	1225
Low Moor	6 40	7 10									1035	11 0	1130	1145			
Bradford arr	7 0	7 30									1045	1110	1145	12 0			

Trains marked a run empty from Halifax to Bradford.   The train marked S will work the Penistone Branch

Two guards commence with S1 train, Penistone and Brockholes, and work all trains marked S

Two guards work K1 train, Huddersfield to Halifax, and all trains marked K.

Two guards commence with L1 train, Holmfirth to Halifax, and work all trains marked L.

Two guards commence with N1 train, Holmfirth to Halifax, and work all trains marked N

SPECIALS—BRADFORD TO HALIFAX.

	O1	P1	Q1	R1	K2	L2	M2	N2	P3	O3	Q3	R3	S4	K4	M1	L4
	am	am	am	am	am	am	am	am	am	am	am	am	am	am	am	noon
Bradford dep	5 30	6 0	6 20	6 50	7 10	7 40	8 0	8 30	9 10	9 45	1016	1040	11 0	1120	12 0	1215
Low Moor	5 40	6 15	6 36	7 0	7 26	7 50	8 10	8 40	9 20	10 0	1026	1050	1110	1130	1210	1230
Pickle Bridge	5 56	6 26	6 46	7 10	7 36	8 0	8 20	8 50	9 30	1010	1036	11 0	1120	1140	1220	1235
Lightcliffe	6 0	6 30	6 50	7 20	7 40	8 5	8 25	8 55	9 35	1016	1040	11 6	1125	1145	1225	1240
Hipperholme	6 10	6 40	7 0	7 30	7 50	8 15	8 35	9 5	9 40	1026	1050	1116	1135	1150	1235	1245
Halifax	6 20	6 50	7 10	7 40	8 0	8 25	8 45	9 15	9 50	1036	11 0	1126	1145	12 0	1245	1 0
Sowerby Bridge	6 30	7 0	7 20	7 50	8 10	8 35	8 55	9 25	10 0	1045						
Huddersfield	7 5	7 30	8 0	8 30	8 40	9 0	9 30	1010	1040	1130						
Holmfirth	7 30				9 0	9 30										
	b	b	b	b	b	b	b	b								

Trains marked b run empty from Halifax (via Sowerby Bridge) to Huddersfield and Holmfirth

Two guards commence with O1 train, Bradford to Halifax, and work all trains marked O

Two guards commence with P1 train, Bradford to Halifax, and work all trains marked P.

Two guards commence with Q1 train, Bradford to Halifax, and work all trains marked Q

Two guards commence with R1 train, Bradford to Halifax, and work all trains marked R

SPECIALS—HALIFAX TO PENISTONE.

	R4	S5	K5	M5	S6	L5	N5	O6	S7	P6	Q5	R6	K7	S8	M7	N7	L7	O8	Q7	P8
	pm	pm	pm	pm	pm	pm	pm	pm	pm	pm	pm	pm	pm	pm	pm	pm	pm	pm	pm	pm
Bradford dep	3 30	3 40	4 20	4 50																
Low Moor	3 40	4 0	4 30	5 0																
HALIFAX						5 10	4 35	5 0		5 35	6 5	6 20	7 10		7 50	8 25	8 30	9 0	9 45	10 0
North Dean		4 0	4 30	5 0		5 20	5 0	5 45		6 15	6 30	7 30	8 0		8 30	8 45	9 10	9 40	10 10	10 30
Elland		4 5	4 35	5 5		5 25	5 5	6 25		6 50	7 10	7 45	8 10		9 5	9 15	9 40	10 15	10 30	11 0
Brighouse		4 15	4 45	5 15		5 35	5 10	6 40		7 0	7 15	8 0	8 45		9 10	9 25	9 50	10 20	10 50	11 10
Huddersfield	4 10	4 30	5 0	5 30		5 45	6 25	6 45		7 20	7 40	8 25	9 10		9 15	9 30	9 55	10 25	11 20	11 40
Lockwood	4 40					6 0				7 30					9 50	9 40	10 5	10 35		
Berry Brow	4 45					6 5				7 35					9 55		10 25	10 50		
Honley	4 0					6 10				7 40					10 0		10 30			
Brockholes	4 55					6 15				7 45					10 5		10 35			
Thongs Bridge						6 20				7 50					10 10		10 40			
Holmfirth						6 25				7 55					10 15		10 50			
Brockholes					6 20				7 50					10 10						
Stocksmoor		5 5			6 30				8 0					10 20						
Shepley		5 10			6 35				8 5					10 25						
Denby Dale		5 15			6 45				8 10					10 30						
Penistone		5 25			6 55				8 20					10 40						
	a	a	a	a		a	a	a		a	a	a	a		a	a	a	a	a	a

Trains marked a run empty from Bradford to Halifax

SPECIALS—HALIFAX TO BRADFORD.

	N4	O5	P5	Q4	R5	K6	M6	N6	L6	O7	Q6	P7	R7	K8	N8
	pm	pm	pm	pm	pm	pm	pm	pm	pm	pm	pm	pm	pm	pm	pm
Holmfirth									6 30	7 0		8 0			
Huddersfield					4 20	5 10	5 40	6 30	6 50	7 15	7 50	8 20	8 35	9 20	10 0
Sowerby Bridge					5 10	6 0	6 30	7 10	7 30	8 10	8 30	8 55	9 20	10 10	10 30
					b	b	b	b	b	b	b	b	b	b	b
Halifax dep	3 10	4 10	4 10	5 10	5 30	6 20	6 50	7 30	7 46	8 20	8 50	9 10	9 40	10 30	10 45
Hipperholme	3 50	4 20	4 50	5 20	5 40	6 30	7 0	7 40	7 56	8 26	9 0	9 16	9 50	10 40	10 55
Lightcliffe	3 56	4 26	4 55	5 26	5 46	6 36	7 5	7 45	8 0	8 30	9 5	9 20	9 55	10 45	11 0
Pickle Bridge	4 0	4 30	5 0	5 30	5 50	6 40	7 10	7 50	8 6	8 40	9 10	9 25	10 0	10 50	11 5
Low Moor	4 10	4 40	5 10	5 40	6 0	6 50	7 25	8 0	8 16	8 55	9 20	9 35	10 20	11 0	11 15
Bradford	4 20	4 56	5 25	5 56	6 15	7 0	7 40	8 15	8 26		9 35	9 50	10 35	11 16	11 30

Trans marked b run empty from Holmfirth or Huddersfield to Halifax, via Sowerby Bridge

SPECIALS—MIRFIELD TO HALIFAX (Via LOW MOOR).

		T1	U1	V1	T2	U2	V2	T3	U3	V3	T4
		am	am	am	am	am	am	am	am	am	am
Sowerby Bridge	dep	a	a	a	6 50	7 15	8 5	8 45	9 20	10 5	10 30
MIRFIELD		5 30	6 0	6 45	7 20	8 0	8 45	9 10	10 0	10 45	11 10
Heckmondwike		5 40	6 10	6 55	7 30	8 10	8 55	9 20	10 10	10 55	11 20
Liversedge		5 45	6 15	7 0	7 35	8 15	9 0	9 25	10 15	11 0	11 25
Cleckheaton		5 50	6 20	7 5	7 40	8 20	9 5	9 30	10 20	11 5	11 30
Low Moor		6 0	6 30	7 15	7 50	8 30	9 15	9 40	10 35	11 15	11 40
Pickle Bridge		6 10	6 40	7 25	8 0	8 40	9 25	9 50	10 40	11 25	11 50
Lightcliffe		6 15	6 45	7 30	8 5	8 45	9 30	9 55	10 45	11 30	11 55
Hipperholme		6 25	6 50	7 40	8 15	8 55	9 40	10 5	10 55	11 40	12 0
HALIFAX	arr	6 35	7 0	7 50	8 25	9 5	9 50	10 15	11 5	11 50	12 15
Sowerby Bridge		6 45	7 10	8 0	8 35	9 15	10 0	10 25			
		a	a	a	a	a	a	a			

Trains marked a run empty from Halifax (via Sowerby Bridge) to Mirfield

Two guards commence with T1 train Mirfield to Halifax, and work all trains marked T

Two guards commence with U1 train Mirfield to Halifax, and work all trains marked U.

Two guards commence with V1 train Mirfield to Halifax, and work all trains marked V.

SPECIALS—CLECKHEATON TO HALIFAX (Via NORTH DEAN).

	W1	X1	Y1	W2	X2	Y2	W3	X3	Y3	W4	X4	Y4	W5
	am	am	am	am	am	am	am	am	am	am	am	am	am
Low Moor	4 45	5 20	5 50	6 30	7 0	7 30	8 10	8 40	9 10	9 50	10 20	10 50	11 30
CLECKHEATON	5 0	5 30	6 0	6 40	7 10	7 40	8 20	8 50	9 20	10 0	10 30	11 0	11 45
Liversedge	5 5	5 35	6 5	6 45	7 15	7 45	8 25	8 55	9 25	10 5	10 35	11 5	11 50
Heckmondwike	5 10	5 40	6 10	6 50	7 20	7 50	8 30	9 0	9 30	10 10	10 40	11 10	11 55
Mirfield	5 20	5 50	6 20	7 0	7 30	8 0	8 40	9 10	9 40	10 20	10 50	11 20	12 5
Cooper Bridge	5 26	5 56	6 26	7 6	7 36	8 6	8 46	9 16	9 46	10 26	10 56	11 26	12 10
Brighouse	5 32	6 2	6 32	7 12	7 42	8 12	8 52	9 22	9 52	10 30	11 2	11 32	12 15
Elland	5 40	6 10	6 40	7 20	7 50	8 20	9 0	9 30	10 0	10 40	11 10	11 40	12 25
North Dean	5 50	6 20	6 50	7 30	8 0	8 30	9 10	9 40	10 10	10 50	11 20	11 50	12 35
HALIFAX arr	6 0	6 30	7 0	7 40	8 10	8 40	9 20	9 50	10 20	11 0	11 30	12 0	12 45
Low Moor	6 20	6 50	7 20	8 0	8 30	9 0	9 40	10 10	10 40	11 20			
	b	b	b	b	b	b	b	b	b	b			

Trains marked b run empty from Halifax (via Low Moor) to Cleckheaton

Two guards commence with W1 train Cleckheaton to Halifax, and work all trains marked W

Two guards commence with X1 train Cleckheaton to Halifax, and work all trains marked X

Two guards commence with Y1 train Cleckheaton to Halifax, and work all trains marked Y.

SPECIALS—HALIFAX TO MIRFIELD (Via LOW MOOR).

	U4	V4	T5	U5	V5	T6	U6	V6	T7	U7	V7	T8
	pm	pm	pm	pm	pm	pm	pm	pm	pm	pm	pm	pm
Sowerby Bridge	...	...	...	5 30	6 5	6 35	7 30	8 5	8 45	9 25	9 55	11 10
HALIFAX ....dep.	3 50	4 25	5 0	5 50	6 25	6 55	7 50	8 20	9 0	9 50	10 10	11 30
Hipperholme........arr.	4 0	4 35	5 10	5 55	6 35	7 0	7 55	8 30	9 10	9 50	10 20	11 35
Lightcliffe	4 5	4 40	5 15	6 0	6 40	7 5	8 0	8 35	9 15	9 55	10 25	11 40
Pickle Bridge	4 10	4 45	5 20	6 5	6 45	7 10	8 5	8 40	9 20	10 0	10 30	11 50
Low Moor	4 20	4 55	5 30	6 20	6 55	7 20	8 15	8 50	9 30	10 10	10 40	12 0
Cleckheaton........	4 30	5 5	5 40	6 30	7 10	7 30	8 25	9 0	9 40	10 15	10 50	...
Liversedge	4 35	5 10	5 45	6 35	7 15	7 35	8 30	9 5	9 45	10 20	10 55	...
Heckmondwike	4 40	5 15	5 50	6 40	7 20	7 40	8 40	9 10	9 50	10 30	11 0	...
Mirfield	4 50	5 25	6 0	6 50	7 30	7 50	8 50	9 20	10 0	10 40	11 10	...
Sowerby Bridge	5 25 *a*	6 0 *a*	6 30 *a*	7 25 *a*	8 0 *a*	8 30 *a*	9 20 *a*	9 50 *a*	10 30 *a*	...	...	...
	a	*a*	*a*	*a*	*a*	*a*	*a*	*a*	*a*			

Trains marked *a* run empty from Mirfield to Halifax, via Sowerby Bridge

SPECIALS—HALIFAX TO CLECKHEATON (Via NORTH DEAN)

		W6	X5	X5	W7	X6	X6	W8	X7	X7	W9	X8	X8	W10
		pm	pm	pm	pm	pm	pm	pm	pm	pm	pm	pm	pm	pm
Low Moor	dep	1 0	4 35	5 5	5 10	6 0	6 25	7 0	7 50	8 25	8 45	9 40	10 20	10 35
Halifax	arr	3 55	4 40	5 10	5 35	6 35	6 5	7 30	8 20	9 10	9 20	10 10	11 10	11 20
North Dean		1 0	4 50	5 10	5 40	6 35	7 10	7 40	8 25	9 5	9 30	10 20	11 5	11 30
Elland		1 0	4 50	5 20	5 50	6 45	7 20	7 45	8 35	9 15	9 35	10 25	11 15	11 30
Brighouse		1 10	5 0	5 30	6 0	6 55	7 30	7 55	8 45	9 25	9 45	10 35	11 25	11 45
Cooper Bridge		1 20	5 10	5 40	6 10	7 5	7 40	8 0	8 55	9 35	9 50	10 40	11 35	11 50
Mirfield		1 30	5 20	5 50	6 20	7 15	7 50	8 10	9 5	9 45	10 0	10 50	11 45	12 0
Heckmondwike		1 40	5 30	6 0	6 30	7 25	8 0	8 20	9 10	9 55	10 10	11 0		
Liversedge		1 45	5 35	6 5	6 35	7 30	8 5	8 25	9 15	10 0	10 15	11 5		
Cleckheaton		1 50	5 40	6 10	6 40	7 35	8 10	8 30	9 20	10 5	10 20	11 15		
Low Moor		5 5	5 50	6 20	6 50	7 15	8 20	8 40	9 30	10 15	10 30	11 25		
		b	b	b	b	b	b	b	b	b	b	b		

Trains marked b will run empty from Cleckheaton (via Low Moor) to Halifax

RETURNING SAME DAY

		am	am	am	am	am	pm	pm	pm	pm	pm
Leeds	dep	6 30	7 0	8 45	10 0	11 0					
		a	a	a							
Low Moor		7 10	7 40	9 10	10 30	11 25					
Halifax	arr	7 30	8 0	9 30	10 50	11 45					

		pm	pm	pm	pm	pm
Halifax	dep	4 15	4 55	6 30	7 25	9 5
Low Moor		4 35	5 15	7 10	7 50	9 30
Leeds	arr	5 15	5 55	7 30	8 30	11 10
		b	b	b		

Trains marked a run empty from Halifax to Leeds.

Those marked b run empty from Leeds to Halifax.

GREAT NORTHERN SPECIAL.

		am	am	am	am
Wakefield	dep	7 30	8 10	8 30	10 0
Low Moor		8 10	8 40	9 0	10 40
Halifax	arr	8 30	9 0	9 0	11 0
				a	

RETURNING SAME DAY

		pm	pm	pm	pm
Halifax	dep	6 0	6 20	7 40	8 33
Low Moor		6 20	8 0	8 0	8 30
Wakefield	arr	7 0	8 40	9 30	
		b			

Trains marked a run empty from Halifax to Wakefield.

Trains marked b run empty from Wakefield to Halifax.

The Wakefield trains run via Gildersome Branch.

ORDINARY AND SPECIAL TRAINS

WILL DEPART

FROM HALIFAX,

ON TUESDAY, AUGUST 4TH, 1863,

AS FOLLOWS :

Ordinary or Special.	Time of Departure.	Destination.
	p. m.	To
G. N. Ordinary	3 10	Leeds and London.
L. & Y. Ordinary	3 25	Huddersfield, Wakefield and Normanton.
L. & Y. Special	R 3 30	All Stations to Huddersfield.
......	H 3 30	Low Moor and all Stations to Leeds.
......	E 3 40	All Stations to Todmorden.
......	N 3 40	Bradford.
L. & Y. Ordinary	C 3 45	Bradford, Low Moor and Leeds.
....	3 50	Manchester and Liverpool.
L. & Y. Special	3 50	All Stations to Low Moor and Cleckheaton Branch.
......	S 3 55	„ „ Huddersfield and Penistone.
......	W 4 0	„ „ Mirfield and Cleckheaton Branch.
......	I 4 0	Low Moor and all Stations to Leeds.
......	F 4 10	All Stations to Todmorden.
......	O 4 10	Low Moor and Bradford.
G. N. Special	4 15	Bowling and Stations to Leeds.
L. & Y. Special	K 4 20	All Stations to Huddersfield.
......	V 4 25	„ „ Low Moor and Cleckheaton Branch.
L. & Y. Ordinary	4 30	Todmorden, Burnley, &c.
L. & Y. Special	J 4 30	Low Moor, and all Stations to Leeds.
......	X 4 35	All Stations to Mirfield and Cleckheaton Branch.
......	G 4 40	„ „ Todmorden.
......	P 4 40	Low Moor and Bradford.
......	M 4 50	All Stations to Huddersfield.
L. & Y. Ordinary	4 55	„ „ Huddersfield.
G. N. Special	4 55	Bowling and Stations to Leeds.
L. & Y. Special	T 5 0	„ „ Low Moor and Cleckheaton Branch.
......	D 5 0	Mirfield, and all Stations to Wakefield and Barnsley.
......	Y 5 5	All Stations to Mirfield and Cleckheaton Branch.
......	A 5 10	„ „ Bradford.
......	L 5 10	„ „ Huddersfield, Holmfirth and Penistone.
L. & Y. Ordinary	5 15	Wakefield and Normanton.
L. & Y. Special	E 5 25	Low Moor and Bradford.
......	R 5 30	All Stations to Bradford.
......	H 5 30	„ „ Todmorden.
L. & Y. Ordinary	5 35	„ „ Bradford and Leeds.
L. & Y. Special	W 5 35	„ „ Mirfield and Cleckheaton Branch.
......	F 5 45	Low Moor and all Stations to Leeds.
......	N 5 45	All Stations to Huddersfield.
L. & Y. Ordinary	5 47	Manchester and Liverpool.
L. & Y. Special	U 5 50	All Stations to Low Moor and Cleckheaton Branch.
G. N. Special	6 0	Gildersome Branch and Wakefield.
L. & Y. Special	I 6 5	All Stations to Todmorden.
......	G 6 15	Low Moor and all Stations to Leeds.
......	O 6 15	All Stations to Huddersfield.
L. & Y. Ordinary	K 6 20	Huddersfield, Wakefield and Normanton.
L. & Y. Special	6 20	Bradford.
......	V 6 25	All Stations to Low Moor and Cleckheaton Branch.
......	A 6 30	Mirfield, and all Stations to Wakefield, Barnsley and Goole.
G. N. Special	6 30	Bowling and Stations to Leeds.
L. & Y. Special	X 6 35	All Stations to Mirfield and Cleckheaton Branch.
......	J 6 40	All Stations to Todmorden.
L. & Y. Ordinary	6 43	Bradford and Leeds.
L. & Y. Special	P 6 45	All Stations to Huddersfield, Holmfirth and Penistone.
......	M 6 50	Low Moor and Bradford.
L. & Y. Special	T 6 55	All Stations to Low Moor and Cleckheaton Branch.
L. & Y. Ordinary	6 57	Rochdale and Manchester.
L. & Y. Special	A 7 0	All Stations to Huddersfield.

ORDINARY AND SPECIAL TRAINS

WILL DEPART

FROM HALIFAX,

ON TUESDAY, AUGUST 4TH, 1863,

AS FOLLOWS

ORDINARY OR SPECIAL	TIME OF DEPARTURE	DESTINATION.
	p m	To
L. & Y. Special	H 7 0	Low Moor and all Stations to Leeds
.	Y 7 5	All Stations to Mirfield and Cleckheaton Branch.
..	K 7 10	„ „ Todmorden
G N Special	7 25	Bowling and Stations to Leeds
L. & Y. Special	I 7 30	Low Moor and Bradford
.	W 7 30	All Stations to Mirfield and Cleckheaton Branch
	N 7 35	All Stations to Bradford
	P 7 35	„ „ Todmorden
	R 7 45	„ „ Huddersfield.
	L 7 45	Low Moor and Bradford.
G N Special	7 40	Gildersome Branch and Wakefield
L. & Y. Special	U 7 50	All Stations to Low Moor and Cleckheaton Branch.
L & Y. Ordinary	7 50	Huddersfield, Wakefield, &c
L. & Y. Special	C 7 55	Mirfield, and all Stations to Wakefield and Barnsley
L & Y Ordinary	8 5	Bradford and Leeds
L. & Y Special	O 8 10	Low Moor and Bradford.
..	G 8 15	All Stations to Todmorden.
.	J 8 15	Low Moor and all Stations to Leeds
	V 8 20	All Stations to Low Moor and Cleckheaton Branch
...	X 8 20	„ „ Mirfield and Cleckheaton Branch
. ..	D 8 25	All Stations to Wakefield
	K 8 30	„ „ Huddersfield
G N Special	S 30	Gildersome Branch and Wakefield
L. & Y. Special	B 8 45	Mirfield, and all Stations to Wakefield, Barnsley & Goole.
.	E 8 45	Low Moor and all Stations to Leeds.
	A 8 50	All Stations to Bradford
	H 9 0	„ „ Todmorden
.. .	T 9 0	„ „ Low Moor and Cleckheaton Branch
	M 9 5	„ „ Huddersfield, Holmfirth and Penistone
G. N Special	9 5	Bowling and Stations to Leeds
L. & Y. Special	G 9 10	All Stations to Mirfield and Cleckheaton Branch
	P 9 10	Bradford
L. & Y. Ordinary	9 13	Rochdale and Manchester.
L & Y. Special	F 9 15	Low Moor and all Stations to Leeds.
.	N 9 15	All Stations to Huddersfield
	W 9 20	„ „ Mirfield and Cleckheaton Branch
	I 9 30	„ „ Todmorden
.	L 9 40	„ „ Huddersfield and Holmfirth
	R 9 40	Low Moor and Bradford
L. & Y. Ordinary	9 45	Huddersfield and Wakefield
L. & Y. Special	G 9 45	Low Moor and all Stations to Leeds
	U 9 50	All Stations to Low Moor and Cleckheaton Branch
L & Y Ordinary	10 7	Bradford and Leeds
L. & Y. Special	X 10 10	All Stations to Mirfield and Cleckheaton Branch
.	V 10 10	„ „ Low Moor and Cleckheaton Branch
	O 10 15	„ „ Huddersfield
.	J 10 20	„ . Todmorden.
	K 10 30	„ „ Bradford
.	H 10 40	Low Moor and all Stations to Leeds.
	Q 10 40	All Stations to Huddersfield
.	N 10 45	All Stations to Bradford
..	E 11 0	„ „ Todmorden
.. ..	P 11 5	„ „ Huddersfield.
.	Y 11 10	„ „ Mirfield
.	W 11 20	„ „ Ditto
...	P 11 30	„ „ Low Moor and Cleckheaton Branch

Superintendent's Office, Wakefield, July, 1863.

SPECIAL INSTRUCTIONS.

TUESDAY, AUGUST 4th.

To Station Masters and Guards

All the ordinary trains to be strengthened as follow :—From Wake-field 10 carriages up to Todmorden, and from Todmorden to be strengthened 10 carriages up to Wakefield

All trains between Halifax and Huddersfield to be made up to 15 carriages

All trains which run between Bradford and Huddersfield to be made up to 8 carriages

Ten extra carriages to be run by all trains between Sowerby Bridge and Bradford, except the 12 35 noon train to Leeds

Signalmen at the stations must keep a vigilant look out and must not leave or attend to any other duty than the working of signals They must have the signals lighted not later than 7.30 p m, the station masters will be held responsible for this being carried out

Inspector of Ways

To place one man every mile, with proper signals, to protect trains between Halifax and Low Moor, Bradford and Cleckheaton Branch, to Mirfield; also between Mirfield and Todmorden, Sowerby Bridge and Halifax, and on the North Dean Branch. To have 3 men placed at proper distances between Copley Station and Dryclough Junction, and one man between all stations from Holmfirth to Huddersfield.

The pilot guard will be held responsible for the safe working of all trains over the single line between North Dean and Dryclough Junction. It is intended for all trains loaded, to and from Halifax, to pass over the single line, and all empty trains to run via Sowerby Bridge. No engine driver must enter on to the single line without **the pilot guard or from his instructions.**

Electric telegraph signalmen at Bowling, Pickle Bridge and Sowerby Bridge tunnels must strictly adhere to the rule, not to allow a second train to enter and be in the tunnel at the same time.

Engine drivers and guards are requested to give particular attention to their workings of trains, they will observe that the trains are alphabetically arranged and numbered progressively according to the number of the train which they will have to work. The driver and guard who commence to work the train marked A 1 continue throughout the day to work every train marked A and no other trains,—the same order applies to all the other letters Every engine will carry a board in front with the letter which particularizes the train On changing engines at Sowerby Bridge and Low Moor the guard will be held responsible for the board being removed from one engine to the other.

To prevent detention with engines running round the trains at Low Moor and Sowerby Bridge, an engine will be kept in readiness to take on all such trains, and the arrival engine to wait and take on the next train in succession. The guard to see the engine head board changed to the succeeding engine

The special trains are not to exceed 17 vehicles, with two guards, one at each end of the train. The head guard to give the engine driver instructions as to the next train they are marked to work.

HALIFAX STATION.

The inspector in charge of the west end of station to have the proper trains brought into the station as per Special Working Time Table, having 3 porters exhibiting, on each train, the "board" informing the public the destination of the said train

The inspector in charge of the east end of station to have the proper trains brought into the station as per Working Time Table, having 3 porters on each train who will exhibit a board shewing the station for which the train is intended.

Five additional platform porters for each up and down platforms.

Additional Booking Office near Canal Street.

Two porters to be in attendance and direct passengers to their trains; also two porters to direct passengers getting off the trains from Low Moor to the new road leading from the station; and on the passengers returning by way of the same new road, direct them to their proper Trains.

Station Booking Office Passage.

Three porters to be in attendance and prevent crowding and confusion of passengers in booking.

Sowerby Bridge Station.

Thirteen ticket collectors are to attend the trains, the present staff to be made up to that number. To collect all tickets for Halifax, and examine tickets in all up trains.

Low Moor Station.

Twelve ticket collectors are to attend the trains, the present staff to be made up to that number, to collect tickets of all trains going to Halifax, when not stopping at intermediate stations.

Mr Boydle, inspector, to assist in despatching the trains to time and in proper order according to Special Working Time Table All trains between Leeds and Low Moor to consist of 10 carriages.

Hipperholme Station.

Fifteen ticket collectors are to attend the trains and collect tickets for Halifax, the present staff to be made up to that number

North Dean Station.

Ten ticket collectors are to attend the trains, the present staff to be made up to that number, and collect tickets for Halifax.

Brighouse Station

Ten ticket collectors are to attend the trains, the present staff to be made up to that number from the staff in the goods department, to collect tickets for Huddersfield of all trains.

Sowerby Bridge and Low Moor Stations.

The station masters must use every exertion to keep the ordinary trains to time, much depends on their skill and discretion in not allowing the special train to leave their station when likely to be in the way to Halifax.

Guards.

Each first guard, with special trains, will be held responsible for having a supply of lamps and fog signals, the lamps to be returned to the station from which they were obtained The tail and side lamps to be lighted and placed on the last vehicle of their trains, not later than 7 30 p m.

AT ALL STATIONS —To have the booking-office windows open at 5 a m., and not to be closed again until the departure of the last train at night The clerk to be prepared and book the passengers as they arrive at the station. To issue *all* return tickets to Halifax, if possible ; but if any passengers are desirous to take single journey tickets by the special trains, they must be booked first and second class fares only. **Any station** where the passengers are not cleared out by the trains, the clerk must immediately communicate by telegraph with Mr. Normington, at Halifax Station.

The locomotive superintendents will be required to provide sufficient locomotive power to meet the requirements of the extra carriages attached to the ordinary trains, a spare engine will also be required for Sowerby Bridge, Low Moor, North Dean, Bradford, and Leeds.

GREAT NORTHERN COMPANY'S SPECIALS.

The G. N. R guards will be responsible for their own lamps being attached to the trains, not later than 7.30 p m. Tickets by the G. N. specials to be collected at Low Moor, approaching Halifax. Return tickets between Wakefield, Leeds, and Halifax, are recognised on the return journey by either company's trains.

On Tuesday, the G. N. Company to have a spare engine at Halifax, to hook on to train arriving from Leeds or Wakefield, and return with it at once—this is to prevent causing a block at the station. All Great Northern trains returning will start from the goods sidings, calling at the station to take up passengers.

Superintendent's Office,
Wakefield, July, 1863.

I remember, in September, 1863, the directors of the Lancashire and Yorkshire Railway Company and the directors of the West Yorkshire, Leeds, Bradford, and Halifax Railway Company, having a meeting at Kirkgate Wakefield Station, for the purpose of considering the advisability of the former Company taking over the latter Company's line of railway. Before our directors went into the office to the meeting one of them came to me, as I stood on the platform, and said, "Normington, what's your opinion as to the advantages to us if we take over this new line?" I replied, "I suppose you have already agreed to do this and merely come over here to the meeting to sign the agreement," when another of the directors said, "No; we have come to try upon what terms we can agree." I then said, "You must take it upon any terms. Whatever they ask, you must give it. It is not a question of price, but have it—my views are so strong that this new line should become part of the Lancashire and Yorkshire Railway system." These remarks led to a round-ring conference on the platform, when they asked me to state my views, and what advantage it would be to us if we got it. I then explained, in the first place, that the congested state of our main line was well known between Wakefield and Sowerby Bridge, which resulted in serious delays both to passengers and goods trains. It would relieve this portion of the main line by diverting the goods traffic at Wakefield arriving from south-east for Bradford and Halifax; and the traffic on the West Yorkshire local line was already paying 6 per cent. Also, if we took it, it would have a tendency to keep other companies off the ground. At this time the chairman of the new company came out of the office and called our directors in. After they had gone into the office I felt very anxious, as though it was my own concern. Some of them seemed to be very undecided what to do. I waited and walked about the platform until they came from the meeting. I saw them come out of the office, and went up to them and asked the result. One of them said they had not taken the line. I really could not conceal my feelings, and I said, "You all ought to have your heads shaved for losing such a golden opportunity." The Chairman of the West York-shire Company happened to be passing at the time, and heard my remark. He turned round and said, "You are right, Normington ; they will rue some day, and regret the business they have done to-day." I learnt afterwards that it was a Lancashire director who gave the casting vote not to have the new line.

In January, 1864, I remember a most remarkable incident which occurred near Stocks Moor Station. I received a telegram at Wakefield from Huddersfield in the early morning to the effect that the 9-30 p.m. passenger train from Penistone had not arrived. I at once got an engine to take me in search of it, and found the engine and train buried under a deep fall of snow, with nothing whatever to be seen but about a foot of the funnel of the engine projecting above the snow. This was in a deep cutting situated between Stocks Moor and Shepley Station. The few passengers who were in the train had been got out the previous night and taken to Shepley Station, where they remained all night I at once telegraphed to the permanent way inspector, at Mirfield, to bring the ballast train with some wagons and men, as the line was blocked with snow. They arrived in strong force in about an hour and a half afterwards, and commenced filling their wagons with snow and taking it away. The line was cleared and opened for traffic about mid-day. In the meantime, the men requiring refreshments, I, accompanied by the locomotive inspector, went to an inn near to Stocks Moor Station On arriving at the house I saw no one about, so went through a passage into the kitchen, and there found a woman sitting in a large old-fashioned oak chair. I asked her if she could supply a few men who were working on the railway with refreshments. She replied, "Yes, I can." Her very strong voice attracted my attention. I stepped forward and stood in front of her; I took off my hat, and said, "Well, I never saw such a woman in all my life." She then said, "When a gentleman takes off his hat to me I must rise," and she rose up from her chair. I was so astonished at the size of her that I called my friend into the kitchen When he got in he stood staring in amazement. I said, "Come forward, and we will try to clasp round her," and we just managed to make the tips of our fingers meet. She then sat down in her chair, and I ordered refreshments for twenty men Whilst the refreshments were being prepared I said I should like to know her weight. She replied "Ha, but I'm not going to tell that; but you being a gentleman from t'railway, I'll tell yo' this · I wor at station t'other week, and there wor yor station master, and porter, and ar policeman wer there. They all three got on to t'scale at t'weighing machine on t'platform; I put one leg on to t'other scale, when they all went up, and that's as much as I'm going to tell yo'." However, we were quite satisfied with what was provided for us, and came away, leaving the old woman sitting comfortably in her chair.

On Whit-Monday, May 16th, 1864, we had a school excursion from Denby Dale to Liverpool. The special train was made up to twenty-five coaches; ten of these were what the public designated as Daw-green reds. They were old third-class carriages, with wooden slides in place of windows, and bare wood seats for the passengers to sit upon. They had been hurriedly re-painted inside and out for the season. The train was well filled with passengers, and those who travelled in the Daw-green reds, after having been seated for five hours, got pretty warm on the new painted seats. On their arrival at Liverpool, many of them on attempting to rise found themselves stuck fast, which resulted in their either leaving part of their clothing or taking away a good sized patch of paint stuck to their dresses and coats like a piece of leather. Of course the Company had the damages to pay.

With the view of forming a through connection from Yorkshire stations to the North via Burnley Branch and Preston, I suggested that a train should leave Bradford at 8-40 a.m., arriving at Preston at 10-25 a.m., in direct connection with the London and North-Western trains to Edinburgh, arriving there at 5-45 p.m. The return train left Edinburgh at 10 a.m., arrived at Preston at 5 p.m., left Preston at 5-15 p.m., due to arrive at Bradford at 6-15 p.m. This train was put on in March, 1865. This gave great satisfaction to the travelling public, and gathered up a good traffic during that year and afterwards.

On April 5th, 1864, as the 4-5 p m passenger train from Knottingley to Leeds was passing over Methley Branch, the engine and train left the rails, doing considerable damage to rolling stock, and a few passengers were injured. On May 20th, I met Captain Tyler, the Board of Trade inspector, at the scene of the accident, for the purpose of making an inquiry as to its cause. Afterwards we went over to Leeds together, and conversed upon railway working generally. During our conversation I happened to say that an additional service of passenger trains had been brought in and out of Bradford Station by the directors having admitted the Great Northern Railway Company, and in some parts of the day the five-minutes' rule could not be adhered to without causing serious delays, as there were four signal cabins within a mile. As a remedy, even without authority, I took the opportunity of testing the question of these short sections being worked on the block system, the telegraph instruments being already fixed in each signal cabin. The arrangement was made by pegging over the needle, which was released by the signalman in advance when the train had passed, and I found it worked most admirably; it not only ensured punctuality, but safety. Captain Tyler seemed to be pleased with the idea, and evidently did not forget the suggestion afterwards, as in 1869 all railway companies were requested by the Board of Trade to adopt the system.

Soon after this a similar inconvenience arose with the five-minutes' rule between Low Moor and Halifax, these being short sections. I applied for permission to adopt the telegraph block system similar to what had been done between Low Moor and Bradford. This was objected to, and I was summoned to attend the board meeting at Manchester, to give an explanation. I accordingly attended, when the chairman expressed his surprise that I should have asked for any such system to be adopted on our line, as he was sure that no one knew better than myself that it was not possible to work the heavy traffic on our line on such a principle I then explained the reason why I had already adopted the system of block working by the telegraphic needle between Low Moor and Bradford, for a test, without authority, and found it not only ensured punctuality, but safety. After this explanation my request was agreed to, thus completing the block working by telegraph system between Bradford and Low Moor and Halifax. This was the first portion of our line worked upon the block principle. Since then our telegraph superintendent deserves credit for the way in which he has developed the principle throughout the whole line.

In January, 1865, I recommended a quick service of passenger trains from Yorkshire stations to Manchester and Liverpool, with the view of giving better facilities to merchants, manufacturers, and tradespeople generally in getting to and from the various markets, and increasing the receipts for the Company, which was only partly agreed to; but even this concession enabled us to compete with the London and North-Western Railway Company for traffic at some of the principal stations.

In January, 1865, the system of working all the tunnels on our system on the block by telegraph was adopted.

In March, 1865, the Great Northern Railway Company took possession and management of the West Yorkshire Railway, including the Ossett, Gildersome, and Batley Branches, and ran their trains to Kirkgate Station, Wakefield.

In June, 1865, according to instructions of the general managers of the Lancashire and Yorkshire, North-

Eastern, and Great Northern Railway Companies, a meeting of their officers was held at Lofthouse, for the purpose of making a joint report on a code of rules and regulations for working the Branch. We met, and submitted a report, as desired, and the branch was opened in August, 1867. This was a branch line constructed between Methley and Lofthouse jointly by the three companies Had our Company complied with the wishes of the chairman and directors of the West Yorkshire Railway Company, and taken over their line when they had the chance, in September, 1863, this short branch might have been utilised with advantage to the Lancashire and Yorkshire Company.

I remember when, in 1865, our Company made an attempt to secure a through line of railway from the busy towns of commerce and population situated on the Lancashire and Yorkshire Railway system to and from London. The connection commenced on the Askern Branch. The new fork line joined the Great Eastern Railway Company's line on the south-east side of Doncaster, passing through Gainsborough, Lincoln, Sleaford, Peterborough, and Cambridge, to London. Although this new route was seventeen miles further round, as compared with the Great Northern Railway from Wakefield to London, it opened out new ground, where wool was produced, and those agricultural supplies and food stuffs required by the manufacturers and thickly-populated towns situated in Lancashire and Yorkshire. During the time this scheme was hatching, I recollect one of the Great Eastern Company's directors calling at my office, at Wakefield, when we talked over the scheme. I pointed out to him the advantage it would be to the public and to both companies I drafted out a time table for him, showing how a service of five trains each way could be run daily from Liverpool, Manchester, Bolton, Oldham, Rochdale, Halifax, Bradford, Huddersfield, Wakefield, and intermediate stations to Lincoln, Cambridge, and London. He was very much pleased with it, and took the rough copy with him, saying it would greatly assist them when the proposed line of railway was considered in committee. However, the two companies were out-generalled, and the committee threw out the bill. If this new fork line of railway had been made, it would have materially enhanced the interests of the Lancashire and Yorkshire Railway Company

If the directors had remained firm to a policy of constructing through lines of railway in place of making so many short branches, as is shown in Yorkshire, it would have been more remunerative to the Company. For instance : The Company constructed a short branch to Holmfirth, one to Meltham ; one to Ripponden ; each of these terminate at the edge of a moor. One short branch was made to Stainland, and terminated in a mill yard ; also one to Clayton West, which terminated in the middle of a field.

I have good reason for remembering being present at the cutting of the first sod for the last-named branch by the late Mr John Kaye, J.P , Clayton West, on Wednesday, November 27th, 1872. After the ceremony, the contractors gave a very sumptuous banquet in Skelmanthorpe Village Schoolroom, when all the gentry and farmers in the immediate neighbourhood were invited After justice had been done to the good things provided, then commenced the usual toasts on such occasions, as shown by the following cutting from the *Halifax Guardian*, Saturday, November 30th, 1872 :—

Mr Burnup, of Cleckheaton, a large shareholder, proposed "The Directors of the Lancashire and Yorkshire Railway," and said that if the gentlemen on the route would support the line when made, he had no doubt it would be cut through Mr. J Sheard responded to the toast, and said that all the landowners, except one, had been settled with, and all the tenants had been arranged with. (Applause). Mr. Clark then proposed "The Engineers and Officials of the Lancashire and Yorkshire Railway." Mr. Swinburne, resident engineer of the line (and who is also resident engineer on the Stainland Branch), responded, and said he had no doubt that if the subject were pressed, the line would be made through. Mr. Normington, traffic manager of the district, also responded on behalf of the officials, observing that railway officials, as a rule, were not accustomed to speech-making, but rather to working When the line was constructed, they would endeavour to work it so that it would benefit both the public and the shareholders He believed, however, that the line would never be fully beneficial until it was carried through to a connection with the Barnsley Branch, when it would be a means of diverting a considerable amount of traffic from a crowded line on to a line that was not so much used, and would better serve the town of Huddersfield and the districts beyond (Cheers). Several other toasts were proposed and responded to, the proceedings terminating a little before six o'clock by the singing of the National Anthem

The week following the above-named banquet, I received a notice from the secretary to attend the next meeting of the board at Manchester. I attended as requested. I saw the chairman cast his eye upon me. He said: "Normington, we have given you notice to attend this board to receive our censure. We have seen in the public newspapers. some remarks you made when at the banquet at Skelmanthorpe, on the occasion of cutting the first sod of Clayton West Branch. You advocated making the line through to Barnsley Branch. This is something we have spent thousands of pounds in opposing, and we do not allow our officers to go to banquets and make public speeches contrary to our opinions" I got up to make a reply The chairman said: No; I could leave the board, and be a good boy for the future. It is most remarkable that since my censure the Company have applied to Parliament twice for powers to extend the line from Clayton West to Barnsley Branch, but failed each time.

It is still my opinion that there is neither population nor trade sufficient to ensure receipts to pay interest for money spent in making the branch. nevertheless, this branch is so situated that if it had been extended so as to be connected with Barnsley Branch, and carried forward to Cudworth, to be connected there with the Midland Railway system, thus giving a direct connection with the neighbourhood of Halifax and Huddersfield, and to Stairfoot, and there to join the Manchester, Sheffield, and Lincolnshire Railway, this would have given three outlets, and would have cultivated quite a new traffic, particularly in coal from South Yorkshire. It would also have given great relief to our congested main line, situated between Wakefield and Sowerby Bridge, and to the public the facilities they have been agitating for for years

In September, 1865, I remember a most peculiar incident which occurred Three wagons loaded with grain, labelled Lincoln to Wakefield, were seen in a field by some platelayers when going to their work in the early morning The field was situated between Featherstone and Crofton The platelayers reported the case to the station masters at each station. No clue whatever could be found as to how they had got there, only they had come off the main line, and run down the embankment. However, after further inquiry, it was traced that the three wagons had been attached to a Great Northern midnight goods train, from Doncaster to Wakefield On the guard in charge of this train being questioned, a few days afterwards, he knew nothing whatever about losing any wagons from his train, but did remember, soon after passing Featherstone Station, his train having broken loose, when he brought the latter portion, about twenty wagons, to a stand with his break. Looking forward, he saw the engine standing with the other portion near to

Crofton Station, and someone coming towards him with a light, which proved to be the fireman. It was then arranged for the front portion to be set back up to the rear portion. The wagons were then coupled together, and they went on to Wakefield On the engine driver being questioned upon the matter, he stated that he was not aware he had lost any wagons on the journey, but did remember the train breaking loose when passing over the line between Featherstone and Crofton, and after bringing the front portion to a stand he could see the latter portion by the lights at a stand towards Featherstone Station. It was arranged for him to set back to the rear portion, when they coupled the wagons together and went on their journey to Wakefield.   Neither the engine driver nor the guard thought it necessary to report the case, as it had only been a break loose.   I may say here, when this occurred there was no station at Sharlestone, or night staff at either Featherstone or Crofton Stations

On Sunday, December 13th, 1865, when at the morning service at St. Mary's Church, Wakefield, a telegram was brought to me to the effect that the Mytholm Bridge Viaduct had fallen, and the line was blocked to Holmfirth.   This viaduct is situated between Brockholes Junction and Thongs Bridge Station, on the Holmfirth Branch.   In the valley, close by, there stood an old corn mill, worked by a water wheel.   The old miller, who lived beside the Mytholm Viaduct, was named England.   He happened to be stirring about early that morning, and on hearing the crash he saw what had occurred, and, fortunately, he had presence of mind to remember that a passenger train was about due to pass from Huddersfield to Holmfirth.   He immediately hastened up the embankment on to the railway, and ran on the line towards Brockholes Junction Station, and was

8

just in time to stop the train, which was leaving at
6-59 a.m. for Holmfirth. The distance from the viaduct
to the Junction Station is about nine hundred yards, on
a very sharp curve Had it not been for the prompt
action taken by the good old miller of the Mytholm
valley, a most serious accident would have happened, as
there was nothing to prevent the engine and train of
carriages running off the line into the valley beneath, a
drop of fifty yards.

On receiving the telegram I immediately left the
church, and went to the station and got an engine, which
took me to the scene of the accident, when I saw that all
communication by railway with Holmfirth was destroyed
for at least twelve months, I began to consider what
was the best thing to do under the circumstances. I
telegraphed at once to the secretary and general manager
at Manchester, giving particulars as to what had
occurred I then took a survey of the surrounding
neighbourhood, with the view of establishing an omnibus
service between Holmfirth and Brockholes Station, in
connection there with the trains; but I found the ground
so rugged, and the roads so narrow and bad, that it was
impossible for an omnibus to travel there. Later on in
the day one of our directors came over, when I told him
what I had done, and that it was not possible to run
omnibuses from Brockholes to Holmfirth. I recommended
that the service of omnibuses should be run between
Honley Station and Holmfirth, which was eventually
agreed to. I then waited upon an omnibus and cab
proprietor, of Huddersfield, and arranged with him for
the omnibus service, six each way per day, He asked
me to arrange to pay the toll bars, there being three to
pass through on the journey. Finding these toll bars
were taken on the contract principle, and the person who
held the contract resided in the toll-bar house at Lock-

wood, I waited upon him there, with the view to arrange to pay monthly, but this he would not agree to, and although I offered him five pounds per month, he still insisted upon being paid every time an omnibus or vehicle belonging to the Company passed through the bar. I thought this would be very inconvenient for the 'bus drivers to do, and knowing that we carried mail bags daily, by trains from Huddersfield to Thongs Bridge and Holmfirth, and that a mail bag cleared the 'bus toll, I at once arranged for a mail bag to be conveyed by every 'bus. A week or two afterwards I received a letter from the toll-bar contractor, to say that since our interview he had re-considered the question of the omnibus service which ran between Honley and Holmfirth, and had decided to accept what I had offered, five pounds per month. I replied that since our interview I had also re-considered the question, and made other arrangements, and could not now alter them. The omnibus service was transferred to the manager of the Manchester Carriage Company on Monday, December 21st. The viaduct was opened for traffic and trains passed over on Monday, March 11th, 1867, thus dispensing with the omnibus service and the old toll-bar contractor, who, from his own avariciousness, lost fifteen five pound notes.

In November, 1865, I suggested that the goods trains should be placed under the control of the passenger superintendent, and in December the directors ordered that the proposal be adopted and carried into effect, and that the general manager should arrange the details with the superintendent. In January, 1866, I met the general manager, along with the goods superintendent for Yorkshire Division at Normanton Station, and arranged the details as ordered. When the general manager laid before the Board of Directors the worked-out details of the transfer, the chairman took umbridge and objected to the scheme   This led to high words between them, and the general manager decided to leave the Company's service, and did so in December, 1867.   On the 21st the officers of the Company, to show their appreciation of his abilities, presented him with a testimonial in the board-room at Hunt's Bank, Manchester   After the presentation he followed me out into the corridor, tapped me on the shoulder, and said, " Normington, I told you that I should leave the Company after what had occurred at the board meeting in reference to our arrangements made when we met at Normanton Station for the better and more economical way of working the line." He further said, " I know your prospects with the Company, but if ever you desire a change let me know, and I will find you a much better position." I thanked him and then we parted.   I have often thought since that the Company had lost a good, sound, practical, energetic, and enter-prising railway manager, and had he remained with them, along with officers then about him, the dividends would never have receded to four per cent.   His abilities showed that.   We only have to follow him to the Caledonian Railway Company to observe his abilities as general manager of a railway.   When he entered that company's service the shares stood in the market at 50, and when he retired they were 130

Prior to this meeting at Normanton Station I remember having a long conversation with the general manager as to the best method of managing a railway.   With the view of ensuring an efficient staff at all stations, and also of the traffic produced within the radius of the station limits, particularly at country stations, I suggested that the basis of a station master's or agent's salary should be first regulated upon the present receipts earned at the station, and afterwards on all increased traffic during the current year they should receive a small commission, or the advantage of an increase of salary or otherwise for keeping down station working expenses. By adopting such a policy, in my opinion, all station masters and agents, if worthy of the position, would always keep themselves in close touch with the trades people and public generally, and at any time when a grievance arose would at once see the persons concerned personally, in the spirit that railways were made for the public, obtaining all particulars of their grievances, reporting fully upon all cases as they arose to the divisional superintendent. who would immediately take action with the view of applying a remedy. I know from my experience with the public in Yorkshire that they are not eager to court railway competition ; they simply desire the necessary facilities so as to enable them to deal punctually with their various trades and industries. The station masters and agents to commence with their commission on the 1st of January yearly. If there should happen to be a decrease in their receipts, a full explanation would have to be given as to the cause or causes.

The West Riding and Grimsby Railway was opened for traffic in February, 1866, between Doncaster and Wakefield, when the Great Northern Railway Company discontinued to run their trains from London and Doncaster via Pontefract to Wakefield and Leeds. On this date they transferred the whole of their service of trains to run over the abovenamed new lines. They not only took all their trains from running over our line, but became keen competitors on our own ground for local traffic at our principal stations, particularly Wakefield, Bradford, Halifax, Dewsbury, and Leeds. This verifies my remarks made to the directors on the platform at Kirkgate Station, Wakefield, in September, 1863.

On March 5th, 1866, a new station at Mirfield was opened for passengers, and was built on the principle I suggested, which was what is called an island platform, with bay sidings at each end for the branch trains to be placed in. The Company have erected many new passenger stations since then, and had they being built on a similar principle, they would have been more convenient, and would have been worked at half the cost.

In April, 1866, the directors resolved that the deputy passenger traffic superintendents were to attend the traffic committee whenever their principals were unable to attend, and that on other occasions they were to be summoned should their attendance be required, and ordered that they were to be summoned to the next meeting of the Traffic Committee. I may say from this time I attended the meetings of the Board of Directors, also represented the Company at general meetings of officers of other companies held in London, York, and other places, for the purpose of making traffic arrangements up to the time of centralisation in 1871.

Whit-Tuesday, May 22nd, 1866, was a great jubilee day at Halifax of Sunday school children, and was held in the Piece Hall. Many children were brought from the country by special trains within a radius of twelve miles. This materially increased the heavy Whitsuntide traffic, and caused us to be short of carriages to meet the extra requirements. We had to get one hundred cattle wagons fitted up with seats, which were mostly used to convey the school children, and gave great offence to the ministers and school managers who happened to be so unfortunate as to have to travel in them. This was a very busy Whit-Monday and Tuesday for Yorkshire district. We had seventy special trains for the two days, and conveyed in and out upwards of eighty thousand passengers without any casualty. I left my home at four o'clock on Monday morning, and was continually on duty until I arrived back at Wakefield on Wednesday at mid-day, and on June 13th I received a vote of thanks from the directors for the safe and efficient manner in which the heavy Whit-week traffic had been dealt with, together with a present of ten pounds.

On Saturday, July 28, 1866, an excursion train was run from Berry Brow to Goole and Hull, which turned out to be a very heavy train. It consisted of twenty-eight carriages, in charge of three guards, conveying over 900 excursionists The special train was due to return from Goole at 8-30 p.m. It being such a heavy train, I went to Goole to meet it, and travelled back with it in the guard's van, next the engine. The night was very dark, and a little rain was falling. On approaching Crofton Station, about 10 p m., running at the speed of about twenty miles an hour, I observed the distance signal for the station at danger, and seeing that the engine-driver and fireman had not noticed the signal, I made every attempt to attract their attention, but did not succeed before the engine had passed round a very sharp curve. It was then too late, there being no continuous brakes on the train, to stop it. The red lights on the guard's van at the rear of a goods train could be seen standing at the station. The engine-driver with the excursion train, after seeing the signals, made every effort to stop his train, but the distance was too short to prevent a collision I got on to the footboard of the guard's van just as the collision occurred, and was pitched off with great force on to the opposite line, jamming my head under the metals in the hollow of the ballast. I laid there unconscious and unobserved for some time. I was just coming to my senses when one of the guards came and helped me up. I asked him to take me to the place to see the worst, and he did so. I saw the engine of the excursion train down the embankment. It had broken away the coupling of the guard's van and rolled down into a field, leaving the driver and fireman on the embankment with very slight injuries. A few passengers who travelled in the first two carriages complained of having received some slight injuries, while the passengers in the rear part of the train were not aware there had been a collision until some time afterwards. On my seeing the goods brake van across the parapet of the bridge on the opposite line. I asked the guard if any one had gone on towards Wakefield to stop the 10 p.m. passenger train from there to Goole. He replied he did not think any one had gone. I said, "Go at once, for the train is overdue;" and away he went. Directly after I heard the train coming towards Crofton. Although half dead, I ran to meet it, and it was stopped just in time to prevent another collision. The extra exertion I had made in running so soon after the severe shock I had just received completely knocked me over. I told the guard and station staff what to do, when reaction returned. I was then put on to the engine that was with the goods train and sent on to Wakefield, and arranged with the station master there to take a doctor and a staff of men to Crofton to clear the line. I then went home, and had to stop there for a few days. I felt the effects of the very severe shock I had received to my head for years after; even yet at times I feel a depressed sensation. I received no compensation for this injury, but did get slightly compensated for my spoilt clothing

On November 12th, 1866, I had been on the line all the day from early morning, arriving back at Wakefield a little after seven o'clock. I had just got home to tea when a telegraphic message was brought to the house, which informed me that the 5-10 p.m. passenger train from Manchester to Normanton was stopped at Cooper Bridge, in consequence of the line being blocked with goods wagons off the road. I immediately went back to the station, and got an engine to take me to the scene of the accident. The driver asked where we were going to. I said, "Cooper Bridge, as fast as you can go," and we left Wakefield about 7-44 p.m. On approaching Horbury Junction the signals were at danger. The driver whistled according to rules, and in a short time they were taken off On approaching Horbury Station the signals were all off, indicating the line was clear to run past the station. On emerging out of the short tunnel, and running over fifty miles an hour, I observed three red lights on the brake van at the rear of a goods train. Before I could speak to the driver the engine came in collision with the goods train. I was pitched from the engine on to the tender, where I lay unconscious for a short time. When I came round I found myself embedded amongst the coals I got out the best way I could, and seeing no one about, I got off the engine and struggled along the line to the station, a distance of about five hundred yards When reaction came on I managed to crawl on to a seat in the booking office lobby, and was immediately surrounded by a number of mill girls, who had come to see the accident. They evidently took me for a drunken man, as one of them called to her friend, "Come here; there's a drunken man." Just at this time a porter came up with a lamp in his hand, and on hearing the girls call to each other he looked over their heads, and on seeing me crouched on the seat he called out, "There is Mr. Normington here," and drove the girls away. The station master then came up to me and said, "We have been looking for you all over the line," and asked where I was injured. I could not answer him, as after the reaction set in I was rendered speechless. I wrote on a piece of paper requesting him to send for a doctor, and he immediately did so. In the meantime I heard the station master explaining to some one the result of the collision. The engine-driver and the fireman with the empty engine had received very severe shocks and cuts, but no bones were broken. The brake van at the rear of the goods train was smashed to pieces, and the guard very much injured, and he had been taken to the Wakefield Infirmary. Eight loaded goods wagons, along with the van, were thrown off the line. It is not often we are glad to see a doctor, but I was somewhat relieved on seeing Dr. Kemp, of Horbury, make his appearance. He said I was very seriously injured, and that I had better be taken to the inn close by and put to bed for a thorough examination. I wrote on a slip of paper, " No, if I am going to die, I will die at home, and you must take me there " An engine and carriage were provided, and the doctor accompanied me to Wakefield On arriving there Dr. Wood and Dr. Fowler were waiting, having been telegraphed for. I was carried home, where the three doctors examined me They retired into another room for consultation After a short time Dr Kemp returned, and whispered into my ear, " Normington, I guarantee you will get better if you keep up your spirits " This remark was a great relief to me. I thought this a palatable medicine, and did as desired On the second day I recovered my speech, and in less than a month I was out on the line again I received no compensation for these injuries—broken ribs and severe shock to the system. But, as before, I received some acknowledgment for my spoiled clothing

In January, 1863, I was asked by one of the directors to draft out a quick market train service, to run between Bradford, Halifax, and Manchester, on Tuesdays, to be only first-class bookings I submitted a scheme to commence on March 1st, and it was agreed to by the directors, the time occupied in running the journey being eighty-five minutes.

On March 1st, 1867, the Great Northern Railway Company transferred the whole of their service of passenger trains, which they despatched from and arrived at their West Riding Station, Bradford, to the Lancashire and Yorkshire Railway Company's Station, at Bradford, thus increasing the number of passenger trains in and out of that station by sixty-four, making a total of one hundred and ten daily; and now, in 1895, the two companies arrive and depart two hundred and twenty-five trains daily.

On Monday, March 11th, 1867, I was summoned to London by the directors to give some Parliamentary evidence upon the passenger train service running between Huddersfield and Halifax and other principal stations in the district. I went by the first train after receiving the telegram, and had an interview with the general manager in the evening, for the purpose of preparing the evidence required. In the afternoon of the 12th, whilst in the committee-room of the House of Commons, I received a telegram from Wakefield, requesting me to return that night to be ready next morning to meet the Board of Trade inspector on the examination of the new line of railway from Dewsbury to Thornhill. There was also to be held at Bradford an adjourned inquest on the engine-driver who was killed in Bowling Tunnel, on the 7th of March, which required my presence. I showed this message to the directors, and explained to them how important it was that I should be at Bradford to be present at the adjourned inquest. They then had a consultation with counsel, and in arguing the matter he saw the importance of my being at the inquest, and said that as he had my evidence sufficiently complete he did not object to my going away. I had only a very short time to call at my lodgings, and catch the last train to Wakefield. On leaving the committee-room, and being in a great hurry, I took a wrong hat; it seemed to fit all right, and I did not observe the mistake I had made until I arrived home, and my wife asked me whose hat I had got. I then looked at it and saw it was rather a broad-brimmed one, and declared it must be John Bright's. After this discovery that hat was only used on very rare occasions

On August 27th, 1866, the Dewsbury Branch line was opened for goods traffic, and on April 1st, 1867, it was opened for passenger traffic. We commenced running a service of passenger trains between Dewsbury, Thornhill, and Mirfield, in connection there with the up and down main line trains. We also commenced to run a service of trains between Wakefield and Dewsbury, in connection with trains from York, Doncaster, Goole, and Barnsley Branch.

In August, 1867, Mr James Shaw, the passenger traffic superintendent for East Lancashire Division, resigned, having accepted a similar appointment at Liverpool, under the London and North-Western Railway Company. A suitable testimonial was presented to him on Friday, the 13th September, by the officers and railway servants of the Company. The public also recognised his abilities, and presented him with a testimonial at Accrington, on Monday, the 25th of November. The Lancashire and Yorkshire Railway Company was again unfortunate in losing a good practical railway servant, and the London and North-Western Railway Company was fortunate in securing one.

On September the 13th, 1867, I became a Freemason in Mirfield Lodge, No. 1102

On Monday, August the 3rd, 1868, Meltham Branch was opened for goods traffic, and closed again in September, owing to one of the embankments giving way. Re-opened for goods traffic February the 6th, 1869, and for passenger traffic on Monday, July 12th. On this day the contractors gave a sumptuous banquet at the Rose and Crown Hotel, Netherton, in commemoration of the final opening. This is only a single line, but it has been a costly construction.

In 1867-8 the traffic both in passengers and goods had greatly increased, with every prospect that it would gradually increase. This necessitated our putting on additional trains, especially for the goods and coal traffic Siding accommodation at all stations was so limited that goods trains had to be shunted from one main line to the other, to clear, to allow passenger trains to pass, which resulted in serious delays to both passenger and goods trains on the opposite lines. This led to increased working expenses, and the directors passed an order that the divisional passenger traffic superintendents should look fully into the matter, and report thereon. For Yorkshire Division I made out a return for one month, showing the delays and the causes, and suggested the only remedy would be that at the principal stations, where goods trains had a good deal of shunting and exchange of wagons to contend with, loop lines should be constructed, and at smaller stations refuge sidings, wherein to place goods trains for express trains to pass, and avoid having to shunt from one main line to another. My view was to give accommodation for each up and down main line to deal with its own traffic, which would be a sure way to prevent delays and accidents, and reduce working expenses. This report was laid before the Board of Directors, together with pen-and-ink sketches showing the idea of the requirements necessary at the several stations. However, the general manager objected to the suggestions, saying he would not recommend the directors to incur such an enormous cost, and so the matter dropped for a time, but force of increased traffic compelled them to do a little of something. The scheme not being yet completed keeps up the working expenses to this day, 1895.

In July, 1868, I completely broke down through the strain of continuous head work, in a dark, unventilated office. I consulted Dr. Lister, of Halifax, also Dr. Wood, of Wakefield, and both advised me to go away for a short time out of the reach of business. They said I had been doing too much, and had not had the rest I ought to have had, after the two very severe shocks I had received to the system in the two collisions I had the misfortune to be in a short time before. I took their advice, and went away, not telling anyone but my wife where I was going to. Dr. Wood undertook to make Captain Binstead and the directors acquainted with the circumstances. I went to the quiet, rural, and picturesque village of Kirk Smeaton, took my daily rambles along the banks of the river Went, and through Brock-o'-Dale Woods, and admired their most beautiful and charming surroundings; also I wandered through and through the magnificent and extensive avenues of Stapleton Park and the beautiful valley and village of Wentbridge, through which the river Went meanders along its quiet and peaceful course. During my eight days stay at this delightful place the weather was charming and all that could be desired. I made a few friends amongst the farmers, and also became friendly with the vicar of the village. They were one and all very kind to me. On the morning of my return home I had purposed walking to the railway station, but on my leaving the house where I had been staying, to my surprise I found the old village blacksmith had sent his horse, carriage, and coachman to take me to the station. The coachman had evidently been hurriedly called from the stable, as he came without coat or hat, and one of his shirt sleeves rolled up. I took stock of the turn

out and accepted the drive for goodwill. We had gone
about half the distance to the station, when I found I was
running the risk of losing my train, as we had been forty
minutes in driving the distance of a mile and a half. I
got out of the carriage, gave the coachman a shilling, and
off I went to the station, arriving there just in time to
catch the train to Wakefield. On my appearance at the
office next day Captain Binstead was delighted at seeing
me back again, and said that Dr. Wood had told both
him and the directors the circumstances of my absence,
and much sympathy had been expressed towards me.
He further said I must take things more calmly, in the
future, and that a clerk had been appointed to render me
every assistance in the office work I also called upon Dr.
Wood, and he further advised me that whenever I felt the
sensation described come over me I was to cease office
work at once, and take occasionally a half-day's recreation,
such as shooting or fishing. This, he said, he had named
to the directors, which gave me the opportunity to again
take up my gun. I feel sure it has been the means of
preserving my health, and I still hope to keep to my dog
and gun. This little outing to Kirk Smeaton resulted in
my having many a day's shooting in Stapleton Park
with the farmers in the immediate neighbourhood, and
with the vicar, who was a true sportsman. I remember
receiving a written invitation for me to join him for a
day's shooting, himself fixing the day and time I replied
the day and time would suit me, and should arrive by
train due at Womersley Station at 8-10 a m During
the night heavy snow had fallen, covering the ground
to the depth of six or eight inches. The boughs of the
trees and the hedgerows were drooping with the weight.
On my arrival at the station there was no trap to meet
me, as I expected However, off I went with my dog
and gun, trudging through the deep snow, a distance of

over three miles, to Kirk Smeaton. On arriving at the
Vicarage, the vicar himself opened the door. On seeing
me he exclaimed, " Well, I never thought you would turn
out on such a morning as this." I replied, " When I
make an appointment for a day's shooting I never let the
weather stop the arrangements." He said, " Well, I am
ready," and away we went, and had a very good day's
sport, arriving back at the Vicarage a little before dusk.
Whilst we were having tea, the Vicar said to his wife,
" My dear, I dare say Mr. Normington would like a glass
of beer." I replied, " It's just what I was wishing for."
She looked at me and said, " I did not think anyone but
my husband could drink beer with their tea, and thought
it was only an excuse to get one for himself." However,
I let her see that I could drink a glass of beer with my
tea, as I had two. The Vicar turned to his wife, and
said, " Ah ' my dear, but you see Mr. Normington is one
of the old sort of sportsmen, with similar ideas to Mr.
Barton, of Stapleton Hall, who once invited me to
join him for a day's shooting in the park. It
happened to be such a morning as this was; the
ground and trees were covered with snow, and I
thought no one would go out shooting on such a morning,
so I did not go. But the next time we met he did not
forget to call my attention to the fact that I did not turn
up for the day's shooting as arranged. I told him I did
not think he would go, it being such a winterly morning,
when he said that an arrangement was an arrangement
with shooters, and that he went himself with the keeper.
I never received from Mr. Barton another invitation for a
day's shooting."

In the latter part of 1868, the general manager for the
Great Northern Railway Company expressed a desire
that I should go over to their company, and take a
division. This was mentioned to our directors. I

received a letter from one of them, in which he expressed a wish to see me. I called upon him the next day, when he asked me if it was my wish to go over to the Great Northern Company. We then talked the matter over. He said it was the directors' wish, and particularly his own, that I should remain with them, because I knew the district and the requirements of the line so well. If I would stay with them I should eventually succeed to a more remunerative position, and with this understanding I decided to stay with the Company. Time has shown that I made a mistake in not following the example of my brother officers, and changing companies when the offer was made to me; but, having faith in the promise in the way in which it was made, I remained with the old Company

In May, 1869, Ravensthorpe Branch was opened. It is situated between Thornhill and Heckmondwike. This line gave greater facilities to the travelling public between Bradford, Dewsbury, Wakefield, and to other lines south-eastwards, by dispensing with the necessity of having to travel the circuitous route by Mirfield, and the saving of time by twenty-five minutes. A through service of passenger trains was established to run between Dewsbury and Bradford, in direct connection at Thornhill with up and down main line trains.

On November the 1st, 1869, North Dean Branch was opened as a double line, when a through service of passenger trains was established to run between Bradford Halifax, Brighouse, Huddersfield, and Holmfirth, in direct connection with the up and down main line trains, either at Brighouse or at North Dean; also a through service of passenger trains was established to run between Bradford, Mirfield, Huddersfield, and Meltham, in direct connection with up and down main line trains at Mirfield.

In June, 1869, I attended a railway officers' meeting,

9

at Euston Station, London. Seven railway companies were represented at the meeting. In the course of arguing matters over in connection with railway traffic arrangements, I introduced to the meeting for discussion the advisability of abolishing second-class accommodation, but the question was not unanimously entertained, and was deferred to a future meeting, but was not minuted. After the business of the meeting, the Midland Company's representative asked me to go with him to have a quiet chat together, as he would like to know what had brought about my idea as to discontinuing second-class bookings. I went with him, and we had a long talk upon railway matters generally. I explained to him that our through service of trains from Yorkshire to Manchester and Liverpool was made up at Sowerby Bridge into a double train, and divided again at Rochdale, which made it a very long train over this section of the line, being seventeen to twenty coaches long, and we often had to send an extra engine to assist part of the way. I had noticed that the second-class compartments were, as a rule, comparatively empty, and that the few who did travel second class generally held return tickets at reduced fares, which meant very little more money than a third-class single fare each way, and concluded that if the train above described had only had first and third class bookings, I could have reduced the length of it by at least six coaches, and saved hauling about empty stock and the assistant engine. The same rule would apply to all branch trains with regard to hauling about empty stock, which would be the means of materially reducing the working expenses, and save the cost of having to build second-class carriages. My view was that the question could be met by slightly reducing first-class fares. The Midland representative was highly satisfied with my explanation, and said he should like to see the principle adopted on their line. The question was afterwards brought before the officers' meetings, but before it got thrashed out I was debarred from attending these meetings in consequence of a change of management. The Lancashire and Yorkshire Railway Company adopted the system of centralised management, in May, 1871, which excluded me from attending in future any officers' meetings of other companies. I lost sight of the question until 1874, when one of the directors called at my office at Wakefield, and said he had just returned from London, having represented the Lancashire and Yorkshire Railway Company at a conference of railway directors to decide the question of abolishing second-class carriages. He said he had voted against the abolition, as he did not think that the discontinuance of booking second class would be satisfactory to the public on our line. I replied I was very sorry that he should have taken that view, and voted against the abolition. I explained to him that I was the first railway officer to suggest the abolition, and the reason why I came to be of that opinion. Although I have not attended those officers' meetings, I have continually urged both the general manager and the directors to adopt the no-second-class principle, being so strongly of opinion that it would have materially reduced the working expenses, at no inconvenience to the public, or any pecuniary loss to the Company. My opinion now is (in 1895) still to abolish second-class carriages, and to adopt in their place workmen's carriages

In December, 1869, the Goole and Staddlethorpe Branch was opened. This branch is situated between Goole, in connection with the Lancashire and Yorkshire main line, and Staddlethorpe, in connection there with the North-Eastern main lines to and from Hull Early in November I accompanied our general manager to Goole, having a meeting there with the North-Eastern

Railway Company's representatives for the purpose of making working traffic and train arrangements, I being under the impression that, as we had running powers over this new branch line through to Hull, it was just the opportunity to establish a through service of passenger trains to run between Liverpool and Hull. With that view I had drafted out a time table showing six trains per day each way, which was submitted to the meeting I was somewhat surprised when the representatives of the North-Eastern Company said it could not be accepted, as we had not absolute running powers over the line. This rebuff made the general manager and myself look rather small, having attended a meeting, and not knowing the extent of the Company's running powers After further consideration I urged the next best thing, to agree to run through carriages by three trains per day between Liverpool, Manchester, and Hull, to be transferred to and from the North-Eastern trains at Goole. This also was objected to, but eventually it was agreed upon to run through coaches by two trains per day. Within twelve months such circumstances occurred, owing to the irregular running of the trains, that the through carriages had to be discontinued. At this time traffic over the whole of our system was very heavy Additional services of trains, both passenger and goods, had to run to meet the requirements, and this, with the main line already overcrowded, made it impossible to get the trains through without serious delays Although rapid strides had been made in utilising the telegraph with the view of facilitating the trains over the line, serious delays occurred for the want of accommodation, such as would have been given by loop lines and refuge sidings being constructed, as recommended in 1868.

In December, 1869, I was summoned to meet the deputy chairman at Manchester I went there and had an interview with him, when he told me they were anticipating making some changes amongst the officers on the line. It had been suggested and talked over by the directors, who considered that I was the most suitable man to come up to Manchester. He did not state definitely what the position was, but from his remarks I concluded it was for the general superintendency. I asked for a short time to be allowed me to think the matter over. He replied, "Certainly, and you can give me an answer in the course of a day or two" The very next day I received a letter from one of the directors, requesting me to meet him at Halifax. I met him, and he said, "Normington, the directors are wanting you to go to Manchester." I said, "Yes, I suppose so, as I had an interview with the deputy-chairman yesterday, and he told me" When he said, "I don't think you would care to leave Yorkshire, you are so well known and respected by the public generally; at least I would rather you would stay in Yorkshire," and from our further conversation upon the matter I was led to believe that it was intended to work the line in two divisions in place of three, and that Yorkshire Division would be extended. I replied, "If that be so, I would rather stay in Yorkshire, seeing that I have worked night and day for the past ten years in devising and organising improved schemes for the general working arrangements throughout the district," and added, "I will stay in Yorkshire extended division," and replied to the deputy-chairman to that effect.

Having observed, since the agreement entered into between the London and North-Western and Lancashire and Yorkshire Railway Companies for a division of competitive traffic, in 1862, to remain in force for fourteen years, that we were gradually losing the through passenger traffic from the North-Eastern Railway Company's system

arriving at Normanton and at Holbeck Junction, also from
the principal stations in Yorkshire Division to and from
Manchester and Liverpool, owing to the London and
North-Western Company giving better facilities to the
public for railway travelling, I, with the view of
retaining the through traffic, revised and drafted out a
quick service of trains to run from Normanton and Leeds
to and from Manchester and Liverpool. This scheme
increased the working expenses by fourteen hours per
day of engine working. This new express train service
was submitted to the Board of Directors. I explained
that if it was adopted, we should not only maintain the
through traffic from the North-Eastern Company's
system—which is over a thousand miles of railway—but
would also give the quick service of trains to the
merchants, manufacturers, and tradespeople which had
long been asked for throughout Yorkshire Division, so as
to enable them to get to and from the various markets.
Nevertheless, after all my explanations, and arguing the
necessity of such a service, but not being backed up by
the general manager, it was resolved by the Board of
Directors not to adopt it, because it would increase the
working expenses; and seeing that an arrangement had
been made between the two Companies for dividing
the traffic, also pending amalgamation. I remember
that after the board meeting the general manager and
myself had some conversation upon the matter. He said
he thought the directors were right in not agreeing to
the express service of trains, particularly when the
amalgamation and division of traffic were considered.
" Why should we incur additional expense in working
the traffic?" I replied, " We have the traffic now, and
we ought to try and keep it, seeing that we get working
expenses in addition to the division. The amalgamation
might miscarry, and the divisional agreement for traffic
will terminate in 1876. If we keep the traffic, we shall

be in a better position at that time to meet the London and North-Western Company in making arrangements for extending the agreement, if it were considered necessary, which could then be done with more advantage to our Company." He replied, "No; we can put the express service of passenger trains on then, and we shall soon get the traffic back." I replied that lost traffic was expensive in trying to get back.

However, the London and North-Western Company grasped the necessity of an express train service from Yorkshire, and put one on in February, 1870, which resulted in their getting the traffic, and keeping it. This was the first step that led to their success in Yorkshire. Our Company objecting to establish an express train service brought on unpopularity, and the gradual loss of traffic.

I observed that the central management, in 1888, put on an express service of trains from Yorkshire, but overlooked making the necessary connection at Holbeck Junction with the North-Eastern Company's trains, and the local traffic seemed to be forgotten altogether.

In 1870 it was anticipated that war would break out between France and Germany, and my views were, if there should be war, it would result in a great increase of traffic on our line, particularly in goods. The line already being in a very congested state, I again urged for loop lines and refuge sidings to be constructed at an early date. The directors ordered that the officers go fully into the question, and report as early as possible at what points additional siding accommodation was required. So far as Yorkshire Division was concerned, I submitted a list of the principal stations recommended for loop lines, and the other smaller stations for refuge sidings, again accompanied with pen-and-ink sketches, showing what was required. I attended the board meeting when the

increased siding accommodation was discussed. During
the discussion, one of the directors made a remark that I
was born before my time. I said, "No man ought to be
a railway manager unless he could see fifty years before
him." Another said, "We might as well double the line
as carry out your suggestion." I replied, "The serious
delays which now occur cannot be avoided until the
additional siding accommodation is provided. If the
suggestions were carried out, and the traffic still goes on
increasing, which we have every reason to expect it will,
it means doubling the line It will then be already half
done." However, the divisional superintendents' recommendations were not backed up by the general manager,
and the directors thought the outlay would be too large.
The schemes were, therefore, deferred to some future
time.

The end of April, 1871, saw the termination of divisional
management of the Lancashire and Yorkshire Railway,
and destroyed the rivalry which was mixed with that
harmony necessary for working a railway to advantage.
Each divisional traffic superintendent was anxious to
show at the end of the year that some improvement
had been effected, and Yorkshire Division always had the
credit of being to the front.

May 1st, 1871.—It is just twelve years since I was
appointed assistant to Captain Binstead, traffic superintendent for Yorkshire Division. I have endeavoured to
carry out the verbal instructions given to me by the
directors in May, 1859. This necessitated me devoting
hundreds of hours at home (after having done a long
day's work on the line) in organising and devising
schemes for the better working of the line with economy,
punctuality, and safety, and giving extended and improved facilities to the public, which had the tendency of
increasing the receipts every year. A five-pound note

was never lost, where it was possible for one to be made. This was plainly demonstrated during the excursion season. All applications were immediately attended to and traffic secured within a few hours after application, and if the schemes and recommendations submitted had been more generally complied with, more money would have been secured and the working expenses materially reduced. To show how anxious I was for the success of of the Company, I ask my readers to give a glance at the eleven years' extracts taken from my diary.

From January 1st, 1860, to the end of December, 1871, the average time I devoted to the interests of the Company (week days and Sundays) was 4,653 hours per annum net, taking 365 days in the year, which averages twelve hours and forty-five minutes daily spent on the line or in the office. This does not include the hours worked at home after leaving the office, which were considerable, in devising schemes for the better and safe working of the line, and schemes for earning more money with reduced working expenses.

After centralised management took effect the position of goods superintendent, who had the arrangement and management of the working of all goods trains, was dispensed with. Soon after this the service of goods trains landed in a chaos of confusion and loss to the Company. Centralised management took effect on the 1st of May, 1871.

Directors.

Chairman, Thomas Dugdale, Esq
Deputy-Chairman, Thomas Barnes, Esq

George Anderton, Esq	The Rt. Hon Lord Houghton
Joshua Appleyard, Esq	John R Kay, Esq
Samuel Fielden, Esq.	B. C. Nicholson, Esq.
Theodore Julius Hare, Esq	James Pilkington, Esq
John Hargreaves, Esq	Joshua Radcliffe, Esq
James Hatton, Esq	Peter Thompson, Esq
William H. Hornby, Esq	George Wood, Esq

Officers.

William Thorley, Traffic Manager
Henry Blackmore, Superintendent of the Line.

George Alsbury, District Superintendent, Lancashire.
Henry Goodier, District Superintendent, Accrington
E. M Grundy, District Superintendent, Manchester
Thomas Normington, District Superintendent, Wakefield

The following newspaper extract, cut from the *Halifax Guardian*, shows the opinion of the public upon the changes made by the new management.—

SUPERINTENDENCE OF THE LANCASHIRE AND YORKSHIRE RAILWAY

Contrary to general expectation, the directors of this railway have appointed Mr. Blackmore, who for many years has been superintendent of the Lancashire portion of the line, to be the general superintendent of the whole line, now that Admiral Binstead has retired The *Wakefield Journal*, of yesterday, alluding to the appointment, says.—"We had hoped, and so, we believe, had the public, that whenever Admiral Binstead retired from the superintendence, Mr Normington, who has so ably conducted the passenger traffic arrangements for a great number of years, would have been promoted to the post This, however, we are sorry to say, is not the case, for the directors have appointed Mr. Blackmore, who has been manager for a number of years of the Lancashire district, manager of the entire line, and Mr. Normington, we believe, is made inspector, with duties very similar to those he has discharged for the last few years We understand, however, that Mr. Normington was offered the post vacated by Admiral Binstead, but clogged with such conditions that he refused it. His case is the harder that he had the offer of a very good appointment on another railway a short time ago. His abilities are, however, well known, and we have the authority of the late Mr Seymour Clarke for the statement that his services would be considered an acquisition by any railway company in the kingdom."

The four district officers proceeded to their respective positions with their hands and tongues tied. Our instructions were not to communicate or make any arrangements for traffic with the public, or to correspond with railway officers of other companies. Our general passes were curtailed, confining us exclusively to our own immediate districts This destroyed all energy and enterprise on the part of the officers. The new system of management was very different to what the directors had previously led me to expect. I therefore made application for a re-arrangement, especially for the Yorkshire Division, and enclosed a written basis for revising the previous arrangement. I was therefore summoned to attend the Board of Directors' meeting, but owing to an accident at Mytholmroyd, and the line being blocked, I unfortunately did not arrive at Manchester until after two o'clock. On making my way to the boardroom I found the directors were leaving the room. One of them asked why I was not there at the time summoned—twelve noon? After explaining the cause, I was told that my suggestions had been considered in my absence, and the question had been left with the general manager, and I was to see him before I returned to Wakefield, and whatever he and I agreed to it would be right to them.

I therefore called upon the general manager, and found him alone in his office. He asked why I was so late, and said the directors had been waiting half an hour for me, and it was not often they would wait for anyone. I explained to him the cause of my being late, and said I had just seen two of the directors, who told me that my question was left with him and myself to decide. He replied, "That is so;" and producing the document containing my suggestions which had been considered at the meeting of the Board of Directors, said, "I cannot agree to these suggestions, as others want power as well as yourself." I replied, "When I drew out these suggestions I never thought about power, but was simply working upon past experience, and I am satisfied my scheme will be the best way of ensuring success for the

Company. The more the line prospers, the more credit
will involve upon yourself, as our line is something like a
beehive of industry, all population and trade, and is still
growing, which requires the best system of organisation."
He again replied he would not agree to the basis of my
suggestions, and would not say what he intended doing
at present. I then said, "If the line is to be worked
upon the principle which seems to me to be intended, the
dividend will dwindle down to 4 per cent, and then there
will be trouble for someone, and I shall be sorry to see a
10 per cent line so reduced for the want of management.
Notwithstanding all this, I shall always take my share of
credit as being one who has worked up the traffic to
enable the Company to pay to the shareholders a $9\frac{1}{4}$ per
cent dividend, and laid the foundation for increasing
traffic, and paying a much higher dividend" I then left
his office, saying, " I will go back to Wakefield and make
the best of it."

I was often waited upon by the public with regard to
excursion trains for workpeople, schools, and institutions,
but being debarred from making any arrangements whatever with the public, I simply noted down the particulars
and forwarded them to the central management at Manchester. After waiting a few days, and receiving no
reply, the parties got impatient and made their arrangements with other companies, thus taking away the
traffic. I had also many complaints from the public
who had written direct to Manchester, and, getting
no reply, had to make arrangements with other companies. This change from divisional management seemed
to me certain to lead to decreased dividends.

The next interview I had with the general manager
was on Monday, December 11th, 1882, when an officers'
meeting was called, to be held at Manchester, to argue
the question of reducing working expenses by reducing

the staffs at the various stations. This reminded me of our last interview at his office in 1871, when I made the remark that the new policy of management would work the line to 4 per cent, and there would be trouble for someone. Since that time I have observed a great deal of experimenting, but no feasible scheme ever adopted for the true interests of the Company.

The foundation laid by the divisional management for increasing receipts and working traffic with economy began to give way in 1872, and the dividends gradually dwindled down as low as 3 per cent, paid to the shareholders in 1889, although the population and trade had grown throughout the whole line.

As I anticipated in 1870, war was declared between France and Germany, and goods traffic became so heavy throughout the line as to render it impossible to work it with any degree of punctuality. I received a letter from the office of central management on the 12th of November, 1871, complaining of the irregular running of passenger trains, requesting an early reply for the directors, with an explanation as to the cause, and suggestions for a remedy. I replied on the 15th, to say the only remedy would be to carry out the recommendations I submitted to the directors in 1870, which were to give more goods siding accommodation at the various stations, and to construct loop lines, so as to avoid having to shunt slow goods trains from one main line to the other, for other trains to pass. I then gave an instance which came under my observation the other day: A goods train arrived at Luddendenfoot Station; the 5-25 p m. express from Manchester to Normanton and the 5-15 p.m express (passenger trains) from Normanton to Manchester were both overdue to pass, and for the want of siding accommodation the goods train, standing on the down main line, had to be kept there until it was seen which

passenger train arrived first. During this time four more
goods trains arrived on the down line. The down express
arrived behind them, and had to wait until the up express
had passed and the five goods trains had been shunted
from the down to the up main line, Whilst these goods
trains were standing on the up main line, two other
passenger trains arrived from Sowerby Bridge, and were
delayed until the five goods trains were shunted back
again from the up to the down main line. Notwithstanding my explanations, very few of my suggestions
were carried out.

Up to January, 1872, the telegraph system had been
greatly developed and utilised with much advantage in
dealing with the heavy traffic passing over the line. Still
unavoidable and serious delays occurred, which gave
dissatisfaction to the public generally. This is demonstrated by the following newspaper cutting from the
Bradford Observer, January 1st, 1872 ;—

THE NON-PUNCTUALITY OF LANCASHIRE AND YORKSHIRE TRAINS

Anticipating that many changes and improvements would take place
in the railway communication and arrangements for this district on the
commencement of a new year, consequent on the pre-amalgamation
arrangement between the Lancashire and Yorkshire and London and
North-Western Railway Companies, we have not thought it necessary
recently to call attention to many great disadvantages which not only
the people of this district, but all those who have occasion to travel or
send goods by the Lancashire and Yorkshire Railway, labour under. We
do not mention this because we thought that by the new arrangements
many of these disadvantages might be removed. It seems, however,
that on this line matters are to remain as they were. The January
notices are out, and with one or two slight alterations the time bills
and arrangements that have been in force during December remain the
same for the first month of the new year, and travellers and others using
the railway may expect again to endure all the ills they have hitherto
suffered. In fact, for any notification to the contrary from the directors
and managers, the whole of the working of the line might be going on

as merrily as a marriage bell ; but those whose misfortune it is to travel on it could tell quite a different tale   The service of passenger trains provided would be a good one, were there the slightest reliance to be placed on their arriving and departing anywhere near the times at which they are announced by the official tables   Train after train, and this day after day, however, are ten, twenty, thirty, and sometimes even sixty minutes behind time, and travellers, whose time is valuable, have it dwindled away by hours in railway carriages   Occasionally a train may start from a terminal station at or about the proper time, but before it has proceeded more than a mile, it has to be pulled up until a goods train, or sometimes two or three, have been shunted out of its way on the other line, and this occurs every few miles, even to express trains. Of course, the goods trains so shunted become a block to trains running on the other line ; and sometimes these goods trains, made up in many instances of trucks containing goods whose delivery is urgent, are kept for hours, see-sawing, as it were, from one line to the other.   Intelligent readers will no doubt ask why a large company, having the immense traffic of the Lancashire and Yorkshire, do not take steps to remedy this evil, by constructing sidings at most of the principal stations, into which goods trains could be turned, and remain without blocking the lines in either one direction or the other.   This is one means by which a great relief would be afforded to the main line, but another evil has come into existence, having arisen out of what was expected to be a good. Eight or nine months ago the management of the line became centralised in Manchester   Previously the line had been managed by three superintendents, living in the district over which they had control, and who had each full power to remedy every defect occurring in their district, and to punish any infractions of the Company's bye-laws committed by the servants   Under this old system the people of any district could at once appeal to the superintendent, and, where necessary, evils were at once remedied   Now, however, all matters of this kind are referred to the central office, in Manchester, and, as everyone knows who has to deal with a large and busy department, long delays will occur, and sometimes the matter written about is altogether forgotten amidst a multitude of other matters   That the centralising system, which has now had eight months trial, has failed, everyone that travels the line has reason enough to know.   Under it, men who had worked the passenger traffic of their various districts with great advantage to the Company and credit to themselves, for nearly twenty years, and from time to time, when the dividend of the line was but 2 per cent, have been displaced, or deprived of all power to be useful, and the result is that the line is blocked with an enormous amount of goods traffic, which seems to be worked without much system ; and through these goods

trains passenger trains have to wend their way as best they can. The
published time tables have become a farce, and the best notice that could
be put up at the stations would be, "Passenger trains will be run as
circumstances and the goods trains permit." Even were this the case,
intending passengers would be in no greater uncertainty as to the time
of arrival and departure of trains than they are at present As a remedy
for many of these evils we would recommend the directors to return to
the old system of local management, which acted so well both for the
Company and the public until last May The centralisation system
(which has resulted in this case in such disorganisation) cannot be
adopted with advantage on a line which, like the Lancashire and Yorkshire, runs through such a large hive of industry, and has such a
network of railways. With such a number of branch lines, and so many
connections, it must necessarily require local management, and that the
person so appointed should be invested with full power to remedy evils
as they daily occur. This is the only way in which the full resources of
the Company can be developed in these populous and peculiar districts,
where such a great spirit of competition exists, and it is also the only
way to accomplish that which is so necessary to both the Company and
the public—the punctuality of passenger trains —*Guardian.*

An assistant passenger superintendent was appointed
under Mr. Blackmore, Manchester, in August, 1872, a man
who had had no experience whatever in the passenger
traffic department. It was considered by many at the
time to be a most injudicious appointment for such a
congested line as ours, and was something like putting a
round man into a square hole—he didn't fit it

In November, 1872, the London and North-Western
and Lancashire and Yorkshire Railway Companies gave
notice that an application would be made to Parliament
in the session of 1873, for the purpose of obtaining an
Act for the amalgamation of the two companies This
notice caused much public excitement, and chambers of
commerce and corporate bodies petitioned against it.
The Select Parliamentary Committee deprecated the
principle, and the bill was withdrawn; only, however, to
be introduced in the following session, 1874, when it met
with an absolute veto. The Lancashire and Yorkshire

No. 663 Engine.

Railway stock, 1872, was quoted at £163, and the dividend was $8\frac{1}{2}$ per cent. If the amalgamation had taken effect, the shareholders of this Company would have received $\frac{5}{8}$ per cent per annum more than the London and North-Western stock holders, owing to an agreement entered into by the two companies in 1862, for a division of traffic at competitive districts, which was to remain in force up to 1876, during this time allowed the North-Western to have the pick of the long through traffic.

The directors, having received so many complaints from the public of delays to their traffic, again instructed their officers to report as to the causes, and to submit schemes for remedies. I again, in 1872, devised schemes more extensive than those submitted to the board in the latter part of 1870, which were for extended siding accommodation, with loop lines at every station, so as to ensure sufficient accommodation, which would prevent hazardous shunting of goods trains from one main line to another. I was summoned to attend the Board of Directors' meeting, and went prepared with pen-and-ink sketches showing the extensions, and with statistics explaining the necessity of my recommendations. In the course of a discussion on the suggestions by the directors and the general manager, one of the directors again said, "We might as well double the line at once" I replied, "There is sufficient traffic to warrant doubling the line," and then explained to them why I had suggested such extensive alterations, and handed my pen-and-ink sketches, along with statistics, saying, "You will find the delays occur for want of the accommodation I ask for, and it is my opinion that we lose more locomotive power in such delays as those described than would work the whole of the goods traffic." The general manager interrupted me, and said he doubted my statement. I replied, "There is no difficulty in your obtaining a weekly return from all

10

stations of such delays, and you will then find that my statement has not been exaggerated" However, the question was again deferred for further consideration, and complaints, delays, and working expenses increased.

From what occurred afterwards it was very evident to me that the centralised management was anxious to show the directors that it was not necessary for them to incur great expense to carry out my suggestions and schemes. They thought they had hit upon a plan (which no doubt emanated from the newly-appointed assistant superintendent), without incurring any additional expense, that would ensure greater punctuality in the passenger traffic When this plan was completed I was requested by the superintendent to go to Manchester to look over it, and to give my opinion so far as Yorkshire was concerned On arriving at the superintendent's office I was shown a revised time table, and on looking over that portion which related to the Yorkshire Division, I was astonished and grieved to find that they had undone what it had taken me twelve years trying to accomplish, viz., to convey the merchants, manufacturers, and the public to and from the various markets in as short a time as possible The superintendent's new scheme was this A train from Bradford to Manchester was shown in the time table to run the journey in seventy-five minutes, but, owing to being delayed by goods trains on the road, as a rule arrived at Manchester fifteen or twenty minutes late. He had given this train twenty minutes more time to run the journey. All other trains were dealt with in a similar way, giving them more time to run the journey. He explained to me the reason why he had given them more time. He said it was based on the actual time taken from the guards' road notes. The assistant superintendent of the line remarked that that was the proper way to time trains. Knowing that he had had no experience, I told him I feared he would find he knew nothing whatever about timing the running of passenger trains, and I said that, in my opinion, to give the trains more time was a most impracticable remedy for the purpose intended, and I should be very sorry to see such a plan or scheme adopted, as it would not remove the obstruction, and so long as that remained the delays would occur, however they revised the time table

The superintendent said they would give the new plan a trial, as it was no use deceiving the public by issuing a time table which was never worked to The new time table was issued by the centralised management in the latter part of 1872, and being their first attempt at the better working of the line, the public were expecting to see great improvements and increased facilities, far superseding those given by the divisional management; in fact, all were looking forward to great results. After this time table had been in existence a week I went to Manchester to see the return of the week's working compared with the week of the previous month, when it was shown that the passenger trains had kept worse time than they did before. The superintendent said he thought it had not had a fair trial, and another week was tried. When the result was compared with the previous month it was shown that the second week resulted in more delay than the first. It was then found that upsetting the old time table had not removed the obstruction, but, nevertheless, the new plan had to produce a clear sheet showing no delays, to be placed before the directors. With a view to obtain this the central management issued instructions to station masters at all junctions that no main line train was to be kept waiting for its connection if the branch train was running five minutes late, or a branch train to wait for its connection if the main line train was running ten minutes late. These instructions, together with the extended time given for the trains to run the journey, created great confusion, and completely upset the public arrangements in getting to and from their places of business and the different markets. This state of things continued for several weeks, when the instructions given to the station masters were somewhat modified, but not before the traffic, both passenger and goods, had to some extent been diverted on to other companies' railways This led to reduced traffic, with increased working expenses and unpopularity, and tended to the advantage of other companies competitive in the Yorkshire district After this mischief had been done a movement was made to construct loop lines and refuge sidings at some of the principal stations, and also to the purchasing of a number of more powerful locomotive engines. This proved more to the advantage of the Company than the new plan of the revised time table

During the excursion season of 1873 the centralised management hit upon another plan with the view, as they thought, to do less work and make more money by advertising increased rates for excursion traffic. They certainly reduced the number of heavily-loaded excursion trains, but they did not succeed in making more money, which was shown by a reduced dividend as compared with the latter half of the previous year. This plan destroyed a good paying traffic from the Yorkshire stations to the West Coast, Belle Vue, Littleborough, and other places, which it had taken years to cultivate. The public found other companies gave better facilities and advantages to Morcambe Bay by the Midland, by the Great Northern to Skegness, and other places on their system, and the North-Eastern to places on the East Coast The traffic thus diverted into other channels has not found its way back to the Lancashire and Yorkshire Company. The action of the Lancashire and

Yorkshire also created a very keen feeling on the part of the inhabitants of Blackpool against the Company, and public meetings were held and resolutions passed condemnatory of the action of the Company, and the aggrieved parties invited other companies to construct and run railways into their town. In addition to this the Company discontinued running weekly excursions from Yorkshire stations to Scarborough, which would average five or six hundred passengers a week, and thus causing the North-Eastern Company to transfer much through traffic from their system to other companies

In 1873 it was decided to establish the principle of absolute block working by telegraph throughout the line. The system was that two trains should not be allowed to be in one section at the same time This necessitated re-signalling with semaphore signals at all stations and junctions. It was also decided to adopt the interlocking principle with points and signals, all to be concentrated into the signalman's cabin, connected there with levers arranged in a frame, and worked by the signalman. This new construction was carried out at an enormous cost to the Company, which arose mainly through not having well-matured plans for the work required before commencing it. I often observed that some of the stations and junctions had to be re-constructed two, and some three, times before they were made workable. To facilitate working the line on the block system, it was found to be necessary that telegraph speaking instruments should be fixed in every signal cabin, so as to enable the signalmen to communicate to each other as to the running of particular trains, and this was done After the instruments had been fixed in the cabins, a rather awkward difficulty arose, as some of the men had not the ability to comprehend the art of working the telegraph speaking instruments, which caused an additional expense by having to place boys in the cabins to work the speaking instruments. However, in 1882, this difficulty was overcome, it being superseded by the telephone. My attention was first drawn to this invention by reading a paragraph in one of the newspapers that a sermon had been preached in the Square Congregational Chapel, Halifax, by the Rev. Dr. Mellor, and that it was recorded in Manchester through the telephone as preached. This struck me at once with the idea that it was just what we wanted in the signalmen's cabins; that there would then be no difficulty in any signalman communicating to another, that this would greatly expedite the work, dispense with the telegraph speaking instruments, and with the boys On making inquiry as to the particulars of the telephone invention, I found that our telegraph superintendent was connected with the inventor. I at once arranged for an interview with him, and asked his opinion as to its suitableness for adoption in signalmen's cabins in place of the telegraph instruments. He said, " I quite agree with you that the telephone is preferable to the telegraph instruments for your work, and if you will get me an order I will have them put in." I then made application for the telephone in place of the telegraph for the signal cabins I urged the question, and explained how it could be readily utilised to advantage on our congested line, and would dispense with the boys who attended to the telegraph instruments in the cabins, and at last, after hard pressure upon the central management, they agreed to give the system a trial. It was found to answer far beyond our expectations, and resulted in the telephone being fixed in every cabin in the Yorkshire district. Barring loop lines and refuge sidings, it was the best scheme ever adopted for reducing delays to trains. I am pleased to record that the Yorkshire Division was the first to test the telephone's efficiency for working railways, and that it gave such satisfaction as to become generally adopted.

Just to show how the public impose upon railway companies in making claims for accidents, I here give an instance.

I remember an incident which occurred in September, 1867, in connection with a one-day excursion from Yorkshire stations to Scarborough. The weather being fine, a large number of people availed themselves of the opportunity of having a day's outing. On the arrival of trains at Wakefield from various parts of the line, they were then made up into one train, which consisted of thirty carriages. All were well filled with passengers, and the train departed from that station about 7-30 a m. It so happened that I travelled with the train. We arrived at and left York about 8-50 a.m., all right. I was seated in the jack-in-the-box, which is an elevation situated in one corner of the guard's van, next to the engine Soon after passing Flaxton Station, on the North-Eastern Railway, I saw several head of cattle on the line. They seemed to be coming towards the engine. I called out and signalled to the driver to pull up the train. He did so, and the cattle, some five or six in number, turned off the line and down a slight slope to the hedgerow, and passed along clear of the train. When the driver gave the engine steam to start away again, the train broke loose about the centre. I, observing this, signalled to the driver, calling his attention, when he stopped the front portion of the train; the latter portion was already at a standstill some two hundred yards back. The first portion was set back and coupled up, and the train then started away to Scarborough, and stopped at Malton Station to collect tickets. Afterwards the station master gave the signal to the driver and guards to go ahead. Just when the train got into motion I saw a passenger hurrying out of the refreshment room with half a dozen bottles of beer in his arms. one of the porters opened the guard's van door and helped him into the van. The train arrived at Scarborough at 10-30 a.m, all right.

Three weeks after this date the secretary of the Lancashire and Yorkshire Railway Company received a lawyer's letter, calling attention to a passenger who was alleged to have received some serious injuries whilst travelling in an excursion train from Wakefield to Scarborough, the accident occurring on some portion of the line between York and Malton. This letter was handed over to me for inquiry and to report as to the particulars, and from inquiry I ascertained that the alleged injured passenger was staying at the Grand Hotel, Scarborough. I went over to Scarborough, and found the gentleman was a solicitor from Wakefield. I gathered from the manager and one of the waiters at the hotel that he arrived there about noon on the 30th September, 1867, had his dinner and went out, and returned again between 10 and 11 at night with a friend, and they had supper together—mutton chops, and other good things followed— and at about midnight he was taken suddenly ill. A doctor was sent for, and the gentleman had been confined to his bed ever since. I also found it was the same gentleman whom I saw hurrying out of the refreshment room at Malton Station with the bottles of beer. On my return to Wakefield I made further inquiries there, and found that he was a married man, and subject to epileptic fits. After the information I had gathered, and particularly as I travelled with the very excursion train, and was a witness to the carriages breaking loose—which was such an accident that could not possibly injure any-one travelling by the train—I was of opinion that he was attacked by one of the fits which it was said he was subject to, no doubt brought on by his excellent supper, and the jollification and excitement with his friend. I reported the facts accordingly, and recommended the Company not to entertain the claim.

Soon after this a claim was made for £1,000 damages I was then instructed to get up evidence to defend the Company in court, when I again went over to Scarborough, and the friend who had accompanied the claimant to the hotel between 10 and 11 was traced. This person was subpœnaed to give evidence on behalf of the Company. I also traced that the claimant was at a school feast at Sharleston a fortnight before the excursion was run from Wakefield to Scarborough. At this festival he was taken with one of his accustomed fits, and was laid up at his aunt's for some days. This aunt was therefore subpœnaed on behalf of the Company. I also traced the carriage he was travelling in at the time the train broke loose. It was one from Denby Dale; and I further traced some of the passengers who were travelling in the same carriage with him at the time of the alleged accident, and on questioning many of them they declared that no one received any injury in that carriage. In fact, the mishap was so slight that several of them were not aware even of the break-loose. Four of these were subpœnaed to give evidence on behalf of the Company; two of them were a man and his wife, both over 80 years of age. When the trial came on at York, and the plaintiff had stated his case to the judge, with an elaborate appeal by counsel and before any evidence was taken for the Company's defence, the judge was of opinion that negligence had not been proved, and dismissed the case, with costs against the plaintiff

I will just give another case which occurred about this time out of many that I had to contend with up to 1871.

A short time after the above case, the secretary of the

Company received a letter from a solicitor at Huddersfield, making a claim for £500 on behalf of a passenger who was said to have received some severe injuries from an accident to the train he was travelling in whilst at Brighouse Station, when on his journey from Blackpool to Huddersfield, which incapacitated him from attending to his ordinary duties as bellman and fish hawker. He had been laid up for some time, and was likely to be so, and was perhaps injured for life. This letter was handed over to me to make inquiry and to report the particulars.

I went over to Huddersfield and traced that the passenger had booked by the Lancashire and Yorkshire Railway Company from Huddersfield to Blackpool, taking a five days' excursion ticket. On his return he travelled in a through carriage from Blackpool to Huddersfield. This carriage was detached from the main line train at Brighouse, and afterwards attached to a branch train for Huddersfield. As the porters were pushing the carriage on the line up to the train, it came rather sharply against the carriage when coupling up, but so slightly that it was impossible to have injured any of the passengers in the carriages. This was the only complaint from any source. Being under the impression that there was an attempt at extortion, and the solicitor saying that the man was unable to follow his ordinary duties, I called upon a friend of mine who kept a corn factor's shop in Huddersfield, who I thought could give me some information upon the subject. I told him my case, and he replied, "Oh, it will be Billy the bellman and fish hawker. I know very little about him, and had not heard that he had had an accident, but I can take you to a place where they will know all about him." This was a barber's shop, where he received his orders for his bell business. I then said it would be just the place to go to to gather the gossip of the town, but if we went together the barber might be suspicious and withhold information which I wanted; and suggested, with a view of helping me to get particulars as to how long the bellman had been unable to follow his ordinary duties, that he should go and get shaved, and after I thought he had been in the shop sufficiently long to get seated and well prepared for the process, I should rush in and ask if the bellman was about, as I wanted him to cry in the town that I had lost a grey rough terrier dog, a very valuable one, and that anyone finding the same and bringing it to the barber's shop, should receive ten shillings reward. My friend agreed, and away we went together. I saw him into the barber's shop, waited outside until I thought he had got well prepared for business, then I went in hastily, and asked for the barber. He said, "I am here; what do you want?" I said, "I want the bellman" He replied, "He is somewhere about; he was here not five minutes since." I saw my friend sitting in the chair: he was well lathered and covered with a white sheet. He pulled the corner of the sheet sideways, and said, "Is that you, Mr Normington?" I said, "Yes; I have not been in the town long, and have lost that grand terrier dog, and I want the bellman to cry the town to see if it can be found before I return to Wakefield." The barber said, "He can be found; I will send for him and have him here directly;" and shortly after in came Billy the bellman. After telling him what I wanted, and giving him a slip of paper with a written description of the dog, and with instructions to get round the town as quickly as possible, promising if he found the dog before I left the town I would give him a shilling extra for his trouble, up went his bell under his arm. He stopped a minute or two to read over the paper to get it well off before starting, and off he went My friend then said, "Oh, Mr. Normington, if you will wait a minute or two, I will go with you." I stopped in the shop looking at the numerous bills, notices of sales, which were hanging on the walls. Of course, I was too busy reading to take any notice of my friend or the barber, but I heard my friend ask the barber if Billy hadn't been in a railway collision. The barber replied, "It is said so, but it is all bosh;" and named two well-known gentlemen in Huddersfield—one was a doctor and the other a lawyer—who had asked him (the barber) to go partners with them in the claim against the Company, the conditions being "No cure, no pay." He declined to do so, saying, "I will have nothing to do with the case, it being a clear case of imposition, as the man can do his work at bell-crying as he always has done, and I can see nothing the matter with him." My friend got squared up, and we left the shop, went to several street corners in the town, and saw and heard that the bellman did his work well: he had a voice that could be heard all over. Being satisfied with this, I said to my friend, "Do you think he hawks fish for Mr. B., the general dealer?" He replied, "It is very likely he will, I know him very well." I replied, "So do I," and we decided to just give him a call and get a few oysters. So away we went, and found Mr. B. in his shop. We went into a little snug in the corner, where we had our oysters. Mr B. joined us, and we got into conversation on the topics of the day, when, of course, Billy the bell-man's case came on for observation. Mr. B. said, "I do not think he ails much, as he comes to my place for fish three nights a week for hawking in the outskirts of the town." I said, "I understand he has not been hawking lately;" when he replied, "I have not missed him, but will look in his book where the transactions are entered." He then went to overhaul his book, which gave me an opportunity of looking it through, and I found the entries all regular and correct for three months back up to that

date. There was one week of no entries, which corre-
sponded with the time he was away at Blackpool. After
this, of course, we had another oyster, and left the shop.
I shook hands with my friend, and thanked him for the
way in which he had helped me, and returned to Wakefield without my imaginary dog, made my report, giving
particulars of my inquiry, with a recommendation that
the Company should entertain no claim whatever

Nevertheless, the lawyer and the doctor pressed their
case, took it to court, and it was tried at the Liverpool
Assizes. Notwithstanding all the above particulars
brought forth in the Company's defence, it was most
surprising that the jury should have given a verdict for
the plaintiff, although it was only for a few pounds as
damages

I often heard it said in Huddersfield afterwards, that
Billy the bellman only got about £5 out of the plunder.

In March, 1874, I attended the annual dinner, by
invitation from the secretary, of the Wakefield Trades-
men's Association. My name was coupled with a toast
in connection with the railway; and I may here give a
summary of my remarks in responding, taken from the
Wakefield Herald.—

Mr Normington duly responded, and, in allusion to the remarks that
had been made on the subject of railways, he said his 27 years' experience
had taught him that the more facilities they gave the public and the
better dividends the shareholders got. He thought, so far as Wakefield
was concerned, they had not very much to find fault with, so far as
passenger trains were concerned. They had over 200 trains at Kirkgate
and over 100 at Westgate Stations, while Halifax had not more than 100
trains per day It was quite correct that the largest revenue was
obtained from third-class passengers. Second-class passengers were
conveyed at a loss, and he would recommend that there be no second-
class carriages.

Shortly after this announcement I received a censure
from the Board of Directors for the remarks I had made, as

recorded in the above extract. This verifies the instructions I received on May 1st, 1871, that the public was not to know there were such officers as district superintendents employed on the railway.

On Friday, January 1st 1875, the Stainland Branch, between North Dean and Stainland, was opened for general traffic, when the inhabitants of the villages of West Vale and Stainland (the only two stations on the branch) made the day a holiday, and the contractors gave a dinner to their friends at the Station Hotel, Stainland

I remember being at Sowerby Bridge Station one day in February, 1875, when the 8-50 a.m. train from Wakefield to Manchester arrived. I was called to a carriage by one of the directors. I went up to the carriage, and saw there were four directors in the compartment I was asked to join them as far as Todmorden, when one of them said, " Normington, I wouldn't advise you to come in here, unless you want a good blowing up." I replied, " That does good sometimes," and got into the compartment, and went with them to Todmorden. The conversation was upon the unsatisfactory working of the railway, and one of the directors wanted to know when the gradually decreasing receipts were going to stop. I got up from my seat, and placing my hands on my back, said, " The decreasing receipts and the unsatisfactory working you complain about commenced soon after the time when you tied the hands and shut the mouths of the district officers, and will continue until you release them." The conversation continued upon matters connected with the railway during the journey to Todmorden The directors said some alterations would have to be made to bring about a better state of things, and I replied that the sooner they did as I had suggested the better it would be for the shareholders.

In March, 1875, it became well known that the superintendent of the line was about to retire from the service of the Company. I thought this an opportune time for the directors to revert to something like divisional management, and on the 23rd inst I wrote to one of the directors the following letter :—

Dear Sir,—Referring to our conversation the other week, whilst travelling together from Sowerby Bridge to Todmorden, I herewith furnish you with a few remarks, with the view to determine something better for the district officers. I am sure you will agree that they ought not to be placed in such a helpless position I hope I may yet realise the position in Yorkshire that I was always led to expect—to have the district with sufficient power to work it, having all the gentry and manufacturers in my favour. At the time when the Board of Directors resolved to give centralised management a trial, I understood that the arrangement was to be so guided that the present district officers would not be superseded or prejudiced. However, this decision has not been adhered to You are well aware that some three years ago an officer from the goods department, a perfect stranger to the passenger department, was placed in the position of assistant superintendent of the line, over the heads of district officers, who had so long and well served the Company, and through their energy and exertions had developed the traffic in their respective districts, which enabled the directors to declare a dividend of over 9 per cent. I think the time has now arrived to put right the great injustice done to the district officers in 1871 Centralised management may be right on a line where traffic is light, but on such a line as ours, which is a beehive of industry and population from one end to the other, local management is required to give necessary satisfaction to the public and to ensure the interests of the Company Centralised management has had its trial, and proved to be an entire failure, both to the Company and to the public I therefore trust that in the event of any revised arrangement being made, in reference to the retirement of the superintendent of the line, the district officers will be favourably considered —Yours, truly,

THOMAS NORMINGTON.

To one of the Directors of the Lancashire and Yorkshire Railway.

It baffled all comprehension that after divisional management had done so well for the Company, in working up the traffic, which resulted in the directors paying a dividend of 8 to 9 per cent, and had laid the foundation for a continuous increase, which would have led to a 10 per cent dividend, that they (the directors) should have adopted the system of centralised management, which destroyed all perseverance, energy, and enterprise.

In June, 1875, the superintendent of the line resigned, and when his assistant applied for the position, backed up by the general manager, one of the directors told me that the majority of them were against the appointment, and in favour of advertising for an official. However, to meet the case, the directors made the general manager the chief traffic manager, which led to the appointment of the general manager's choice Shortly after this appointment a friend of mine told me of a little incident which occurred whilst congratulating the new superintendent on the platform of Victoria Station, Manchester. While they were in conversation one of the directors walked past them some eight or ten yards, and then stopped to read a paper which he had in his hand. The new superintendent then left my friend, and walked along the platform, passing the director a few yards, and then doubled and came back to where the director was standing. Taking his hat off and bowing most graciously he thanked him for his recent appointment as superintendent of the line The director held up his head, looked at him with abhorrence, and said sharply, " You have nothing to thank me for ; I have done nothing for you,' and walked away. This little incident, coupled with what one of the directors had told me prior to the appointment, convinced me of the injustice practised by centralised management

The tactics applied by the general manager in this new appointment brought back very forcibly to my mind the time in 1871, when the Board of Directors had discussed my suggestions in my unavoidable absence, and requested me to see the general manager; which I did, and we disagreed as to the new policy of management. It was clear from that time I was kicked out of the line of promotion, and kept out. Nevertheless, this changed policy of management brought down the dividend from 9 to 4 per cent, as I predicted.

The public were disappointed that I should again have been overlooked in the changes made, and determined to compensate me to some extent for the great injustice the Company had dealt out to me by presenting me with a substantial testimonial, in recognition of the services I had rendered to the travelling public, and also to show the directors that I had their sympathy and appreciation. The following is a copy of the proceedings on the day of presentation, and I may add that I received many letters of congratulation from friends, who expressed their disappointment at not being called upon to subscribe to the testimonial.

LIST OF SUBSCRIBERS

TO A

TESTIMONIAL

CONSISTING OF A

CASKET OF GOLD,

AMOUNTING TO £610,

TOGETHER WITH A

GOLD WATCH AND APPENDAGES,

PRESENTED TO

MR. THOS. NORMINGTON,

District Superintendent of the Lancashire and Yorkshire Railway,
Yorkshire Division,

IN RECOGNITION OF HIS UNIFORM COURTESY, KINDNESS,
UNTIRING ZEAL AND ENERGY IN THE INTERESTS OF THE
TRAVELLING PUBLIC, FOR NEARLY THIRTY YEARS

T. K. SANDERSON, M P., Chairman

PUBLIC RECOGNITION

OF THE SERVICES OF A

RAILWAY SUPERINTENDENT.

On Saturday afternoon, a large and representative gathering of gentlemen, well known throughout Lancashire and Yorkshire, took place at the Bull Hotel, Wakefield, when a really substantial recognition of services rendered in the interests of the travelling public, for now nearly thirty years, on the part of Mr Thos. Normington, superintendent of the Yorkshire division of the Lancashire and Yorkshire Railway, was made. The recognition consisted of a beautiful Algerian marble casket, surmounted with gold, and containing six hundred and ten sovereigns, together with a valuable gold watch and appendages, the whole being accompanied with a suitable illuminated address on vellum, in an elegant case. This unusually handsome gift was in no way connected with the railway service to which Mr Normington is attached, but was subscribed for entirely by gentlemen who use the line over which Mr. Normington is a superintendent. We believe no official of the Lancashire and Yorkshire service was canvassed to become a subscriber, and no railway official but Mr. Normington was invited to be present.

The presentation ceremony was preceded by a sumptuous repast, after which Mr. T. K. Sanderson, M P for Wakefield (chairman of the Testimonial Committee), and the vice-chairmen Mr. T. Wilton Haigh, Many Gates House, Wakefield, and Mr. John Kelly, Heckmondwike, presided. Amongst the other gentlemen present were Mr. T. Normington (the guest of the evening, who sat on the right of the chairman), Aldermen W. H B Tomlinson J P., and Joseph Wade, Wakefield; Councillors Sam Armitage, Dewsbury, and J Howden, W. H. Milnes, and Simpson, Wakefield, Messrs James Atkinson, Cleckheaton, T. Beaumont, Dewsbury, Jno Crossley, Halifax, Ralph Crawshaw and E Dent, Heckmondwike, T Davies, Dewsbury Moor, Holmes Emmott,

Elland; J. B. Eccles, Huddersfield, H. J. Fearnley, G. B. Fearnley, Dewsbury; Josh. Garside, Liversedge; G. Greoves, Huddersfield; T. Wilton Haigh, Wakefield, David Hanson, Stainland, George Heaton, Joe Heaton, Heckmondwike; John Hoyle, Mytholmroyd, Henry Johnson, Manchester; John Johnson, York, Chas. E Johnson, Huddersfield; Richard Kershaw, Clifton, Ralph Kelly, John Kelly, Joe W. Kitson, and Samuel Loxdale, Wakefield; James R Moffatt, Mirfield; Joseph D. Nowell, Savile Park, Halifax, T. R. Normington and Wm. Pettinger, Wakefield, F. Pratt, Heckmondwike, Joseph F. Simpson and John Simpson, Wakefield, John Shaw and John Edward Shaw, Sowerby Bridge, G A. Shaw, Elland, Henry Smith, St. John's, Wakefield; Henry Smith, Agbrigg, Thos. Smith and J. T. Smith, Wakefield, Hy. Skelton, Mytholmroyd, Stevens and Sons, London; Matthew Thackrah, Mirfield, Capt Taylor, Coroner, Wakefield; Robert Todd, Bradford; Joseph Whitehead and William Wilcock, Hebden Bridge; Alfred Wiman, Dewsbury, &c., &c.

Letters of apology for non-attendance were read from Sir Geo. Armytage, Sir Hy. Edwards, Mr J. Beswick Greenwood (chairman of Quarter Sessions), Mr. Stanhope, M P., Mr. Ripley, M P., Mr. L. R. Starkey, M.P.; Major Waterhouse, M P ; and Mr. Bentley Shaw, J.P.

Mr. T. K. Sanderson, M.P, in presenting the very handsome testimonial, said it was very gratifying that they had met, not in few numbers, but in a body fairly representing the great bulk of Yorkshire (a voice: Lancashire as well") commercial centres. He was almost surprised to see so many assemble together to do his friend honour. He had known Mr. Normington for many years. He first came to Wakefield when a friend of his (Mr Sanderson's), Admiral Binstead, was superintendent, and he knew that he was of immense service to the admiral, who was a good and active worker for the company, and whose loss was very much regretted They would not have met together that day to make such a presentation to a public servant, unless it was felt that he had worthily done his duty, and everyone in that room and amongst the outside public were of that opinion, and that Mr Normington possessed the confidence of his friends, of his directors, and of the public. (Hear, hear) From his knowledge of Mr. Normington, extending over a great number of years, he knew him to be an honourable, straightforward, and upright man. As a Churchman, he had always been an earnest and active worker in its interest, and he did not suppose that those in the room belonging to the Masonic order would be sorry to find that he was a brother (Applause) Having presented the casket and a beautifully-illuminated address, amidst the heartiest applause and demonstrations of good feeling, Mr Sanderson presented the watch and appendages, remarking that the only thing he could say against the Lancashire and Yorkshire Company was, that he hoped the presentation of the watch would be the means of causing them to keep better time in future (Laughter) Mr Sanderson read the illuminated address, which was as follows (the watch also bearing a similar inscription) —

List of subscribers to a testimonial, consisting of a casket of gold, amounting to £610, together with a gold watch and appendages, presented to Mr Thomas Normington, District Superintendent of the Lancashire and Yorkshire Railway Company (Yorkshire division) in recognition of his uniform courtesy, kindness, untiring zeal and energy in the interests of the travelling public for nearly thirty years Signed, T K Sanderson, M P, chairman Wakefield, January 29th, 1876

Mr Normington, who was received with cheers then replied. He said I am really so overwhelmed with gratitude for the kind feeling manifested towards me by the gentlemen and public of the Yorkshire district through which the Lancashire and Yorkshire railway runs, that I cannot possibly find words that would in any way be adequate to give expression to my feelings on this occasion The emotion caused by your generosity is too much for me, I therefore hope you will forgive me, and accept the will for the deed (Cheers) Since entering this room, and seeing so many kind friends before me, I have frequently asked myself, "What have I done to merit such generosity?" I have simply endeavoured to do my duty both to the public and the company, in the sphere in which it has pleased Providence to place me, and if this is a public acknowledgment that the little attention I have at times given to their requests, has so far been satisfactory, I only wish I had had sufficient power, which would have ensured their wants being more favourably dealt with (Cheers) This being so, I accept this magnificent testimonial with many thanks I wish to express my sincere thanks to you, Mr. Chairman, and to the two hon secretaries,— (applause)—who have done so much; and thanks to all my kind friends who are here present to assist in the presentation, also to the many kind friends who are prevented from being present The gifts you have presented to me are of far greater magnitude than anything I could possibly have conceived, and I believe no such presentation emanating from so many subscribers has ever been made to an officer on any railway. (Hear, hear) I assure you that it will always be a pleasure to me to attend to your requests at any time when brought under my notice. (Cheers.) Mr Normington then proceeded to give an account of his connection with the railway service, from the time he commenced, in 1847, at Brighouse Station, to the present He entered the service of the Lancashire and Yorkshire Company in 1847, at Brighouse Station, and in October of that year was removed to Oldham, where, as station master, he opened the Mumps Station on the 1st November the same year. In

1849 he was drafted to Mirfield, and there acted as guard up to 1854, when he became station master at Sowerby Bridge. Whilst he was a guard he had charge of the first passenger train to Bradford, on May 9th, 1850, and also had charge of the first passenger train to Holmfirth on 1st July, 1850. He remained at Sowerby Bridge up to April, 1856, when he came to Wakefield, and on the 1st May that year was appointed Assistant Superintendent under Captain (since Admiral) Binstead, whom he succeeded on his retirement. He concluded—On first entering the service of the Railway Company, I decided that my policy should be that of progression and conciliation—(hear, hear)—and one that should do good to all about me. That policy I have endeavoured to carry out, and the result is seen to-day when it is acknowledged by the public and shareholders in Yorkshire. I can only add, therefore, with the renewed expression of my thanks, that the truest and best policy of any railway company, is that which throws progression into their system and working, and a conciliatory spirit to their customers and the public. (Cheers.)

Amongst the list of 281 subscribers, were two Baronets, eight Members of Parliament, and forty Justices of the Peace. The following is a list of the subscribers :—

SUBSCRIBERS.

BARONETS.

Armytage, Sir George, Bart, Kirklees Hall, Yorkshire
Edwards, Lieut.-Col Sir Henry, Bart, Pye Nest.

MEMBERS OF THE HOUSE OF COMMONS.

Beaumont, Wentworth Blackett, M P, Bretton Park

Fielden, Joshua, M P, Stansfield Hall, Todmorden

Leatham, E A M P, Whitley Hall

Ripley, W H, M P, Acacia, Apperley Bridge

Sanderson, Thos Kemp, M P, Wakefield.

Stanhope-Spencer, W T W, M P, Cannon Hall

Starkey, Lewis Randle, M P, Becca Hall, South Milford

Waterhouse, Major, M P, Hope Hall, Halifax

JUSTICES OF THE PEACE

Balme, E B W, J P, Cote Wall, Hopton

Barker, Major, J P, Holme Field, Wakefield

Blakeley, William, J P, Woodhouse Hall, Huddersfield

Carter, Alderman, Mayor of Barnsley

Charlesworth, J C D, J P, D L, Chapelthorpe Hall, Wakefield

Cook, Thomas Hague, J P, Mirfield

Creyke, Ralph, J P, Rawcliffe Hall

Critchley, R Illingworth, J P, Dewsbury

Day, Henry, J.P, Dewsbury

Fielden, John, J P, Dobroyd Castle, Todmorden

Firth, F, Alderman, Mayor of Dewsbury

Foster, Major, J P, Lightcliffe

Gill, William Henry, Alderman, Mayor of Wakefield

JUSTICES OF THE PLACE—*continued*

Green, Edward, Heath Old Hall
Greenwood, J Beswick, J P, Dewsbury Moor. Chairman of Quarter Sessions
Greenwood, Thomas, J P, Dewsbury Moor
Holdsworth, Saml, M D, J P, Wakefld
Hurst, Josh S, J P, Copt Hewick Hall, Ripon
Norris, William, J P, Stansfield House, Sowerby Bridge
Kay, John, J P, Clayton West
Moxon, Richard, J P, Pontefract
Newall, Henry, J.P, Littleborough
Newsome, Mark, J P, Dewsbury
Peel, William, J P, Ackworth Park, Pontefract

Rawson, W H J P, Sowerby Bridge
Ridgway, Alderman, J P, Dewsbury
Riley, Thomas, J P, Mytholmroyd
Rothwell, William, J P, Halifax
Shaw, Bentley, J P, Huddersfield
Skilbeck, Robert, J P, Crosland Hall
Stanfield, A. W, J P, Wakefield
Sutcliffe, Captain, J P Hebden Bridge
Tomlinson, W H B, Alderman, J P, Wakefield
Wayman, T, Alderman, J P, Halifax.
Westerman, G H, J P, Sandal
Wheatley, Charles, J P, Mirfield
White, I Tolson, J.P Normanton
Wickham, Lamplugh, J P, Lowmoor

GENTRY.

Allatt, Peter, Rastrick
Alsbury, G, Southport
Anderton, William, Cleckheaton
Armitage, Sam, Dewsbury
Armitage, George, Mirfield
Ashton
Atkinson, Henry, Cleckheaton.
Atkinson, James, do
Baldwin, Thomas
Baldwin, William, Greetland
Baldwin, John, Greetland
Banks, Thornton and Garside Liversedge
Bannister, John, Snaith
Barber, Fairless, Rastrick
Barber, H J, Brighouse
Bastow, B, Cleckheaton
Blart, B, Leamington
Bennett, Dr, Cleckheaton
Berry, J I, Southport
Bradbury, Charles, Heckmondwike
Brook, Major, Kirkburton.
Brown, George, Goole
Booth and Reynolds, Wakefield
Birkby, Joseph Liversedge
Binns, Edward, Eastwood
Bates, J, Alderman, Dewsbury
Beaumont, I, Dewsbury
Blackburn, William, Cleckheaton
Bottomley, J Carr Brighouse
Bottomley Bros, Elland
Burnup, Thomas, Cleckheaton.
Cadman, Heaton, Ackworth
Camm, W and A, Brighouse

Chambers and Chambers, Brighouse
Child, Rowland, Wakefield
Clay, R O and Sons, Dewsbury
Clayton, Joe, Wakefield
Clayton, William, Sandal
Clay and Sons, Sowerby Bridge
Crawshaw, Ralph, Heckmondwike.
Crossley, J R, Elland
Crossley, John, Lightcliffe
Crossley, George, Cleckheaton
Crowther, J P and J, Mirfield
Croxall, James H, Bradford
Coggin, W, Wakefield
Cuthbert, W, Councillor, Wakefield
Dent, E, Heckmondwike
Dixon, Benjamin, Deputy Clerk of the Peace, Wakefield
Dixon, John H, Deputy Clerk of the Peace, Wakefield
Dymond, J, Liversedge
Ellerton, G V Wakefield
Emmott, Holmes, Elland
Farrer Brothers, Henley
Framley Jonathan and Sons, Dewsbury
Fernandes, C B L, Wakefield
Firth, Arthur, Cleckheaton
Foster, Abraham, Dewsbury
Foster, A C Halifax
Fox, D, West Vale
Fox, F and Sons, Sowerby Bridge
Fox, Marmaduke, Mirfield
Forge, John, Wakefield
France, James, Dewsbury
Frazer, John, C E, Leeds

GENTRY—*continued*

Friend, A, Leeds
Friend, A, Wakefield
Gledhill, Ashworth and Co, Bradford
Goldthorpe, E, Cannes, France.
Good, Joseph D, Dewsbury
Greame, —, Hull
Greaves, J O, Wakefield
Greenwood Brothers, Mytholmroyd
Greenwood, Joseph, Sowerby Bridge
Greenwood, William, Cleckheaton
Good, J H, Leeds
Hadwen, G B, Sowerby Bridge
Haigh, John, Alderman, Dewsbury
Haigh, T Wilton, Councillor, Wakefield
Hanson, Thomas, Lowmoor
Hanson, David and Co, Halifax
Heaton, James and Sons, Heckmondwike
Hebblethwaite, G H, Huddersfield
Heckmondwike Manufacturing Company, Limited
Helliwell, T W, Brighouse
Heslop, Richard, Huddersfield
Harrison, S F, Sandal
Hemingway, John, Dewsbury
Hirst, David, Cleckheaton
Holt, Elias, Alderman, Wakefield
Holt, Edmund, Horbury
Holt, P. S, Ripponden
Howarth, Joseph W, Wakefield
Howgate, Joseph, Wakefield
Howgate, E. Smith, Mirfield
Horsfall Brothers, Mytholmroyd
Horsfall, Richard, Halifax
Howden, Joe, Councillor, Wakefield
Hirst, Samuel, Ferry Bridge
Hinchcliffe, R and H
Hoyle, John, Mytholmroyd
Holliday, Thomas, Huddersfield
Ibberson, J K, Heckmondwike
Ibberson, Joe, Dewsbury
Ingham, E I, Horbury
Jackson, George, Cleckheaton
Jackson, William, Hebden Bridge
Jeffries, E, Lowmoor
Johnson, Joe Marshall, Mirfield
Kaye, Anthony K, Councillor, Huddersfield
Kelley, Fairfax, and Sons, Heckmondwike
Kershaw, James, Elland.

Kershaw, Richard, Brighouse
Kilner, John, Wakefield
Kilburn, James, Meltham
Kitson, Joe W, Wakefield
Lamb, George, Elland
Law, Samuel, and Sons, Cleckheaton
Lodge, Henry, Barugh
Loveday, James, Wakefield
Mackie, Robert and Sons, Wakefield.
Maude, John, West Vale
Mann, Henry, Cleckheaton
Marsden, John, Wakefield
Mander, George, Wakefield
Marsh, John, Sowerby Bridge
Meller, Benjamin and Sons.
Milner, J F, Elland
Milnes, W H, Councillor, Wakefield
Milthorp, Councillor, Wakefield
Moffatt, Alfred, Mirfield
Moffatt, J R, Mirfield
Morton, E G, Hipperholme
Moxon, W H Thomas, Pontefract
Moxon, George Dunhill, Pontefract
Naylor, J, Warley
Newton, George, Wakefield
Norriss, H A, Sowerby Bridge
Nowell, J D, Halifax
Oates, J. F, Heckmondwike
Ogden and Lumb
Ormerod, T T, Brighouse
Ormerod, Hanson, Brighouse
Outram's Executors
Park Coal Company Limited, Heckmondwike
Pearson, S and Sons, Bradford
Pearson, George, Pontefract
Pettinger, William, Wakefield
Pollard, A, Ossett
Poppleton, Richard, Orbury
Radcliffe, P, Todmorden
Rhodes, John, Featherstone
Ringrose W C and L, Hull
Roberts, Charles, Wakefield
Roberts, John, Birmingham
Robinson, J G, Elland
Rockett, J H, Snaith
Royle, John, Heckmondwike
Saxby and Farmer, London
Shackleton, James, and Sons, Hebden Bridge
Shaw, E P, Wakefield
Shaw, G A, Sowerby Bridge

GENTRY—continued

Shaw, John, Elland
Shaw, J L., Sowerby Bridge
Shaw, J Sandal
Shaw, Walker and Co, Gook
Sheard, Joe, Huddersfield
Simpson, W and J, Wakefield
Skelton, Henry and Son, Mytholmroyd
Sladen, Asheton, Halifax
Smith, Henry, Aglaigg
Smith, Henry, Wakefield
Smith, Thomas, Wakefield
Smith, J R, Wakefield
Smithson, Joseph, Lightcliffe
Smithson, Joshua Lightcliffe
Smithwaite, Captain, Wakefield
Stainclitfe, John, Mirfield
Stevens and Sons, London
Stewart, William Henry, Alderman, Wakefield
Stewart, William, Wakefield
Stott, Henry, Halifax
Sutcliffe, John and Sons, Grimsby
Sugden Thomas and Sons, Brighouse
Sunderland, G, Halifax
Sutcliffe, William, Blackpool
Sutcliffe, William Todmorden
Sweeting, J T, Wakefield
Swire, R and J, Cleckheaton
Tadman, R, Wakefield
Tattersfield J, Mirfield
Taylor, H Dyson, Huddersfield
Taylor, R A, Cleckheaton
Taylor, Thomas, Wakefield.
Tennant, C A Dewsbury
Tonge, S H, Sowerby Bridge

Townsend, H, Luddendenfoot
Townsend and Phythian, Greetland
Teall, William, Bridlington
Terry, B, Bradford
Todd, Robert, Bradford
Thackrah, Matthew, Mirfield
Thackrah, William, Mirfield
Wade, Joseph, Alderman, Wakefield
Wainwright, Joseph, Wakefield
Walker, John, Thornhill
Walker, John, Holy Well Green
Walker, Richard, Dewsbury
Walker, Tom, Wakefield
Walker, T S, Halifax
Walker, T J, London
Waites and Son, Clayton West
Wharton, Alfred, Mirfield
Walsh, Joe, and Son, Halifax
Wheatley, Henry, and Sons, Mirfield
Wheelwright, J W, Ripponden
Whitaker, Frederick, Halifax
Whitehead, J, Wakefield
Whitworth Brothers, Heckmondwike
Whitworth, Joshua, Councillor, Huddersfield
Wilcock, John, and Sons, Mytholmroyd
Williamson, Captain, Mirfield
Wilman, Alfred, Dewsbury Moor
Widdop, W W, Brighouse
Wilson, Joseph, Elland
Wrigley, H and E Netherton
Woodhead, John, Wakefield
Wooler, C, Mirfield
Yates Thomas, Cleckheaton

On receiving this most handsome testimonial I determined to become a shareholder of the Lancashire and Yorkshire Railway, and took up shares accordingly.

I remember the great Conservative demonstration at Nostell Priory, the seat of the late Rowland Winn, Esq, M P, on the 23rd of August, 1884. I was requested by a sub-committee to deal with all companies in making railway arrangements to convey the members of the various clubs and associations in Yorkshire I worked hard to make it a success, and it was calculated that the various railway companies conveyed over thirty thousand people, which, together with those who went in all kinds of conveyances, and others who journeyed on foot, it was estimated there were not less than ninety thousand persons assembled in the park It was said that this large and enthusiastic gathering saved the House of Lords. I have great pleasure in recording that, when on the balcony, I was thanked for the energy I had displayed in the Conservative cause by the Right Honourable the then Chancellor of the Exchequer (Sir Stafford Northcote, Bart , M P.) and Rowland Wynn, Esq., M.P.

The experimenting policy adopted since 1872 resulted in loss of traffic and diminished receipts, which brought forth loud complaints from the shareholders at the half-yearly meeting held in Manchester on the 21st of August, 1878. After the Chairman had opened the meeting and tried to explain away the cause of the reduced dividend, one of the shareholders said he agreed that the directors had no control over the state of trade, but they had great control over the expenditure. He pointed out that the North-Eastern and London and North-Western Companies, with large decreases in traffic, had during the last half-year been able to effect reductions in the working expenses, amounting in the first case to £118,000, and in the second to £95,000, whereas the Lancashire and Yorkshire Company showed a positive increase in the working expenses of £12,000. He could not but feel that this was most unsatisfactory and discouraging to the shareholders. Another shareholder congratulated the directors on having declared the worst dividend they had had for fifteen years, and asked if the competition of other lines had had anything to do with the loss of traffic He could not understand why there had been so large an expenditure. If they looked at other lines, they found that in the case of the Manchester, Sheffield, and Lincolnshire Railway the working expenses amounted to 52 per cent, the North-Eastern 52½ per cent, the Midland 53 per cent, the London and North-Western 54 per cent, while on the Lancashire and Yorkshire line they amounted to 56½ per cent. These things demanded explanation. Another shareholder attributed the present state of things to the management of the directors. All classes agreed in finding fault with the management, and it was generally declared the worst managed line in the kingdom. He asked the directors if they were too old to take a lesson from the management of such lines as the London and North-Western and the North-Eastern Companies

The following letter appeared in the Manchester *Examiner and Times* in 1878 :—

LANCASHIRE AND YORKSHIRE RAILWAY
To the Editor of the Examiner and Times.

Sir,—The efficient management of railways is a subject which concerns the public and shareholders alike The first in respect to their convenience, safe, cheap, and expeditious travelling, and the quick transit of goods and minerals , and the second in reference to the dividends and the reputation of their lines The policy pursued by the Lancashire and Yorkshire Railway management since 1871 is fast reducing the value of the property, and will, if persisted in, very shortly leave nothing for the ordinary shareholder in the shape of dividend, which has now been reduced to 4? per cent The raising of the passenger fares 7½ to 50 per cent during the present serious decrease of wage-earning power by the masses shows such a lack of knowledge of the true economy of railway management as to be a wonder the directors would sanction it. I may be told that it is only the fares from 1d. to 1s that have been increased such an excessive percentage , to which I reply they are just the fares that are in the balance between walking, omnibuses, and railways; and their loss is making a considerable proportion of the present traffic decrease. It might have been thought that the advisers to the directors would have taken a lesson from the penny post and cheap press in catering for the public, but this is too much to expect from a management which takes three days to remove goods and coals about twenty miles, and to which a gentleman representing a firm paying to the Company about £20,000 a year has to call three times before he can see a chief officer, and then only under a threat of going to see the directors.

The next blunder is the attempt to reduce the wages and increase the hours of enginemen and firemen, a piece of parsimony which is very foolish to say the least of it. To reduce these men to a semi state of starvation and exhaustion, who have such important duties entrusted to them, and who have to face all the varied inclemencies of the weather, from a blazing hot sun to a blinding snow or hail storm—men who go to work with their lives and those of the public in their hands, the constant strain on whose nerves in attending to the engines when travelling, the argus-eyed vigilance required to detect and attend to movable and fixed signals when travelling at the rate of 40 or 50 miles an hour, the nerve and pluck required and displayed in moments of danger, to remedy the errors of pointsmen, platelayers, and others, are matters of daily if not hourly occurrence, yet, forsooth, the efficiency and vigour of these men is to be kept up by starving and overworking them Woe to the public and the shareholders if the better judgment of the directors does not prevail. I shall be curious to note the saving effected when the butcher's bill is paid, from the safety and lives of the public being entrusted to an enervated half-starved body of engineers and firemen. The wages and hours of these men are the same as they were in 1867, when their hours were reduced from 12 to 10 per day, so that they have enjoyed no benefit from the recent inflated prosperity of the country. It is the management, not the men, that is at fault. In 1871 the cost of working a train was 7 25d per mile ; and for the six months ending June 30, 1878, it was 10·39d per mile, or an increase of 3 14d per mile, equal to £72,400 for this six months—wages and hours of the men of both periods being the same, and this in face of the fact that the sum of £2,500,000 had been expended upon the lines open for traffic, in providing improvements and facilities for working it. The London and North-Western Railway locomotive expenses in 1871 were 7 57d. per train mile ; and for six months ending December 30, 1877, were 7·92d., or an increase of 0·35d, solely due, in my opinion, to a more efficient management.

After the severe criticism at the half-yearly meeting held at Manchester, on the 21st of August, 1878, upon the policy of management, it brought forth a circular from the chief traffic manager to all stations upon the question of reducing wages and staff. When he drew

out that circular I wondered whether it reminded him of
the prediction I made to him in 1871, that if he adopted
his intended policy of management, it was my opinion he
would work the line down to 4 per cent, when there
would be trouble for someone. I was very sorry when I
saw the circular, which was intended to improve the
dividend out of the hard-worked and under-paid class of
servants. However, the reduction took effect I need
not say this caused great discontent and dissatisfaction
amongst the servants throughout the line. I am sure
the shareholders would not thank the directors for an
improved dividend obtained from such a source. This
policy simply increased the Company's unpopularity, which
is shown in the following extract —

RAILWAY ECONOMY

To the Editor of the Examiner and Times.

Sir,—Kindly allow me to lay before your readers the following
remarks relative to the cheeseparing policy now being pursued by the
Lancashire and Yorkshire Railway Company At the last half-yearly
meeting of this Company the shareholders generally complained of the
low dividend declared, as compared with previous half-years, and attributed this state of affairs to mismanagement. Since that meeting the
directors have reduced the wages of their staff in certain departments,
and promise shortly to treat other of their men in like manner. In the
case of their goods guards the hours have been increased from 60 to 66
hours for a week's work, and fortnightly reckonings substituted for
weekly, so if 100 hours are worked one week and 40 hours in another,
the overtime can be reduced by making up the two weeks to 132 hours,
and eight hours overtime, or two weeks and one day overtime In the
case of pilot men their wages have been reduced very considerably
Doubtless all this has been done with the object of showing a good
dividend at the next meeting of shareholders There is, however, in my
opinion, no wisdom in this mode of reducing expenses, inasmuch as it
causes the men to lose interest in their work, and to shirk it ; neither is
there justice in it, seeing, as in the case of goods and passenger porters,
they receive but meagre pay, and can only hope to obtain any higher
amount by reason of long servitude, steadiness, and ability Indeed, I
greatly mistake if some of these men would not prefer to be put on short

time, or even dismissed the service, to submitting to this paltry reduction of 1s. weekly, which to most of them represents the difference between comparative comfort and discomfort. Depression of trade should not affect a railway in the same ratio as a private firm, if the directors properly considered their business, for the system may be altered at any time to meet the exigencies of trade A reference to and consideration of this Company's working time tables will show that many trains—goods and passenger—could be either abolished or amalgamated with others, without detriment to the public convenience, and without extending the long hours of the goods and passenger guards, which are at present much too long A peep into and thorough examination of the several depôts would convince the directors that changes could be made which would in no way interfere with the thorough and effective management and conducting of the system , as, for instance, a reduction in the staff of travelling inspectors could be effected with safety and a gain to the Company, because, if traffic be so much less, there is no need for these men to be kept up at the full strength, as in seasons of good trade. Their services would be of use as ordinary inspectors, shunters, and signalmen, also as guards and drivers—whatever class they belong to. Again, to examine the various depôts, and see what could be done there I am told by men in this Company's employ that at least 20 per cent could be saved in the expenses in this direction, which would enable the directors to advance men's wages in place of reducing them, and at the same time enable them to pay a dividend of not less than 6 or 7 per cent. It would be advisable for this and all other companies to revive that good rule which encouraged any of their staff to suggest freely improvements in working the system, for does it not sound to reason that their experienced servants could throw out many useful ideas if opportunity were only afforded them? It would also be well if they discouraged favouritism, which is the curse of the railway service, and let ability, not influence, guide them. This would encourage men to remain in the service It would also be an encouragement for men if the aged servants were treated with some little consideration, in lieu of being turned into the cold world after 30 or more years' faithful servitude, merely because they have passed 50 years of age, as has just taken place at the Salford Goods Station with several of their old servants. Perhaps the shareholders will deal with the questions herein raised at their next meeting, and, for the sake of those servants who have to earn the dividend, insist that the loss should not all fall on the working staff, but that equal justice should be dealt all round. This will redound to their credit, and to the prosperity of the Lancashire and Yorkshire Railway Company.—Trusting I have not trespassed too far on your space, I remain, yours truly,   JAMES CORDWELL.
104, Morton Street, Longsight, November 7, 1878.

Holding very strong views on the policy of reducing the wages of already underpaid servants, I think the central management ought to have brought forward schemes which would have produced more money, or even adopted those which had been submitted by the district officers; as I had submitted many such schemes with that view which were never carried out in their entirety The small portion they selected as a rule spoiled the object in view. However, they did one good thing, which was brought about through pressure and a great deal of criticism from the press, by reverting to the old system of running week-end excursions from Yorkshire stations to Blackpool. But it was "too late", the traffic had gone for six or seven years to other companies. These companies appreciated the increase, gave the necessary facilities, and kept the traffic.

The *Blackpool and Fleetwood Gazette* of September 18th, 1878, commenting on this matter, says:—

BLACKPOOL RAILWAY ARRANGEMENTS.

Up to 1871, when centralisation took place, the Lancashire and Yorkshire Railway Company ran trains from the Yorkshire district daily, at 7s. 6d for 14 days, which enabled the holders to return any day except Sunday , tickets available from Saturday to Monday, at 3s. for the double journey. These excursions were run for three or four months in the summer season, and they carried a weekly average of 2,500 passengers It is very probable that this number would have doubled itself by this time had the same accommodation continued ; but up to the beginning of this month the Lancashire and Yorkshire Company had from 1872 issued only monthly tickets to excursionists, at a cost of 10s 9d each. Only a month ago we pointed out in these columns that the discontinuance of these week-end trips, notwithstanding that passengers were still brought from West Yorkshire at pretty nearly the same fares as from East Lancashire, might have a serious effect upon the fortunes of Blackpool This probability seemed increased by the knowledge that the Midland Company takes passengers from Leeds to Morecambe at 9s. for two months , from Bradford to Morecambe at 8s. for the same term, and run day trips from those places at 2s. 6d. each, no doubt diverting much of the traffic to Morecambe which would have come to Blackpool had the Lancashire and Yorkshire continued the facilities and low fares which prevailed up to 1872. Much as we wished a return to the system of week-end trips in the interest of Blackpool, we did not venture to hope for such a speedy recurrence as has come to pass, the less so because the London and North-Western Company was, as it had been all along, in league with the Lancashire and Yorkshire Company on the point. Indeed, it is said to be a fact that it was the London and North-Western to whom we were chiefly indebted for the long cessation of the week-end trips, the directors of that concern, which has comparatively little excursion traffic, urging the directors of the line that feeds Blackpool to the course, on the specious plea that in reality nothing was gained by the excursion business, since it led to accidents year after year, which swallowed up all the profits. It will be remembered that that was before the days of the block system, and, as might have been expected, the discontinuance of excursion traffic was not found a perfect cure for railway collisions, so that the loss of traffic was added to loss from accidents. After a lapse of six or seven years, it is noticeable that it is not Blackpool that first calls out for recurrence to the old state of things, but Southport, favoured as it has been by the Lancashire and Yorkshire Company in the past, for no better reason, as people say, than that certain of its prominent officials are identified with the place. We notice that the shareholders, too, have been demanding the restitution of week-end trips, and it will be gratifying to our readers to learn that they are again advertised to run from Manchester and other places. We are glad of this for the sake of the Lancashire and Yorkshire Railway Company itself, for its indifference to the interests of Blackpool for some years past has caused many to look with wistful eye towards the Midland Company, and others to talk of the construction of an independent line. But we trust a better and more cordial understanding is setting in between Blackpool and the line that meets its requirements. In addition to the week-end trips, we notice that a later train is announced by way of Lytham, and it is to be hoped that the extended summer service and increased winter service, which we pleaded for not so very long ago, and which the Town Council petitioned for a few weeks back, will be granted. Besides, it is whispered—and there is never smoke but there is fire—that we are to have a new station exclusively for passenger traffic, which is an object greatly to be desired. While we can never forgive the oversight that permitted the Lytham extension to disfigure so much a length of what is really frontage, we trust we shall have in the new station some amends for the irreparable injury thus done us.

12

I am certainly of the same opinion as the writer of the foregoing leading article, that the London and North-Western Railway Company may have had something to do with the cessation of running the week-end trips. But surely a general manager ought to know the best course to be adopted to enhance the interests of his own company, and not to be misled by managers of other companies.

The Great Northern Company having withdrawn the service of trains which they ran over our line between Doncaster, Knottingley, and Leeds, the Lancashire and Yorkshire Company established in its place a local service. The local traffic proved to be very light over this section of the line, and with the view of working those trains to advantage in 1879 I suggested that the Company should bring Askern more prominently before the public by advertising improved railway facilities, and offering reduced fares similar to what the North-Eastern Railway Company have done for Harrogate. Askern is well known in all the towns and villages throughout Yorkshire for its most beautiful surroundings, for drives and walks, and for its picturesque lake and baths, also its sulphur springs, which have long been celebrated for their curative effects in cases of rheumatism, indigestion, and cutaneous disorders. These curative properties are well known to doctors, who recommend their patients to go and take the waters, which have proved beneficial. I went over to Askern, with a view of giving my suggestions a start, and had an interview with a few of the influential residents in the village. In talking matters over they agreed to render every possible assistance, and formed themselves into a committee for the purpose of getting up a grand fête, athletic sports, and fire brigade demonstration as an attraction, provided the Company would give railway facilities by running special trains at reduced fares. The date was fixed for Saturday, July 19th. On my return to the office I wrote to the central management at Manchester on the 11th of June, and explained everything that was intended to be done by the committee. I also suggested to the central management what the Company ought to do to ensure the affair being a success and to bring Askern more to the front, and I submitted a special service of trains, with half-day excursion fares, to be quoted from the stations on various sections of the line in Yorkshire. Receiving no reply, I wrote again on the 16th, and received an answer to the effect that my suggestions could not be agreed to. On the 17th I wrote again and submitted further suggestions, quoting the fares similar to those charged to Littleborough. I was surprised to receive a reply on the 19th, saying that it was not the intention of the Company to run specials at reduced fares, as proposed by me, at the Company's risk. I had then been waited upon by the Askern committee, also by the captain of the Yorkshire Fire Brigade Association. I wrote again to the authorities at Manchester on the 23rd, asking for a re-consideration of the question, stating that a guarantee would be given to run the specials at the rates previously quoted by me, and referred them to my letter of the 11th, which gave them all particulars. On the 28th of June, not having had a reply to this letter, and time being on the wing, I wrote again and mentioned that a guarantee would be given. The next day I received a proof bill from Manchester, showing stations east of Wakefield only, and at fares and times quite different to those I had submitted, and no allusion was made as to their agreeing to run a guaranteed special. On July 1st I again wrote calling their attention to the necessity of running special trains west of Wakefield, where the population was, and where the fire brigades were coming from, also to the high rate of fares quoted for a half-day trip, as shown in the proof bill. We had then entered on the month of July, the sports were fixed for Saturday, July 19th, and the railway arrangements were not completed I waited upon the Askern committee and explained matters to them, and although they had got their programme into print, they decided to put off the sports until Saturday, July 26th On July 2nd I wrote to Manchester stating the particulars of the change of date. Having had no answer to this letter or the one of the 1st July (asking for special facilities to be given to stations west of Wakefield), or to the one of June 28th (which offered to guarantee the special trains from stations where the brigades where coming from), I again wrote on the 4th of July, strongly recommending that the propositions should be at once entertained, as the delays would have a tendency to spoil the traffic, and the future interests of the Company. I received a letter and the bills for stations east of Wakefield on July 7th, with an intimation that there was no intention to include stations west of Wakefield or to give any facilities whatever, and no mention was made as to the guaranteed special. I wrote again on the 8th, to say that if special trains were not run from stations west of Wakefield, where the population resided and the fire brigades were coming from, we could not expect to have the traffic. Having had no reply to my letter of the 8th, I wrote on the 12th for the result of the re-consideration of my previous correspondence as to facilities for stations west of Wakefield, On the following day I received a letter with a proof bill attached for stations west of Wakefield, but again nothing was said as to the proposed guaranteed specials. On the 14th I returned the proof bill, and suggested that the trains should not be run at such high fares, as it was my opinion the traffic at such fares would not pay the expenses On July 17th I wrote again and enclosed a programme of the sports, and again urged a reduction of fares, in which event I anticipated from two to three thousand people would travel by the trains, also pressing for the bills to be issued to the public early. On July the 18th I received a reply to say the bills were out and could not be altered. On July 19th I wrote again, expressing my opinion that the fares were prohibitory, and my apprehension was the affair would be a complete failure in consequence. My opinion was verified by the return showing the number of passengers conveyed from the stations west of Wakefield, which was ten, and the receipts amounting to £1 9s. 4d., and from three special trains. This is another instance of increased working expenses.

From the above facts it will be observed that my intention of permanently increasing the traffic over this section of the line, with the view of compensating for the loss sustained by the withdrawal of the Great Northern Railway Company's trains, and also bringing Askern and its baths more prominently before the public, was completely frustrated by the central management. There were thirty-eight days of correspondence in reference to the proposed special arrangements for Askern.

It will be noticed that the sports had to be put off a week, waiting the decision of the railway arrangements, and that the high rate of fares quoted by the Company prevented the fire brigades and the public from coming to Askern. I received a censure from the general manager on the 31st of July, for writing to the Askern committee, cautioning them as to incurring extra expense in providing horses for the fire brigades on their arrival with the fire engines, as I feared the high fares quoted

LANCASHIRE AND YORKSHIRE RAILWAY.

ASKERN SPORTS.

On Saturday, July 26th, 1879,

CHEAP

HALF-DAY EXCURSIONS

WILL BE RUN AS FOLLOWS :—

FROM	Times of Starting.	Fares to Askern and back, the same day only.
	a.m.	THIRD CLASS.
Bradford (Exchange Station)	11 45	**3s. 6d.**
Low Moor.................................	11 55	
	p.m.	
Cleckheaton	12 1	3s. 2d.
Liversedge	12 5	3s. 1d.
Heckmondwike	12 8	2s. 11d.
Huddersfield.............................	12 5	3s. 6d.
Halifax	11 40	3s. 11d.
Brighouse	12 7	3s. 4d.
Mirfield.............	12 21	2s. 11d.
Thornhill	12 28	**2s. 8d.**
Dewsbury (Market Place)	12 20	

RETURNING FROM ASKERN AT 8-9 P.M.

CHILDREN ABOVE 3 AND UNDER 12 YEARS OF AGE HALF-PRICE.

The Company will not be responsible for Luggage.

WM. THORLEY, Chief Traffic Manager.

Manchester, July, 1879.

would prevent them from coming, which was the case, causing besides great disappointment to the public and loss to the Askern committee   Under divisional management the whole railway arrangements required would have been completed in twenty minutes time ; Askern would have been served, and the Company's reputation saved.   The following is a copy of a letter on the subject from the *Doncaster Chronicle,* August, 1879 :—

ASKERN NEGLECTED.

To the Editor of the Doncaster Chronicle.

Sir,—Nearly every town and village has its sports—athletic or otherwise, flower shows, cricket matches, or demonstrations of some kind or other   It is characteristic of Englishmen to delight in these outdoor exercises and gatherings   Now, when these events happen, we find facilities given by the railway companies to the pleasure-going public at reasonable fares   This is but fair to the promoters of these gatherings, and no doubt is mutually satisfactory to the railway companies in a financial point of view.   Askern not being so well known as Blackpool, Southport, Harrogate, Scarborough, and other places, a committee of gentlemen was recently formed to bring more prominently before the public Askern, its charming neighbourhood, and its peculiar characteristics   Everything has been done, I believe, by the committee to make it a success, but, of course, this is only one side of the picture.   The other side is wanting, viz, the railway arrangements   It should be stated that Askern is, as to its railway communication, in the hands of the Lancashire and Yorkshire Railway Company.   The district superintendent of that line was communicated with, and we believe has, so far as lies in his power, afforded every assistance to the committee, with a view of strengthening their hands, by running special trains at reduced fares from Leeds, Bradford, Halifax, Sowerby Bridge, Brighouse, Huddersfield, Holmfirth, Dewsbury, Wakefield, &c.   The Lancashire and Yorkshire Company, whilst running these special trains as announced by their bill, have set forth the fares at such prices that it is utterly impossible to carry into effect what was originally intended This, therefore, precludes not only the general public taking advantage of the occasion to visit Askern, but likewise prevents those who would otherwise have taken part in the programme of the day, including the firemen of the Yorkshire district, as mentioned in the bills of the committee.   Now, here is a district exclusively in the hands of that blessed Lancashire and Yorkshire Railway Company, and this is how poor Askern, trying to raise itself in the estimation of the public, is supported by that Company. I see by the Great Northern Company's bills that they run to Skegness, Lincolnshire, and back, on half-day excursions from Bradford and other places, for 2s , a distance of about 120 miles. Yet from Bradford to Askern, a distance of 35 miles, the fare charged for a few hours on a Saturday half-day trip is 3s 6d.; Halifax, about the same distance, 37 miles, 3s. 11d , and so on. Our brigade at Doncaster and others in the district were anxious to take part in the proceedings, and to meet their brother firemen from a distance. This, therefore, is a disappointment to them as well as others. The fault is not theirs, and the committee of the sports will no doubt suffer, and it will be a loss to the Railway Company as well.

The first half-yearly meeting of the Lancashire and Yorkshire Railway Company for 1879 was held at Manchester, on August 21st, when the directors declared a dividend at the rate of 4 per cent. These gradually decreasing dividends created no little uneasiness amongst the shareholders, and one of them called the attention of the directors to the working expenses of this Company's line, saying they were far greater than the working expenses of any of the principal railways in England similarly situated with regard to traffic. The outcome obtained by reversing the policy pursued up to May, 1871, had been to reduce the dividends on the ordinary stock of the Company 3 per cent per annum in the current half-year. Another shareholder remarked that the reversal of the policy of management has led to an extravagant expenditure of capital and revenue, and to diminish dividends. It will be for the shareholders to decide whether the expensive and inefficient policy of management is to continue until the dividend is nil.

I agree with the shareholder's remark that the present policy of management is quite capable of reducing the dividend to nil; although the line runs through the best districts for railway traffic in England. It is evident that the shareholders are beginning to observe that the changed policy of management is not working out to their advantage, which was again shown at the second half-yearly meeting for 1879. One of the shareholders said he confessed to a feeling of considerable disappointment at a beggarly 5¼ per cent dividend. He used to look upon the Lancashire and Yorkshire line as one of the very first in the kingdom, but he was sorry to say that it was not maintaining its position. He did not think the chairman had sufficiently explained to them how it was that last year the directors should be able to declare 6 per cent, and this year only 5¼ per cent. They had not gone through any worse times than the Midland, and yet that company had declared for the past half-year a dividend of 6¼ per cent, as against 5¾ per cent for the corresponding period last year; and the London and North-Western Company were giving 7½ per cent, as against 7 per cent for the corresponding half of last year. The latter company thought that the Lancashire and Yorkshire at one time was much superior to their own, and they had an impression that if the line had been managed as they could have managed it they would have been able to give the shareholders 12s. 6d. per share more than the shares of their own line. Could it, therefore, be surprising that the shareholders of the Lancashire and Yorkshire were very much disappointed with the results? He was afraid that the working expenses were much heavier than those of other companies. He thought that the Lancashire and Yorkshire Company required a little change in the management. They had educated some of the best general managers in the kingdom, but they had let them slip one by one through their fingers Before he sat down he would say he saw it stated yesterday that Mr. Pearson, the new director, had entered upon his duties with great zeal and energy, and that the management of the Lancashire and Yorkshire Company was going to

be in future for the advantage of the trading community
Another shareholder said he thought the last speaker had
hit the right nail on the head. He had observed with
regret that the traffic from the North-Eastern Railway
system had passed from the Lancashire and Yorkshire
line to the London and North-Western. That was a
state of things which could not commend itself to the
shareholders. He was sorry the directors were trying to
save money by curtailing the wages of the under-paid
servants. Another shareholder said the line from Liverpool to Southport was the best paying part of the system,
and yet the directors seemed to pay very little attention
to the demands of the Southport people. The dividends
had fallen from 9¼ per cent in 1872 to 5¼ for the half of
1879, and he did not know what grounds the chairman
had for telling them that the prospects were brightening.
He warned the directors that if greater attention was not
paid to the demands that came from Southport, they
would at some time have to compete with another
company.

The Board of Directors and managers in office at the
end of June, 1880, were —

Chairman, Thomas Barnes, Esq
Deputy-Chairman, Joshua Radcliffe, Esq

Joshua Appleyard, Esq	Theodore Julius Hare, Esq.
George John Armytage, Esq	William Himmers, Esq.
Samuel William Bulteal, Esq.	William H. Hornby, Esq
Robert Daglish, Esq	The Rt. Hon. Lord Houghton
Samuel Fielden, Esq.	John Pearson, Esq
Edward Green, Esq	James Pilkington, Esq.
William Foster, Esq	Henry Yates Thompson, Esq.

Officers

William Thorley, Traffic Manager.
John Maddock, Superintendent of the Line.
George Holgate, District Superintendent, Lancashire
J. Livesey, District Superintendent, Accrington.
Thomas Normington, District Superintendent, Wakefield

I was very pleased to observe that the express service of trains from Yorkshire stations to Manchester and Liverpool, which I submitted in 1870, and which was then rejected, after being shelved for ten years was brought forward by the central management, who sent me a copy (somewhat revised) for my perusal and further remarks. On perusal I found there were five express trains each way between Yorkshire to and from Manchester and Liverpool, but they had omitted to make the connections at Holbeck Junction, Leeds. with the North-Eastern Railway Company's system, also the intermediate local stations in the district With a view of making the service complete, I revised the times of the running of branch trains, and submitted a local service of trains to run between Halifax, Sowerby Bridge, and Rochdale, to be in direct connection at those stations with the express trains, thus completing the service by giving facilities for passengers at local stations to travel by the express trains.   But, as usual, they only adopted a portion of my suggestions, which brought forth loud complaints from the public, and loss of traffic from the tradespeople.   This resulted in the Company having to patch up the defective local service by putting on at extra cost additional trains to meet the requirements.   However, the manufacturers and tradespeople generally, especially on the Spen Valley line (Cleckheaton Branch), were not satisfied with the patched-up service of trains, as it did not meet their purposes.   They were continually complaining of being neglected and debarred from the necessary railway facilities, which had a most serious effect upon their various industries   Deputations waited upon the centralised management at Manchester to express their grievances. I also submitted recommendations, and if such had been adopted they would have met the requirements of the public.   Notwithstanding this pressure, very little was

done for them This led to great agitation, and to public
meetings throughout the valley The inhabitants and
manufacturers decided to invite the Great Northern Railway Company to construct a line up the valley in connection
with their line at Batley, and in 1882 application was
made for Parliamentary powers to construct the line. Of
course this application was opposed at a great cost by
the Lancashire and Yorkshire Railway Company After
the Spen Valley bill was lost in May, 1882, the general
managers of the Lancashire and Yorkshire Railway Company proposed to the Great Northern Company that if
they would abandon the Spen Valley scheme they might
have running powers over the Lancashire and Yorkshire
line This offer took the manager of the Great Northern
Company by surprise, and when he asked, " Are you in
earnest, and quite willing that the Great Northern shall
have the opportunity of utilising the existing lines ? "
the general manager of the Lancashire and Yorkshire
Railway Company replied, " Yes, I am quite willing that
you should go to Halifax by our line." This led to the
following agreement —

The Great Northern Railway Company shall have running powers
for all description of traffic over the Lancashire and Yorkshire Railway
lines, including the use of the Lancashire and Yorkshire passenger and
goods stations, from Crofton Junction, near Wakefield, to Halifax, via
Mirfield, Brighouse, and North Dean, and from Thornhill Junction to
Low Moor via Heckmondwike, Liversedge, and Cleckheaton.

This arrangement of admitting additional service of
local trains upon an already congested line led to a loss
to the Lancashire and Yorkshire Railway Company, not
only in delays to their own trains, but a continuous loss
of traffic by being diverted from their own immediate
lines. All this loss and inconvenience, and the ill-feeling
created amongst our best customers, might have been
avoided had the central management considered the

interests of the shareholders by giving to the public what was in their power, and what it was their duty to do, namely, increased railway facilities. I know from my personal and immediate acquaintance with the inhabitants of Spen Valley they did not court or want railway competition, but simply to be assisted by our Company with railway accommodation for their important and varied industries. This is another instance of centralised arrangements, which led to what the shareholders are continually complaining about—diminished dividends I, as a district officer, felt somewhat degraded that another company should have been brought on to the line to show us how to meet the public's requirements

In October, 1880, another attempt was made to increase the dividend by reducing the staff and wages at stations, and throughout the line generally.

The half-yearly general meeting of proprietors, ending December 31st, 1880, was held at Manchester on Wednesday, the 23rd February, 1881, and, although an increased dividend had been declared compared with previous corresponding half-years, the shareholders considered it to be unsatisfactory, and one of them said he felt disappointed as to the amount of the dividend, because, after all, $5\frac{3}{4}$ per cent was a very paltry affair when they remembered, as they were told by the chairman, that during the past year they had carried nineteen million passengers, whilst the London and North-Western Company, with their much greater mileage, carried only twenty-five millions. Out of their nineteen million passengers he thought they ought to have riddled more than $5\frac{3}{4}$ per cent, seeing that the London and North-Western paid 8 per cent. He did not see why the Lancashire and Yorkshire Company should not be at the expense of sending the general manager to the United States, so that, if possible, he might bring back a few

Yankee notions which would enable them to declare a larger dividend than 5¾ per cent

Another shareholder said there was still much cause for anxiety and regret at the wasteful expenditure of capital and revenue that was now going on, and from the increasing desire shown in the report to depart from correct commercial principles, and to mystify the shareholders and cloak the shortcomings of the management by multiplying replacement accounts No doubt many shareholders were asking themselves how it was that the London and North-Western directors were in a position to pay 8 per cent to their shareholders, when the Lancashire and Yorkshire only paid 5¾ to their shareholders. This arose simply from the fact of the working expenses being so much higher than the London and North-Western Company's

These criticisms of the management were well deserved I, as a shareholder, desired a good dividend, and was also anxious for the welfare of the Company, and knowing so well the inclinations and requirements of the public in Yorkshire, I submitted every year well-matured schemes for making money at the least cost, both for ordinary passenger trains and excursion traffic. But these schemes were never adopted; the central management always put their veto upon them, and adopted experimental schemes in their place, which not only led to the loss of traffic, but to expensive working. Bills announcing day excursion trains were seldom issued to the public until the day before the trip was run.

On Saturday, May 15th. 1880, the Denby Dale new stone viaduct was opened for traffic. It was built by Messrs Naylor Brothers, contractors This replaced the old wooden structure which formerly spanned the valley, and is about a thousand yards long, at a high elevation throughout the greater part of its length, the highest part being 26 feet from the ground to the rail level. The stone work is snecked rubble throughout, and the arches are formed of parpoint masonry. Owing to its elevation the viaduct forms a striking object in the landscape, and is of a substantial and imposing character.

The first half-yearly general meeting of the proprietors for 1881 was held at Manchester on Wednesday, August the 24th, when the directors declared a dividend at the rate of $4\frac{1}{4}$ per cent. This dwindling dividend again caused unpleasant remarks from the shareholders. One of them said he was disappointed at the small dividend, and he did not think that the true reason for it had been given Although the working expenses and the cost of coal had increased, the trade of Lancashire had wonderfully improved, and a great many more spindles and looms were working this year than twelve months ago. If, with the present trade, the Lancashire and Yorkshire Railway Company could not increase its dividend, but had actually to decrease it, he was afraid there was not much prospect of better dividends in the future The chairman told them that coal cost more because it had to be carried further, in consequence of the colliers' strike. He had a different belief to that given by the directors as to the reason why the Company was not paying a better dividend. He was sorry to say that wherever persons could deal with the London and North-Western Company they did so, in preference to dealing with the Lancashire and Yorkshire Company. He was interested only in the Lancashire and Yorkshire, and he had tried to prevail upon friends to have their goods carried by that Company, but he had failed to persuade them. One reason was that they were not fairly treated, and another was that their goods were not so quickly delivered as by other companies, One of his clients said he would not be paid to allow the Lancashire and York-

shire Company to take his cotton from Liverpool to
Blackburn, as it took three days to deliver it, whilst the
London and North-Western would have it at his mill the
next morning. With an increased trade, the shareholders
of the Lancashire and Yorkshire had a decreased dividend,
and he was afraid that unless the directors discovered
some way of expediting the delivery of goods and the
officials of the Company were more obliging to their
customers than at present, the Lancashire and Yorkshire
Railway Company would continue to be a byword in
people's mouths. Another shareholder said that meagre
and disappointing as the dividend was, even that amount
could not be paid out of the current revenue. The
diminished dividend was caused by the reckless expenditure of capital upon unproductive works, the high rate of
working expenses, and the loss of traffic from bad management and abortive amalgamation. The whole management
of the Company seemed to be in a muddle. Another
shareholder said that one of the mills in the Whitworth
Valley had cotton conveyed by canal from Liverpool to
Rochdale, and carted from there, although their mill was
within fifty yards of the Lancashire and Yorkshire Company's Station. He considered that a scandal to the
Railway Company. He was afraid their dividends would
not increase while that kind of management continued.
The unpopularity of the Company was likewise apparent
in the verdicts given against them everywhere. He
advised the directors to improve the management of the
Company's concern, and try to cultivate a spirit of
courtesy among the officials. One of the shareholders
alluded to the Blackburn collision on the 8th of August,
1881, and said that in his opinion the way of working
and of signalling trains at Blackburn Station was calculated to court such lamentable occurrences, and not
prevent them.

After reading these and other remarks made by share-holders at the half-yearly meeting, which were very strong upon the management, I thought this was bringing trouble to somebody, as I predicted in 1871 it would. The Board of Trade inspector, who investigated the cause of the Blackburn collision, was of opinion that the accident arose from the imperfect working of the Blackburn Station. The evidence demonstrated that the accident was the result of experimental management.

Ripponden Branch was extended to Rishworth, and opened as a single line for traffic on March 1st, 1881.

Clifton Road Branch, situated between Wike and Bradley Wood, was also opened for traffic on March 1st, 1881. There are two stations on this branch, Baliffe Bridge and Clifton Road. This new line gave a direct route between Bradford and Huddersfield, saving the circuitous route by Mirfield, and running the journey in thirty minutes, being a saving of time to the public of fifteen minutes. It also enabled the Company to put on a service of passenger trains to run between Bradford, Huddersfield, Penistone, to Sheffield and London. This was considered by the public to be a step in the right direction, and gave general satisfaction.

The half-year ending December 31st, 1881, general meeting of proprietors was held at Manchester on Wednesday, February 22nd, 1882, when the directors declared a dividend of $5\frac{3}{4}$ per cent. Some of the share-holders again expressed their dissatisfaction. One of them said that the dividend for the half-year was a disappointing one, especially when compared with the dividends of other and similar companies, such as the London and North-Western, who paid 8 per cent; the Midland, who paid $6\frac{1}{2}$ per cent; the Great Northern, who paid $6\frac{1}{4}$ per cent; the Great Western, who paid $7\frac{1}{2}$ per cent; and the North-Eastern, who paid $8\frac{1}{2}$ per cent. The

13

territory covered by the Lancashire and Yorkshire Railway was far superior to the districts covered by the companies he had mentioned, and, as he had repeatedly pointed out, the line only required good management in order that better results might be obtained from it. Owing to bad management, there had been a diversion of coal traffic between Liverpool and the Wigan coalfield from the lines of that Company to those of the London and North-Western Company ; and the accident at Shaw was another example of the bungling policy pursued. The shareholders had much cause for dissatisfaction. Another shareholder said he also was of opinion that the dividend was very small. Looking at the line from a trade standpoint, he regarded it as the worst-managed line in England. He was informed by a manufacturer that goods sent from Bolton to Burnley, only a short distance, reached their destination at the end of five days Was there under these circumstances any wonder that the line paid a poor dividend ? If the line was properly managed, there was no reason why a dividend of 10 or even 12 per cent should not be paid.

I observed another severe criticism by the shareholders at the half-yearly meeting upon the bad management and dwindling dividends, which resulted in a third effort being made since 1878 to increase the dividend by reducing the wages and staffs at the stations—even this time those servants who had grown grey and spent the best part of a lifetime in the service of the Company This seems to be the only way that central management can see how to increase dividends, instead of adopting schemes which would increase the receipts If they even went back to divisional management, they would ensure a reduction of working expenses. The London and North-Western Company still adheres to that good old policy of management, which enables them to pay a satisfactory dividend.

The general meeting of proprietors, for the half-year ending June 30th, 1882, was held at Manchester, on Wednesday, August 23rd, when the directors declared a dividend of $4\frac{3}{4}$ per cent. The question of poor dividends again caused loud complaints from the shareholders. One of them said there was no time for delay on the part of the Company if it intended to meet the requirements of the public, and to prevent their traffic being taken from them by other companies There was an amount of inactivity which ought to have been remedied. During the last decade their dividends had been dwindling down. There had been bad times, it was true, but not bad for the Lancashire and Yorkshire Company only, and notwithstanding these bad times, the London and North-Western Company were paying $7\frac{1}{2}$ per cent, and the Lancashire and Yorkshire Company only $4\frac{3}{4}$ per cent. He was not content for the directors to pine away in solitude at home, but was rather in favour of their doing all they could to bring about a more satisfactory condition of the affairs of the Company. Were they to sit quiet and see traffic taken from them? He said " No." There had been an increase in their third-class passenger traffic, and no doubt if the wants of such passengers were attended to that traffic would be further increased. It was necessary not only to increase the number of trains, but to accelerate their speed. The time for action was at hand, no longer could they linger on their oars. Though their line would vie with that of the London and North-Western, their dividends were decreasing. Another shareholder remarked that, like the gentleman who had just spoken, he was not content with the position of the Company. He had not come there to talk about his own interests he had in the Company. The chairman told them at the last meeting—and he had thought about it very much since, for it had amused him very much—that the directors represented £2,000,000 of the capital of the Company If he understood the purport of that remark, it was that, inasmuch as the directors represented £2,000,000 of the capital of the Company, everyone of the shareholders must keep their mouths shut. He represented people who held more than £2,000,000 interest in the Company, and these people believed that if the directors did not use their powers to the best advantage, their interests would suffer. If all the other shareholders were like him, they would soon alter the directorate and management. If they had carried on like the London and North-Western Company, they would have been enabled to pay the same dividend; and if they did not alter their centralised policy, their dividends would soon fall below 4 per cent. Another shareholder asked, How was it that the London and North-Western Company were able to declare $7\frac{1}{2}$ per cent this half-year, while the Lancashire and Yorkshire could not pay more than $4\frac{3}{4}$ per cent? He was told immediately after the London and North-Western meeting on Saturday, that if the Lancashire and Yorkshire line had been under the same management as the London and North-Western, they could have paid a dividend of $7\frac{1}{4}$ per cent with the greatest ease. There must be some fault somewhere, and he did not think that the fault rested with the servants. Another shareholder said the management maintained its unenviable reputation for having the highest rate of working expenses and the least dividend of any of the principal railways in England. With one of the best traffic-producing districts in the whole country, the net result was the miserable dividend of $4\frac{3}{4}$ per cent, owing to the excessively high rate of the working expenses. This showed bad management of the traffic and of the business generally, and no doubt explained the seven collisions during the last two and a half years, in three of which there had been seventeen persons killed and one hundred and twenty-seven injured. This had occurred notwithstanding the Company had expended about £700,000 to prevent blunders of this kind. There had been £26,962 paid in compensation. The London and North-Western Company during the same period did not kill a single passenger In the last ten years, since the changed policy of management, the ordinary stock of the Company had depreciated something like £4,000,000 , whilst the stock of the London and North-Western. the Midland, the Great Western, the North-Eastern, and all other leading companies' stocks had risen in value, to the satisfaction of their shareholders.

Another half-yearly meeting of the proprietors of the Lancashire and Yorkshire Railway has passed. The dissatisfaction and criticism of the management were much stronger than at the previous meetings. The remarks made were correct and to the point, but still no attempt was made by the directors to improve the policy of management. But with a view of improving the dividends for the coming half-year the central management resorted to their old policy of reducing wages and staffs at stations throughout the line, which took effect in December, 1882, and January, 1883.

I remember an incident which occurred on the night of Monday, December 4th, 1882. Three passenger and two goods trains had to remain at Denby Dale Station all night, owing to a very severe snowstorm. The snow had fallen and blocked up the line in three places, which necessitated my being on duty all night.

For the half-year ending December 31st, 1882, the general meeting of proprietors was held at Manchester on Wednesday, 21st February, 1883, when the directors declared a dividend at the rate of 5 per cent. The continual dwindling down of dividends compared with the London and North-Western Railway Company, who then paid 8 per cent, again brought forth some very unpleasant remarks from several of the shareholders. However, the chairman in moving the adoption of the report, stated they were about to make some alterations in their directorate by electing two new directors, also a new chairman. It was evident from the chairman's concluding remarks that the directors anticipated a stormy meeting, which was verified by the severe remarks made by many of the shareholders upon the disgraceful management. One of them exposed the management adopted since 1872 so correctly, that I consider it worthy of record, and needs no further comment from me. He expressed my views, that centralised management had brought ruin upon a railway which runs through one of the best traffic-producing districts in the whole country. He said he had noticed without surprise the apologetic tone adopted by the chairman. He could not imagine any body of shareholders receiving with satisfaction the continually reducing dividends of the Company. It seemed to him that the chairman in the course of his address had touched on issues which were comparatively trivial, and ignored others on which he would have been heard with much interest. The chairman had not given them one ray of hope as to what they might expect for the future. The present was the most unsatisfactory dividend which had been declared since 1871. The present condition of the Company was the more serious when they took into account the favoured position of the line locally. There was certainly no line in the country which ran through a district so fertile for railway enterprise. It was the most populated part of the kingdom, the richest out of London, and the heart of manufacturing industries. How populous a neighbourhood it is would be seen in the fact that the Company had carried during the previous six months no fewer than 21,560,000 people over its 493 miles of rails, while the London and North-Western Company, with a mileage four times as great, viz , 1,667, only carried 27,388,211. The Company used to stand well both financially and in public estimation. In 1872, under divisional management, when the dividend paid was 8¾ per cent, the Company then bore so good a name in the financial world that in the proposed amalgamation with the London and North-Western Railway Company the suggested union was based on the principle that the Lancashire and Yorkshire shareholders should receive 12s. 6d. per cent per annum beyond the dividend yearly paid to the holders of London and North-Western stock. He presumed that the London and North-Western Railway Company saw that by the introduction of management similar to that of their own company they would be able to make it very valuable. The medium prices of the respective stocks in 1872 were—Lancashire and Yorkshire, 158 ; London and North-Western, 148 The prices in 1882 were—Lancashire and Yorkshire, 130 ; London and North-Western, 178 , or, in plain terms, the London and North-Western, which ten years ago was considered worth 10 per cent less than Lancashire and Yorkshire, is now 48 per cent higher. Look at the dividends in 1872 ? The Lancashire and Yorkshire paid 8⅝ per cent, and the London and North-Western 7¾ per cent. The past year the Lancashire and Yorkshire had shown a miserable return of 4⅞ against 7½ per cent dividend of the London and North-Western. This retrogression on the part of this Company had not been a sudden one, and was not in any way traceable to extraordinary or special disaster. The decline in the value of the stock and the decrease in its dividend payments had been gradually increasing year by year. As each report had come out the shareholders had seen their property dwindling down till it required no supernatural vision to prophesy it going down to par in a few more years, unless some strong hand was raised to save it from the ruin which threatened to engulf it. Who, then, was responsible for the present state of affairs, and how could an alteration be brought about? The only persons to blame for the decadence of the property were the present directors. They wanted experienced railway men, and not amateurs, to manage their line. He could not understand why the Lancashire and Yorkshire line should always be in the experimental stage. They had been told that day that they were experimenting with heavier wagons and carriages, but, in the name of common sense, had they not had experience enough up to the present time to show them the best engines and wagons to use? This experimental business had been going on during the last eight or ten years, during which the continued loss in dividend had also been going on. He believed that the general manager of the Company was not a gentleman who had been trained in the early stages of railway work. It seemed to him, as he had said, that there was too much of the amateur in connection with the line. Nothing was more needful than that there should be a first-class general manager to guide the Board of Directors, and on the Lancashire and Yorkshire system such a man seemed to be lacking. He pointed to the example afforded by the Great Western Company, when in 1871 its fortunes were at a very low point indeed. The shareholders then took the matter in their hands and elected Sir Samuel Gooch as their chairman, who had learnt his business on his back in the firebox at the Crewe engine works. What was the result? That line had from 1871 to the present time continued to steadily advance in prosperity under the guidance of that

experienced gentleman, whilst the Lancashire and Yorkshire Company had gone on in exactly the reverse direction. The increases in the price of stocks on the other
lines that had taken place since 1872 were The Metro-
politan was 51 per cent higher, the Great Eastern 29
per cent, the North British 30 per cent, Dover 28 per
cent, Great Western 21 per cent, South-Western 21 per
cent, London and North-Western 30 per cent, while the
Lancashire and Yorkshire was 28 per cent lower. The
dividends paid by the Lancashire and Yorkshire during
the past eleven years had been as follow : 1872 (at the
time of the changed policy of management), $8\frac{3}{4}$ per cent ;
1873, $7\frac{1}{4}$; 1874, $6\frac{1}{4}$; 1875, 6 ; 1876, $5\frac{7}{8}$; 1877, $6\frac{1}{8}$; 1878,
$5\frac{3}{5}$; 1879, $4\frac{3}{8}$; 1880, $5\frac{3}{8}$; 1881, 5 , 1882, $4\frac{7}{8}$ Now,
that was a serious state of affairs. The dividend had been
going down for years, and the shareholders were to be
faced in the early future by an enormous demand for
about two millions of money. It was time, he said,
there should be an end of this, and he hoped they would
exercise their common sense by calling in to their aid
some railway experts, who would thoroughly understand
the position of affairs, and be able to do something to
remedy matters. He had, with that view, the following
resolution to propose : "That the report be received, but
in consequence of its unsatisfactory character this meeting
is of opinion that a change in the policy of the administration is absolutely necessary, and believe it is of the most
vital importance that a gentleman possessed of railway
experience be invited to join the board as chairman, and
that such position be offered to Sir Edward Watkin for
acceptance, and that a committee be formed to report
to an adjourned meeting of the shareholders, and that
this meeting be adjourned for one month pending such
report."

Another shareholder said he had never before seen the proposer of the resolution, but he was quite prepared to second his motion. They would have noticed that the chairman, during the whole of his speech, had simply been giving them reasons why they should be content with the existing state of things Many of them would remember that twelve months ago he sketched to a considerable extent the position of the Company, and twelve months' experience had only verified what he then said. It had been stated that they did not derive the traffic they ought to do from Yorkshire, but the chairman had not told them the reason He had not told them that the policy of management pursued had completely separated Yorkshire from them, and that if people there could send traffic by any other company, they would do so. What was wanted was to develop the traffic in the populous districts, and this could only be effectively done by divisional management, as formerly.

Another shareholder supported the resolution, and said he had been dissatisfied with the state of the Company, and had called in a public accountant to his aid. The result was rather astonishing to him when he made comparisons between the Lancashire and Yorkshire and London and North-Western departments, the latter being acknowledged to be one of the best managed lines in the kingdom. He found that had the two companies been equally well managed the difference in the half-year to the Lancashire and Yorkshire Company would have been only £5,500. He went through all the items to see what would be the saving effected had the Lancashire and Yorkshire been as well managed as the London and North-Western throughout, and found that the total saving would have been £28,262 He agreed that one of the reasons of the diminished dividend arose through the want of additional lines to work the traffic.

The chairman put the resolution to the meeting, which was lost by 84 votes to 116.

Another shareholder moved: "That in the opinion of this meeting it is desirable that the chairman of the Company should also hold the position of managing director, with an annual salary, and, in view of the retirement of our present chairman, the directors be requested to summon a special general meeting of the shareholders, to be held 28 days from the present date, to fix the amount of salary and make such appointment, and that the directors be also requested to recommend to such meeting the name suitable for the appointment"

This motion was seconded by another shareholder

The motion was supported by a shareholder, who said that when the resolution was proposed he expected it would have finished with a vote of want of confidence in the Board, and the meeting was no doubt surprised at the moderation of his amendment He believed the Board had better accept the amendment. They appeared to him not to be a very happy family.

The Chairman suggested that the amendment should be withdrawn The proposer agreed to the withdrawal, but his seconder would not, and upon being put to the vote it was declared carried.

I have observed many stormy half-yearly meetings, and severe criticisms upon the management by the shareholders since the policy of centralised management was adopted in May, 1871, but this half-yearly general meeting, with the still dwindling dividends, brought matters to a crisis. Resolutions were put to the meeting and suggestions made that a gentleman possessed of railway experience be invited to join the Company, and that it was desirable that the chairman of the Company should also hold the position of managing director, with an annual salary. I consider this verifies my remarks made to the general manager, in his office at Manchester in May, 1871, that his intended policy of management would reduce the dividend to 4 per cent, and there would then be trouble for some one. Since that time, although population and trade has materially increased throughout the whole line, central management has allowed the dividend to dwindle down as I predicted. Ten years of central power of management have passed, and who can say it has not proved a miserable failure

The following notice to the shareholders appeared in the *Manchester Examiner and Times*, calling attention to the adjourned general meeting to be held at Manchester.—

LANCASHIRE AND YORKSHIRE RAILWAY

The dividend for the past half-year at the rate of 5 per cent, as compared with 5¼ in 1881, has caused much disappointment, and it again places the Lancashire and Yorkshire in the unenviably prominent position of showing the greatest retrogression amongst the leading "heavy" English lines. As I pointed out last month, a steady deterioration has been going on since 1871, when an amalgamation with the London and North-Western was on the eve of being carried, the basis of which was that Lancashire and Yorkshire Ordinary Stock should be entitled to ¾ per cent more dividend than North-Western If such was the estimate of their relative values then, and we now find Lancashire and Yorkshire Stock fallen from 155 to 128, while North-Western has advanced from 145 to 175, it is scarcely surprising that great discontent should prevail Many communications have been addressed to me by proprietors during the month as to the unsatisfactory state of this railway as compared with its neighbours, and it is remarkable that nothing should have been done by them long since to bring about a change Shareholders, however, rarely seem to realise the authority they possess, and even if they do they are, as a rule, so averse to oppose their directors that they apparently prefer to suffer in silence rather than enter into a conflict. That they do possess a power, however, and one which can be exerted by themselves for the good of their property, has been abundantly proved over and over again, and notorious instances of this have come prominently under my own notice, viz, in the London, Chatham, and Dover Railway, and the Grand Trunk and Great Western Railways of Canada. In these companies shareholders combined for their own benefit, and practically carried measures which never could have been accomplished unless they had taken the initiative.

It is apparently agreed on all hands that the administration of this railway is not what it should be, that the retrogression during the past twelve years, while other leading lines have advanced in prosperity, is not explainable by any special or exceptionally adverse events with which it has had to contend, and that its natural advantages should entitle it to take the very highest position amongst English railways If, as my correspondents' communications indicate, such views generally prevail, shareholders should bestir themselves and give expression to their opinions on the subject at the forthcoming meeting An earnest and united effort on their part cannot fail to be productive of much good, and I should therefore advise all who can to attend the meeting on the 21st inst. As there is every probability of an interesting and animated discussion, it is my intention to be present, and I hope to be in a position to make certain suggestions calculated to benefit the property

The adjourned special general meeting of proprietors was held at Manchester on the 23rd of March, 1883, The Board of Directors elected for their new chairman, John Pearson, Esq., and George John Armytage, Esq., deputy-chairman. Mr Pearson not being at home, Mr. Armytage, deputy-chairman, presided, He said that, as they would be aware, the meeting had been called in consequence of a resolution passed at the last half-yearly meeting. Since then the directors had considered the resolution submitted, and they had thought over the whole subject, and while they did not think that the chairman should be in the position of a managing director, they did think that he should have an adequate remuneration, to enable him to devote the whole of his time, or as much as possible, to the affairs of the Company. In their conference with the proposers they had shown this, and he (the chairman) thought they rather agreed with them, that it was merely a matter of words more than anything else, and they had acceded to, or rather agreed with, the resolution which the Board proposed on the subject. Assuming that such be the case—that the proprietors agreed with the resolution which would be moved by a shareholder—then came the question as to what the remuneration should be. That would be a matter on which the mover and seconder would have something to say, and the question was one upon which the Board would like to hear the opinions of the shareholders.

One of the shareholders said that what the chairman had stated was correct, but the Board seemed to take objection to the term managing director. He therefore moved the following resolution · "That a salary be paid to the chairman of the Board for the time being in consideration of his devoting continuous attention to the affairs of the Company." He had heard that the new chairman of the Company was a large proprietor of collieries. and reputed to be a man of good business habits. At the previous meeting the question was raised—what peculiar qualification a colliery proprietor had for being appointed managing director of a railway company?

Another shareholder seconded the resolution. He said the directors appeared to take some objection to the term managing director, appearing to think that it was putting on the Board a paid servant with the status and position of a director. Now, this was not what either he or the mover intended by the term managing director. What they wanted was an able man, one experienced in railway affairs, and competent to exercise a controlling power over the management of that Company. He was not disposed to dispute with the directors the term to be applied to the chairman, as they appeared to virtually admit the principle for which the shareholders were contending. Taking an impartial view of the Company's affairs, he thought everyone must admit it was time there was a strong hand in the directorate. The candle seemed to be rather burning at both ends. The working expenses, instead of being lessened by the capital outlay, had gone up, and the traffic receipts had not increased as they ought to do. Comparing the system with other companies, he thought it showed they were losing traffic at some corner or other. They heard a great deal of abuse of directors, but he thought the blame should be rather laid at the doors of the different departments, After all, the Board must be very much in the hands of their advisers, and they might depend upon it that the departments needed a thorough overhauling, as none appeared to be in a vigorous condition except the department for spending money.

Another shareholder said he thought, before the meeting voted a salary to the chairman, the most prudent course to adopt would be to give him a little probation, and see what he did. Let him earn his salary before he got it. He took it that was what any honest man would prefer to do, and if the new chairman was a good business man, and capable of bringing about improved returns to the shareholders, he would no doubt be more pleased to show what he could do before accepting a salary. It was not a difficult matter to vote away salaries, but it was a difficult matter to earn them, and as the shares of their line were already falling, it behoved the proprietors to be somewhat careful.

Another shareholder inquired whether the new chairman had had any experience of any other railway besides the Lancashire and Yorkshire.

The Deputy-Chairman replied : Not that I know of; he has been a director of the Company about three years.

The resolution on being put to the meeting was approved.

Another shareholder moved "that the remuneration of the chairman be fixed at such a sum not to exceed

£2,000 per annum," taking into consideration that Mr.
Wilson, during his term of office as chairman received
£1,000 per annum, and the Company was then in a most
prosperous condition But since that time their capital
and business had increased at least double, although
dividends had dwindled down, and he did not think that
£2,000 was too much for the chairman to have if he did
his duty.

Another shareholder seconded the motion. He said
he would rather that it had been a little more peremp-
tory in that the chairman should not have less than
£2,000 per annum, because he wanted him to feel he had
a duty to perform, and that he was paid for performing
it. There were, no doubt various reasons to be urged on
the other side, that it would be well to leave the matter
a little open. He took it that the intention of the
directors was, if the resolution were carried, that the
chairman should not have less than £2,000 a year. As
to commencing with a low salary, and increasing it afterwards, he would begin with what he was prepared to
pay, and if the chairman did not deserve it he would
discharge him.

Another shareholder said he was quite certain that if
the Company continued to pay 5 per cent dividend during
the next two years, it would be paying out of capital and
not out of earnings.

The resolution was then put to the meeting and
carried.

The mover of the resolution said that the remuneration
of the new chairman should be fixed, so as not to exceed
£2,000 per annum. He was pleased to observe the
allusion to Mr. Wilson, who, during his term of office as
chairman, received £1,000 per annum, and the Company
was then in a most prosperous condition. He might

have gone further, and said at that time the line was managed under the policy of divisional management.

The business done at this special general meeting of shareholders is worthy of some note, it having been called for the purpose of deciding upon a more business-like policy of management. I observed with surprise that no resolution of want of confidence in the directors was brought forward. After ten years of the experimental policy of centralised management which had done so much mischief, and been condemned over and over again, not only by the public but by the proprietors of the Company, which brought forth at every half-yearly general meeting severe criticism upon the wretched policy—a policy that is said to have reduced the value of their property by four millions of money, and the dividends from $9\frac{1}{4}$ to 5 per cent, in face of an increased population and trade throughout the whole line.

A shareholder suggested, at the half-yearly general meeting, held on Wednesday, February 23rd, 1881, that the Lancashire and Yorkshire Company should be at the expense of sending the general manager to the United States, so that if possible he might bring back a few Yankee notions ; and at the half-yearly general meeting of shareholders, held on Wednesday, February 21st, 1883. another shareholder said that the decadence of their property was from the want of an experienced railway manager, and not an amateur, as they had at present ; and a resolution was put to the meeting, that it was of opinion that a change in the policy of the administration was absolutely necessary, and that it was believed to be of the most vital importance that a gentleman possessed of railway experience should be invited to join the Company. Yet, notwithstanding all this, and other strong remarks made by other shareholders at previous half-yearly meetings, upon the bad management, and the fact

14

that a special general meeting of the proprietors had been called for the very purpose of condemning and altering the policy of management, however, after the deputy-chairman had had a conference with the proposer and seconder of a resolution, there was not a shareholder present who had the courage to bring forth a definite resolution of want of confidence in the Board of Directors, or in the policy of centralised management, which had so ruinously acted upon their most valuable property. The meeting simply ended with a blessing by giving a vote that a salary of £2,000 per annum should be paid to the newly-appointed chairman in consideration of his devoting continuous attention to the affairs of the Company. It was admitted by the deputy-chairman that the only railway experience, so far as he knew, that the newly-appointed chairman had, was gained during the three years he had been a director on the Lancashire and Yorkshire Railway. I thought this was not a very commendatory recommendation, seeing that the only tuition he had had was from the wretched policy of management which this meeting of proprietors was called together to condemn

This reminds me of the time when the shareholders voted to the general manager a substantial advance of salary, with the view of producing better management, but things went gradually worse. We shall see what this additional £2,000 for salary will do.

The result of this special meeting was most disappointing, not only to the public, but to the servants of the Company, who were looking forward to an altered policy of management, something like the old divisional one, which would have restored that efficiency, energy, enterprise, and harmony which are most essential for maintaining the best interests of the Company. I, being anxious to arrest the ruinous tide of policy which was gradually penetrating into the most vital parts of its

valuable property, and also being an old officer, a shareholder, and an earnest wisher for the Company's
prosperity, ventured to write upon the subject to the
deputy-chairman, as follows :—

February 10th, 1883.

Dear Sir,—The question being so strong on the increased working
expenses on our line compared with other companies, I thought, as you
had not been so long a director, it was quite possible that you would not
have observed comparative statements that were made out in years gone
by for the information of the directors ; I therefore enclose three copies
for your information and perusal, for 1870, 1871, and 1872, which were
the last three years the line was worked and managed in three divisions.
At that time the Lancashire and Yorkshire Railway Company held the
highest position in England , but since the alteration in the management, as you no doubt are well aware, the line has not improved in its
position, or been satisfactory to the shareholders. I do think that if you
had similar comparisons made out for the year 1882, you would then
obtain a knowledge of the different railway workings in every particular,
which would serve you in arguing the questions.

I afterwards, as opportunities occurred, drew his attention to the great mischief which centralised management
was doing to the Company's property and had done for
the last ten years I pointed out that the policy had
proved to be most unequal to the requirements of the
densely-populated districts through which the railway ran,
and that such a policy could not possibly or efficiently
supply the various wants of the industrial and immediate
districts. I also suggested to him that it was essentially
necessary that the districts should have a resident
divisional officer ; and indicated that now was an opportune time to arrest depreciation of the property, and to
pacify the proprietors by reverting to the policy of
divisional management.

Directors, July, 1883.

Chairman, John Pearson, Esq
Deputy-Chairman, George John Armytage, Esq.

Thomas Birnes, Esq.	William Henry Hornby, Esq.
Samuel Fielden, Esq	The Rt. Hon. Lord Houghton
William Foster, Esq	S M. Milne, Esq
Edward Green, Esq	James Pilkington, Esq
Theodore Julius Hare, Esq	Henry Yates Thompson, Esq.
William Himners, Esq	

Officers

W. Thorley, General Manager
J Maddock, Superintendent of the Line
Thomas Normington, District Superintendent. *Yorkshire Division.*
Thomas Collier, *Lancashire Division*
W. Livesey, *East Lancashire Division*

A copy of the summer alterations of trains for 1883, emanating from the Central Office of Management, was sent to me to look over and correct, so far as Yorkshire District was concerned. I returned it with the necessary corrections inserted, and suggested some alterations of branch and other trains to meet the requirements asked for by the manufacturers The altered time table was issued to the public, to commence on July 1st. But, as usual, very few of the corrections or suggestions were carried out, which resulted in numerous complaints from the public, and the traffic being diverted to other companies. The usual routine in such cases was put in motion—canvassers sent out to beg back the diverted traffic, and special notices issued, printed in red ink and large type, that special trains would be run at the times the public had previously asked for. It is this sort of blundering and patching up which loses the traffic and increases working expenses.

The meeting for the half-year ending June, 1883, was held at Manchester on Wednesday, August the 8th. The directors declared a dividend of $4\frac{1}{2}$ per cent This being the first appearance at the half-yearly meetings of the newly-appointed chairman, there was a very large attendance of shareholders, expecting to hear of some intended improved policy of management After the new chairman had opened the meeting, he said : " It is probable you may expect me to make some reference to the position I occupy to-day, and to the future administration of the affairs of this Company. I need scarcely remind you that upon the occasion of the last half-yearly meeting our then respected chairman announced his intention to retire from the chair. At a subsequent special meeting a resolution was passed, on the motion of a proprietor holding a large stake in the undertaking, to the effect that the chairman should give his continuous attention to the business of the Company At that time I was abroad, and during my absence my colleagues did me the honour of electing me to this very responsible position. Had I consulted solely my own comfort and inclination, I would certainly have shrunk from taking upon myself duties of so arduous a kind, but as it was represented to me that it was the unanimous desire of my colleagues that I should accept the office, I consented, and to the best of my ability I am prepared to do my utmost in endeavouring to promote your interests, relying upon your forbearance consistent with the unfavourable circumstances which attends my entry upon the duties. As this is the first time I have had the pleasure of meeting so many of my fellow-proprietors, I think it is due to you that I should explain briefly my views as to the course which ought to guide us in the future, and in doing so I desire to speak with perfect firmness and straightforwardness, treating you as fellow-partners, having met together for the purpose of considering our common interest. I do not propose to go into the past, believing that no useful purpose would be served by entering into questions which might give rise to a good deal of unprofitable debate. No doubt, gentlemen, mistakes have been made and opportunities of developing the line have been allowed to go by, but we must bear in mind that some at anyrate of those errors in judgment have arisen from an over desire to consult the wishes of the shareholders. For instance it would have been better if, instead of paying the good dividends of former years, a portion had been retained for the renewal of rolling stock and stations, and in making proper arrangements for facilitating the conduct of the traffic. Had these works been done at that time, they would have been done at a far less cost than they can be done now, and the probability is that you would have been receiving a better dividend to-day. You will remember that during the years I have referred to you received better dividends than the shareholders of the London and North-Western Railway Company received. That company, instead of dividing to the uttermost, acted prudently and put their line in order; and had the same course been adopted in your case, I venture to say there would not have been the difference in the dividends of the two companies that exists at the present time. But my advice is, let bygones be bygones; we cannot recall the past, and we shall act wisely if, instead of deploring it, as is the continual burden of some of the speeches we hear at these meetings, we address ourselves to the future, in resolutely facing our difficulties and in vigorously promoting the required improvements, and in adopting a spirited policy of determination to maintain our position as one of the foremost railways in Great Britain. No doubt our first duty as directors, having charge of this enormous property in trust for the shareholders, is to endeavour to earn for them a fair dividend, but we must not leave out of view the fact that the public, who are our customers, are entitled to proper and sufficient accommodation. In some districts we have, I am sorry to say, a reputation for illiberality, although I don't think this is altogether deserved, for it must be patent to everybody who has observed our line for some time past that we have been doing much to make our line, which you know is for the most part an old one, more in accordance with modern ideas, and in renewing rolling stock and stations. But, gentlemen, I must be frank with you, and say that a great deal yet remains to be done, and that for some time to come there must be a considerable outlay, both on account of capital and revenue. In order that our traffic may be worked efficiently and economically, we must have relief lines in some places and additional sidings and station accommodation in others. The passenger trains, which you know in order to meet the requirements of the public are more numerous and quicker than formerly, come so thickly on some parts of our line that the goods trains have frequently to be shunted, and sometimes for a considerable period, adding very much to the working expenses. Now, this state of things must be remedied. Now, gentlemen, I think I ought to remind you that we have many difficulties to contend with In the first place, our railway passes through a country that rendered its first cost greater per mile than any other in the kingdom. Competition, both by railway and canal, is keen, public requirements and Government interference keep growing. The distance over which our traffic is conveyed is but short, while stations and junctions are numerous, involving a very expensive block system of working. But notwithstanding all these drawbacks, gentlemen, I am by no means desponding as to the future. With such a hive of industry as our line passes through from one end to the other, and with the increased facilities which these works I have indicated we are about to commence will give us,

I believe, by perseverance, judicious expenditure, economy
in working, diligent attention to the requirements of our
customers—in fact, good management, we shall overcome
all our difficulties, and in a few years be able to hand
over to our shareholders a fair return for their invest-
ments. In the meantime I must ask you to give us your
confidence and support. We, the directors, on the other
hand, assure you that nothing shall be wanting on our
part to bring about this desirable result. I have had
little time since my return to go into the details of the
working of each department. But I am happy to tell
you that the chiefs have each assured me of their hearty
co-operation, and I am resolved, with their assistance, to
go into the working of each department with the view of
securing the most economical and efficient management.
I do not propose to relieve these gentlemen of any
responsibility whatever, believing that to obtain good
management the responsibility must rest on the right
shoulders: but, as you have put me in a responsible
position, I intend to make myself master of the details
of the different departments, so that I may be of assistance
to the chiefs, and that any advice I may offer may be of
value to them. Gentlemen, I will now pass on to the
report, and as usual the gist so far as regards the financial
result of the working of the past half-year is in the first
two paragraphs You will see the almost stereotyped
sentence that we have been doing much more work for
less money. This is shown to be the fact by the detailed
figures of the traffic." After having given detailed particulars to the meeting, the chairman continued. "Now,
gentlemen, as regards the working expenses, which
amount to $56\frac{1}{2}$ per cent. I am almost ashamed to come
before you and state this, but it is a fact, and therefore
it must be stated. I do hope, and, in fact, I have every
reason for hoping, that we shall be able to reduce this

considerably in time. With regard to the general
expenses, I have already told you that I intend to go
into details of the management of each department, and
with the assistance of the chiefs and of my colleagues
will do my utmost to reduce those expenses I have
already referred to our Parliamentary work as far as
regards what concerns ourselves in promoting bills, but I
have not referred to what we have done in the way of
opposition. You will see that reference is made in the
report to the Manchester, Sheffield, and Lincolnshire
Railway Company having succeeded in obtaining the
sanction of Parliament for the extension of a railway from
Wigan to Longton, thence running over the West Lancashire to Preston and Southport. Most of you will
know the direction in which this line runs, and I think
you will see that there is something more than Preston
in view. We have reason to believe—and, in fact, Sir
Edward Watkin was kind enough to tell us so in the
address to the shareholders of the Manchester, Sheffield,
and Lincolnshire Railway—that the Blackpool people had
asked him to give them a leg up. To this the directors
of the Lancashire and Yorkshire rather object. We
desire the continuance of a good understanding with the
Manchester, Sheffield, and Lincolnshire Railway Company, and with all railway companies I do not exactly
see, however, how such a feeling is to be maintained if
such aggressive invasions of our district are carried out,
and, although the Lancashire and Yorkshire Company's
policy has hitherto been non-aggressive, I am sure you
will concur with me in saying that if this aggressiveness
be carried on, it may become necessary for the directors
to consider what course to recommend for the protection
of your interest. Now, gentlemen, I think I have said
all that it is needful to say upon this occasion, and I
shall be very glad to give any further information which

any proprietor may require With these remarks I beg
to move the adoption of the resolution, which the
secretary will read."

The Secretary then read the report The Deputy-
Chairman seconded the resolution. The Chairman then
said " Before putting the resolution I will ask if any
proprietor wishes to make any remarks."

Some of the proprietors availed themselves of the
opportunity One of them said Mr. Chairman and
Gentlemen,—I should like to say a few words with
reference to the report We have been told in former
years that we had such a vast amount of traffic offering
that we really could not carry it, but we see now that ten
or twelve years of continuous outlay does not increase our
revenue, neither do our working expenses diminish in
consequence of this great outlay on lines, a great portion
of which are already open for traffic. What is the secret
of this? Now, Leeds, if I may be allowed to use the term,
is the funnel where the traffic over the enormous
gathering ground of the North-Eastern centres, and,
although we run to that town, nearly the whole traffic
coming off the North-Eastern goes over the London and
North-Western, and all the west bound traffic. It appears
to me that this is a state of things which ought to be
remedied. I am told—I cannot exactly get to the bottom
of it—that there is some sort of an agreement or alliance
between this line and the London and North-Western.
It appears to me that that is one of those mysterious
alliances which we sometimes hear of in human affairs,
where one party gets all the advantages, and if the other
protests is threatened with being turned adrift. In fact,
I am told—I don't know whether it is exactly true or
not—that there is a general impression abroad that the
Lancashire and Yorkshire can neither stir hand nor foot
in either of the two counties without having to consult

the London and North-Western. If that is the case, it ought to be remedied.

Another shareholder said I was very much pleased with the address our chairman gave us I say that if the Lancashire and Yorkshire system is properly managed, by spending a large sum of money on increased facilities, it will never be in the power of any passenger to take his traffic away, because it will be so well managed by the Lancashire and Yorkshire that no other people can compete with them. The people are willing to put themselves out of the way to take their traffic away from the Lancashire and Yorkshire just because it is so badly done

Another shareholder said : I quite agree with the sentiments you have expressed that bygones should be bygones. I am not quite sure, after all you have said, that you have entirely satisfied the public or the shareholders how it has come to pass that the Lancashire and Yorkshire has descended from the high position which it occupied a few years ago, and fallen to the low position which it occupies now. Now, sir, it is not ten years ago that the shares of the Lancashire and Yorkshire stood at 160, and the shares of the London and North-Western at 156. The Lancashire and Yorkshire to-day are not worth 118, and the London and North-Western are worth 176. To-day the Lancashire and Yorkshire propose a doubtful 4 per cent dividend, and the London and North-Western are paying 7 per cent. It is very difficult for anybody to understand how such a transformation has been brought about. However, with the attention which you propose to give to every department, I am quite sure that you and the chiefs ought to keep each other in order. It has occurred to me that I could not do better than make some little inquiry into the way in which the North-Western Board managed their business. I have been led to believe that the committees of this board are very large committees, and something tantamount to the whole board They have sectional committees, and the chairman has great control over his colleagues, and I hope, sir, that the time is not far distant, if it has not already arrived, when you will have the same control over yours. As far as possible, each director on the North-Western is made responsible for a certain length of line adjacent to his place of residence.

Another shareholder said · Allow me, Mr. Chairman, to congratulate you this morning on having acknowledged the blunders of the past. I have frequently at this meeting pointed out the cause of the downward course which has been pursued, and you on this occasion have acknowledged that in the main I was right There is one point I should like to draw your special attention to, and that is this During the last ten years there have been six and a half millions expended on lines open for traffic, and four and a half millions, in round numbers, on new lines, and the result of that latter expenditure is that you have a net increase in receipts above expenditure of £2,425 Now, sir, this is what I want to guard against—injudicious expenditure.

It was somewhat gratifying to me to observe that the new chairman, in his first address to the proprietors, admitted that the line had receded from its high position amongst railways owing to the mere lack of management, and also acknowledged the blunders of the past, and asked for a period of forbearance. He also admitted that if my repeated recommendations to construct loop lines, submitted since 1869, had been carried out, the line would have been paying a better dividend to-day, and that he was ashamed to have to state that for the past half-year the working expenses amounted to 56½ per cent. He further admitted that if the

Lancashire and Yorkshire Company had continued the vigorous policy of divisional management similar to that of the London and North-Western, there would not have been the difference in the dividends between the two companies which exists. Notwithstanding this neglect and inefficient management, he had faith, with such a hive of industry as the line passes through, that the increased facilities they were about to commence would enable them by perseverance, judicious expenditure, economy in working, diligent attention to the requirements of our customers—in fact, good management—to overcome all their difficulties.

It baffled all comprehension how the new chairman was going to accomplish all the grand reforms hoped for if he was going to depend upon the chiefs to guide him, those very managers who had during the past ten years reduced the dividends from 9 to 3 per cent. In his remarks to the shareholders, he clearly showed that the depreciation of their property had solely arisen from the want of a vigorous general manager, one who comprehended railway requirements, and had the ability and the will to enforce them through the directors.

The chairman invited remarks upon the report from the shareholders, and one of them asked for an explanation as to why there was no increased revenue, after twelve years' continuous outlay, and diminished working expenses. He was also rather suspicious that this Company did not reap due advantages from the mysterious alliance with the London and North-Western Company.

If this speaker was alluding to the alliance made by the two companies in 1862, I am of the same opinion, that the London and North-Western got the advantage. The revenue also was lost to a great extent in 1873, when central management reduced facilities and increased the railway fares to Blackpool and other places, which diverted the traffic from the principal stations in Yorkshire to Morecambe Bay, Skegness, and other stations on the East Coast; and this created a bad feeling against the Company amongst the residents in Blackpool. They memorialised other companies to come to the rescue by constructing competitive railways; to wit, the new chairman announced at the half-yearly meeting that Sir Edward Watkin had said in his address to the shareholders of the Manchester, Sheffield, and Lincolnshire Railway Company that the Blackpool people had asked him to give them a leg up. Thus it is observable that the Lancashire and Yorkshire Company not only lost revenue, but created a hostile feeling amongst the public against them, as I have already said, while they incurred a great cost in opposing competitive companies in Parliament, to prevent them from obtaining powers to construct new railways. This is something like the dog in the manger; they won't do the work themselves, but rather be at a great expense in preventing the work being done by others.

The new chairman did not suggest the abolition of centralised management, which was very disappointing, not only to the servants on the line, but to the public generally, this policy having proved again and again to have been the cause of the whole mischief on the line. Neither did the proprietors, at the special meeting, propose or suggest any different policy of management, although the meeting had been called for that purpose; they simply complained of the bad management, agreed to the appointment of the new chairman, and awarded him a salary of two thousand a year and the title of managing director. How could the proprietors expect better management, or better dividends, after allowing the wretched policy, which they had so often condemned, to continue? However, time will show the great mistake they have made.

The new chairman did not explain in what way he purposed to alter the policy of management, so as to enable him to carry out the grand changes which he had announced in his address to the shareholders, to ensure bringing the line back to the high position it once held amongst railways. It was clear, however, that he afterwards found it necessary to have further information than that which he had obtained from the chiefs of the central management, whom he had previously consulted, as he had a meeting called for Thursday, October the 4th, 1883, at which all the district officers of the line were to meet him at Manchester. This conferring with the district officers showed the earnestness of his intentions. There was a full meeting, and railway matters were well argued. He impressed upon us all the necessity of rendering him every assistance possible, and he was sure if we all put our shoulders to the wheel we should accomplish the object desired. We one and all acquiesced in his remarks. The next day we each received a copy of instructions for our future guidance. The meeting that day was evidently satisfactory to him, as it led to his paying a personal visit to every station on the line. He was in the Yorkshire Division three days. I accompanied him to all the stations, and explained to him the serious delays occurring both to passenger and goods trains, arising principally through the limited accommodation we had at most of the stations to deal with the numerous trains. I made him aware that with the view of relieving those congested stations and reducing working expenses, I had repeatedly since 1869 made recommendations and submitted plans to construct loop lines and refuge sidings, and said it was still my opinion that was the only course to adopt to ensure safety and punctuality, and to economise the working of locomotive power, especially in working goods trains. He made notes of all the necessary requirements I pointed out to him at the various stations. I further called his attention to the great loss of traffic in both passengers and goods, in consequence of the slow running of passenger trains from Yorkshire in connection with the North-Eastern Railway Company's system at Normanton and Leeds to and from Manchester and Liverpool, and told him that, with a view of keeping the good passenger traffic we had in 1870, I had revised the time of the running of passenger trains, and submitted a service of five express trains to be run each way per day. This recommendation not being backed up or supported by the general manager, the directors had objected to it. However, the London and North-Western Company established a quick service of trains, and they got the traffic. I had repeated similar schemes every year for the better running of passenger trains, but they were always marred by reducing recommendations and adding what was not required, so that when the time table was issued to the public it caused great dissatisfaction, and resulted in traffic being diverted to other companies' lines. The chairman made a note of all these remarks After visiting all the stations we finished at Wakefield, when we had a long talk together upon railway workings generally. When we parted I had a strong impression that he would eventually adopt a policy of divisional management

It was remarked at the last half-yearly meeting that the new chairman had hitherto well succeeded in all his business undertakings. I thought now was an opportune time, on his taking command of this most important railway at a very critical moment in its downward history, not merely to further his own reputation, but to confer an acceptable benefit on all the shareholders of the

Company, some of these being widows and orphans who had to live and be maintained, and could ill afford the dwindling away of their dividends

The first work of constructing double lines of way was done between Thornhill (London and North-Western Junction for Dewsbury and Leeds), passing through Mirfield Station to Heaton Lodge (London and North-Western Junction, for Huddersfield, Stalybridge, and Manchester), but this was done through pressure of the London and North-Western Railway Company, and the first portion was opened on February 3rd, 1884, and the second portion on Monday, October 15th, 1884.

After a great deal of pressure from the Huddersfield Chamber of Commerce, an improved service of trains from Bradford and Huddersfield, _viâ_ Penistone, to Sheffield and London, commenced on March 1st, 1884, which seemed to create some little surprise in the Bradford district As you will observe from the following extract, which appeared in a periodical at the time, it became the general conversation amongst the commercial travellers at the various hotels, and this one in particular, where a number of gentlemen were discussing the best route to London   Some said the Great Northern ; others said the Midland ; when one of the commercial gentlemen, who travelled for a Bradford house, said, " I don't think either the Great Northern or the Midland are in it compared with the new route, both for scenery and shortest time on the journey."   It was asked, "What new route?" The Bradford traveller replied, "The Lancashire and Yorkshire route."   "Just listen to the man," said one, a wool buyer ; "he's talking about going to London by the Lancashire and Yorkshire, and, to all appearances, he's quite sober !"   " I suppose he's thinking of a short cut round by Manchester, or somewhere where he can have a

15

night's rest on the way," observed another of the party, in a tone of intended sarcasm. "You may laugh, gentlemen," said the traveller for the Bradford house, "but I stick to my original statement the most attractive route from Bradford to London is by the Lancashire and Yorkshire." "But what length of time does it take? that's the question," said the wool buyer. "No longer than by the Midland." "Nonsense!" "It's true, for all that; just you try it the next time you're called up to town, any of you." "Well," said one of the speakers, "I've to go up on Monday next, and I'll try it, for I am fond of new experiences." "I'm going up on that day myself" said the wool buyer; "and if you will meet me at the Lancashire and Yorkshire Station, I'm your companion" "So be it," and they shook hands upon it

On Monday, the 10th, the Bradford traveller and his companion met at the Exchange Station, Bradford, and took tickets for London, and travelled by the 1-27 p.m. train. They arrived at, and departed from, Huddersfield at the time recorded in the time table; when the Bradford traveller said to his companion, "Sit you there, with your face towards the engine, and just keep your eyes about you for the next half-hour or so;" and on they went, making remarks and expressions all the way to London, as follows —

"It was not long,' says the person who tells the story, "ere I began to be so deeply interested, that I asked myself what I had been doing all these years not to have explored this region before, as we travelled through tunnellings and rocky cuttings, to veer round the edges of precipices, and dash across lofty bridges; but as you pass forward by Lockwood, Berry Brow, Honley, Brockholes, and other strangely-named places, you are taken through scenes of surpassing loveliness, some of them of an almost alpine character; glen after glen, and ravine after ravine are passed, with pretty manufacturing villages nestling here and there, looking far more pleasing to the eye than the villages of the worsted districts. The situation of some of the mills is picturesque in the extreme, and their surroundings are in perfect keeping. Not only are factories noticeable for their clean and neat aspect, but for their architectural beauty, which, unfortunately, is not too common a feature of this class of building Nature has been so kind, indeed, to the dwellers in these regions, that it would have been nothing short of desecration to have erected mean-looking buildings there. As it is, the whole district seems to have been lovingly and tenderly treated by the traders who have had the building up of its prosperity, and whichever way the eye wanders there is something to be seen that appeals strongly to its sense of beauty.

"'Is there anything on the Great Northern or the Midland to compare with this?' demanded Fred, over and over again, as we passed scene after scene of striking beauty. 'Certainly not,' I confessed. 'Look there!' he would cry; 'what do you think of that?' as we came in sight of a tossing, foaming beck, as it leaped out from the wooded hill side; and at some points we should both be seen with our heads craning out of the window, taking the fullest possible view of some spot of extraordinary charm. Presently we found ourselves rushing through Denby Dale, with an immense panorama stretching to the right and to the left, full of picturesque details; and then we came to a brief halt at Penistone, where we ran into the Manchester, Sheffield, and Lincolnshire line, and so forward to Sheffield, which smoke-hued town we reached about 2-50. 'Now, this is the only awkward part of the journey; there's a few minutes to wait,' said Fred

" At five minutes past three we were off again, this time in a smoking compartment, where Fred was free with his Havanahs 'Now you'll see a bit of splendid running,' he said, as he lit his cigar And I did On we were borne at what it is customary to call 'lightning speed,' past signal boxes, through stations, across meadows, over bridges, into cuttings, along embankments, dashing, steaming, flying through space as if the furies were at our heels. The men at work in the fields turned round to wonder at us, the young lambs in the meadows regarded us with an innocent surprise that was quite charming. The course was perfectly clear Not a signal against us anywhere. And the road was good, the train was comparatively steady, and the carriage was one of luxury From Sheffield onward the scenery became less interesting, and by the time we merged into the Great Northern system at Redford it had become monotonous The prospect was pleasant enough the fields were green, the woods were plentiful, and the houses were pretty, but one square mile of flatness had such a likeness to the next square mile of flatness, that it was impossible to feel that interest in it that we felt in looking upon the changing hills and valleys, glens and waters, which marked the country between Huddersfield and Sheffield. So we smoked and chatted, and were happy in the thought that we were being taken to London as fast as it was possible to be carried consistent with safety ? 'What,' I exclaimed, when we cleared Retford without stopping, 'don't we stop at Redford ?' 'No, sir,' said Fred, 'we don't. You'll not find many beastly stoppages by this train, I can assure you.' No, we did not stop until we got to Grantham, the run was clear from Sheffield. 'This is about half-way, I think,' I ventured to say. 'Right,' said Fred; 'about another hundred miles, and then we're there.' 'Tickets, gentlemen, please,' said a collector, opening the door. 'For London,' I said, not wishing to have the trouble of looking in all my pockets before I found the bit of pasteboard, as is my general experience. 'You give them up here sir,' said the collector. 'And how shall I do when I get to London,' I inquired. 'Oh, King's Cross is the next stop, sir,' said the man, and, somewhat bewildered with the business, I found my ticket, and handed it to him, following it up with the offer of a very small silver coin. 'No, thank you, sir,' he said, and passed on, leaving me more amazed than ever. 'This beats all,' I remarked. 'I knew you'd be astonished before you'd done,' said Fred. We now set off once more, and were not long in attaining our former 'lightning' speed, which was kept up with little variation throughout the remainder of the journey. When we neared Peterborough the train slackened, and I was not slow to remind Fred that he had evidently been mistaken about the non-stopping. He merely smiled, and the train went slowly forward through the station; then the steam was put on again, and we dashed forward through Huntingdon, St. Neot's, Biggleswade, and Hitchin in turn, and the time seemed very short since we left Bradford. 'Something like a run this, eh?' said my friend, and I acknowledged that it could not be better. After leaving the chalk hills of Hitchin we are soon diving through the tunnels at a 'deil-take-the-hindmost' pace; the straggling village of Stevenage is passed, the stately towers of Knebworth are seen looming through wooded landscape, the picturesque hollow in which lies the lovely village of Welwyn is left behind, then come the suburban retreats of Barnet, Oakleigh Park, and Wood Green; then the shuddering walls of Colney Hatch glide by, then Finsbury Park and Holloway recede from the gaze; and, finally, you are brought to a standstill in King's Cross Station, and the journey is completed. 'What's the time?' asked Fred. 'Half-past five,' I said, 'to the minute Splendid. Just five hours' 'And if they'll only alter that Sheffield delay, they'll equal the Great Northern as to time, while as to pleasantness and comfort they'll beat everybody. Which way will you return?' 'The same way, to a certainty, and I'm much obliged to you for showing me another way of going to London.'"

On Thursday, May 1st, 1884, the new portion of the Victoria Railway Station, at Manchester, which had been three or four years in course of construction, was opened, when a direct service of express trains was run in communication with York, by Normanton, and the North-Eastern Company's system. This was a great improvement upon the express train service adopted in 1880, so far as York was concerned, for traffic by Normanton But central management again ignored the traffic from the North-Eastern system via Leeds, by destroying the connections at Holbeck Junction, with altering the trains from Leeds to Manchester and Liverpool, and cutting off the connection, thereby giving a great advantage to the London and North-Western Company. The York service afforded additional facilities to the travelling public This showed a tendency to a policy of progress. But why a service of trains was not established, as I had so often recommended, to run through from Liverpool to Hull, via Wakefield and Goole, I could never understand. I had frequently pointed out that such a through service between the two great seaport towns was most essential to the Company. With the view of giving the public at the local stations in Yorkshire the opportunity of participating in the facilities given by running the improved express train service, I submitted a dovetailed local train service to run between Halifax, Sowerby Bridge, and Rochdale, and *vice versa*, in direct connection at those junctions with the revised express train service. But central management objected to the scheme. However, when the new time-table books were issued to the public, the passengers at the local stations were very much annoyed to find that their requirements had been so much neglected; in fact, they were ignored altogether. This caused loud complaints and diversion of traffic, and again led, as usual, to additional cost to the Company, through having to patch up, by putting on additional trains, to meet the local requirements

The improved facilities given by the express train service, which commenced on May 1st, took the public by surprise, and brought forth this comment from the *Leeds Mercury* of Tuesday May 6th.

IMPROVEMENTS ON THE LANCASHIRE AND YORKSHIRE RAILWAY.

The management of the Lancashire and Yorkshire Railway in the past has not always escaped adverse criticism. There is probably no railway company, at least in the North of England, which has had so many hard words to bear. The lack of punctuality in the running of trains, comfortless carriages, frequent changes, even on a journey of no great distance, and long waiting in cheerless stations—these and other alleged inconveniences have formed the subjects of complaint from an exacting travelling public. The enterprise of other railway companies has tended to place the Lancashire and Yorkshire in a still more unfavourable light. It could not be denied that the directorate — assuming that the adverse criticism reached their ears—bore it with a good deal of equanimity. They did not seem in any great hurry to adopt the advice which was from time to time gratuitously offered by those who had first abused them. Those most concerned would perhaps admit that there was some ground for complaint, and that it was not to be wondered at that comparisons unfavourable to the Company should be made between its management and that of other companies. The times have changed, however, and condemnation of the Lancashire and Yorkshire, such as we have been accustomed to hear, in now unjust. There are few companies in England which are at present paying greater regard for the convenience of the public than the Lancashire and Yorkshire. The spirit of enterprise has taken possession of those who are entrusted with its management, and they are now as energetic as they were formerly considered to be tardy in doing what they deemed to be necessary for the improvement and development of their important system. This gratifying change followed the appointment of the new chairman, a man of quick perception and energetic disposition. He has apparently gained the full confidence of his colleagues, who with him have seen that it would be imprudent any longer to allow rival companies to continue unchallenged in their competition for public favour. To a share of that favour the Lancashire and Yorkshire is now entitled, and its rivals will have to look to their laurels in view of what it still proposes to undertake. During a comparatively short time great improvements have been made in some of the principal stations on the line. There has also much been done to facilitate the interchange of traffic with other companies. The situation of many of the towns which the Lancashire and Yorkshire passes, as well as the unceasing railway service which their industrial life demands, render it very difficult to carry on the traffic without subjecting passengers to the inconvenience of changing trains. It is not like a great through line. What can be done to obviate inconvenience in this respect is being undertaken, and the success which has already attended efforts in this direction inspires one with hope that the Company will be able to accomplish still more. At the beginning of the present month a new service of through express trains between Manchester, Liverpool, and York was commenced, and by means of it the great port on the West has practically been brought much nearer the East Coast than it was before, connection with the North-Eastern at the ancient capital of Yorkshire giving ready access to the towns lying upon that system. The character of the carriages of the Lancashire and Yorkshire has been greatly improved; very few of the old comfortless vehicles are now in use. Within a short period half of the whole of this part of the Company's rolling stock has been renewed, and now no more comfortable carriages than these new ones are to be found on any of our lines of railway. The trains are fitted with the vacuum automatic brake, and in all other respects those running on the through lines are well appointed. We understand that so far the new service has been conducted with punctuality. Judging from the experience of other railway companies which have sought to serve the public interests as far as practicable, the Lancashire and Yorkshire will receive its reward for the enterprise it is now displaying.

This writer's comment and criticism on the past twelve years' policy of management would not be very pleasant reading or very gratifying to the managers. The management having unfortunately been placed in the hands of those who had not the capacity to comprehend good railway generalship, brought about the whole mischief that has overtaken the interests of the Company. They never produced any schemes that would either increase receipts or reduce working expenses, and in making traffic arrangements with other companies seemed, as a rule, to be out-generalled. In trying also to convince the travelling public that they were made for the railways, and not the railways for the public, they got the Company into bad repute Even when the central management produced the new service of express trains to run between Liverpool, Manchester, and York, they did not display much regard for the convenience of their important local traffic. However, the above writer seems by his concluding remarks to have faith in some altered policy of management since the appointment of the new chairman. He says great improvements have already been made, and the spirit of enterprise has taken possession of those who are entrusted with the management, and that it would be imprudent any longer to allow rival companies to continue unchallenged their competition for public favour. I fear I cannot join in the faith which the writer of the comment expresses, as central management policy will prevent, as hitherto, the Company gaining public favour.

The new chairman will have to contend with the same policy of management, with the same managers, which have been condemned by the shareholders for the last twelve years, and so long as this policy continues the new chairman will never raise the Company as he desires, to the position it formerly held amongst railways.

The first half-yearly meeting for 1884 was held at Manchester on the 11th August, when Mr. John Pearson, the newly-appointed chairman, presided. The report of the directors was submitted, and by consent of the meeting taken as read

The Chairman, in moving the adoption of the report, said he trusted that the result of the working of the past half-year, as shown in the report and accounts, would not be disappointing to the shareholders. When they considered that at the commencement of the past half-year there was a strike among the cotton operatives in the East Lancashire district, which for several weeks seriously affected their traffic, and when they considered that during the whole of the half-year trade had been in a very depressed condition, and taking also into consideration the circumstances attending the Company at this particular period of its history, when they had to pay interest upon a large amount of additional capital, he thought, taking all these matters into account, they would come to the conclusion that to maintain the same dividend as they paid last year, and to carry forward £11,000 more, was not an unsatisfactory state of things, It was true that a 4 per cent dividend was not a high dividend, but he had no doubt the shareholders remembered that twelve months ago, when he took the position of chairman, he reviewed the circumstances under which they were situated as a Company, and ventured to intimate an opinion that for several years to come they must not expect increased dividends. He was still of that opinion. But while saying that he by no means took a pessimistic view of the future. All that he wanted to do was to guard them against being too expectant, and to desire them to have patience with the directors. They might be assured that whatever dividend was recommended would be honestly earned, and that the

directors would not attempt to bolster it up by neglecting
to do any repairs or make additions to works and stock
which they might consider in the interest of the Company. Some of the additional passenger train mileage
and expense was consequent upon the new service of
quick trains which they had established from Liverpool
and Manchester to Bradford, Leeds, and York. Before the
Company took that step they were under a disadvantage
as regarded the traffic exchanged with the London and
North-Western Railway Company. By the new arrangement they had made, to run through to York by way of
Normanton, they were placed in as good a position as any
other company for obtaining a fair share of the traffic of
the very large and important districts served by the
North-Eastern Railway Company. He was happy to
add that even at so early a period of the work, only
two months, it had proved a success. He was also glad
to say the reduction of costs of working expenses had
been, as compared with the previous year, from 56 to 54
per cent. He thought that should give them encouragement. Although they were at a very large outlay at the
present time, that expenditure would not last for ever,
they hoped the increased business would last, and that
when business did revive they hoped to derive advantage
from their increased facilities. He mentioned that to
show that they were justified in the outlay they were
incurring. In conclusion, he desired, on behalf of himself
and colleagues, to express their hearty acknowledgment
to those gentlemen who had the executive management
of this great enterprise, for their zealous and efficient
services, and for their loyalty in carrying out the policy
of the directors. While saying this for the chiefs, they
desired also to remember those officers who, although
subordinate to the chiefs, had most efficiently seconded
their efforts. He had had many opportunities during

the past twelve months of noticing the conduct of their officers, and could not refrain from bearing testimony to their constant endeavour to do all in their power to promote the interests of the Company. Only those who had to do with the inner workings of railways knew the incessant demands on the thought and anxious care of the responsible officers, and this was especially the case on their line. There was no railway in the kingdom which required greater vigilance, watchfulness, and skill in its management, than the Lancashire and Yorkshire Railway.

The way in which the chairman reviewed his past experience was quite satisfactory to the proprietors, and one of them proposed a vote of thanks to the chairman, deputy-chairman, directors, and officials of the Company. He congratulated the chairman upon the very admirable manner in which he had conducted the affairs of the Company since his appointment to the office which he now held. The shareholders were deeply grateful to him for the present position of the Company. He was pleased also to hear the chairman refer to the valuable services of the officials. The resolution was seconded and passed unanimously. The meeting terminated harmoniously.

From the chairman's remarks in his review of his first year's experience, he seems to have comprehended the cause which had led to diminished receipts and dividends, and the cause of the increased working expenses, which had gradually grown since the altered policy of management adopted in May, 1871, namely, the want of a more vigorous and far-seeing manager, who would have prevented the line from drifting into such a chaos of confusion. He asked the shareholders not to be too expectant, and to have patience, and give him time to lift the broken-down management out of the rut. The chairman eulogised the central management, yet he did not forget the subordinate officers, as he termed them. No doubt this remembrance emanated from his having visited the several districts, having the district officers with him, and inspecting every station, where he made notes of all suggestions or alterations, with a view of giving better facilities in dealing with the traffic to and from the stations This one visit was more than the general manager had given (so far as Yorkshire was concerned), for the past twelve years. In my conversation with the chairman, with a view of curtailing working expenses, I learned that he was in favour of abolishing second-class accommodation In his concluding remarks he verifies my opinion of the necessity of a responsible officer, with power to act, being located in the districts.

I remember Saturday, the 16th August, a great reform demonstration was held in Thornes Park, Wakefield, when the managing committee applied to the railway companies—the Great Northern and the Lancashire and Yorkshire—to offer facilities for conveying the public to Wakefield from the various districts.

On Saturday, August 23rd, I noticed in the *Wakefield Express* the following comment upon railway facilities. "With one or two exceptions, there is no place of importance within a five-mile radius of Wakefield which is not in direct railway communication with the town, and therefore the committee naturally turned to the two chief companies—the Great Northern and the Lancashire and Yorkshire—and asked for the usual facilities of conveyance for the several contingents who were to take part in the demonstration. The first-named company readily forwarded the views of the committee, and, with their proverbial courtesy and efficiency, made such arrangements as met the requirements of the visitors The same cannot be said of the latter For reasons which are obvious enough, as little as possible consistent with the show of compliance was done, and done, too, in such a fashion that it might perhaps have been better left undone."

On perusal of the above comment, it reminded me of the one I had read previously, which appeared in the *Leeds Mercury* of May 6th, where the writer said: "A gratifying change has taken place in the management of the Lancashire and Yorkshire Railway Company. They are going in for competition for gaining public favour." It is evident that this policy had not yet reached Yorkshire up to this date August 23rd, although a quick service of express trains had been running since May 1st. However, if the management had carried out my suggestions, that would have saved the comment which appeared in the *Wakefield Express*.

In September, 1884, I submitted a series of alterations of trains for the better working, with a view of punctuality and earning more money. The new time tables were issued on the 1st of October, but minus my suggestions, which again brought forth loud complaints, the public being very much dissatisfied when the usual process of patching-up had to be resorted to.

On October 17th I received a letter from the office of central management, complaining of the passenger trains in the Yorkshire district running so unpunctually. I replied on the 18th October, drawing their attention to the alterations of the running of trains submitted in September, and to my often-repeated recommendations for ensuring the more regular working of passenger traffic, and asserting that had the suggestions been carried out in detail the result would have been most satisfactory to the public, and more beneficial from a financial point of view to the Company. "These observations are verified by the return which you have sent me for the fortnight ending the 9th October. The few of my suggestions which were carried out proved of incalculable benefit, both to the public and the Company."

I have often observed that at the Chamber of Commerce meetings at Halifax and Huddersfield the railway facilities are generally brought under discussion, and complaints often made about being shut out from direct railway communication between North and South. These two large and important towns, with their various industries, are placed at a great disadvantage, being situated on what they term side lines, and are constantly agitating for some company to come forward and construct the requisite link. Several schemes have been devised, and applications made for Parliamentary powers to do so, at a great cost to the Lancashire and Yorkshire Company in opposing them. However, after the new line of railway was opened by the Great Northern Company between Halifax and Keighley, in 1884, I devised and submitted to the central management a service of express trains, three each way, to run between Keighley and Sheffield, viâ Halifax, Huddersfield, and Penistone, in direct connection at Keighley with the Midland Company's express trains to and from Edinburgh and the North; and at Sheffield with the Manchester, Sheffield, and Lincolnshire, and the Great Northern Railway Companies' express trains to London and the South, the distance of the through journey being about 410 miles. This may be compared with the distance by the Great Northern Railway Company from London, viâ York, to Edinburgh. Arrangements could have been made to run through trains.

I could not help but note at the end of 1884—although a new chairman had been appointed, whose anxiety was to improve the system of managing the railway—that he seemed to have forgotten he had undertaken to do this under the old method of management, which was in force prior to his appointment With all his efforts and good intentions, central management still continued their blundering As usual, when a day excursion was about to be run to Blackpool or elsewhere, it was often the case that the bills were issued to the public the day before the trip was to be run, which lost the traffic and increased the working expenses.

The meeting for the half-year ending December 31st, 1884, was held on Wednesday, the 11th of February, 1885. The Chairman, in his opening remarks to the shareholders, said " I will ask you if you will take the report as read. In moving the adoption of the report, I have to remark that the past half-year has been one of considerable anxiety to the directors of the Lancashire and Yorkshire Railway Company It is to be hoped that, taking into consideration the very depressed state of trade and the weight of capital expenditure we are incurring for necessary improvements and extensions we are absolutely required to make, you will consider the account we have presented to you and the dividend we recommend, 4½ per cent, is fairly satisfactory. Our gross receipts exceed those of the corresponding half-year by £20,000, and although it has cost us a considerable amount of extra working expenses to help up and increase the traffic, I think it is a very encouraging proof of the vitality of the Lancashire and Yorkshire Railway that even in times like these the additional facilities we are giving to the public bear fruit in augmented receipts I am convinced that it is largely due to the increased facilities we are giving that our receipts have kept up as they have done, and that it would be very false economy if we were to diminish the accommodation. You must not suppose from these remarks that I am defending extravagance. No one can be more anxious for the economical working of the line than your directors. But we feel strongly that in adopting the policy of acting up to the reasonable requirements of the travelling public we are promoting the true interests of the Company. The popularity of third-class travelling continues to grow. We quite recognise the change in the habits of the travelling public, and must do our best to meet the altered conditions of things by providing the requisite progression of third-class accommodation. That a change must be made, either by the abolition of the first and second classes, one or both, or by a modification of the fares or some other scheme to induce people to ride in these classes, is very certain. We have arranged with the London and North-Western Railway Company to recommend the making of a line, about five miles long, from Kirkham to Blackpool. This will shorten the distance three miles and save a large expenditure which would otherwise have to be made at Poulton. It will place us in a position to work the large traffic to and from Blackpool efficiently. It will also, we think, effectually minimise the effect of the opposition threatened us by the line for which powers were obtained last session. You all know that Blackpool is becoming the most popular seaside resort for our Lancashire and Yorkshire people, and the traffic is enormous. When the line we now propose is completed it is difficult to see what probability there can be even of 1 per cent dividend for our opponents. I have only further to say that you may rest quite satisfied that your directors are fully alive to responsibilities they have to face in the present circumstances of the Company, and that they recognise that the present rate of capital expenditure renders it difficult to keep up the dividend. But they feel that in order to put

16

the system into a proper position they cannot recommend any deviation from the policy I indicated, when I first took the chair at the meeting in August, 1883 We think that when the works absolutely required have been completed the proprietors may fairly look for a reward for the patience they are now exercising."

Several shareholders expressed their opinion on the chairman's speech. One of them said " There is one subject to which you have referred which seems to me to demand serious attention, and that is the question of first, second, and third class fares, You have already intimated to us the extent to which third-class passengers have increased during the past half-year, and the decrease of first and second class. It does appear to me to be really a very serious matter, and I fear that railways have largely contributed to the manufacture of third-class passengers out of first-class material. It should be the endeavour of this Company to make first-class passengers out of third-class material I am quite aware that any alterations you might think proper to make should have your very serious consideration. I am sorry you have not a better dividend for us this time, but I hope it will be the smallest dividend you will ever have to offer us."

Another shareholder said : " I am very much pleased to hear the chairman allude to the necessity of action on the subject of first and second class fares. I have at some of our previous meetings ventured to ventilate the subject. I was then told that the matter was under the serious consideration of the Board. I had supposed that it was still under the serious consideration of the Board, but I have seen no attempt made to grapple with the subject. I see that in the present half-year we have lost in first-class traffic £11,000, and in second-class traffic £2,740. The decrease shows no sign of diminution, but rather of an increase. I think the natural inclination of the people is to ride in a higher class than they can afford, but when they look at the difference, they say, ' Oh ! the accommodation in the second and third class is the same ; I won't pay the extra fare.' It is all very well to keep using expressions of sympathy with shareholders, and throw the responsibility for low dividends on bad trade, but it's my opinion there are other reasons for a great part of the diminution "

Another shareholder said : " I scarcely agree to closing the capital account of a great and growing Company like this ; we must go on. To do this means allowing other Companies to come in and take a portion of our traffic. We cannot afford to do it. There is no question about it that the extensions you are now making and which you have alluded to this morning, and to which also reference is made in the report, are to my mind wise and sensible extensions. If you can choke off the competitive line to Blackpool by shortening your own line between the manufacturing districts and Blackpool, you do a very good thing for the Company. I agree very much with what the last speaker said as to first, second, and third class passengers He recommended you to have a conference with other railway companies Why, sir, did the Midland Railway confer ? Did they consult with any other company when they did away with their second-class passengers altogether ? No. A gentleman behind me says it was a mistake. It has not been proved to be a mistake for the Midland Company, at all events. Now, sir, I was not sorry when I saw in your report that you had at last disentangled yourself from the arms and embraces of the London and North-Western Railway Company, and had got into the arms of their great rival, the Midland. We know that the London and North-Western have in times past invaded the Lancashire and Yorkshire districts, and it appears that the Midland now want to have a share of the good things of this district. Well, sir, I for one quite approve of the agreement you have made with the Midland Company. No doubt, though the terms are not disclosed, you are getting a proper *quid pro quo*, because you are giving them a considerable advantage. You say we are admitting them on terms—on very satisfactory terms. I hope it may be so You may depend upon it it will be a great thing for the Midland to have that through traffic to Scotland. I hope that my friend behind me may be gratified in having an increased dividend. This is about the poorest dividend we have had, but we had better say, Let us be thankful for small mercies."

My observations upon the remarks made both by the chairman and the shareholder at the half-yearly meeting showed that the chairman had been working hard this half-year to improve the Company's affairs, but the fates seemed against him His remarks to the proprietors showed that he had struggled hard, with the view to produce a more favourable report to the meeting, although surrounded with difficulties. He said he had faith that in time the results would be more favourable. Of course the management of the line had gradually gone from bad to worse for the last twelve years and must take some time to regain its former position. His views were correct that giving greater facilities to the public would increase the receipts, and giving more extended accommodation for working the traffic would reduce delays and working expenses I was glad he admitted that Blackpool was the most popular seaside resort for Lancashire and Yorkshire people. He also grasped the necessity of giving the travelling public every possible facility in getting to and from Blackpool, with a view of keeping other railway companies out. He also saw the necessity of reversing the policy adopted by the central management in 1872-3, which policy created a hostile feeling, and did a great injury to the Company when they advertised prohibitory fares to Blackpool. Since that time we have lost traffic, and the Company had been at a great expense in trying to prevent competition. A great deal was said at this meeting upon the question of abolishing second-class accommodation. Neither the chairman nor the shareholders seemed to be prepared to express an opinion, but they were all satisfied that it was necessary that some alteration should be made. One of the shareholders said that before the Lancashire and Yorkshire Company could abolish second-class accommodation they would have to confer with other companies. Another shareholder said that the Midland Company adopted the principle without conferring with any company. The latter remark was not correct, as from the time of my suggesting the principle in 1869 the subject had often been argued at the railway officers' meetings, and prior to the Midland Company adopting the principle a railway directors' meeting was held in London to decide the question, and a well-known director represented the Lancashire and Yorkshire Company.

On his return from London he called at my office at Wakefield, and said to me that he attended this meeting, and the majority was against the abolition. He further said that he had voted with the majority. I replied I was very sorry he had done so, as I was the first railway officer to suggest the abolition, and I explained to him my reasons, which were that I had noticed that second-class carriages as a rule were hauled about the line comparatively empty, and to abolish them would save the cost of building such a carriage and thousands of miles of empty running over the line. It was my opinion that if adopted the shareholders would receive a better dividend by at least 1 per cent every year.

I observed that one of the shareholders was curious to know if the arrangements made with the Midland Railway company would be to the advantage of this Company. The chairman explained that this Company would receive 75 per cent and £81,500 a year for the use of Manchester, Liverpool, and Blackburn Stations. This arrangement was open to question. Why should we pay another company for working our local traffic, and bring on to an already congested line additional trains, which must increase the delays and necessitate extra cost in working our own traffic? It was my opinion that this Company would never improve the dividend from the arrangements made with the Midland Railway Company.

The Hull, Barnsley, and West Riding Junction Railway was opened July, 1885, forming a junction with the Lancashire and Yorkshire Railway Company's line at a point $1\frac{1}{2}$ miles on the Goole side of Hensall Station. They run a service of passenger trains from Hull to and from Hensall Station, in connection with the Lancashire and Yorkshire Company's trains to and from Wakefield. I suggested this service should run through to Wakefield and form a connection there with the whole of our system. However, eventually the service of passenger trains was extended to Knottingley.

On July 16th H.R.H. the Prince of Wales travelled from Ripon to Preston. The London and North-Western Railway Company provided the royal saloons and carriages for the special, which started from Ripon at 10-10 a.m., *via* Leeds, and left Leeds at 10-55 a.m., passing off the London and North-Western line on to the Lancashire and Yorkshire Company's line, passing Mirfield Station, and again joining the London and North-Western line at Heaton Lodge junction, all passing off with punctuality and safety.

The first half-yearly general meeting of the proprietors

of the Lancashire and Yorkshire Railway Company for 1885 was held at Manchester on Monday, August 10th. The Chairman said that, while other railway companies have had to report diminished revenues from the working of the past half-year, arising from the continued depressed state of trade, most of them have had the satisfaction of being able to state that their working expenses have also been more or less reduced I am sorry to say this is not the case with the Lancashire and Yorkshire, and have no doubt that, since the issue of our report and accounts, your attention has been directed to this, and you have naturally asked why, with a diminution of receipts, have increased expenses been incurred? I will endeavour to explain clearly and frankly the causes which have led to this unfavourable result, and will give you details as to the terms of increased cost, with the reason of such increases But first, you may like to have some particulars as to the receipts. The decrease in our receipts is in round numbers £25,000, arising principally from badness of trade, and to some extent from the greater competition to which we are now subjected. I will now explain the increase in the working expenses I need hardly say we have not to wait until the end of the half-year to know how the expenses are going on, as I indicated two years ago, when I first had the honour to preside It is absolutely necessary that our property should be put into and maintained in a thoroughly efficient condition. You know we are carrying out that line of action, and are making great efforts to increase the efficiency of our working, and to improve our rolling stock. Inconvenient though it may be, especially in times like the present, we believe that it will be found to be the true interests of the Company in the long run to go forward in the course we are pursuing. The report of the directors was approved and confirmed. One of the shareholders said : Will you just allow me to make a remark or two on what has fallen from you to-day, especially with reference to the abolition of second-class fares I want you to be kind enough just to consider what you are about before you make that arrangement. Also I want to refer again to the fact that I can see no sufficient supervision that many people travel over your line without having paid for their tickets at all. I have pretty frequently to travel on the Lancashire and Yorkshire, and, as I have said, I do not see that any one properly looks after the tickets. Now, so far as my observation goes, that matter is not attended to on this line. Every gentleman who has a business to look after knows that these small matters make a great deal of difference at the end of the year. Small in themselves, they mount up to a very large sum at the end of the year And it is a further indication when you find little matters like these unattended to, that there is not a proper system in operation in other directions, and that the same thing prevails in other departments of the line and its management It is all very easy to come to a meeting and say bad trade is the cause, but that is a very vague statement, which wants a bit of something definite to convince people that they have no reason to expect a better return."

The chairman was again in a difficulty in finding a satisfactory explanation for the shareholders as to the cause of the diminished receipts with increased working expenses. He seemed to claim sympathy because other companies had to report diminished revenues. He was very sorry to say it was not the case with the Lancashire and Yorkshire to have reduced the working expenses. They had been spending money in maintaining the line in a thoroughly efficient condition Surely, after spending three and a half millions of money since 1872, the line ought to have been in an efficient condition, if the money had been properly laid out, to have reduced the working expenses. He seemed to forget that other companies had also to battle with bad trade and maintain their lines in a thoroughly efficient condition. Although bad trade prevailed, more money would have been made if suggestions submitted to the central management had been carried out; also working expenses would have been reduced by abolishing second-class accommodation and reducing train mileage in accordance with schemes submitted. As to having to deal with competition, this had been brought upon the company by bad management. There was also money lost and locomotive power wasted by neglecting to get excursion bills out in sufficient time, announcing day trips to the public, to the various resorts. These bills were rarely posted more than one or two days before the excursions were run I noticed on Saturday, the 6th of June, that the time for special trains to be run from stations in Yorkshire to Blackpool and Littleborough was inserted in the special workings when the bills in this case were never got out This is a sample of central management. I was pleased to observe that one of the shareholders called the attention of the chairman to the lax way in which passengers' tickets were examined and collected, although I had submitted schemes from time to time which, if they had been adopted, would have prevented frauds which were continually taking place such as those described by the shareholder

The first portion of the new station at Halifax was opened on Sunday, October the 25th, 1885, and completed and opened on June 1st, 1886.

An important revising of the passenger train service was done in September, particularly the Sunday service, which was to take effect on the 1st October I submitted a list of alterations so far as Yorkshire was concerned, but, as usual, when the revision of the train service was published to the public to take effect on October 1st, 1885, the alterations to the trains previously submitted were not made. This brought forth loud complaints from the travelling public, who insisted that the alterations which had been made were not at all suitable for business purposes. The old system of patching up the inadequate service of trains began with issuing small bills with red letters, stating that extended additional trains would be run with a view to meet the several complaints This blundering led to the increase of the working expenses, and to the dissatisfaction of the public

The meeting for the half-year ending December, 1885, was held at Manchester on Wednesday, February 10th, 1886. The chairman, in moving the adoption of the report, said: "It is most disappointing to have to offer you so serious a decline in the dividend as $1\frac{1}{4}$ per cent. It is our misfortune that while so much necessary reconstruction and additional work is going on we have to face so large a diminution in the receipts for the half-year as £59,854. The principal reason of the decline is one over which we have no control—the exceptionally protracted depression in trade. The working expenses are undoubtedly very high, but the difficulty of reducing them is great. Shareholders will remember the loud complaints made against the Company three or four years ago, not only by the public outside but by the shareholders at these meetings Complaints were made of want of punctuality of trains and slowness in speed, bad carriages and stations, insufficient train service and delays in transit, and delivery of goods. All these things are charged against the management, but I venture to say that the same causes of complaint do not now exist. The locomotive expenses are very unsatisfactory, and, I fear, there is no hope of doing this work economically until we get out of our old and badly contrived workshops at Miles Platting and Bury. We look for a great improvement when we get into our new works at Horwich. Having had some 18 months' experience of our express train service from Manchester and Liverpool to York and Leeds in connection with the North-Eastern Railway Company's system throughout the East Coast, and believing that it is appreciated by the public, and largely conduces to the interests of this Company, we have concluded an arrangement on fair terms with the North-Eastern Company, by which we continue to run our trains over their lines from Normanton to York, with the use of the station at York and intermediate stations. The agreement is for a term of 25 years The advantage of this arrangement is that we practically extend our line without any additional capital cost "

Some of the shareholders expressed their opinion on the chairman's remarks on the report. One of them said : "I find that since 1882 the capital account of this Company has been increased by nearly four millions of money, and the dividend has fallen from from 5 to $3\frac{1}{4}$ per cent That is mainly due to the reckless expenditure of capital, and the extravagant working expenses of this Company. If your expenses had been on the same ratio as the Midland and other companies you would have been able to pay $2\frac{1}{2}$ per cent more this time. It is time the shareholders roused themselves and refused to be satisfied with such a state of things as you lay before them from time to time. You may depend upon it that if this policy which is being pursued is continued, there will soon be no dividend at all. I have warned the directors at meeting after meeting of this Company, and have shown them their errors of omission and commission and bad management. It is time for a change and that change must come. Out of every one pound you are receiving for goods and passengers. parcels, mails, minerals, and live stock 5s goes in traffic expenses. That is a point which wants attention. I have called the attention of the board repeatedly to it We have the highest traffic expenses of any company in the country, and we ought to have the lowest I move that a committee of shareholders be appointed to confer with the directors on the present position of the Company"

Another shareholder, in seconding the motion, said· "I think there has been an enormous amount of extravagance in this Company I hope gentlemen will not go away from this meeting without carrying into effect what is now suggested—appointing a committee to look into matters, and the vast extravagance that this Company has committed itself to. We came here to-day to hear a very fine speech from the chairman, and to receive a paltry dividend of $3\frac{1}{4}$ per cent I say the time has come when this reckless management ought to be stopped."

Another shareholder said . "A good many years ago I was an occasional speaker at our half-yearly meetings, and the great grievance at that time was the antiquated character of the directors. That grievance to some extent has been set aside, nevertheless the result is not at all satisfactory. Instead of improving we seem to go from bad to worse It must be remembered that in 1872 the dividend for the corresponding six months was no less than $9\frac{1}{4}$ per cent, and to-day we are asked to receive $3\frac{1}{4}$ per cent, very little better than one-third. That is a melancholy state of things I was reading the report of the Great Western Company, which shows a falling off in revenue of £88,000 on the last six months, but, on the other hand they absolutely saved £28,000 in their working expenses. There is one shareholder who has just made a practical speech on this subject, he has certainly made some statements which, I think, require answering. He foresees that if we go on at this rate we shall have no dividend at all. I am not here to suggest any remedy. I can only speak of what is the feeling outside, and the feeling amongst shareholders is that we really want a radical change. I, for my part, am quite willing to consent to this committee which has been proposed. I think it is high time we took some action in the matter."

Another shareholder said: "Since 1872 we have increased our capital account £16,000,000, and practically spent it on the same line, whilst I do not see that our net traffic earnings have increased anything at all. Our working expenses this half-year are 57 per cent, and any gentleman who knows what working expenses are must be of opinion that this is a most outrageous state of things. Other companies can reduce their working expenses. Whether the committee that is proposed will do any good or not I do not know."

Another shareholder said: "Our friends have anticipated a good deal of what I had proposed to say on this occasion regarding the condition of the Company; but in view of the disastrous state of affairs here, and considering that we are pointed at by the finger of scorn by other companies, I want to enforce what has been previously so well said, and also to get from you, Mr. Chairman, a somewhat more satisfactory answer than has hitherto been given to us. The question is, 'What is the cause of our reduced dividend, and is it in any way attributable to preventible causes, or is it altogether beyond the control of the directors?' I have been a shareholder from the beginning, and have had great experience at these meetings, and I ask, 'How is it, seeing that we have done so much less work, that our charges have increased so enormously?' Twelve months ago our expenses were 55 per cent, and now, with much less traffic, they have got to 57½ per cent. That is a point that is not satisfactory to me I want a proper explanation as to why, with such a diminished traffic, the working expenses should have gone up so enormously."

Another shareholder said : " I was very glad to see that the first gentleman who spoke proposed to form a committee. Now, as I understand that gentleman, what he suggests is that the committee is to work, not in hostility to the directors, but, if possible, to assist them "

Another shareholder said : " I do not think that if we sit here an hour or two longer we can get another ¼ per cent dividend, therefore our best plan is to accept whatever we can get, angry though we may be, and go home. A few meetings ago I ventured to express an opinion that if the directors went on at the reckless rate they were going, the shares would be down at par. I am not quite a prophet, but I think to-day they are 102, and I thought they would have been only 100. I cannot say that I am disappointed at the dividend ; it is just what one might have expected—nay, indeed, I scarcely expected it to be as much as 3¾ per cent."

It is evident from the strong remarks made upon the management by the shareholders, that stormy half-yearly meetings were again coming to the front, and that the directors were finding out that the remedy they applied in 1883, by appointing a managing director at £2 000 a year, had not been successful, neither was it successful when they advanced the general manager's salary a few years before The remedy does not lie in giving large salaries to certain individuals, but in adopting a policy of divisional management, which was in force prior to 1872, when the directors paid a dividend of 9½ per cent.

The shareholders were not satisfied with the chairman's

stereotyped explanation of bad trade, which he alleged was the cause of the gradually-diminished receipts and dividends, with increased working expenses. One of them asked for a more definite explanation, and wished to know if it was in any way attributable to preventible causes, or was it altogether beyond the control of the directors? The chairman gave no reply, but I think he might have replied, because, in my opinion, there are, in addition to bad trade, other causes which have been created since the adoption of centralised management, that have eaten up all vitality, energy, and perseverance throughout the whole line, the management being placed in the hands of persons who had not the ability to comprehend the necessary requirements of an increasing and industrial population. This was, I think, the real cause which led to the Company's unpopularity and diminished dividends since 1872. The public were continually complaining of the inadequate railway facilities given them, which had a tendency to seriously curtail their various industries. No heed being taken of their complaints, and the railway assistance not being forthcoming, brought forth ill feeling, agitation, and memorialising other companies to make new lines and invade the district. This led to the traffic being diverted from us to other railways and the canal; also to this Company giving running powers to other companies over our already-congested system.

I could never comprehend why this Company should not have given the public the necessary facilities, and done the work themselves, and so increased our own receipts, and prevented additional trains being brought on to the line by other companies, which added to delays and greatly impeded the working of our traffic. I have often noticed the additional trains brought on to our line by other companies being allowed to proceed immediately in front of our own trains, taking up and putting down traffic for local stations, on which, it is said, they are allowed 25 per cent for working it, whilst our own trains follow immediately after comparatively empty, thus showing that the money collected on our own local line goes partly to the other companies. Such arrangements result in diminished receipts, and this, coupled with the increased working expenses, is another cause of diminished dividends.

A shareholder stated that since 1872 the capital account had been increased by £16,000,000, and the chairman explained this had been applied in increasing the rolling stock, extending the accommodation at the various stations on the line, and adopting the improvements required by the Board of Trade in preparing the line to be worked on the block system. I thought this a remarkable explanation, as very little had been spent out of this £16,000,000 in constructing refuge sidings, loop lines, and extending siding accommodation at the most congested places on the line in Yorkshire, which works were recommended in 1869 with a view of facilitating the traffic and reducing working expenses.

Another shareholder complained of an enormous sum of money being expended on new engines. In twelve months, he said, they had had 77 new engines, and had spent £138,000 The chairman might have explained that many more engines were required to meet the serious delays which occurred, particularly to goods trains, from the want of siding accommodation, as already described It often happened that an engine sent out for its 10 hours day's work was, through delays, 15 hours or 20 hours in completing its journey. In preparing the line to be worked on the block system in Yorkshire, a large amount of money was wasted for want of a practical man who could comprehend the requirements before the various places for alterations were handed over to the contractors. I could not help observing that when alterations were in progress they had to be done two or three times over before they were made workable, particularly in building signal cabins and fitting up the signals. Similar waste of money took place in regard to many stations which have been rebuilt and altered, and yet the accommodation at the various stations altered is not equal to the requirements for dealing with the increasing passenger traffic, nor for facilitating the through traffic past the stations This is another cause of increased expenditure and diminished dividends

Another shareholder called attention to the fact that in 1872 the Company paid a dividend of not less than $9\frac{1}{4}$ per cent. He might have followed this up and said that at that time the line was worked on the principle of divisional management, and since then dividends had dwindled to $3\frac{1}{4}$ per cent, although the population and trade had enormously increased throughout the line

The chairman replied, and said it was an unfortunate circumstance for the Company that they ever paid $9\frac{1}{4}$ per cent. He further intimated that if the Company had spent more money on extensions at that time he would have had a 6 per cent line to day.

It was quite true it would have been better if more money had been spent in extensions at that date, but the principal cause of the low dividend arose through reversing the policy of earning money since 1872, after which time the policy had been extravagant and wasteful

This meeting was a very stormy one, and attended by a large number of shareholders. A resolution was proposed and seconded that a committee of shareholders be appointed to confer with the directors on the present position of the Company's affairs, but it was lost by a

17

small majority. At this time I wondered what were the feelings of the general manager, who was then seated with the directors, and who heard the unpleasant remarks made by the shareholders. I also wondered whether the conversation I had had with him in May, 1871, was still fresh in his recollection, when I said, "If the line is going to be worked upon the principle it seems to me to be intended, the dividend would be reduced to 4 per cent, and there would be trouble for someone, and I should be sorry to see a 10 per cent line so reduced for the want of better management."

On Monday the 15th March, 1886, the shares were below par. They were quoted in the newspapers at $99\frac{1}{2}$, whilst in March, 1872, they stood at $165\frac{1}{2}$.

The meeting for the half-year ending June 30th, 1886, was held at Manchester on Wednesday, 11th of August. The Chairman said · "As you may have observed from the report, this is the hundredth half-yearly meeting of this Company, and it may be interesting to the shareholders if I give a few figures to show the growth and progress of the undertaking. The Act for the construction of the Manchester and Leeds Railway, which was the original title of the Company, although it never owned a line to Leeds, was obtained in 1836, and the capital authorised by that Act was £1,733,000. This has increased in the last 50 years to the amount shown in our accounts to-day, £41,778,000. The line was opened to Littleborough in 1839, and to Normanton in 1841 I find that from that year dividends have been paid every half-year continuously varying in rate according to the circumstances of the times, but averaging for the whole period $5\frac{1}{4}$ per cent per annum. The first dividend paid was at the rate of 6 per cent, and in four years afterwards (in 1845) it reached 8 per cent, while in 1850 it fell to 2 per cent, again rising, with occasional fluctuations, until 1872, when £8 7s. 6d. was paid. Since then, as you know, there has been a gradual decline to what we recommend for your acceptance to-day (3 per cent). Although it would be unwise to say that we had reached the lowest, I think we may fairly and reasonably entertain the hope that as after 1851 there was a steady improvement, so, when we have gone through the difficulties which have occasioned the fall of dividend, there will be a recovery. I must, however, acknowledge the exertions which our officers have made to carry out our instructions to economise in every way. The results are manifest in the reduction in the working expenses for the past half-year, and there will be no relaxation of our efforts in that direction for the future. I beg to move that the report of the directors now read be received and adopted."

Some of the shareholders were again dissatisfied with the chairman's explanation as to the cause of the diminished dividend. One of them said, " I should like to know how it is that our working expenses are higher this half-year as against the June half-year in 1882 in your goods traffic, although you have a decrease in the receipts of £43,000. I find that in the June half-year of 1882 you paid a dividend at the rate of $3\frac{1}{4}$ per cent. The dividend has dwindled down at the present time to 3 per cent, but I find, taking the items for 1882 and 1886, commencing with salaries and other expenses, that you have an increase of £8,302 in 1886 over 1882, although you have such a large reduction in goods traffic. That does not look like a diminution of expenses. I have no doubt the depression in trade is aggravated by competition. I pointed out in February, 1880, that the London and North-Western Railway Company were taking the greater part of the North-Eastern traffic, but I am glad to find that since that time you have taken measures by which this Company are getting their fair share of that traffic   With the traffic on a line like the Lancashire and Yorkshire you ought to pay a dividend at any rate equal to the London and North-Western, and it would do so if properly managed "

Another shareholder said . " I suggest that possibly you could see your way to graduate the salaries of the higher officials, not that they might receive less than they do now, but more.   Let them have more because the dividend is more.   It requires so much energy to attend to every detail, and the public have such organisations to pull us down that you really require, on the part of your officials, the utmost energy in order to be able thoroughly to cope with them, and to meet them on fair terms on behalf of the shareholders "

The chairman again found himself in a difficulty how to give a satisfactory explanation to the shareholders as to the real cause of the dwindling dividends   He still continued to express his opinion that the cause was bad trade   He seemed to overlook the fact that other companies had also to battle with bad trade, and incur expenses in maintaining the efficiency of working the traffic over their railways, and yet they still managed to pay a fairly satisfactory dividend.   The chairman did not seem to grasp the inner workings of a railway, or else the central management was too much for him, as this management still seemed to waste money in many ways in carrying out what were intended to be improvements in working the railway.

In April and June, with a view of economising the working, and giving some improved facilities to the travelling public, and inducements to local excursionists, I submitted recommendations with a view of increasing the receipts in the district, but, as usual, the central management declined to entertain the suggestions.   It had been the policy to ignore local suggestions from the officers who were acquainted with all the public requirements, and the most able to make working arrangements with economy. These are particulars which I have no doubt have been kept from the knowledge of the chairman

The meeting for the half-year, ending 31st of December, 1886, was held at Manchester, on Wednesday, 16th February, 1887 The deputy-chairman presided. He said . " Before commencing the business, I am sorry to have to announce that our chairman is unable, owing to the state of his health, to be present. For some months he has been suffering, but we had hoped that he would have been sufficiently recovered to have presided to - day. Unfortunately, however, this is not the case. In consequence of his absence the duty of presiding at this meeting devolves upon me. I will now ask the secretary to read the notice of the meeting " The seal was affixed to the register of shareholders The deputy-chairman then said · " I can congratulate you on the somewhat better state of affairs than last year, there having been the very substantial increase of £39,000 in the gross receipts, and the additional traffic has been worked with an increased expense of only £987, which enables the directors to declare a dividend at the rate of 4 per cent. You are probably aware that under the provision of one of our Acts of Parliament, it is enacted that when this Company shall have paid an average dividend of 8 per cent for three consecutive years, the Board of Trade may revise rates as would be likely to reduce the profits to 8 per cent, and you may be quite sure that we shall not surrender this position without a struggle I cannot conclude without telling you how much we are indebted to our officials for the circumstances which have enabled us so materially to reduce the percentage of our working expenses. They have all worked with a thorough will and a hearty desire to promote your welfare It would be invidious to select any one department; they have all done their duty We intend, if possible, to continue the steady policy which we think we have got on foot, and to avoid alternate fits of heavy expenditure and parsimony, and I venture to think if we can do this and keep on the present good terms we are on with our neighbours, the shareholders will have no cause to regret the confidence they have placed in us "

This was a very quiet meeting. It is clear that the shareholders had made up their minds to be satisfied with what they could get. However, a few remarks were made by the shareholders. One of them said. "On the statement you have made to us to-day, we may, I think, congratulate ourselves and the directors that the statement is one of which we have all a good right to be satisfied' Another one said· "It is somewhat disappointing that so many as half-a-dozen accidents have occurred during the half-year, especially when we consider the enormous sums spent in providing signalling apparatus, a fine permanent way, good rolling stock, and the best brakes in the country. In view of all this it is, I say, a little disappointing that we should have so many accidents ' The resolution was put and adopted.

The deputy-chairman in his remarks to the shareholders appeared to be quite jubilant at having achieved, as he thought, a marvel in having a substantial increase of £89,000, at an increased expense of only £987. It did not seem to occur to him that in such a densely-populated district as that through which the line ran, with its various and numerous industries, that there should be any difficulty in showing such increases yearly, or even more than £89,000. The deputy-chairman was so delighted with such an unusual occurrence that he was led to say it was the largest increase of any railway in the kingdom He said he was sure they had now got on a proper track, and intended, if possible, to continue that steady policy which they thought they had got on foot, also to avoid alternate fits of heavy expenditure and parsimony. The shareholders seemed to be fairly satisfied with those remarks. I also thought with the shareholders that a better time was coming, and decided to test the question with a view to assist the chairman in carrying out the steady policy which he said they had got on foot, knowing the dissatisfaction which existed amongst the travelling public, because of the inadequate local passenger train service, and their complaints not being attended to, which resulted in their travelling less upon our lines, and also diverting their goods traffic to other companies. I again revised the local service of ordinary trains by dove-tailing them in connection, at the junctions, with all the express trains east and west. I also renewed schemes which I had for several years placed before the central management for extended facilities to the excursionists from Yorkshire stations to Blackpool, Southport, and the west coast during the summer season. These schemes embraced the whole of our stations in Yorkshire district, including Sheffield and other stations from the M. S. and L. and Hull and Barnsley Co.'s lines. But when submitted to the central management for adoption in April, 1887, I received a letter on April 21st, with the usual rebuff, "not agreed to." This brought forth the following reply from me. "I have perused your letter containing the list of answers you have sent me respecting my suggestions for train alterations, after which I could arrive at no other conclusion than that I never saw such an attempt to frustrate the best interests of the Company. I proposed nothing in the train alterations but what was practicable and required to serve the public convenience, which would have been to the best interests of the Company. However, I note your decision."

From my observations, centralised management never did devise schemes for earning more money, or even adopt methods for keeping what traffic they had. Whatever they had done in the way of making money, had been forced upon them from the outside public, and that was the true cause of dwindling dividends since 1872. Their policy had been well developed in spending money extravagantly, not only in the working expenses, but in carrying out extensions, &c.

BOARD OF DIRECTORS AND OFFICERS, JUNE, 1887.

Directors.

Chairman, George John Armytage, Esq
Deputy-Chairman, William Tunstill, Esq

Heywood Bright, Esq	S M. Milne, Esq
Louis John Crossley, Esq	Joshua Radcliffe. Esq.
Samuel Fielding, Esq	Sir David Radcliffe
Sir Edward Green, Bart	John Ramsbottom, Esq.
William Himmers, Esq	Hy Yates Thompson, Esq.
Wm. Hy Hornby, Esq	

Officers

General Manager, W Thorley, Esq
Passenger Superintendent, J Maddock, Esq
Central District Passenger Superintendent, J Bolland, Esq
Yorkshire District Passenger Superintendent, Thos Normington, Esq
East Lancashire District Passenger Superintendent, Jno Whitehall, Esq

On Wednesday, 10th August, 1887, the half-yearly meeting ending June 30th, was held at Manchester, and a dividend declared of 3¾ per cent. The Chairman said · "At the commencement of the business of the last half-yearly meeting I had to announce that our chairman (Mr. Pearson) was unable owing to the state of his health at that time to be present I expressed a hope that his health would soon be completely restored, but I regret to say that that hope has not been realised, and it becomes my painful duty to report to you that he never recovered from the illness that he had suffered from. No words of mine can express to you the great loss you have incurred by his death. His whole-heartedness in the interests of this Company was far beyond the ordinary qualifications of mankind, while his kindnesses, good nature, and courtesy, made working with him a pleasure which those who have not experienced it cannot understand. His thoughts at the latter part of his life were wrapped up in this Company, and almost to his last day he employed himself in consulting plans and reading reports relating to our businesses. The directors at their first meeting after his death sent a resolution of condolence to his family, and it has occurred to me that we, as proprietors, at our first meeting, would naturally wish to place on record our feeling at the loss the Company has sustained, and express our sympathy with Mr. Pearson's family, whose grief we can only measure by our own loss. I therefore beg to move 'That the proprietors present desire to express their deep regret at the loss the Company had sustained by the death of the late chairman (Mr. Pearson), and to record their high appreciation of the unremitting zeal and energy and great ability which he devoted to the business of the Company, and, further, that the chairman be requested to convey to his widow and family the assurance of the sympathy of the shareholders in their bereavement ' "

Mr Alderman Walmsley (shareholder) said : " I feel highly honoured in being requested by you to be the seconder of this motion. I much regret that it has not fallen into more able hands, but I will not give way to any gentleman in my respect for the late chairman, and show a desire to pay him the last compliment it is open to us to pay him, and at the same time we may to some extent give comfort to his widow and family. I am sure that all the shareholders as well as myself must have been highly gratified with the way in which Mr Pearson infused new life and vigour into the Lancashire and Yorkshire Board. Would that he could have lived to see carried out the schemes which he began. But I live in hopes that the new life and energy to which I have referred may not have died out with the late chairman, and that you, sir, holding the position which he has held, will profit by the good example he set, and that that infusion may spread over the whole Lancashire and Yorkshire Board I second the resolution with great pleasure."

Another shareholder said "I am quite sure there is one feeling among us about the loss we have sustained Mr Pearson sacrificed his life to the anxiety which, as the chairman of this company, fell upon him Mr. Pearson had confidence in the future of the Company The result contemplated by his policy must be waited for, it cannot be hastily gathered, but must be the slow fruit of time. While we regret our loss we hope that the business of the Company will not suffer in consequence."

The resolution was carried unanimously

The chairman then moved the adoption of the report He said ' On referring to the report of previous half-yearly meetings I find it is just four years ago when the late Mr Pearson first presided, and on that occasion he referred to what he considered was the proper course to adopt in the future administration of the Company, and he laid down the principle that the line, works, and stock of the Company should be placed in a thoroughly good condition and so maintained, and as this is the first occasion on which I have had the honour to preside as chairman, you will no doubt expect that I should also give you some indication of the policy which, in my opinion, should guide us in the management of the affairs of the Company. I have no hesitation in saying that the principle expressed by our late chairman, on the occasion referred to, embraces in every way my own views on this subject, and I believe I am correct in saying that they have received the approval of the proprietors generally. But, while saying this, I feel bound to remind you that the conditions under which railway companies now work are such that keeping down expenses is daily becoming more difficult. However, our working expenses have been 1 per cent less than a year ago, and for the past half-year we had the very handsome increase of £100,000."

A shareholder said, "I have listened with very great pleasure to your speech—I mean to the delivery of it I may say that if these gentlemen do not go home to-day pleased with the position of the Company, it will not be because you have not endeavoured to make them pleased with it. Now, I have not been in this room for four and a half years. A policy was adopted then which I tried hard to stop, but the majority of the shareholders agreed to that policy, and a new gentleman was placed at the head of affairs, and I do not think it fair, when a new course is sketched out, for gentlemen to offer a factious opposition to the carrying out of that course, but to see, fairly, whether that course has resulted in the prosperity of the Company as was then anticipated, and as indicated by you this morning With the prosperity that you have named I disagree, and I am very sorry that Mr. Pearson is not here I had far rather he had been in that chair than yourself to-day, though I feel quite satisfied that you are able to meet anything that can be laid before the shareholders to-day. I have been looking into the matter in connection with the policy pursued by the Board under Mr. Baines for four years before Mr. Pearson took the helm, and for four years afterwards, and I have drawn my own conclusions from it. I leave it with the shareholders to either be satisfied or not satisfied with the progress which has been made during the last four years I find that Mr. Baines declared from that chair in 1880 a dividend of 5 per cent I find that the net earnings—the earnings that ought to pay interest on borrowed money, and shares, and preferred shares—were £612,117. To-day you have declared a dividend of 3¾ per cent and the net earnings have been £652,388. Here you have an increase in net earnings of £40,271, and you have a decrease in dividend of 1¼ per cent Perhaps these gentlemen, when they get home, will look into their reports and examine them to see if they can come to the same conclusion that you have to-day, namely, that we are going on very comfortably and ought to rest satisfied. Now, you talk about the flourishing way in which this business is being conducted. Why, the fact is that for the last four years, under the chairmanship of Mr. Baines, the shareholders received in dividends 20 per cent. In the four years of improved progress, which has been so much eulogised by our chairman this morning, improved management has resulted in our receiving 17 per cent, or 3 per cent less than under the management of Mr. Baines I find that in 1880 you had sixteen directors, and that they received £5,000 for their services. I find also that the manager, accountant, secretary, and clerks in the head office in 1880 received £22,900 for their services. I find now that with thirteen directors they receive £6,500, or with three directors less they receive £1,500 more. I find further, that the manager, accountant, treasurer, secretary, and clerks received in 1887 £25,911, or an increase of £3,011. Now, you will see, gentlemen, that while your dividends are going down their salaries are going up I suppose I shall be informed that this increase is owing to the salary given to the late managing director; in other words, there are two Richmonds in the field—two persons to manage your affairs, and the result of the management is this, they have increased your expenditure while you have £103,000 more capital to pay 1 per cent upon, and have reduced your dividend, as a consequence, $1\frac{1}{4}$ per cent. You directors are placed there simply because you occupy positions in the country, and have respectable connections, and large connections, and the next thing you think is this, 'Is he quiet; can we manage him; has he got no ideas that he will want to thrust forward, if he has we will keep him off.' There is no business qualification required to make up a director or manager."

Another shareholder remarked, "I am sure that the shareholders as a body will agree with me that the paltry sum paid to Mr. Pearson for the hard work he has done for this railway has not compensated his family for the life given, for, as far as I can judge, he killed himself in looking after our interests."

I noted one of the shareholders remarked, that since 1880 the directors, managers, and others in the head office had had an increase in pay to the amount of £4,511, while at the same time the shareholders' dividends were dwindling down.

He might have gone further, and said that there was another class of men connected with the railway whose dividends were dwindling down, that since 1878 a reduction in staff at stations, and wages reduced of the under-paid servants on the line, had taken effect not less than three times   This comparison shows that bad management does not affect the managers financially.

The death of Mr. James Pearson, the chairman, was much regretted by the railway servants, and seemed to cast a gloom throughout the whole line, as we were all looking forward to see important reforms introduced, which would have led to something like divisional management, as was in force prior to 1872. He worked hard with a view to carry out the policy he declared at his first meeting in August, 1883, but finding the strong prejudice set against reforms by the central management, and the dividend still dwindling down, and working expenses growing, no doubt had its effect upon his breakdown in health and unexpected death The mistake was made by the shareholders at the special general meeting held in March, 1883. That meeting, instead of appointing a managing director at £2,000 a year, ought first to have broken down the wretched management which had existed for the past fifteen years, and which the shareholders had denounced at every half-yearly meeting. That management, named centralised management, which had wrought so much mischief upon their valuable property, was too much for any one man to battle with and bring back the concern to the high position it once held amongst railways. If a resolution had been passed at that meeting abolishing centralised management and restoring divisional management as formerly, under the direction of Mr. Pearson, the shareholders would have done some good for the Company and themselves, and have obtained railway experience which would have enabled Mr Pearson to carry out the policy he declared at that meeting, and he no doubt would have been alive now. The chairman at the opening of the meeting spoke very feelingly when referring to the death of Mr. Pearson, and expressed his sense of the value of his work in many ways in enhancing the interests of the Company, in which remarks I quite concurred I could not but admire the way in which the chairman eulogised the officers of the Company for their zeal and energy in looking after the Company's interests, and thought this would hardly compare favourably with the suggestions and schemes which had been submitted for the Company's interests to the central management, which had met with the usual rebuff, "not agreed to," and which brought forth my letter dated April 23rd, 1887. My view was the chairman would have to obtain a better knowledge of the inner workings of central management before a satisfactory dividend could be realised for the shareholders

From a conversation I had had with Mr. Pearson I had reason to believe that he would, with a view of reducing working expenses, have abolished second class accommodation and adopted the principle of two classes only, namely first and third; also that he was paving the way to again adopt the policy of divisional management. At any rate, had he been living at the time of the general manager's death, in 1891, some alteration in the management would certainly have taken effect. He was determined to adopt a line of policy which would lead to the prosperity of the Company, and his unexpected death was a great loss in many ways, particularly to the shareholders.

One of the shareholders severely criticised the management of the Company, and exposed many defects. He said he could not understand the Company paying a 5 per cent dividend upon net earnings of £612,117 and yet only paid a dividend of $3\frac{1}{4}$ per cent upon net earnings of £652,388. He also considered something was wrong in paying salaries to two general managers, and complained about £11,000,000 being laid out which did not produce 1 per cent for the Company. I quite agreed with the shareholder that some of those millions had not been judiciously laid out. Some of the millions might have been spent in widening the lines at the most congested places by constructing loops and refuge sidings, which would have prevented the serious delays which daily occurred, particularly of the goods trains. This would have had a tendency to ensure the goods traffic having a more punctual delivery. There would also have been fewer engines required to work the traffic, which would have materially reduced the working expenses.

On Wednesday, July 20th, 1887, the general manager summoned an officers' meeting, at Manchester, to meet the newly-appointed chairman in the boardroom. I attended for Yorkshire district. The chairman declared the policy on which he intended working the railway, which would be the same laid down by the late Mr. Pearson, and he hoped that every officer would render him that assistance which would ensure the line being worked satisfactorily, and he would be glad to hear any remarks they might wish to make. Several of the officers took the opportunity, and made appropriate remarks on the working of railways. I remarked: "You are the eighth chairman I have had the pleasure to serve under. It has always been my study and endeavour to devise schemes and give suggestions which would work out to the best interests of the Company, and I have, in times past, received the best thanks of the then board of directors I shall still continue to submit suggestions and schemes which I consider, if carried out, will be to the best interests of the Company, so long as I remain in the service." The meeting ended harmoniously.

On January 23rd, 1888, for the second time I met the Duke of Clarence and Avondale, at Normanton, on his way from York to Barnsley He was on a visit to Wentworth Castle. I took charge of the special train from Normanton to Wakefield and Barnsley, arriving there safely and with punctuality.

The half-year ending December 31st, 1887, the general meeting of proprietors was held at Manchester, on Wednesday, February 15th, 1888. G. J Armytage, Esq., the chairman, said . "I am very glad to meet you this half-year with a better report than we have had for

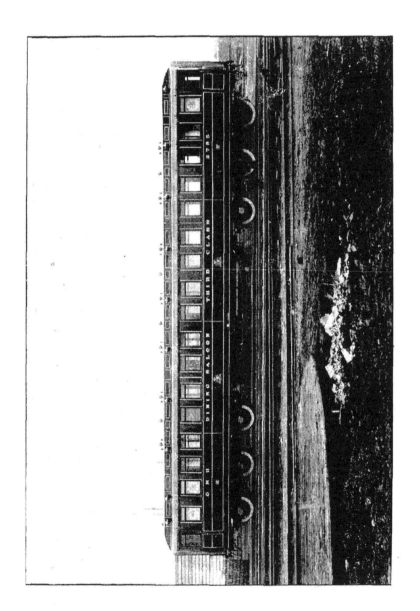

MODERN THIRD-CLASS DINING SALOON CARRIAGE (1895).

some time past, and to be able to declare a dividend of 4¾ per cent, which is a higher rate of dividend to the extent of ¾ per cent more than at the corresponding period last year; but I should not like to raise your hopes too high, for there can be little doubt that the increased amount, £79,034, arises from the successful exhibition which has been held in Manchester. The working expenses have increased by £13,878. This is the first occasion on which the receipts for one half-year have exceeded two millions of money, and I congratulate you on this circumstance "

The chairman announced to the shareholders that there had been an increase in receipts of £79,000, which enabled them to declare a dividend at the rate of 4¾ per cent. This seemed to have pacified the shareholders to some extent, as only one or two made remarks, which were in reference to having expended eleven and a half millions of money which only realised 1½ per cent. I was rather glad to find that the chairman did acknowledge that the increased receipts had arisen from the Manchester Exhibition, and not from ordinary traffic. This increased dividend came at a very opportune time, as the chairman and deputy-chairman had to be re-elected as directors of the Company.

Mr. Tunstill, the deputy-chairman, said : " I now move that Mr. George J. Armytage be re-elected as a director of this Company. In doing so, I beg to be allowed to say that a more honest, single-minded, and pure man as a public man does not exist ; and as to his capability in respect to his chairmanship of the board, you might ride a horse to death and not find such a man. It gives me very great pleasure to propose his re-election as a director of the Company."

A shareholder said . " I beg leave to second the nomination, and to endorse every word uttered by my predecessor in commendation of the chairman."

18

The chairman (Mr. G. J Armytage), then said : "I thank you very much for this mark of your confidence; and I have to propose to you that Mr. William Tunstill be re-elected a director of this Company. I can say for him ten times as much as he said for me, and it will be sufficient for me to tell you what a very happy thing it is for me and the directors to have such a colleague. I hope you will re elect him without exception."

One of the shareholders seconded the resolution. The resolution was carried unanimously.

Mr. Tunstill said : "Gentlemen, you have had a great opportunity of changing the policy of this board to-day; you could have refused to reappoint the chairman and deputy-chairman, and then I think you might have gone on new lines : you have not chosen to do so, and I thank you."

One of the shareholders said : "During the ten years ending 1887, I find you have expended eleven and a half millions of money, and the receipts on that expenditure do not quite equal $1\frac{1}{2}$ per cent, so that the difference between what you are paying for the money you have raised (eleven and a half millions) and the earnings, has to come out of the pockets of the ordinary shareholders. Now, it is time the directors gave strict attention to this matter of capital expenditure, and put their foot down upon it, for, however good may be the earning power, there is a limit to it. Adding year by year a million to your capital account, the Lancashire and Yorkshire Company will be, as it is, one of the poorest-paying lines in the country, considering the large amount of traffic—it has a traffic which exceeds that of any other provincial line in the country. If this traffic was worked at the ratio of other companies, there would be better results to the shareholders "

Another shareholder said "I have not risen for the

purpose of uttering complaints, but to draw attention to an ominous paragraph in the report, that you are going for powers by a new bill to raise capital of one and a half millions, together with the usual borrowing powers. I did not think a year and a half ago that we were then within a measurable distance of getting towards the close of our large capital expenditure. The late chairman, I believe, led us to think that we were within a measurable distance. Here, gentlemen, we have a demand for no less than two millions. What is it for? The chairman has not explained." At this point the chairman called out, "I cannot hear you" The shareholder continued : "It seems to me, gentlemen, if the directors had come before us twelve months ago with this proposal they would have met with a rather hostile reception." At this point the chairman again complained that he could not hear. The shareholder continued : "I think the directors would not have ventured to come before us with a bill proposing to go in for so large a capital expenditure twelve months ago You have picked your opportunity very well. We have had a good year, but the increased traffic is very much to be attributed to exceptional circumstances. You have had a charming exhibition in Manchester, which, as the chairman has said, has materially contributed to the receipts. The result of all these fortunate circumstances is that the total amount of dividend for last year is fully $4\frac{1}{2}$ per cent. You cannot take the half-year and say it is $4\frac{3}{4}$, and I am afraid we cannot look for this prosperity to go on. The state of our capital account is not satisfactory. I see from account No. 1 we have a total unused stock of £350,000 only with the Liverpool station unfinished ; with the Pendleton and Hindley railway only half finished ; with the Blackburn Station unfinished ; Bradford Station unfinished ; and, I have no doubt, sundry other little lines. I cannot come to any other conclusion but that these works, authorised by Acts of Parliament, have exceeded their estimate." The chairman here again called out: "I cannot hear you." The shareholder replied: "I cannot come to any other conclusion than that the estimates under which you are authorised to make these works by previous Acts are fallacious; that, in fact, the works have exceeded the estimates." The shareholder continued, and said "The chairman was recently present at the cutting of the first sod of the Halifax high level line, and must have heard the remark of a railway director present, who stated their great anxiety was to cut down capital expenditure." The chairman again called out, "I cannot really hear a word that you say, and I am not deaf." The shareholder said; "I have pretty nearly finished my remarks, tell me what you did not hear."

The 4¾ per cent dividend proved to be a great pacifier to the shareholders, although one of them said they had not earned more than 4½ per cent; but the 4¾ per cent was an advantage to the chairman and directors on the re-election of the chairman and deputy-chairman, for directors who nominated themselves. It was quite perceivable how they eulogised each other, and from the remarks made by the chairman and deputy-chairman on returning thanks for being elected it was quite evident that they comprehended the necessity of some altered policy of management, and rather feared the shareholders might have availed themselves of the opportunity to force a change. Nevertheless, I liked the remark made by the deputy-chairman, as it gave me some hope that the directors were beginning to perceive that the policy of management adopted since 1872 was gradually consuming all chances of prosperity to the Company. This ruinous policy of management had been apparent to the shareholders for some time, hence the severe criticism at the half-yearly meetings. The few strong remarks made by one of the shareholders were evidently too strong for the chairman, as he repeatedly interrupted them by saying, "I cannot hear you." It may be convenient to some people, when strong remarks are made, to be hard of hearing.

On Tuesday, August 7th, 1888, His Royal Highness Prince Albert Victor visited the Yorkshire Agricultural Show, held at Huddersfield. He travelled from York by the 9-50 a.m. ordinary train to Mirfield. I made up a special train there to convey His Royal Highness forward, which I took charge of, and left Mirfield at 11-15 a.m., arriving at Huddersfield at 11-25 a m. I afterwards took charge of the special train, which consisted of a Great Northern saloon and breakvan, which conveyed His Royal Highness through to London. It left Huddersfield at 3 p.m. the same day, arriving at Penistone at 3-25 p.m., the saloon being attached at Penistone to the 3-51 p m. Great Northern ordinary train to London

In February, 1888, it was considered desirable to reduce engine mileage, with a view to reducing the working expenses. I submitted a scheme for Yorkshire in March, which reduced the mileage to the extent of over two engines' work, and still maintained an efficient service for the travelling public; in fact, it improved materially the local service between Halifax and Rochdale, which had often been memorialised for, but when submitted to the central management I received the usual reply "could not be agreed to." However, a portion of the suggestions were adopted, which spoilt the whole scheme, and after the time book was issued to the public it simply called forth loud complaints The usual mode was adopted to patch up the defects by running additional trains, which resulted in more cost than if there had been no alterations made.

The half-year ending June, 1888, the general meeting of proprietors was held at Manchester, on Wednesday, the 15th August, 1888. Mr G J. Armytage, chairman, said : "In moving the adoption of the report I propose to explain to you as usual the principal features in the accounts in the order in which they are entered. In the first place we have increased our capital account during the half-year by £277,612, and we have expended on our main line and branches, and other lines and works in course of construction, £389,282, against the estimate of £510,608 In the revenue account our receipts show an increase of £53,864. You will find that this increase is almost entirely in goods and minerals, the passenger traffic being less than in the corresponding half-year, notwithstanding a good Whitweek traffic, and notwithstanding that there has been an additional day in the half-year. Our expenses on revenue account have increased £32,978, and this increase is divided in pretty even proportions amongst the various spending departments. Let me tell you that every inch of your system is completed with the block system and signals interlocked, and, as I previously told you, every carriage is fitted with the automatic vacuum brake. All that we can do is being done to make travelling as safe as possible, and it is a pleasure to find such a satisfactory result in the reduction of this account. You will see by the report the Midland Company has commenced from the 1st July running with Scotch traffic to and from our stations in Liverpool and Manchester, so that in the current half-year in future we shall not only receive the rent they pay us for the use of our stations, but also the proportion of the receipts, that we have agreed with them for the use of our line. I will now only allude to the satisfactory assistance which the Company have received from its officers. The more I know them the more I feel how much they have your interest at heart, and I am sure you can ask them to do no more for you than to continue to conduct your business in the future as well as they certainly are doing at present. I should have been pleased if we could have managed to have increased our dividend slightly, but I think you will agree with me that it is preferable to have good property in good condition with improving prospects than to strain a dividend at the risk of not making provisions for the perfect maintenance of the property. I now beg to move the first resolution."

Some of the shareholders were dissatisfied with the dividend of 3¾ per cent, and one of them said : " You have an increased traffic of £53,800, and the whole of that increase goes in working expenses and additional interest upon capital expenditure, and you require to draw from the balance drawn from last year's account to the extent of £7,800 to enable you to pay 3¾ per cent this half year; and you have been constructing sorting sidings at Aintree to marshal the goods wagons at Liverpool. There was to be a great flourish of trumpets at the opening of the sidings, but lo ! they would not work, and your traffic was delayed. I wish to ask what has been the cost of putting these sidings down, and what you have paid for loss of traffic and detentions owing to this kind of procedure ? The sidings have been altered at considerable expense, and, even now, are not equal to the London and North-Western. They run their trains up, the engines are at once uncoupled, and all is right, whereas you have still to shunt before you can arrive at their process. Your expenses are continually increasing, and it is a fact with regard to your working expenses that they are the highest of the large companies in the kingdom If these matters were put on a satisfactory basis you would have at least 2 per cent more dividend for your shareholders than you now have."

Another shareholder said : " I am rather a believer in the last speaker's criticism, and quite second the observations made. We are only anxious to see an increase in dividend I do not know that it matters so much whether it is well or badly managed ; all we want is a good return for our money."

It was very observable that the chairman on opening the business of the meeting was not so jubilant as at the previous half-yearly meeting When he read the report for this half-year, he found there had been no special causes, such as Manchester Exhibition, or any other special cause to increase the receipts ; therefore the ordinary cause not being sufficient, the passenger traffic resulted in being less than the corresponding half-year ; nevertheless there had been an increase in working expenses divided amongst the various spending departments of £32,971, which swallowed up the small increased receipts. This, no doubt, accounted for his mildness in opening the meeting, and yet he eulogised the officers of the central management, and said he could not ask them to do more than they were doing. Although they existed amidst a hive of industry and population, they seemed not to have the ability to perceive the vast valuable field of traffic which lay within their reach, nor to be able to develop it in such a way as would ensure increased receipts every year.

A shareholder called attention to a large expenditure in constructing a series of sorting sidings, and when the new sidings were opened it was found they were not workable. This called for another large expenditure to be laid out before the sidings could be utilised. This verifies my previous remarks that in any alteration or new works constructed, they had to be done two or three times over to make them workable, which arises from the want of a practical hand to sketch out the real requirements before being handed over to the contractor. Similar waste of capital occurred in completing the block system and signal interlocking.

The chairman alluded to the Midland Company commencing to run its Scotch traffic to and from our stations in Liverpool and Manchester, but he said nothing about allowing that company to work local traffic. From such an arrangement the Midland Company seemed to reap all the advantages

The half-year ending December 31st, 1888, the general meeting of proprietors was held at Manchester, on Wednesday, February 20th, 1889, when a dividend was declared for the past half-year at the rate of $4\frac{1}{2}$ per cent per annum. The chairman said, in moving the adoption of the report and the approval of the accounts: "I propose, as usual, to explain them to you in the order they are entered. There is a special feature in the capital account to which I will direct your attention—an item of £1,496,955, which appears this half-year for the first time; also, on referring to the revenue account, you will find our receipts show an increase of £13,109. We do not think this is a bad return considering that we are comparing with the traffic which we obtained from the Manchester Exhibition. The working expenses have increased by £8,524, the percentage being the same as in the corresponding period, viz., 54 per cent It is a pleasure to find again so large a decrease in our passenger compensation: the amount we have spent this half-year is only £1,487. This is the lowest amount for thirty years, the amount in 1859 having been £1,426, but in 1859 we carried only $7\frac{1}{2}$ millions of passengers; in the past half-year we carried 22 millions, or about three

times the number, besides the contract-ticket holders."
In conclusion, the chairman said : "I think I have now
gone pretty fully into all matters which it occurs to me
are likely to interest you I may tell you generally, that
I feel pretty hopeful that our business will improve We
have had a considerable turn in the tide as regards our
traffic receipts since the commencement of the year. If
we can keep our capital expenditure under control, our
working expenses down in proportion to our traffic, our
stock and line in order, and if the Board of Trade and
Parliament treat us fairly as to our rates, I do not fear
for the future. I now beg to move the adoption of the
report and accounts "

Some of the shareholders criticised the chairman's
report, and one of them said. "The present report is
very unsatisfactory The necessity of reducing the
capital expenditure is clearly demonstrated in your
report, where the increased interest last half-year is
£11,600, and absorbs nearly the whole increase of traffic
receipts—£13,109. That cannot be a satisfactory position. The interest on the increased capital has covered
the increased receipts What would you say of any
gentleman managing a concern of your own who expended
£10,000 in earning £9,700 ? If you will just refer to the
report, under the head of 'Traffic Expenses' you will
find you have told us there has been an increase of
£12,309 in salaries and wages in earning this £10,000 of
railway receipts. Since you handed over the best part of
the traffic to the London and North-Western Railway
Company, your management has reduced the dividend
from 9 per cent to 4½ per cent Now you are going a
step farther You are handing over to the London and
North-Western Company your proprietary rights in the
North Union, and the best-paying portion of it too. Is
that the way and style to manage the business? I say

it is time there was a change in the management; and, whatever the opinion of the chairman is, such things as these will not commend themselves to the shareholders."

Another shareholder said · "I would like to know if there is any satisfactory reason why the receipts under the head of 'Goods, Minerals, and Live Stock,' should be £2,000 less than in the corresponding period of last year? The chairmen of other companies have been able to congratulate their shareholders on a large increase in the goods and mineral traffic, and to give very gratifying accounts of an increase in trade all over the country. This was the case with the Great Western, the Midland, the North-Eastern, and the London and North-Western. For the last eight years we have had a very large outlay of capital which has increased our facilities for traffic, and here we are at the end of a half-year, when a very large amount of trade has been done, without seeing much reflection of it in our accounts"

Another shareholder gave a comparison of the dividends paid over the sixteen years from 1874 to 1889 inclusive. The London and North-Western Company's distribution had averaged £6 17s, the line being worked upon the policy of divisional management; and the Lancashire and Yorkshire Company's distribution averaged £4 17s. 3d., the line being worked upon the policy of central management.

The chairman made an effort to make the best of an unsatisfactory half-yearly report when explaining it to the shareholders. He said it was not a bad return having increased receipts of £13,109 with only increased working expenses of £8,524, and for this he lauded the officers of central management for their energy in obtaining this high position. However, some of the shareholders were not of the chairman's opinion, and were not going to be led away from their view of the management.

One of them said that after the very large outlay of capital to give increased facilities for traffic, and with a very large amount of increased trade throughout the country, there ought to have been a better result than a dwindling dividend. He should like to know, with this good trade all over the country, the cause. He also doubted the energy of the officers, as he found in the half-yearly report, under the head of "Goods, Minerals, and Live Stock," is shown £2,000 less receipts than last year, although the chairmen of other companies congratulated their shareholders on a large increase in this traffic.

Another shareholder pointed out the extravagant manner in which the working of the line was managed. This shareholder often criticised, and pointed out in a practical form at the half-yearly meetings, the very expensive mode of management, and said, if continued, the policy must lead to the ruin of the line I could never understand why so few of the shareholders came forward to back him up in his remarks. I often wondered what object the chairman had in view when he referred back to 1859 for comparison in passenger compensation account with the year 1889. In the former year the line was in its primitive state, was worked upon the policy of divisional management, and paid a dividend of 5 per cent per annum. The latter year (1889) the line was in its most progressive days, was worked upon the policy of central management, and although since 1859 population and trade had more than doubled throughout the line, the dividend paid was only 4½ per cent. Also the Company had spent upon the line more millions of money with a view to prevent accidents than the millions of passengers conveyed in 1859, and still a less amount was paid for passenger compensation, and a better dividend paid to the shareholders in 1859 than in 1889.

It was very observable, the way in which the chairman

eulogised the officers of central management at the conclusion of his remarks on the half-yearly report to the shareholders, when he said they did so much and so well that he could not ask them to do more. I was sure he knew very little about the inner working of this department, otherwise he would not have said so much. It was evident some of the shareholders did not coincide with the chairman, as one of them said in his criticism of the management, "What would you say of any gentleman managing a concern of his own who expended £10,000 in earning 9,700?" The chairman might have answered, had he known the inner workings, that this excessive expenditure arose in many ways I will here give an instance, one out of many, which often occurs simply in the staff changes, just to show the expensive way they are dealt with by the central management. In the first place, the district officers have to select men or boys, and arrange them to fill up vacancies as they occur at the various stations on the line, and to submit the arrangement to the central office. A vacancy occurred on April 8th at station A, wages 15s. per week. A porter was drafted from station B, who had 14s. per week, to fill up the vacancy at 15s. Another porter was drafted from station C, wages 11s. per week, to fill up the vacancy at 14s. per week. Another porter was drafted from station D, and he had 8s. per week, to fill up the vacancy at 11s., and a new appointment made for station D, at 8s. per week. This arrangement advanced three porters who were applicants for an advance in wages. This was submitted for approval to the central management on April 17th, but was not agreed to until June 18th. All this time, eleven weeks, correspondence was going on, and a temporary man was put on to fill up the vacancy at an extra cost to the Company, to say nothing about the inconvenience of station working. This lax way of dealing with staff changes materially adds to the working expenses.

In consequence of opening the new route from Liverpool and Manchester to Halifax, Bradford, and Leeds, the express train service running between these places was accelerated, commencing June 1st, 1889 I was requested by the central management to attend a trains' meeting on Monday, April 8th, with the view to arrange the local train service expected to run in connection with the express trains I submitted the alterations required, so far as concerned Yorkshire district, but, as usual, they were objected to, and I left the meeting without agreeing to anything On May 5th I received a letter from the central management, with proof copy of the revised express train service for June time-book. I was to consider carefully the train service in my district, but I was to distinctly understand that there was now no time to discuss additional train alterations However, I looked over the new time-table, and found the local train service had been ignored altogether, also several important trains, to and from Leeds, had been severed from connection at Holbeck Junction with the North-Eastern Company's trains to and from their system, thus throwing important through traffic over to the London and North-Western Company. After what occurred at the meeting on April 8th, and the contents of the letter I received on May 5th, I simply did nothing but call attention to the great mistake they were about to make with the accelerated service of express trains. The new time-table for June was issued, and the alteration of trains gave great dissatisfaction to the travelling public, and caused numerous complaints to be made, and traffic again diverted to other companies, in fact, there was a complete chaos throughout the district. Of course, the usual process was resorted to, at a great cost to the Company, of patching up an inadequate arrangement, and still it was unsatisfactory. It was very unpleasant to me to find that the public attributed the blundering to myself, as I was inundated with complaints, both verbal and written, and was almost ashamed to go on the line. I forwarded the written complaints to the central management at Manchester, with my remarks, and on June 19th I was requested to attend a trains' meeting at Manchester. I went prepared with the necessary local train alterations. Prior to this meeting I submitted a copy of the alterations I intended bringing forward at the meeting, and said that, if agreed to, they would cover the ground of all the complaints contained in the attached letters which I had received One important alteration was to run a service of local trains between Halifax, Sowerby Bridge, and Rochdale, in direct connection with all the express trains—at Rochdale, to and from Manchester and Liverpool; at Halifax, to and from Bradford and Leeds; also to make the necessary connections at Holbeck Junction with the North-Eastern Company's system of trains to and from the North. However, after so many complaints had been made, and traffic lost, I was sorry to find the central management still objected to the suggested remedy. The revised time-table was issued to the public on July 1st, containing part of my suggestions. The public had been looking forward to some more satisfactory alterations; but, on looking over the revised time-table, they were very much disappointed to find so little had been done to meet their requirements. Patching up the defective time-table had again to be resorted to by adding additional trains, at an extra cost to the Company.

On Monday, January 28th, 1889, I was having a day's covert pheasant shooting, in High Hoyland Woods, near Clayton West. About 2-30 in the afternoon I heard a voice hallooing in the woods that I was wanted. A telegraph message was delivered to me to the effect that Prince Albert Victor was travelling from York to Barnsley, and would arrive at Normanton Station about 4-30 p m, and I was requested to meet him there and convey him, by special train, to Barnsley. I at once gave up my gun, and made all haste to Haigh railway station, two miles away, where I obtained an engine which ran me on to Normanton. Arriving there, I at once made up a special train, took charge of it, and conveyed His Royal Highness, arriving at Barnsley Station at 5-20 p.m., amid loud cheering on his alighting from the train. He shook hands, and heartily thanked me for my attention. He was then escorted to the carriage waiting to take him forward to Stainborough Castle.

On Monday, July 15th, the Miners' Demonstration took place at Barnsley, but owing to the blundering way in which the centralised management dealt with the miners' representatives, the miners at Sharlston—a colliery close to our station—and neighbourhood walked over to Normanton Station, a distance of a little over two miles, and were taken from there by the Midland Railway Company to Barnsley. We ran two advertised specials from Normanton to Barnsley, but they were very lightly loaded, the Midland Company having secured the traffic. This resulted in another loss to the Company, and added to its bad reputation.

The half-year ending June 30th, 1889, the general meeting of the proprietors was held at Manchester, on Wednesday, August 7th, when a dividend was declared of 4½ per cent per annum. The chairman said : " I now beg to move the adoption of the report, and the approval of the accounts I will now take you to account No. 9— the revenue account—which I venture to think will give you some satisfaction. Our traffic receipts have increased during the half-year by no less a sum than £81,144, and we have been enabled to work this by an increase in the expenditure of £18,949. One result of these accounts is that we are enabled to recommend you to divide a better dividend by one-half per cent than we did this time last year; and inasmuch as we brought a smaller balance into the account than we propose to take out, there can be no doubt we have fairly earned every penny of it, and I shall have pleasure, after you have passed this resolution, in moving that we pay a dividend of 4 per cent for the past half-year. It is the best that we have been able to pay for the first half-year since 1882, and I sincerely hope that we may not see a worse one for some time to come." In conclusion he said: "Now, gentlemen, I think that completes the remarks I have to make on our last half-year's working. We have, no doubt, been fortunate in earning this increased dividend at so small a cost. Although our receipts for the current half-year appear up to the present to be satisfactory, I cannot hold out to you the hope that we shall be able to work at so low a rate of working expenses, for you must be aware that all materials are considerably advanced in price; at the same time let us hope that the better state of trade which causes this enhanced cost will give us such traffic as will enable us to maintain, and, if possible, increase our dividends. I need hardly say that you are all much indebted to our officers for the satisfactory results of the past half-year; they have not only worked well, but they have worked well together, and it appears to me to be the uppermost thought with each one how he can best use his abilities for your interests" The report was unanimously adopted.

One of the shareholders said: "I beg to move a vote of thanks to the chairman for his courteous conduct in the chair. I am glad to see that the directors have been enabled to reduce the working expenses, which have

19

hitherto been a trifle excessive. I have been pleased to see so marked a change, and I hope it will continue."

Another shareholder said. "I wish to second the resolution, and to say a word or two. I am, very likely, the only individual in the room who is an original shareholder, and I think it becomes my duty on this occasion to say to you what a remarkable circumstance it is that we should have a meeting like to-day. I never was at a meeting where the resolution of the board was so unanimously carried."

On perusal of the chairman's remarks in his explanation to the shareholders upon the half-yearly report, I find he thought that having increased receipts of £81,144, and an increase in the expenditure of only £18,949, ought to be highly satisfactory Even the shareholders were pleased to see such a marked change in reducing the working expenses; but I fear this reduction is too good to continue, although a very large amount of money has been expended with the view of reducing working expenses. It certainly was a most remarkable circum stance for the half-yearly meeting to have concluded without any criticism from the shareholders upon the management. However, I could hardly agree with the chairman's concluding remark, when lauding the officers of the central management for the satisfactory results of the past half-year This remark was intended to convey to the shareholders that the officers had done the best that could be done for their interests, yet I knew that more money could have been earned, and a reduction in working expenses made The receipts certainly ought to have been more favourable considering the good trade there was all over the country, and would have been had the suggestions submitted by the district officers with that view been carried out I submitted a series of half-day local excursions, and also recommended giving more favourable facilities in travelling from Yorkshire, to and from Blackpool and Southport, so as to enable us to compete with the Midland Company (from Leeds and Bradford to Morecambe Bay), the North-Eastern Company (from Leeds to Scarborough, Bridlington, and to stations on the east coast); and the Great Northern Company (from Leeds, Bradford, and Halifax to Skegness) These three companies, giving better facilities and advantages, got the best share of the seaside traffic. The next suggestion I submitted was a local train service to run between Halifax and Rochdale, in direct connection with the revised express service of trains, to and from Manchester and Liverpool. This recommendation was also not agreed to, which resulted in loss of traffic. This is a specimen of what had been going on since 1872; therefore it hardly bore out the chairman's concluding remarks concerning the officers. Similar inattention to the recommendations made by the other district officers materially accounts for what the shareholders had complained about at the half-yearly meetings since 1872.

On Thursday, August 15th, I was requested by the central management to attend a train-alteration meeting at Manchester. I did so, prepared with the necessary alterations required for Yorkshire, having previously submitted a copy of them to the management at Manchester; but, as usual, nothing was agreed to at the meeting. This unsatisfactory state of things continued month after month, which led to the inadequate local service of trains.

One of the members of the Local Board at Todmorden was deputed to wait upon me to ask what could be done to give them in Todmorden valley a more suitable service of local trains, which would enable the manufacturers to get to and from Manchester and Liverpool markets. He said they had already written numerous letters to the authorities at Manchester, but could get no satisfactory reply, and asked if I could do anything for them. I told him I had already submitted a scheme of local train service, and showed him a copy, when he said if that was adopted it would satisfy everyone. I, seeing the Company was losing traffic all round, kept on urging that the local train service should be adopted, but still nothing was done. The complaints being so numerous and strong, the inattention to them had a serious effect upon the interests of the Company, and led to the diversion of goods traffic, and the establishing an omnibus service to run between Hebden Bridge. Mytholmroyd, Luddendenfoot, Sowerby Bridge, and Halifax. This being the case, in January, 1890, I made another effort to get the local train service adopted, and with the view to secure this, on January 11th I submitted a copy of my recommendations to the chairman; and, early in March, I received a letter from the central management to say that my scheme had been again considered, but the whole of it could not be agreed to   On March 5th I received a telegram from one of the members of the Todmorden Local Board, asking if I had succeeded in obtaining my local train service.   I replied, on March 8th, as follows : That I had received a letter from Manchester to say my scheme of local service of trains had been again considered, but the whole of it could not be agreed to   On March 10th I received a letter from the member of Todmorden Local Board, as follows :—

March 10th, 1890.

DEAR MR NORMINGTON,—I am in receipt of yours of the 8th, and must thank you for the great trouble you have taken in this matter, but I see that your board are almost immovable.   I am very sorry that they will not give us a better train service at Walsden.   I cannot find that they have put a single addition to what there was before   They have altered a few, but not one of them that we wanted altering   Not having received a reply from you before our Local Board meeting last Wednesday, the matter was brought before them, and they ordered Mr.

Eastwood, the cleik, to write to your Company for a better service, but I am afraid it will be of little use , at the same time, I think that it is a shame that we should be between two and thiee hours several times during the day without a tiain , and I can assure you that tradespeople here will diveit all their goods by some other route so long as they are so badly treated by your Company —Fiom yours respectfully,

FIELDEN.

The half-year ending December 31st, 1889, general meeting of proprietors was held at Manchester, on Wednesday, Februaiy 12th, 1890, when a dividend was declared at the rate of $4\frac{3}{4}$ per cent per annum.

The Chairman said· " I beg to move the adoption of the report and the approval of the accounts, and I will endeavour as far as possible to explain them to you in the oider in which they are entered. The total capital of the Company at present chargeable to revenue is £46,035,876. The revenue account. Our total receipts show an increase of £82,645 ; working expenses for the same period of last year show an increase of £54,058. I think you will agiee with me that this is satisfactory, considering the abnormal high prices we have had to contend with in increased cost of fuel and wages" The chairman concluded his remarks on the half-yearly report by saying : " It is a great pleasuie to look back upon the past few years, and to see how, in spite of capital expenditure which we have been compelled to undertake, we have slowly but surely improved our position , and if you will be good enough to give us in the future, as you ceitainly have done in the past, your confidence in the policy we are pursuing, I do not think you will have any cause to iegret having done so. I am very sorry to tell you that our general manager, Mr. Thorley, has for some time past suffered from ill health, and, under the advice of his doctor, has obtained leave of absence for a visit to the South of France. We sinceiely hope that he will shortly be restored to health, and be able to undertake his duties with renewed vigour This enforced absence has naturally thrown upon the other officers of the Company more work and responsibility; but it is an ill wind that blows nobody good, and it certainly has given me an opportunity of seeing how heartily and loyally they are all attached to your interests. It is a pleasure to me to be able to inform you how well they have all, from the highest to the lowest, done their duty " The adoption of the report and the approval of the accounts were agreed to.

Some of the shareholders made a few remarks upon the report One of them said " I find that the Lancashire and Yorkshire Company, although it has the largest traffic receipts of any of the large companies per mile, is paying the lowest dividend The London and North-Western Company pay 8 per cent; the North-Eastern, $8\frac{1}{4}$; the Great Western, 8 , the Midland, $6\frac{3}{4}$, the Great Northern, $6\frac{1}{4}$; the Manchester, Sheffield, and Lincoln-shire, $5\frac{1}{2}$; the Lancashire and Yorkshire, only $4\frac{3}{4}$ That is not a state of things that can commend itself to this side of the table, though I do not know if it does to the directors' side. There is another point. I find that of this £82,645 increased receipts, $65\frac{1}{2}$ per cent is absorbed in increased working expenses, and this in face of the fact that during the last few years you have expended millions of money to provide increased facilities for carrying on your business "

The chairman was evidently disappointed with the past half-year's results (1889); although the increased receipts amounted to £82,645, he did not like the £54,058 increased working expenses, particularly when he knew the very large amount of money there had been expended on the line with a view of reducing the working expenses. But what else could he have expected from the expensive method in which the traffic had been worked for the past half-year, and, comparatively speaking, very little had been done in the shape of loop lines to facilitate and help the punctual working of goods trains? There had been a good trade throughout the country, and the increased receipts ought to have been much higher, and would have been had the local requirements of the public been properly attended to at the time of the accelerated express train service in 1883 and 1889. It was evident that when the express passenger train service was revised, that nothing had been considered only the through traffic. This was not a comprehensive scheme, but simply calculated to accomplish one object at the expense of losing a very large local traffic, and one most valuable to the Company.

One of the shareholders compared our dividend with other large railway companies' dividends, which showed that we paid the lowest, even $\frac{3}{4}$ per cent less than the Manchester, Sheffield, and Lincolnshire Company. Surely this of itself ought to have attracted the attention of the directors, and to have convinced them that there was something radically wrong in the management

Half-year ending 30th June, 1890. The general meeting of proprietors was held at Manchester, on Wednesday, 6th August, 1890, when the dividend was declared at the rate of 4 per cent per annum.

The Chairman said "I will, if you please, follow the usual course, and refer to the accounts in the order they are entered. We are still continuing our policy of putting our stations into proper order to meet the requirements of the traffic by degrees. Then, as to the revenue account, it is hardly necessary for me to point out to you that although our gross increase of receipts amounts to £68,225, it has all been swallowed up in the increase of expenses, which amount to £87,861, but you will naturally require some explanation of this. I may say at the outset that it is generally accounted for by the increase in cost of coal and materials, and the extra wages to the Company's servants, necessitated by the present high price of labour. I think I have now entered pretty fully into the matters that have affected us in the past half year. We have had the good fortune lately to slowly but steadily increase our dividend, and I can assure you that I feel very much that we have to make a slight retrogression in this respect, but I venture to think that you will be satisfied that it is from no want of care or attention on the part of the directors or officers of the Company that we are unable to maintain the same payment as this time last year. The greatest care has been taken by all in the management of your business, and I have reason to hope that with favourable weather this autumn and increased traffic, and with a due regard to economy in our capital expenditure, we shall overtake the inflation in the cost of wages and materials from which we are now suffering." The resolution having been passed, the Chairman said "I should have been very glad if we had been able to have kept that ¼ per cent dividend, but depend upon it we shall do the best we can for you in the future."

Some of the shareholders again justly criticised the management One of them said : " I do not see that you have favoured us with any more information than we can find in the report. The increased receipts are £68,225 and the increased working expenses £87,861, which, with the further sum of £12,353, make £100,000 altogether. The decrease in the dividend is ¼ per cent. I think that will scarcely commend itself to you all. The remarks from the chairman are almost identical with what we have heard meeting after meeting during the time the dividends have been dwindling from 9 or 8 per cent— more receipts, less dividend The conclusion to be drawn is that the business has got beyond the grasp of the management. The Midland pay an increased dividend, and the Great Northern no less, but the Lancashire and Yorkshire is on the down grade again.' Another shareholder said: "I wish to call your attention to the very unsatisfactory manner in which the Bury division of your railway is attended to The local service of passenger trains is not at all satisfactory, and you are losing passengers and a lot of other business. I wish to call your attention to that matter, and it behoves you to look into this even better than you are doing. You ought to pay over 4 per cent, and I am one who will be satisfied with 5, but you want some change somewhere or other, and it will have to come." Another shareholder said: "I think this is a singular instance of having reduced dividends with increased traffic. The reasons given for it no doubt are very sound. One can see plainly that the working expenses have increased faster than the traffic has increased. One item is coals, and I would merely ask on that point whether you did not make any contract for coal, as prudent people who consume such a quantity of it generally do ?"

Another disappointing half-yearly report to the shareholders. It was obvious from the chairman's remarks that he was at a loss to explain the cause of the increased working expenses, which more than absorbed the £68,225 increased receipts, resulting in a dwindling dividend. He attributed the causes to the increase in cost of coal and materials, and extra wages to the Company's servants However, other companies had similar contingencies to contend with, and they managed to pay a satisfactory dividend to the shareholders. Some of the shareholders were not satisfied with the chairman's explanation. One of them said, "The conclusion to be drawn is that the business has got beyond the grasp of the management."

The Chairman concluded his remarks on the report, as usual, by saying that the diminished dividend had not arisen from the want of care or attention on the part of the officers of the Company. "The greatest care has been taken by all in the management of your business." This remark is not borne out by the shareholders' remarks, as one of them said that the train service in the Bury division was very unsatisfactory, and the Company were losing passengers and merchandise traffic in consequence. This shareholder confirms the views expressed in my criticism on the half-yearly report of June, 1889, that the local traffic in other districts than Yorkshire is neglected, and lost in consequence The chairman tried to explain away this unsatisfactory local passenger train service, but the shareholder was not satisfied with the explanation, and said, "I know it can be done, and I can regulate it, if you cannot." Had the management comprehended and adopted the suggestions supplied to them, this would have helped the chairman to have kept what he was most anxious to do—that $\frac{1}{4}$ per cent.

On Thursday September 4th. 1890, the Halifax High Level Railway was opened with great pomp and ceremony, the length of the line being a little over three miles. The line was worked conjointly with the Lancashire and Yorkshire and Great Northern Railway Companies. On the opening day a special train left St. Paul's Station, King Cross, with the directors, contractors, and friends, for Holmfield Station, where the line forms the connection with the Great Northern line, Halifax and Bradford. Holding the position of district superintendent for the Lancashire and Yorkshire Railway Company, I was invited to join in the ceremony. We assembled at St. Paul's Station about 1-30, when a presentation was made to the Mayor (Alderman James Booth) of a massive silver jardinière Afterwards a special train left St. Paul's

Station to Holmfield and back, when the line was declared open by the Mayor for public traffic. The invited guests then made all haste to Belle Vue, the residence of the late Sir Francis Crossley, M P., where a most sumptuous luncheon was provided. After due justice had been done to the good things, the usual loyal and patriotic toasts were given and responded to, coupled with every good wish of success to the new line of railway.

I could never understand the Lancashire and Yorkshire Railway Company being joint owners of the line between Halifax and Holmfield, and afterwards from Holmfield to St. Paul's, a line that could never be worked to the Company's advantage, and declining to be joint owners of the new line from Holmfield to Keighley, a line which would have been utilised to the great advantage of the Company and the public, as this would have completed the link in connecting a through line from North to South, which the Chambers of Commerce, both of Halifax and Huddersfield, have been agitating for for years

The general manager, Mr. William Thorley, died September, 1890, after serving the Company for a period of forty-two years. Mr. J. H. Stafford was appointed to succeed him in October, 1890.

I attended a time-table meeting on January 15th and 16th, 1891, prepared with the necessary alterations, with a view to improving the local traffic, but, as usual, very few of my recommendations were agreed to.

For the half year ending 31st December, 1890, the general meeting of proprietors was held at Manchester, on Wednesday, the 11th February, 1891, when a dividend was declared at the rate of $4\frac{1}{2}$ per cent per annum. The Chairman said : " I have very little doubt that the first thing that will have struck you on receiving the report for the past half year is that our increased expenditure has been greater than our increased receipts. I will not

depart from my usual habit of considering the accounts
in the order they are entered. The accounts show our
total receipts to be £2,210,546, which is an increase of
£75,542, with an increased working expense of no less
than £88,850 In looking carefully into the accounts, it
will be apparent that this arises from the high price of
coal and materials, together with the advance in wages.
There has been a steady development in our passenger
traffic during the past half year. We have carried, inclusive of season ticket holders, 24,000,293 passengers.
Shortly after our last half-yearly meeting we lost the
services by death of our late general manager, Mr. Thorley.
He had been in the service of this Company for a period
of forty-two years, and obtained a knowledge of its affairs
which, I suppose, was not possessed by any living man.
He had been in the position of traffic and general manager
for twenty-three years, and you can easily understand
the loss we felt at his decease. He discharged his duties
most zealously, and was, without doubt, a most faithful
servant of the Company. We have appointed to the
vacancy Mr Stafford, who was well known to you as the
late secretary. I cannot help thinking that this appointment will meet with the approval of the proprietors, and
I can, with confidence, say that in no particular have we
regretted the choice we made He and all the other
officers of the Company have used their utmost endeavours
to further your interests in every way. I should have
been glad if we could have maintained our 4¾ per cent
dividend, as in the corresponding last half year, but,
under the circumstances, I think we are taking the
prudent course by declaring 4½ per cent and carrying
forward a good balance "

The report was adopted,

Some of the shareholders again criticised the report and
management on the extraordinary working expenses.

One of them said : " This is one of the best railways and one of the best paying lines in the country, and it is being crushed by this unprofitable expenditure you are constantly involving us in. We have expended millions in the last few years in giving increased facilities to working traffic, and you come and tell us practically you cannot work the additional traffic It takes £88,000 additional money to earn £75,000. Practically, £50,000 of this is passenger traffic, where there ought to be a very trifling increase in expenses, if any. You tell us the cost of coal and materials has caused the falling off of dividends. I tell you that it is want of management that has caused it. In 1872 and 1874 the price of materials was one and a half to three times what it is now. In 1872 you paid $9\frac{1}{4}$ per cent dividend ; in 1874, $6\frac{1}{2}$ per cent, in the December of that year. Coal in 1872 was double the price it is now ; steel and iron were one and a half times ; the price of rails in 1872 and 1874 was £14 per ton, and it is now about £5 per ton , and you come before us and tell us it is the price of materials. It is want of management that makes this position. If it were not for the wage-earning class, if it were not for the exertions they make, dividends would be lower still ; but it is their officers sending out trains from sidings to stations, and having to bring them back again, because there is no room in the stations to place them , sending their men out on a bit of line like the Lancashire and Yorkshire, where drivers and firemen and guards have to change beds three times a week, and where men, after such a severe winter, have to turn out in wet clothes It is these things that tell against you— the want of management."

Another shareholder said : "I am not at all surprised that there should be a little disappointment at this meeting—disappointment because, while our receipts have been so much increased, our dividend has been diminished.

I anticipate a greater amount of extra traffic will be sent over the Lancashire and Yorkshire line this year than we have probably ever had before, and I wish to ask, and hope that you will be able to give, every facility for carrying goods on the main line, so providing that they can as easily as possible be conveyed to where they are wanted without delay."

Another shareholder said "I should like to ask a question, whether the Lancashire and Yorkshire Railway, which is mainly a local line which has arrangements with trunk lines, and which is crowded with traffic, gets a proper remuneration for the traffic it receives from the trunk lines, or does it do a great deal of work which other companies get paid for? It has often struck me—of course you know best—whether the arrangements are of the best kind to the interests of the Lancashire and Yorkshire—that other companies may have the best of the bargain. I will tell you why. Sometimes I have to inquire about some little reductions of rates on the Lancashire and Yorkshire in connection with the trunk lines, and I have been told, ' If we make you any concession at all, it will be all that we get out of the traffic—we get a very small portion of it.' Other people seem to be getting the dividends, and you are doing the work."

Another shareholder said "I should like to ask about the delay to traffic on this line. I myself pay this Company a large sum a year for traffic. I put all the traffic I can on the line, but I have never been so much bothered by my friends here as I have been by those who say they will send their traffic by other companies, on account of the great delays which occur on the line"

It is very apparent that a great change has overtaken the management and the feeling of the shareholders since the meeting of 7th August, 1889. At that meeting every one seemed to be very highly satisfied and jubilant. No criticism was made upon the management, all being pleased to see such a marked change, to have been able to earn £81,144 with an increased working expense of only £18,949, and they hoped it would continue. But I had no faith in this apparent prosperity. At the very next meeting the increased receipts were £82,645, at an extra cost in working expenses of £54,058; and the following half-year the increased receipts were £68,225, to earn which the increased working expenses were £87,861; and this half-year increased receipts £75,542, increased working expenses no less a sum than £88,850. The last two half-years the increased working expenses have absorbed more than the increased receipts by £32,944. This again roused the temper of the shareholders, which caused a rather strong and stormy meeting, and many important remarks were made to the chairman. The chairman found it difficult to explain why there was a diminished dividend in the face of increased receipts. He attributed it to the same cause as last half-year, namely, to the high price they had to pay for coal and material. I was glad this explanation was challenged by one of the shareholders, who said he could not see how that explanation could be accepted, seeing that in 1872 coal and material were more than double the price they were then paying, and in those days they paid a dividend of $9\frac{1}{4}$ per cent, and now they have to be satisfied with $4\frac{1}{2}$ per cent. Another shareholder pointed out what he considered added much to the increased working expenses, namely, bad management in the arrangement of the working of goods trains, and the want of siding accommodation wherein to place rolling stock after finishing the day's work. He was afraid, too, that the Company got the worst bargain in making working arrangements with other companies, the Company having to do a large amount of work which other companies got paid for, and also asserted that, in consequence of great delays which occurred on the line, many of his friends diverted their traffic to other companies These correct and pithy remarks by the shareholders at meeting after meeting ought to have had some effect upon the directors, with a view of altering the management, and adopting a better policy for working the traffic on the line, but still they went on in the old and unsatisfactory mode The chairman announced at the meeting the loss the Company had sustained by the death of their late general manager, Mr. Wm. Thorley, and eulogised his worth for the Company. However, I had known him a much longer period than the chairman, and I quite agree with him as to his zealousness in doing his best for the interests of the Company, but he lacked the ability to comprehend, as a general manager, the necessary tact of railway management His idea was that the public was made for the railway, and not the railway for the public; otherwise he would never have allowed one of the richest 500 miles of railway for traffic in England to have drifted down from its high position when paying $9\frac{1}{4}$ per cent, to the low one of 3 per cent during the 18 years it was under his management His policy was to work the line upon theory rather than by practical experience. He destroyed all energy, enterprise, and rivalry not only amongst the officers, but throughout the whole line, when he discontinued the district officers' monthly meetings. From the time the Company adopted the policy of central management up to the time of his death I had only been called to his office twice; each time was for the purpose of considering the best way of reducing the staff and their wages, that seemed to be his idea of reducing working expenses Had he called meetings of the district officers, with a view to have devised schemes for earning more money on the line, the shareholders would have been much more sure of a better dividend than by adopting the policy of lowering the servants' wages and reducing the staff.

The directors appointed the Secretary (Mr. J. H. Stafford) to be general manager in October, 1890, in place of the late Mr. William Thorley. Mr. Stafford commenced a policy of management by restoring the monthly conferences with the district officers. They had to be prepared with an agenda of subjects to be discussed at the meetings. This reminded me of days gone by, when the line was growing in its prosperity. I thought the new general manager was adopting the correct policy to ensure the working of the line being again placed in · its proper position Yet, to the astonishment of not only myself, but of all the district officers, after the second meeting orders were received to discontinue submitting agendas Since then we have still attended monthly conferences, and have sat at the table like dummies, only to speak when spoken to. I often thought, when sitting at those meetings, what a great mistake the general manager had made when he discontinued the agendas, by which he destroyed arguments which would have been brought forth, not only to his own advantage, but to the best interests of the Company.

Mr. John Maddock, superintendent of the line, died 17th February, 1891. He was appointed assistant superintendent in 1872. Mr. Blackmore retired in 1877, when Mr. Maddock was appointed his successor. This appointment emanated from Mr. Thorley, the general manager. Mr. Maddock not being a practical man in the passenger department led to an enormous waste of money in experimenting, and which added materially to the working expenses.

Mr. Charles J. Nicholson, assistant superintendent, was appointed to succeed Mr. Maddock in March, 1891, as

20

superintendent of the line. He had only been in the service some six years, and prior to that, it was said, he was manager for a tramcar company. The making of such an appointment to this important position on so busy and congested a line as the Lancashire and Yorkshire baffled all comprehension, and gave rise to anything but satisfaction amongst the officers, who had served the Company both long and well, and were looking forward to better positions. Filling up important positions such as the above with practically inexperienced men is not the way to keep down or reduce the expenses of working the line.

Observing that stormy half-yearly meetings were again coming forth, in consequence of the dwindling dividends and the enormous and unreasonable increase in the working expenses, I thought it an opportune time, seeing that a great change had been made in the officers of central management, to venture once more to call the attention of the chairman to this matter. In February, 1891, I drew his attention to the importance of the system of management being reorganised and the district officers being recognised in the management of the railway. It follows, as a matter of course, that the development of the working, alike in its economy as in its money-making, rests to a very great extent on the emulation of the district officers. I received a reply on February 23rd, 1891, to the effect that my desire to benefit the Company was fully appreciated, but nothing was said about any intention to alter the policy of management. After this I determined to offer no suggestions upon the management in the future.

On Thursday, April 30th, 1891, the Duke of Clarence and Avondale visited Wakefield for the purpose of formally opening the Technical and Art School, followed by his planting a tree in the public park. The Mayor and Corporation determined to make it a memorable day by its adoption as a general holiday, and most elaborately decorating the streets and public buildings, and along the highways to the park, a distance of a mile. The railway company decorated the station, with its approaches, and erected a raised platform in the entrance yard covered with crimson cloth, where an address of welcome was to be presented to the distinguished guest by the Mayor. A quantity of dirty-looking bunting was sent to me from Manchester not at all suitable for the occasion, and not half sufficient to cover the entrance of the approach road. I applied to Manchester for a further supply, but got no reply until late in the day prior to the visit, when I received a telegram to say they could not send any more, and that I was to make the best arrangements I could. To save the Company's reputation, I arranged with the man who had undertaken to decorate the town for the Corporation to find the necessary bunting and do the needful in putting up the decorations, &c., for £25. He did the work very well, and the Company got credit, as was shown in the newspaper reports upon the decorations in the station and its approach. The royal train arrived at Wakefield at 12-55 p.m. from York. I attended to supervise the arrangements for receiving the train conveying the royal prince. The railway programme, which I received from Manchester, giving particulars of the arrival and departure of the royal train, was contrary to the Corporation programme—fifteen minutes on arrival and one hour on the return journey—which was a stupid mistake on someone's part, and made it very difficult for me to meet the requirements punctually.

After the prince had planted the tree in the park, the ceremony concluded with a hearty vote of thanks to the prince The procession again re-formed, and his royal highness was conducted back to the Kirkgate Railway Station, where the royal train was in waiting to convey him to York. On his royal highness arriving on the platform, his Worshipful the Mayor introduced me to the prince, who shook hands, and after thanking me for my attention, he entered the carriage amidst loud cheering The royal train left for York at 5-15 p m., with another outburst of cheers from the spectators on the platform.

On receiving the bill from the decorator against the Company of £25, I forwarded the account to the authorities at Manchester, there to be dealt with; but to my surprise the account was returned to me with the communication that I should have to pay it myself, not having had authority to make such arrangements. However, after further communications had passed, the Company paid the bill

For the half-year ending June 30th, 1891, the general meeting of proprietors was held at Manchester, on Wednesday, August 5th, 1891.

Directors.

Chairman, G. J Armytage, Esq, Clifton, Woodhead, Brighouse.
Deputy-Chairman, William Tunstal, Esq.

Heywood Bright, Esq	Thomas Fielden, Esq.
Sir Edward Green, Bart , M.P	Joseph Lees, Esq.
W H Hornby, Esq.	S M. Milne, Esq
J. W Naylor, Esq.	James Priestley, Esq
Sir David Radcliffe	John Ramsbottom, Esq.
E. Wilfrid Stanyforth, Esq	H Yates Thompson, Esq

Officers.

J. H. Stafford, General Manager.
C. J. Nicholson, Superintendent of the Line.
Thomas Normington, Superintendent Yorkshire District
John Bolland, Superintendent Lancashire District.
John Whitehall, Superintendent East Lancashire District.

The Chairman said : " When we met here six months ago, I said I anticipated our working expenses, during the severe weather we were then having, would be heavy, and I felt that we were not entering upon a very prosperous half-year. I should have been glad, indeed, had I turned out to be a false prophet. We have not only lost money, owing to the extreme severity and great length of the past winter, but our holiday season has been most disappointing. Our receipts show an increase of £34,682, and the working expenses have increased by £72,152. The only comfort is that other companies have been similarly affected; but it would have been far more satisfactory if we had been able to declare the same rate of dividend as last half-year. I have told you generally the cause of the increase in our expenditure. I am prepared to answer any questions that you may like to ask me. I can only say that it has been a very anxious time, and though the results are not so satisfactory as we could wish, you may rest assured that you have had during the past half-year the most careful service of the board and the officers of the Company." The resolution was seconded, and the half-yearly report and accounts were passed.

The shareholders were very much disappointed. One of them said. " I am sure that we cannot congratulate ourselves on the present report. I think it is one of the most disappointing we have had for many years. It is not only accompanied by a reduction of dividend, but it is accompanied by a speech which gives us precious little encouragement. I am the more surprised to see from this report that we are asked to give our consent to a further large capital outlay. I have told you where you would land yourselves—that you were spending too much on too limited an area—and the result is a very disappointing and unsatisfactory dividend. During the last twenty years we have increased the capital account 86 per cent. These are the figures given before a Parliamentary committee of the House of Commons, and our gross earnings have only increased 56 per cent. Where is it to land us? There is a little poor line. called the North Staffordshire, which a few years ago was a byword amongst companies. 'Poor thing'' it was said; 'they don't know what to do with it.' But we have got below it. Their stock is at £125, and ours is at £112. Not only in price, but in earning money they are better, their dividend of 4¾ comparing well with our 3½ per cent. I am sure the directors have met with the fullest confidence of the shareholders They have never asked for money but we have granted it They cannot complain of any reluctance on our part. It may be said that we have approved of their conduct. I do not think we have. We are not in a position to know the requirements of the Company. They have had new engine works; capital has been supplied to them without stint; and the miserable result is that we are going down, and down, and down, and yet they are asking us for £1,200,000 more. I am of opinion that we are running too many express trains, chasing each other over the line between Liverpool, York, and Leeds They say it pays; but I doubt if anybody knows whether it does, because of the indirect cost The delays to trains—to goods trains—are something awful. I do not know whether you hear complaints, but I do. A great many of my friends are large shareholders, and they ask, 'Where is this all to end? Are we to drift until there is no dividend at all?' And as for ladies and people of small means, it is pitiable to hear their expressions of dissent and dissatisfaction."

Another shareholder remarked. "I think the dividend can hardly be satisfactory to you on this occasion: 3½ per cent are the net earnings for six months for the Lancashire and Yorkshire, one of the best lines in the land, with great traffic from one end to the other, but it seems the more traffic we have and the less dividend. How does this arise? I have pointed out before that it has been through excessive working expenses, and these are continued and maintained till the present time. It is want of management that is ruining this grand line of ours. I find you are paying 40 to 50 per cent more for materials than they can be bought for in the open market. With regard to the question of wages, I am not in favour of reducing the working man   I believe in 'good hands, good hire,' but I do not wish to see two men doing one man's work."

Another shareholder said. "I am a very poor man and a small shareholder, and I came to ask one question, which is this· About eleven months ago I had one thousand pounds to spare, money which I had made and saved with great care and labour. I was induced to invest that money in the Company's shares, which I bought then at 120   Now those shares can be bought at 112½, and I should like to hear from you, or any other gentleman in the room, the cause or causes which have led to so great a fall in so short a time."

The shareholders' criticisms upon the management at this half-yearly meeting will hardly bear comparison with the remarks made by the shareholders at the half-yearly meeting in 1889, when they accorded a vote of thanks to the chairman and directors for having managed to earn £82,144, with only an increase in working expenses of £18,949. Since that time the working expenses have more than absorbed the whole of the increased receipts, as it will be observed that the past half-year has taken £72,152 to earn £32,682. This bears out my remarks made upon that meeting—that it was too good to continue —and that the chairman was under the same impression is evident from his remarks when he said he could not hold out any hopes that they would be able to continue working the traffic at so low a rate of working expenses. He seemed to think the unexpected circumstance was a lucky hit, and a piece of unexpected good fortune. His explanation as to the cause of such rapidly increased working expenses since 1889 was very vague The shareholders' remarks were very appropriate to what was daily occurring on the line—delays to trains, working expenses over-running the money earning. This management might well create dissatisfaction amongst lady shareholders, and others of small means, who gave expressions of dissent, as the poor dividends naturally make them also poor. This might all have been prevented had the management carried out suggestions and recommendations submitted years ago More money would also have been earned had they adopted a local service of passenger trains to run between Halifax, Sowerby Bridge, and Rochdale, and this, no doubt, would have been the means of preventing an omnibus service being established. I very much sympathised with the poor man shareholder, who said he had bought shares at 120 a few months ago, and now they were only worth 112½. This reminded me of the time when I bought shares at 145 and had to sell them for 117. I need not say what a loss this was to me, and a great annoyance, especially as I knew that the depreciation in stock had arisen from bad management.

On Friday, the 4th September, I received a letter from Henry F. Beaumont, Esq , M.P., of Whitley Beaumont, Huddersfield, requesting me to meet his Royal Highness the Duke of Cambridge, who was expected to arrive at Wakefield by train due at 5-12 p m. on Monday, the 7th. He was coming on a visit for the week to Whitley Beaumont. I met his royal highness as desired, and on the arrival of the 4-30 p.m. express train from York to Manchester, due at Wakefield at 5-17, I saw him into the carriage, and travelled with the train to Mirfield, which

WAKEFIELD, 1841.

stopped to put down his royal highness, and Mr. Beaumont, who had his carriage waiting, drove him away to his residence. On Tuesday, the 8th, a special train from Manchester to Doncaster stopped at Mirfield to take up his royal highness, Mr. Beaumont, and his party. I travelled with the train to and from Doncaster, which ran to time both ways. On Wednesday, the 9th, a special express train from Manchester to Doncaster again stopped at Mirfield to take up his royal highness, Mr. Beaumont, and party. I travelled with the train to and from Doncaster, which again ran well to time both ways. On arriving at Doncaster, I had the pleasure of having ten or fifteen minutes conversation with his royal highness, which was principally upon the traffic arriving and departing on the Leger day. He seemed to appreciate my remarks to him. On Thursday, the 10th, I had to make special arrangements for the occasion. I made up a special train for his royal highness, Mr. Beaumont, and party, and left Mirfield about 12 noon, arriving at Westgate Station, Wakefield, at 12-30 p.m. The saloon carriage was there attached to the Great Northern 12-37 p.m. express train for Doncaster. His royal highness and party returned from Doncaster by the Great Northern 5-32 p.m. train to Wakefield, and from Wakefield by the Lancashire and Yorkshire 6-15 p.m. local train to Mirfield, arriving there at 6-40 p m On Friday, the 11th, the special train from Manchester to Doncaster took up his royal highness, Mr. Beaumont, and party, at Mirfield, and I again accompanied the train to and from Doncaster. I gave the noble duke my special attention for five days. On Saturday, the 12th, he left Mirfield by train, for the North, when his royal highness handed a letter to Mr. Henry F. Beaumont, M.P., of which the following is a copy.—

September 12th, 1891.

My Dear Beaumont,—Before leaving Whitley Beaumont this morning I must write you one line to ask you to express to the railway authorities in this district my sincere thanks and acknowledgments for the excellent arrangements made by them for assisting us all to get so comfortably backwards and forwards to Doncaster. My sincere acknowledgments are due to all concerned

I remain, with sincere thanks to yourself for all the trouble taken on my account, yours most sincerely, GEORGE

A little incident occurred in the arrangements on Thursday, the 10th We had no ordinary train suitable to convey His royal Highness the Duke of Cambridge, Mr. Beaumont, and party from Mirfield to Doncaster, and this being the duke's first visit on our line in Yorkshire, I thought we could do nothing less to oblige him than run a special to Wakefield, a distance of nine miles, there to catch the Great Northern train to Doncaster ; but to my surprise, on the 13th October, I received a letter from the authorities at Manchester, to say that I should have to pay the cost of running the special from Mirfield to Wakefield, or call upon Mr. Beaumont to do so. The special not being ordered by Mr. Beaumont, I did not feel disposed to degrade myself or the Company, so I paid the money—19s However, this amount was refunded to me on January 28th, 1892, but without thanks for my anxiety to maintain the reputation of the Company.

A new station at Northorpe, on the Cleckheaton Branch, was opened December 1st, 1891 There were no time tables either for trains arriving or departing, or booking offices ready. The waiting rooms were only partly built, and no lights whatever provided on the platforms or elsewhere about the station, which had to be lighted up temporarily with torchlights ; whilst the trains stopped by guess, and the passengers had to go without tickets This is an example of central management in opening new stations.

This is a most remarkable station for a branch line out in the country, having only a small population, and receipts per week under £5. The station is built of scoured ashlar stone, dovetailed in a peculiar and costly manner. The building is more fitted for a bishop's palace than a country railway station, and it was said cost at least £10,000, whereas, only being for a passenger station, it might have been built quite equal to the requirements for the next fifty years at a cost of less than £2,000 This is another instance of wasting the Company's money, and note, the contract was let at a time when the Company's shares were below par

For the half-year ending December 31st, 1891, the general meeting of proprietors was held at Manchester, on Wednesday, 10th February, 1892, when a dividend was declared at the rate of $4\frac{1}{4}$ per cent. The Chairman said. "I now beg to move the adoption of the report and the approval of the accounts, and I propose, as usual, to explain them to you in the order in which you will find them in the balance sheet. The receipts are increased £42,860, and the working expenses are increased by £51,952. You will see by the report that we have intro- duced a bill into Parliament. We propose to construct a fork line to connect our Barnsley Branch with our main line at Horbury, so as to enable the traffic between Barnsley and any part of our main line west of Horbury to be sent direct without shunting at Horbury Junction, which takes both time and money in doing. We shall widen the line at Horbury, and make the Wooley Edge Tunnel, which is now only a single line, into two lines of way. We obtained powers some years ago for widening our entrance into Wakefield, which powers have now expired, and we have renewed them in this bill. There is one more Parliamentary matter which I think I should explain to you. This Company many years ago invested a sum of £100,000 in the ordinary stock of the Hull Dock Company. Since the competition which arose with the opening of the Alexandra Docks at Hull, there has been but a small dividend paid on this ordinary stock. Looking at the fact that we have ample running powers into Hull, and to all parts of the Dock Estate, and having agreed with the North-Eastern Company that our position shall in all respects be as good in Hull as it is to-day, we gave our consent to the proposed purchase of the Alexandra Docks by the North-Eastern Company." The chairman concluded with the usual lament of a diminished dividend, and assured the shareholders that no pains had been spared by the directors and officers in looking after the business of the Company. The chairman also replied to a question asked by one of the shareholders. He said, "There is no doubt whatever about it, that properly-spent capital will bring you in a return commensurate with the expenditure; the great point is where to spend it—where it requires spending most. We have taken much trouble this half-year in going very carefully into the question as to where the most congested parts of the line are, and we had a most carefully-prepared scheme showing the points where our traffic is most delayed and congested, and it is our duty to deal with these first."

Some of the shareholders were not satisfied with the chairman's explanation about the gradually dwindling dividend, and one of them said "I am going to make an observation or two. You know for the last ten or fifteen years we have been laying out an enormous amount of capital upon a small length of line, and my opinion has always been that we shall never get an adequate return on this too limited area. I think we have tried it for a very long time, and the result is not satisfactory. The thing is, What is the best remedy? My proposition is this:

Why should not the line be leased to some of the big companies who will guarantee us a fixed dividend? I am convinced of this, that we shall never be able to get a return for the millions of money we keep spending on the line. There is only one of two things, either extend the line or lease it. I have no doubt this concern would be worth 6 per cent, and pay 6 per cent on the ordinary stock to any other company. The time is coming when the shareholders will button up their pockets and reduce the outlay, because it won't pay. On the present lines we are making no progress, but going back. The despised old North Staffordshire Railway is paying 5¼ per cent, and we, for the last twelve months, have gone down to this present state. It is not satisfactory."

Another shareholder said: "I have no doubt if this line were leased to the Midland Company we should get 7 or 8 per cent; or even to the London and North-Western Company, whose dividend, I find, with all their lines, is 7¾ per cent, the same as in the corresponding half-year, and they have got the same ratio of increased traffic as on this line. Can you stop this down grade in dividend earning? My opinion is that it ought to be, and can be, stopped, for this line, as far as traffic goes, is one of the best in the kingdom—in fact, it goes through the very best traffic-producing country outside London."

Another shareholder said: "I hope that by the management of yourself and the gentlemen surrounding you, times may mend, and things may improve I look at the amount of traffic you have. Sometimes I cannot find a seat in a train; and occasionally I walk through this Manchester Station, and if I happen to be there when a train is coming in, I am almost swept away. Then, you are quite overdone with goods traffic If, with all this property, things get worse and worse, then I think the unfortunate shareholders will be in the position which has been described as 'between the devil and the deep sea.'"

Another shareholder said : "I may say a few words on what a previous shareholder has already said, as to the line being leased to some of the big companies. There is not the slightest doubt if we could have that arranged it would be a good thing, but I should like to give the directors another trial, and to see whether we can find one or two of those shrewd Yorkshiremen who have been so successful in getting the Midland Company to its present state, or to borrow, buy, or steal one or two of those directors, so that they can improve our property. I can say this, and quite agree with the previous shareholder when he tells of what this Company has to spend. Particular attention will have to be paid to the local traffic Trains are kept waiting 10, 15, and 20 minutes outside stations, dislocating the whole of the traffic, and I think we should be in a very different position from this. You are spending millions of money in grappling with the situation, but with very little benefit to the shareholders. I should like to impress upon the directors the advantage of finding one or two of those shrewd capable Yorkshiremen to get us out of our difficulties. I should say, Attend to your local traffic ; you have a gold mine in it ; and if you do not attend to it, lease the line either to the London and North-Western or the Midland Company, or else you will find the shareholders in a few years from now will not get much more than $2\frac{1}{2}$ per cent."

From the chairman's remarks, it was evident that he did not much like the diminished dividend ; but what else could he expect when the money was not earned that might have been, at any rate in Yorkshire, and a much less cost in working expenses incurred ? At every half-yearly meeting, and this in particular, strong remarks were made by shareholders on the management, and the chairman's explanation as to the causes of the continued decay of their once most prosperous railway line in the kingdom was not satisfactory to the shareholders, who seemed clearly of opinion that the best was not done that might be done It might be the best so far as the then management comprehended, but that was not sufficient. As one of the shareholders said : " We have tried it for a very long time, and the results are not satisfactory; and I propose as a remedy that the line shall be leased to some of the big railway companies." Another shareholder confirmed this by saying it would be a good thing if the line could be leased to some other company. It was evident that the shareholders were finding out the great mistake they made at the adjourned half-yearly meeting held at Manchester, March 23rd, 1883. Instead of breaking up the policy of management which was gradually bringing the line to ruin, and which management they had condemned for years, they simply passed a resolution that a salary be paid to the chairman of £2,000 a year, which was tantamount to giving him the title of " Managing Director"; as one of the shareholders remarked, "placing two Richmonds in the field." Surely they are now satisfied that they ought to have altered the policy of management. It is not one or two high-salaried officials who work a busy railway like the Lancashire and Yorkshire to advantage At this crisis the proprietors ought to have passed a resolution that this railway be leased to some other company, or that a different policy of management be adopted.

I observed that one of the shareholders properly remarked that the Company had spent millions of money with a view to facilitate the working of traffic, and still trains were kept 10, 15, and 20 minutes outside the stations, dislocating the whole of the traffic. The Chairman, replying to this remark, said : " We have taken much trouble this half-year in going most carefully into the question as to where the most congested parts of the line are; and we have had a most carefully-prepared scheme showing the points where our traffic is most delayed and congested, and it is our duty to deal with this" I thought this explanation most remarkable, as the management seemed to have only just found out where the traffic was most congested. Had the pigeon-holes in the general manager's office been overhauled, no doubt schemes would have been found which had been submitted in 1870, showing where delays occurred and what were the congested points of the line, so far as Yorkshire was concerned. These schemes were accompanied by pen-and-ink sketches, showing where it was necessary to construct loop lines and refuge sidings—the principal stations to have loop lines, and smaller stations refuge sidings; but in consequence of not being backed up by the general manager, the schemes were deferred. Schemes were again submitted on a more extended scale in 1872, accompanied with pen-and-ink sketches, pointing out the serious delays which occurred at the several stations on the congested parts of the line At this meeting I told the directors that we lost more locomotive power in delays than would work the whole of the goods traffic. Again, not being backed up by the general manager, the schemes were deferred. Since then the traffic has been seriously delayed, and the working expenses gradually increased If the plans for building stations and for extensions in siding accommodation had been well matured before being handed over to the contractors, in my opinion the money spent during the past fifteen years would have been sufficient to have completed the whole scheme of alterations required in Yorkshire.

I was much surprised that the Company was about to

construct a fork line to connect the Barnsley Branch with the main line at Horbury Station, and purposed doubling the line at Woolley Edge Tunnel, with the view of enabling the traffic to be run direct from Barnsley Branch to stations westward. To spend such a large amount of money for such a purpose was, in my opinion, a great mistake. In the first place, the coal beds on the Barnsley Branch were getting worked out ; secondly, to turn the trains from off the Barnsley Branch over the fork to Horbury would not relieve a congested main line or reduce mileage from Barnsley, with traffic going westwards. What was really required for the benefit and best advantage of this Company, was what I had urged again and again, that was, for the Clayton West Branch to be extended and connected with Barnsley Branch near to Darton Station, a distance of about three miles, and have continued the new line on to Cudworth, there to connect with the Midland Company's main line for stations southward ; also a fork line ought to have been made to Stairfoot, there to join the Manchester, Sheffield, and Lincolnshire Company's line. This would have opened out a new route for traffic from the South Yorkshire coalfields, and would have been the means of preventing the numerous projected schemes of new railways by other companies between Barnsley, Huddersfield, and Halifax, and would have saved the Company expense from having to oppose those new schemes in Parliament. It would also have enabled the Company to run two trains of coal from Barnsley Branch to all the stations west of Mirfield in the time now taken up in running one train, and would have greatly relieved the congested main line between Wakefield, Horbury, Mirfield, and Brighouse It would also have met the suggestions of the shareholder who said, "There is only one thing for us to do, either for us to extend the line or to lease it to some other company."

21

In my opinion, the cost of extending the Clayton West
Branch would be very little more than constructing the
proposed fork from Horbury Station to Barnsley Branch,
and doubling the line through Woolley Edge Tunnel, and
the Company could have utilised the Clayton West
Branch to advantage in giving relief to the main line, and
increasing the traffic.

I noticed that the chairman called the attention of the
proprietors to the large amount of money (£100,000)
which had been invested in the ordinary stock of the
Hull Dock Company, and said a very small dividend was
paid on this ordinary stock. He also said that the Company had ample running powers into Hull. This being
so, surely the Company had sufficient interest in Hull to
have warranted the central management in establishing a
through service of passenger trains to run between Liverpool, Manchester, and Hull. This would have been an
extension of our main line, such a service as I submitted
in November, 1869, a month prior to the opening of the
new branch line from Goole to Staddlethorpe, there to
join the North-Eastern Company's main line to and from
Hull. The local traffic on our system could have been
worked to and from Wakefield, and dovetailed in to work
with the express trains. This would have ensured a good
paying traffic between the two large seaport towns, Liverpool and Hull, and to some extent compensated for the
loss of dividend in the dock shares. The management
did not seem to grasp the importance and advantage it
would be to this Company if such a service had been
established, not only in passenger traffic, but in goods
traffic. The Manchester, Sheffield, and Lincolnshire
Company established a through service of passenger
trains to run between the two large seaport towns; and
the London and North-Western Company saw it was too
good a thing to be allowed to pass by, and they estab-

lished a service of passenger trains to connect the two large seaport towns. The Lancashire and Yorkshire Company were accordingly left out in the cold although their line was much the shorter route, and would have given the Company more mileage charges for traffic, than of handing it over to the North-Eastern Company at Normanton.

I never experienced such a want of loop lines and siding accommodation as I witnessed in Christmas week in 1891, the traffic being very heavy, and a fog prevailing continuously for several days. The traffic came to a deadlock throughout Yorkshire. Some of the passenger trains never ran at all, and the goods trains took two or three days to run the journey. I again took the opportunity of writing to the management, pointing out the necessity of the schemes submitted in 1869, 1870, and 1872 for siding extensions being carried out, showing that if part of those schemes had been acted upon, it would have saved locomotive power and prevented the delays which then occurred.

The half-year ending June 30th, 1892 the general meeting of proprietors was held at Manchester, on Wednesday, August 10th A dividend was declared at the rate of 3¼ per cent. The Chairman said · "I beg to move the adoption of the report and the approval of the accounts. You will find that our gross receipts show an increase of £23 957, and the working expenses an increase of £20,396. We have an increase in second-class passengers of 15,682. I think this is sufficient to convince you that we have done right in not making any alteration in the second class, the increase being greater on this occasion than we have experienced for the last three years. The power for the short line at Horbury has been sanctioned by Parliament. I am sorry that we have not been quite able to maintain the same dividend

as last year, and I have explained to you it is entirely
from the depression of trade, and the extra cost we are
put to by reducing the hours of labour. These are
matters which give us great anxiety, and which receive
due attention from our officers, to whom we are much
indebted for the pains they have taken in looking after
the affairs of the Company. No stone has been left
unturned to economise as much as possible, always bearing in mind the importance of maintaining our system
efficiently." The chairman also stated that the Company
were making alterations to the passenger stations at
Hebden Bridge and Hipperholme.

Some of the proprietors made a few remarks. One of
them said: 'I think the dividend is unsatisfactory to
the shareholders, considering the low price of materials.
Although there may be an advance in wages, I think
that with efficient management the dividend ought to be
considerably more than $3\frac{1}{4}$ per cent. I have drawn
attention on previous occasions to the excessively high
rates for maintenance of locomotive and traffic expenses.
These will require the serious attention of the directors.
I am sure $3\frac{1}{4}$d. per train mile for coal is excessive."

Another shareholder said. "I regret that we cannot
congratulate ourselves on stopping these continually-
diminishing dividends. We seem to meet from half-year
to half-year for the purpose of recording the gradual
decline of our dividend. I do not intend to go into that
matter, because you know my views. It is, of course,
because we have spent a great deal of capital not on
judicious lines"

Another shareholder said. "I should like to ask with
regard to the alliance between the Lancashire and Yorkshire and the Midland Company. You have now had the
experience of this alliance for a considerable time. Are
you in a position to say what is the effect on your pocket

of this alliance? I read a short time ago of a conversation between the general manager of the Midland Company and one of the directors of the London and North-Western Company, referring to the great increase of traffic on the Midland The director asked the manager, 'How have you managed?' 'Well,' was the reply, 'when the other companies are not looking we help ourselves.' That is our policy. The Midland are never satisfied unless they have their fingers in the pockets of their neighbours; and, unless you are particularly careful, I apprehend you will find those nimble fingers are in the pockets of the Lancashire and Yorkshire."

On reviewing the Chairman's explanation and remarks, made on the half-yearly report, together with the few remarks made by the proprietors, it was evident that the hope which he expressed at the half-yearly meeting held February 20th, 1889, when he said, "I feel pretty hopeful that our business will improve," being so long deferred, made their hearts ache, and they seemed to have given up in despair all prospect of a better dividend. As one of the shareholders said: "We seem to meet from half-year to half-year for the purpose of recording the gradual decline of our dividend." The dividends certainly ought to be considerably more than $3\frac{1}{4}$ per cent. The chairman seemed to make a great point of having conveyed 15,682 second-class passengers during the half-year, which he thought ought to be sufficient reason for not making any alterations in second-class accommodation. He seems to overlook the fact that had there been no second-class accommodation these 15,682 passengers would have travelled in company with others either first or third class. If the accommodation had been abolished, they might have been discomforted to the extent of being deprived of travelling in a carriage or compartment to themselves, and, had they been so inconvenienced, it would have resulted in a great saving to the Company, and would have materially reduced the working expenses, and added to the shareholders' dividend.

One of the shareholders was very jealous with regard to the alliance between the Lancashire and Yorkshire and the Midland Companies. He was afraid the latter company would be too wide awake and out-general the Lancashire and Yorkshire with the arrangements, and that the advantages would be against us. I, myself, had been under the impression that admitting other companies' trains to run over our crowded and congested lines, and picking up and putting down our local traffic, the advantages to this Company could not be very large. At any rate, since the alliance was made with those companies, the London and North-Western, Great Northern, and the Midland, it will be observed that the dividends of those companies had gone up, and our dividends had dwindled down. This looked as if the Lancashire and Yorkshire Company had been out-generalled in the arrangements.

At the beginning of 1892, the traffic being at such a low ebb, and shareholders complaining of poor dividends, I again submitted a scheme to run excursion trains between Huddersfield and the park at Lockwood. This park, which Mr. Henry F Beaumont, M.P , presented to the Corporation of Huddersfield, consisted of about 20 acres of most beautifully-wooded and picturesque land, dotted along a steep hillside with rugged rocks, and with streamlets of water rippling down into the valley below. The Corporation gladly accepted the gift, and had it tastefully laid out, making a most beautiful resort for the public as a recreation ground. After the opening of the park by His Royal Highness the Duke of Albany, the

Corporation were wishful to have a station erected near to the park on the Meltham Branch. The Board of Trade regulations prohibited this being done on account of the branch line being on such a steep gradient. The scheme referred to above was with a view to developing the local traffic with advantage to the Company. I suggested and urged that the Company should construct a siding on a level from Meltham Branch Junction, Lockwood, to run from there along the park side, a distance of some 800 yards, and a small station at the end, arriving the passengers in the park grounds, which could have been done at a very little cost to the Company I submitted a scheme for working the traffic, there being many trains that terminate at Huddersfield and have to wait an hour or more for the return journey. Such trains could have been utilised to work local trips to and from Huddersfield and Beaumont Park If faies were advertised to attract pic-nic parties and half-day excursionists from the various parts of the district, such as Halifax, Bradford, Leeds, Dewsbury, Wakefield, &c., during the summer season, a large amount of money might have been earned at very little extra cost in working expenses However, the scheme suggested was not entertained by the management.

With the view of improving the Blackpool and Southport traffic from the Yorkshire stations during the summer season, I submitted a scheme which covered the whole stations in Yorkshire, in 1892, the first train starting from Goole at 8-52, arriving at Blackpool at 1-10, thus taking up all stations, including Barnsley Branch, Stainland and Ripponden Branches, returning from Blackpool at 2-40, arriving at Goole at 7-50. This would have covered the ground with one engine and train for the day's work. The second train would start from Sheffield at 8-56, taking up all stations from Penistone,

Holmfirth, Clayton West, and Meltham Branches, and local stations from Brighouse to Todmorden, to return from Blackpool at 2-45 p m , arriving at Sheffield at 7-45, this engine and train thus covering this ground. The third train was intended to start from Leeds at 10-5, joining the Bradford and Dewsbury and Cleckheaton Branch portion at Low Moor, arriving at Blackpool at 12-37, returning from Blackpool at 5-10, arriving at Leeds at 8-5, this third engine covering this ground These three services to be run daily, Sundays excepted. On Saturdays an additional train was to leave Wakefield at 2 p m , arriving at Blackpool at 5-40, taking up all the stations from Wakefield to Todmorden, returning on Sunday at 6-30 p m., arriving at Wakefield at 10-13, and a special train to leave Leeds at 2-30, taking up Bradford at Low Moor, with Cleckheaton Branch and Stations to Sowerby Bridge, arriving at Blackpool at 5 p-m , returning on Monday at 7-5 a m , arriving at Leeds at 9-40. If this scheme had been adopted in its entirety, it would have kept the passengers from being mixed up in other trains, and prevented them from being delayed on the journey, and their luggage lost when changing at the several junctions, and would have saved 2,600 empty mileage, which were run this season to meet central management arrangements

On March 10th, 11th, and 16th, 1892, I attended a train alteration meeting, but I was unable to prevail upon the management to adopt the scheme suggested in its entirety of the ordinary local train service submitted to run between Halifax, Sowerby Bridge, and Rochdale; neither would they agree to adopt the scheme I submitted for improvement of the summer season service of trains from the Yorkshire stations to Blackpool, Southport, &c

The general meeting of the proprietors for the half-year

ending the 31st December, 1892, was held at Manchester on Wednesday, 8th February, 1893. A dividend was declared at the rate of 4 per cent per annum. The Chairman said : " I propose, as usual, to take you through the accounts in the order in which you will find them in the report. You will find that our gross receipts show a decrease of £11,642 as compared with the corresponding period of 1891, and the working expenses a decrease of £2,805. This is the first decrease on this side of the account that we have been able to show since the half-year ending June, 1886. I am not aware there is any other matter after having explained the report to which it is necessary for me to call your attention. In my opinion the property of the Company is in a thoroughly sound condition, and I hope that when the state of trade will permit us to carry more traffic than at present we shall be able not only to maintain but increase the dividend that we are now recommending."

Some of the shareholders were again dissatisfied, and made some strong remarks upon the management. One of them said· "Up to now I have not devoted the attention to the annual meetings that perhaps I ought to have done, but I find that although we possess a line passing through a country equal to that of the London and North-Western, yet that company so far exceeds us in profits that I cannot but think there must be some mismanagement somewhere. My friend on the left has referred to outlays on stations which are adjacent to this city. I will refer to what I consider extravagant outlays on stations in smaller towns. I will refer to the Thorn-hill and Heckmondwike Stations, two stations that have cost an immense amount of money, and yet are as bad stations as can be. To Thornhill Station you have no satisfactory access ; you have to tumble down to the line twelve or fourteen yards ; you cannot get passengers luggage to or from it. You have a station some 600 yards long, the ladies' waiting-room is at the east end, and if a lady is coming to Manchester she has to run some 300 or 400 yards along the platform to get to the train, and if a gentleman is going to the east he also has to run 300 or 400 yards to get to his train The accommodation is most wretched As for Heckmondwike Station, it is equally bad, or worse My friend on the right, if his statements are anything approaching correctness, has accounted, to my mind, for the reduction of dividend coming to us half-year by half-year, and we shall get down at this rate from what ought to be a first-rate property to a third or fourth rate property Mismanagement there must be somewhere, and in my own mind I can only put it on the chairman and directors. I am not going to put it on the servants of the Company. You, gentlemen, meet perhaps once a month, and discuss matters laid before you by the servants of the Company, and you probably know no more of the line between Wakefield and Goole than I do That for any railway company to have been guilty of an extravagant expenditure on such places as I have pointed out, without the prospect of a farthing a year increase, is guilty of an expenditure not one of you would have laid out in the same fashion on your own property."

Another shareholder said : " It is rather late to protest, as a gentleman here has done to-day, against the reduction of dividends he should have come to assist me when I have been knocking at it for years and years, protesting against such extravagant outlays I can point to lots of stations besides those mentioned, but I have been alone in protesting, The outlay of capital has been a million a year for the past fifteen years. The money is spent, and you have only yourselves to blame for it. You have the monkey on your back, and you will have to carry it."

Another shareholder said : "I think all the share-holders would be very much gratified if you would give them a good reason why the dividend of the Lancashire and Yorkshire is so poor as compared with the Great Western, the Midland, and other companies, which, I suppose, is 6 per cent. They have the same difficulties as you have about rolling stock, high wages, and frosty weather, and yet their dividends go on increasing. Ours never increases. I would like a good reason why this happens."

Another half-yearly meeting, calling together the pro-prietors, it may be, for the purpose of recording the gradual decline of dividend. Nevertheless, the chairman seems to be highly satisfied at being able to show a decrease in working expenses of £2,805, but he did not say how this had arisen, from good management or by a fluke. One of the shareholders asked for a real reason for the diminished dividends. The Chairman replied : "The reason is this, that our concern cost £90,000 per mile." Surely the reason given could not be expected to be a satisfactory explanation, as the line had cost the same amount of money on making it when they paid a 9¼ per cent dividend, as everyone knows it is the traffic and good management which makes the dividend. Another shareholder called attention to the extravagant outlay in building inadequate new stations—to wit, at Thornhill and Heckmondwike. The chairman replied it was the Board of Trade that compelled them to dispense with the level crossings that existed at each of those stations. This was certainly no answer as to the extrava-gances. It is quite true that both these stations are in-adequate for the purpose required, particularly Thornhill Station (which is on the main line), where a great waste of money occurred in not having well-matured and practical plans for the guidance of the contractors. I will name another new station which has been built—at Hebden Bridge, on the main line. At the time of laying the foundation stone for this station I called the attention of the authorities at Manchester to the fact that a great mistake was about to be made in building the new station on the plans the contractor showed to me This station ought to have been built on the island platform principle, the area of ground being so limited, and so well situated for such a station. One set of waiting rooms would have answered for both up and down lines, and would have been worked at a much less cost than the two-platform station Also, had it been built on the island platform principle, sufficient ground would have been left to construct four lines of rails through the station, which have long been required to facilitate running trains through it, this being one of the most congested parts of the main line between Sowerby Bridge and Todmorden The two-platform station has simply blocked up the ground for widening-out facilities, and working the traffic with punctuality. Nevertheless the Chairman concluded with the usual stereotyped remark: " We and the officers do the best we can for the Company " But this best they can do is poor consolation for the shareholders, and how the chairman and directors could rest and be satisfied with the management after those continuous tumultuous half-yearly meetings, and having to sit and listen to the many expressions of disapprobation, and never make the attempt to improve the policy of management or the position of the Company, is a problem I could never solve. If the management had deferred the building of new station houses, and spent money in widening-out facilities for working the traffic on the congested lines, delays would have been considerably reduced, and the working expenses would have been materially curtailed. Also, to have adhered to the policy of earning money, the management would then have been in a position to build new stations, and would not have blocked the line by taking up the ground which ought to have been appropriated for constructing working traffic more punctually They would then have prevented the dwindling dividends of the shareholders.

Mr. Appleyard has very clearly grasped the cause of the gradually declining position of the Company, and urges the shareholders to take action before it is too late. I heartily concur with his remark that this railway passes through the two best counties in England for traffic, and it is a disgrace to the management that they have allowed such a once prosperous line to dwindle from a 9¼ per cent to a 3½ per cent dividend

On Saturday, November 19th, 1892, a paragraph appeared in the *Barnsley Chronicle*. One of the members of the Chamber of Commerce said : " It is 20 years this month since the first sod of the Clayton West Branch was cut by Mr. John Kaye, J.P., and on that occasion the opinion was expressed by Mr. Normington who represented the Company, that the line would be of comparatively little value until such time as it could be extended to the Barnsley Branch. I at the same time expressed a hope that the directors would be induced to see their way to carry the line further, and hoped that the powers now asked for would be granted." (These remarks are quite correct. See my explanation of November 27th, 1872.)

On January 9th, 1893, a letter appeared in the *Halifax Courier*, signed C. Raymos Appleyard, advising the shareholders to take immediate action to lease their system at a fixed rental to some other company. They will get better terms now than they would later on. There are a host of reasons which could be adduced in favour of the line being leased to some other company, and I shall be glad to hear from the shareholders in the Company who are favourable to take active steps in the matter It is a well-known fact that the Lancashire and Yorkshire Company runs through two of the best counties in England--the two counties which the name of the Company signifies—and permanently stand head and shoulders over any two other counties in England as far as population and commerce are concerned

The half-year ending June 30th, 1893, general meeting of proprietors was held at Manchester on Wednesday, 9th of August, 1893, when a dividend was declared at the rate of $3\frac{1}{4}$ per cent The Chairman said : " I beg to move the adoption of the report and the approval of the accounts. The decrease in the receipts is £12,716, which has been caused by the stoppage in the cotton trade, and the working expenses have decreased £25,736. We have given the closest attention to the working expenses, and I venture to think that this result will be satisfactory to you. In connection with this account, the saving in all departments is out of all proportion to the net loss of traffic. This is accounted for by the increase being in the passenger department. I think you will agree with me, that, considering the difficulties that we have to contend with, we have had a fairly satisfactory half-year, and although we have been successful in effecting considerable economies in the working expenses, you may rest assured that in no case has this been done at the cost of inefficiency, nor will it ever be so long as I can help it."

The shareholders again made some dissatisfied remarks concerning the affairs of the Company. One of them said " We have been so accustomed to have a little shedding of our dividends, generally a quarter at a time, that I should not have been surprised if on this occasion we had got down to the sweet simplicity of the 3 per cent At any rate, I am agreeably surprised, and the fact points a moral "

Another said : " I am a shareholder of something like 35 years' standing. I am very much disappointed with the dividend earned by the Company for such a long period. If every station on the line is so grossly mismanaged as Poulton, no wonder our dividend is so small. At present wagon covers lie on the ballast for six or seven weeks together, covered with brickbats and rubbish, cart wheels go over them, and horses trample them under their feet In my opinion there are a great deal too many inspectors knocking about the line It used to be said that this railway was the nursery for good railway managers. Has it been so of late ? I trow not."

Another said : " While sympathising with the directors in the loss of traffic caused by the cotton strike, I can congratulate them on the small economies which reduce the working expenses by £25,736. I must say a dividend of 3¼ per cent is unsatisfactory. We want something different in management. If the working expenses were brought to a proper rate, the shareholders would be receiving a dividend of 5 or 6 per cent even out of present receipts, and unless you have men who can return something like a dividend to the shareholders, it is time there was a change."

Another said : " I should like to know what the directors were doing about taking away the second-class carriages. I came on a train this morning nearly empty I think if you would study that matter, and see if you could not take a little less for first-class passengers, and let the second-class passengers go in the first, you would recoup yourselves, as you would not have to keep up so many empty carriages running, which cost a great deal for wear and tear."

Another 3¼ per cent dividend, and this for the first half-year in 1893, and still the Chairman said. " I venture to think that this result will be considered satisfactory

by the shareholders." It was evident he had come to
the same conclusion which the shareholder had who said,
" We are a long-suffering, patient, and abiding people."
However, from the remarks made by other shareholders,
it was very clear they were not satisfied with the half-
year's results. One of them properly called attention to
the numerous travelling inspectors on the line, who, however, could not observe the irregularities taking place at
Poulton. The reply to this is, that this arises through the
policy of management, and needlessly adds to the working
expenses. He further remarked that the Lancashire and
Yorkshire Railway was formerly the nursery for good
railway managers. I can say this is quite correct, and
that nursery being destroyed has something to do with
the dwindling of the dividends. Another shareholder
called attention to the hauling of empty carriages about
the line, to accommodate second-class passengers when
there are any. A remedy for this had been suggested
years ago. Had it been adopted it would have materially
helped up the dividend by reducing the working
expenses. In consequence of a reduction in working expenses of £25,736, a vote of thanks was proposed to the
chairman. In returning thanks, he said, " We will
continue to do as well as we can ; we will do our best."
I fear the shareholders will find this great reduction in
working expenses is too good to continue, in the face of
neglecting to widen out facilities to enable the traffic to
be worked without delays.

In January, 1893, I found myself in great difficulties,
after hard struggling with family matters over which I
had no control. Just as I was getting clear of my undertaken obligations I received a letter from a solicitor,
demanding from me £210 19s. 9d., and saying I was
responsible for this amount, having signed my name to a
document on Sunday, the 22nd November, 1891, as surety

for a friend of mine, who was also a solicitor, for that amount. I considered this a most dastardly fraud practised upon me, and refused to pay it. Nevertheless, I found myself jammed between two solicitors, and the affair cost me a large amount of money and trouble to get out of. I can say here, "From such friends good Lord deliver us."

With a view to earning more money and reducing working expenses, I again brought forth my revised scheme for giving extended facilities from Yorkshire stations to Blackpool and Southport, which I submitted in 1892, to be adopted for the summer season of 1893, but it was again objected to.

In addition I also submitted a revised scheme, giving extended facilities for passenger traffic for the summer season from all Lancashire and Yorkshire stations to Bridlington, Filey, and Scarborough, the trains to run over the new line of the Scarborough, Bridlington, and West Riding Junction Railway. It was suggested for the special train to run daily, Sundays excepted, leaving Liverpool at 10-30 a.m., Manchester 11-25, and Wakefield 12-50, arriving at Bridlington at 2-33, Filey 3-1, and Scarborough at 3-20 p.m.; and to return from Scarborough at 4-35, Filey 4-50, Bridlington 5-20, arriving at Wakefield 7-1, Manchester 8-35, Liverpool 9-30 ; but this was not agreed to

The old system of working the summer season traffic to Bridlington and Scarborough was continued, resulting in the ordinary trains being overcrowded. Serious delays, inconvenience, and loss of traffic occurred, which also resulted in having to run empty mileage (usually termed in the workings, "special relief trains"), in order to meet expected requirements on the return journey.

I again renewed a scheme which I had previously devised and submitted, of local half-day excursions from

22

the various towns where the shopkeepers closed during
one day in the week for half-day holidays ; also on
Saturdays to the various places of attraction situated in
Yorkshire. This was only partly agreed to, and for what
was adopted prohibitory fares were inserted in the bills,
which had their effect upon the traffic where competition
existed. As an instance, Halifax or Bradford to Askern,
distance 35 miles, fare 1s. 9d. Other companies' half-day
trips from same towns to Cleethorpes or Morecambe Bay,
distance over 70 miles, fare 2s ; and even from Heckmondwike to Askern, half-day trip, distance 29 miles, 1s. 9d.
I suggested that the fare should not exceed 1s 4d. The
half-day excursion traffic was greatly marred in consequence of the competitive companies taking more
reasonable fares for much longer distances.

The half-year ending December 31st, 1893, general
meeting of proprietors was held at Manchester, on
Wednesday, February 7th, 1894, when a dividend was
declared at the rate of 3 per cent per annum.

The Chairman said : " I beg to move the adoption of
the report and the approval of the accounts. You will
find that the receipts show a decrease of £30,844, and an
increase in working expenses of £53,522. There is a
further item of serious importance. We have the obliga-
tion put upon us by the Board of Trade as to signalling,
brakes, and other matters of that kind. We have also to
contend with shorter hours of labour and higher rate of
wages, all tending to enhance the cost of working the
traffic. I regret, as you all will, the unfortunate circumstances which cause our dividend to be so low, but we can
do no more than look matters fairly in the face, and, in
view of the satisfactory increase which has taken place in
our traffic during the last few weeks, let us hope that we
may see better times in future."

The shareholders again seemed to be very much disappointed with the small dividend. One of them said : " Before the report is passed I should like to make a few remarks. Every shareholder in this concern must, with the directors, regret sincerely the cause which has led to a reduction in the profits. Notwithstanding, it strikes me the shareholders in the Lancashire and Yorkshire Company are a long-suffering and patient, abiding people, because if you compare the Lancashire and Yorkshire Railway some 30 years ago with its own brother, the London and North-Western, you will see the Lancashire and Yorkshire still runs through as prolific a country for providing traffic as the London and North-Western. Why should the Lancashire and Yorkshire have fallen into the position it holds to-day, and the corresponding line have maintained the position it held ? That is a question you must ask for yourselves. My opinion of the difference between the Lancashire and Yorkshire and the London and North-Western is this, that the management is somewhere wrong. Certain of one thing I am, it is not mismanagement of the holders of the ordinary stock, but must be the mismanagement of your Board of Directors. I think, if I am not mistaken, some 30 years ago the Lancashire and Yorkshire worked their line principally by district managers, and a certain number of directors divided the line into districts and looked after the management of your affairs. Now the whole management is in this building. Thirty years ago I do know if any customer, say at Cleckheaton or Dewsbury, and other towns in Yorkshire, had any grievance and took away his traffic, in much less time than a week he would be seen and reconciled. If any accident occurred on the line, the district manager was there to look after your interests, and appoint energetic men to look after the interests of the ordinary shareholders. I have heard and read some remarks made by a Mr. Johnson, and it strikes me his remarks have more weight than you have taken into account. Bear in mind, the majority of these gentlemen on the board can afford to see the line worked as it is, with their interests in the debentures and preferred shares, and fees for sitting behind that table, and you must now consider what you are to do in the future."

Another shareholder said · "We are met together to-day under extraordinary circumstances. I suppose we meet to regret the greatest drop in the dividend which has occurred at any one time in my recollection. We may not receive it with gratitude, but we may with resignation."

The half-year ending December 31st, 1893, will long be remembered by the shareholders—the best half-year for traffic, on one of the best lines in England, it being, as one of the shareholders remarked, a "gold mine," and "running through the very best traffic-producing country outside London"; yet the chairman has to-day declared a dividend of 3 per cent per annum.

This was as low a dividend as was paid in the last half-year of 1852, when the capital account was £11,809,360, as compared with £48,661,571 to-day. This is much worse than what I predicted in 1871 This half-year shows decreased receipts of £30,844, and yet we have an increase in working expenses of £53,522. The Chairman explained that this arose principally through carrying out the Board of Trade's requirements and other matters, with shorter hours of labour and higher rate of wages. Surely he knows that other companies have similar contingencies to contend with and they manage to pay dividends satisfactory to the shareholders. One of the shareholders put several important questions to the chairman. He asked, Why should the Lancashire and Yorkshire have fallen into the position it holds to-day?

He said mismanagement was somewhere. Some 30 years ago the Lancashire and Yorkshire worked their line principally by district managers, who appointed energetic men to assist them in looking after and working the traffic. I can vouch that in those early days referred to, wherever a £5 note could be made in the Yorkshire Division, the chance was never missed. It was this policy which enabled the directors to pay a dividend of $9\frac{1}{4}$ per cent. He also mentioned some other shareholder who had often made remarks at previous half-yearly meetings, which he considered ought to have had more weight than had been taken into account. I knew well the shareholders alluded to who had often given particulars of mismanagement, and had pointed out to the chairman that if their present policy was continued it would bring the line to ruin. Had he been now living he would have seen his prediction just on the verge of being realised. The Chairman concluded the meeting with the usual remark, " Let us hope we may see better times in the future. We do our best for you." Notwithstanding the chairman's concluding remarks, I know that more money might have been earned with less cost in working expenses had suggestions submitted to the management been carried out.

I remember passing a certain station in Yorkshire, when I observed some merrymaking and laughter on the platform, and on ascertaining the cause I could not help joining in the laugh. At this station there is a water tank or cistern for the purpose of supplying locomotive engines with water. The water float in the tank had got a little out of order, and, the water escaping, the matter was reported to headquarters. A few days afterwards a man was sent to look and ascertain what was wrong. After a few hours he returned to headquarters and came again the next day, bringing a mate with him. The two spent the day in repairing this float, and had to take lodgings for the night, managing to complete the work next day (the water being wasted by escaping most of the time), when they both returned to headquarters. It will be observed that this would be equal to five days' work for one man, and two nights' lodgings and expenses, and 300 miles travelling, I was told that formerly this work would have been done by a permanent-way man on the spot in less than three hours' time. I thought this was an example of how working expenses grew.

The half-year ending 30th June, 1894, general meeting of proprietors was held at Manchester on Wednesday, the 8th of August, 1894, and a dividend was declared at the rate of 3½ per cent per annum. The Chairman said: "I now beg to move the adoption of the report, and the approval of the accounts, and with your permission give my explanation thereon in the usual order. The increased receipts are £82,531, and the working expenses increased by £44,174. Taking into consideration the fact that the balance brought into the net increase account from last half year is £7,432 less than it was twelve months ago, and that there has been an increase in the interest and dividend on additional capital of £11,601, the result of the half-year's working, which enables us to recommend the payment of a dividend of 3½ per cent on the ordinary stock, an increase of ¦ per cent on the corresponding half-year, carrying forward a larger balance, may, I think, be considered satisfactory, and I have pleasure in moving the resolution." The resolution was passed

My remark is this: It was the quietest half-yearly meeting that had been held for years, and proved the assertion made by one of the shareholders at the last half-yearly meeting, that the shareholders in the Lancashire and Yorkshire Railway Company were a long-suffering, patient, and abiding people. Not one criticised the policy of management; they seemed to all have made up their minds to rest and be thankful for small mercies; even the chairman was satisfied, and pleased to say that the result of the half-yearly workings enabled them to pay a dividend of $3\frac{1}{2}$ per cent; this, he considered, ought to be satisfactory. A vote of thanks was accorded to the chairman, and was passed unanimously.

I received notice that on the 1st of January, 1894, train alterations would all be dealt with at the Central Office, at Manchester. Nevertheless, I was summoned to attend a time table meeting on Wednesday, the 31st January, 1894. I attended the meeting prepared, and submitted, as usual, many local train with other alterations, with the view of serving the public by running in direct connection with the main line express trains to and from Manchester, Liverpool, Hull, and York. However, when the time books were issued to the public for July 2nd, I received a revised time book on Saturday, June 30th, and had to be at the office all day on Sunday, preparing the workings for the men concerned. On looking over the new time table, I found very few of my recommendations carried out The local services of trains were severed from their connections at the several junctions, which caused a complete chaos of confusion to the public. Some of the main line trains were diverted into branch trains, the branch trains into main line, and the flow of passenger traffic diverted from its legitimate course, causing many changes and delays to passengers in their journeys, which gave dissatisfaction throughout the whole district, and resulted in loss, not only of passenger traffic, but goods also. The traffic canvassers were set in motion to get it back again, and the usual patching up to meet part of the requirements was resorted to at an extra cost of putting on additional trains—the usual mode of experimenting. The July time table, which only came out (with its numerous and important summer alterations) on Saturday, June 30th, was a grand specimen of the knowledge the management had in devising a time table with a train service which would serve the public requirements. I was surprised that this blundering did not draw the attention of the general manager or the managing director, so as to have adopted a different policy of train arrangements for the future. The connections from Bradford, Cleckheaton Branch, Huddersfield, and Dewsbury, where there is keen competition, had been left out altogether in the cold. The passengers from the above-named towns had no other alternative but to travel by the competitive companies, having no satisfactory connection with the express trains This, coupled with the unsatisfactory local train service, in my opinion was a great loss to the Company, a much greater loss than the gain realised by the express trains running to and from York and Scarborough. The two named services of trains ought to have run in harmony together to have ensured the best interests of the Company. I again submitted the summer season service of trains (which I had recommended in 1893) to be adopted in 1894, but it was again objected to, which resulted, as usual, in empty mileage being run for the Blackpool service this year of 2,100 miles.

The Company not earning the money they might and ought to do (which was within their reach) by cultivating more local traffic, which was said by a shareholder to be "a gold mine" in the district, I again submitted, in 1894, the scheme suggested for 1892 and 1893, of running half-day excursions, at reasonable fares, from the various towns on their half-day closing days, to the various places of note and attraction But I observed, on the bills being issued to the public, only part of the scheme had been adopted, and this was again spoiled by prohibitory fares for the distances travelled. The management have yet to find out that money-making pays the dividend

The revised time table for July caused great inconvenience to Barnsley tradespeople. Several members of the Chamber of Commerce complained to me verbally. They said the altered trains which ran between Barnsley and Wakefield meant simply locking up the branch line so far as business people were concerned. I called the authorities' attention to these complaints, and submitted a revised service, with the view of complying with their requirements, which could have been worked without putting on any additional engine power, but this was not agreed to. It led to the members of the Chamber of Commerce forming a deputation to wait upon the directors at Manchester, to state their grievances. At their next meeting, on Thursday, August 23rd, they reported the result. The following account of the interview appeared in a Barnsley newspaper on Saturday, August 25th, 1894 :—

BARNSLEY AND DISTRICT CHAMBER OF COMMERCE.

This chamber met on Thursday, at the Town Hall. Mr W. Batty was in the chair, and present were the Mayor (Dr. Halton), County Alderman Brady, Aldermen Wray and Woodcock, Councillors Brady and Foulstone, and Messrs. R D Maddison, A. Fawcett, H. B. Nash, T Fox, J. Bycraft, G W. Cuming, C. H Hutchinson, — Wright, C A. Moulton, secretary, &c.—The Chairman said he, Mr Cuming, Ald. Wray, and Councillor Brady went to Manchester on the 12th inst, as a deputation to the directors of the Lancashire and Yorkshire Railway Company, in regard to train services between Wakefield, Newcastle, York, Scarborough, &c , and the Clayton West extension   After various delays they were ushered into the august presence of the chairman of the directors, and before he (the speaker) had said half a dozen words he was asked to be as brief as possible, and they showed as briefly as they could the inconveniences travellers were put to by the delays at Wakefield, the Clayton West extension seemed to be the more important question to the Company. They came away not feeling satisfied with the reception they had met with.—Alderman Wray said they were much disappointed   The Company boycotted Barnsley by delaying passengers at Wakefield, and neither bringing them nor allowing any other person to bring them to Barnsley, and the only way to obtain a remedy was to boycott the Company by taking all the traffic they could off the line —Councillor Brady agreed as to the scant courtesy of their treatment and the means to obtain greater consideration. He suggested fast trains to Barnsley, and was told they would be run if the deputation would guarantee them paying —A letter was read from the Company saying nothing could be done, and, on the motion of Alderman Wray, seconded by the Mayor, a resolution expressing great dissatisfaction was passed The M. S & L. Company promised to consider the question of workmen's trains to Barnsley from Chapeltown, Birdwell, and Dovecliffe during the making of the new railway The appointment of delegates to the meeting of the Associated Chamber of Commerce at Huddersfield, on the 11th and 12th September, was left with the chairman and secretary. The resolution on the Lancashire and Yorkshire Company's question was finally drafted as follows · "That as various applications have been made to the Lancashire and Yorkshire Railway Company to provide reasonable and proper connections at Wakefield for the Barnsley Branch trains, in order to avoid the delays caused to passengers between Barnsley, Scarborough, York, Newcastle, and the North, and the council in consequence having appointed a deputation to wait upon the directors, to make another appeal to them on this subject, and, further, to request them to carry out the long needed Clayton West extension, and this chamber, now finding that the directors have again disregarded the just demands of the town respecting the Wakefield connections, and altogether ignoring the question of the Clayton West extension, hereby expresses its regret at the unsatisfactory nature of the reply, which, in its opinion, is not calculated to increase or maintain the pleasant relations which have hitherto existed between the traders of the district and the Company."

From the above extract it will be seen that the deputation were not very favourably received, which gave great dissatisfaction, and resulted in traffic being diverted in various ways from the Company's line, and also did not improve their reputation. The centralised policy of management in this did not harmonise with that laid down by the late chairman, Mr. John Pearson, at the half-yearly August meeting. 1883, when he said, notwithstanding this neglect and inefficient management, he had faith, with such a hive of industry as the line passes through, that the increased facilities they were about to commence would enable them by perseverance, judicious expenditure, economy in working, diligent attention to the requirements of their customers—in fact, good management—to overcome all their difficulties. However, nine months after the lost opportunity, the Barnsley people were surprised when they saw bills posted in the town, in large red letters, announcing three additional trains to be run every day, Sundays excepted, between Barnsley and Wakefield, to commence April 1st, 1895. This was done with the view of recovering lost traffic; but this came too late; it had gone for ever. The putting on an additional engine, guard, and trains, which had no immediate connection at Wakefield with main line trains, did not serve their requirements, and was simply adding to a congested line and working expenses.

The general meeting of the propietors for the half-year ending 31st December, 1894, was held at Manchester 6th February, 1895. The Chairman said, in moving the adoption of the report and passing the accounts, that last year they had to content themselves with a reduction in their dividend, caused by the unfortunate stoppage in the coal trade; it was therefore the greatest pleasure to him that day to meet the shareholders with a more satisfactory report. Now that they had returned to a more normal state of affairs, they could declare a dividend of $1\frac{1}{2}$ per cent more than in 1893, and a $\frac{1}{2}$ per cent more than in 1892. "The report shows an increase of £131,964, and the working expenses a decrease of £19,164, which enables us to declare a dividend at the rate of $4\frac{1}{2}$ per cent per annum. The decrease in working expenses is partly accounted for by obtaining coal at a lower price than in 1893, and the engines, being of an improved type, are enabled to deal with heavier loads, and are worked with more economy. The shareholders must not raise their hopes too high as regards the future" So far as the management of the line went, he thought they might claim that they had brought it, as regards its stations, permanent way, and rolling stock, into as good condition as any in the country, and if care and energy on the part of their officers would do it, they would keep it so. The chairman and directors passed over what might be termed another quiet half-yearly meeting. However, some of the shareholders made a few remarks. One of them said : "I do not know if you, Mr Chairman, or any of the directors, have been at Knowsley Street Station, Bury, since the alterations and enlargements were finished I would recommend you to go and see it. I would see, before I would make any alterations, whether I could not spend the shareholders' money to more advantage. I consider, on the Knowsley Street Station especially, the money you have spent might as well have been sent into the gutter. It is ten times worse than before the alterations." The Chairman explained that the Corporation agreed to the plans. The shareholder replied, "They took what they could get from you" The Chairman then said, "They are not grateful," and closed the meeting by putting the resolution.

Another shareholder said : "I should just like to say that, with regard to the management of this Company, it may be a pleasure to some of the shareholders to know that directors of other companies, and especially those who are in London, have several times remarked to me that the Lancashire and Yorkshire Company was now looked upon as one of the best managed companies in England But, gentlemen, I want us to remember that because we have received a dividend larger than the past, we must not therefore rest on our oars. We have a lot of hungry people outside, who are everlastingly clamouring. I have always said to these hungry wolves outside that if they could find a private concern as well managed as this Company, I should be glad to hear of it."

The Chairman seemed to be very pleased at being able to announce to the shareholders that the directors were in a position to declare a dividend at the rate of $4\frac{1}{2}$ per cent, which, he said, made it 4 per cent for the year, and expressed himself highly satisfied with the past year's results. He is again sure they have now arrived at a more normal state of affairs, but still he has not much faith in the future management, as he warns the shareholders not to place their hopes too high. However, one of the shareholders thought that, having had a 4 per cent per annum dividend declared, they ought to pass a vote of thanks to the chairman and directors, because they always do their best. This resolution was seconded and passed. Whether the final words in the resolution were intended as a joke or not I leave to conjecture; but the chairman, in acknowledging the vote of thanks, made use of the words he generally uses at the conclusion of the half-yearly meetings—"We have done the best we can." However, doing the best they can is not always synonymous with either good management, prudence, or wisdom. The increased receipts and dividend may be satisfactory under certain circumstances; but if the management had adopted suggestions submitted, and had not created a bad feeling on the part of the public, more money would have been earned at a further reduction of working expenses. In addition to the increased dividend, it would have been still more gratifying to the shareholders if it had been intimated at the close of the meeting that such alterations in the management had been made as would ensure in the future keeping pace with the public requirements. To have done this, he would then have had no need to be afraid of the cost of increased wages, with shorter hours, for the Company's servants. It was stated that the rolling stock was as good as any in the country. I do not think any railway company possesses a better stock of locomotive engines and railway carriages, taking them all throughout, than the Lancashire and Yorkshire Company. I wish I could say the same with regard to the new station houses that have been built I noticed one of the shareholders called the chairman's attention to the extravagance and inadequacy in the new stations built in the Lancashire district. This, coupled with what had been done in the Yorkshire district, shows that the waste of money in this department exists throughout the line; also that he was not satisfied with the reply that the plans had been approved by the Corporation. The Chairman concluded abruptly, by saying they were not grateful. It was said at the meeting that the Lancashire and Yorkshire Railway Company was looked upon as one of the best managed companies in England. Although the line passes through districts that are gold mines in themselves for traffic, the directors have managed to bring down the dividends from $9\frac{1}{4}$ to less than 4 per cent. If a private concern managed their affairs in such a manner, they would very soon find they would collapse altogether. Allusion was made to what was termed a lot of hungry wolves outside. I suppose this refers to the poor widows and orphans, whose livelihood depends upon the dividend paid by the Company It should be remembered that to this class of shareholders a poor dividend makes all the difference to the ease and comfort of their existence

I have often heard it said by the powers that be that when divisional management paid a dividend of $9\frac{1}{4}$ per cent the line and rolling stock were greatly impoverished; but surely, after having spent twenty-eight millions of money over it since 1872, it ought to have recouped itself long ago, and have enabled the directors to pay a dividend of 10 per cent at the end of June, 1895. The great waste of money in building inadequate new stations, and in making other alterations at the various stations on the line, will account to some extent for the increased working expenses. The general manager or the superintendent of the line rarely visited the districts, to have the necessary interviews with the district officers. The management preferred employing numerous travelling inspectors, and acted upon the information obtained from them, which resulted in their never adopting any definite policy, but always acting upon the principle of an expensive experimenting management. If the Board of Directors which were in authority had existed up to 1872, the Company would never have been allowed to drift to so low a position as it now occupies amongst railways.

The Board of Directors and officers at the end of June, 1895, were as follow —

Directors.

Chairman, George John Armytage, Esq
Deputy-Chairman, William Tunstill, Esq.

Heywood Bright, Esq.	J. W. Naylor, Esq.
Thomas Fielden, Esq	James Priestley, Esq
Sir Edward Green, Esq.	Sir David Radcliffe, Esq.
Wm. Henry Hornby, Esq.	John Ramsbottom, Esq.
Joseph Lees, Esq.	E. Wilfred Stanyforth, Esq.
S M. Milne, Esq.	Henry Yates Thompson, Esq.

Officers.

General Manager, J H. Stafford, Esq
Passenger Superintendent, C. J. Nicholson, Esq.
Central District Passenger Superintendent, J. Bolland, Esq
Yorkshire District Passenger Superintendent, Thomas Normington, Esq.
East Lancashire District Passenger Superintendent, John Whitehall, Esq.

The half-year ending June 30th, 1895, half-yearly meeting of the shareholders was held at Manchester, on

Wednesday, August 7th, 1895. The Chairman moved the adoption of the report and the approval of the accounts

He said : "You will observe that the amount of our capital chargeable to revenue is £53,277,765, as against £48,922,573 last half-year, although the amount actually expended is only £258,277 This large increase is accounted for by a nominal addition of £4,132,664 to our debenture stock, which is brought forward by the conversion of that stock from 4 per cent to 3 per cent This, however, does not lead to any additional charges upon revenue. The past half-year shows increased receipts of £6,281, and the working expenses a decrease of £8,488. The directors recommend the proprietors to declare a dividend at the rate of 3¾ per cent per annum. There has been a decrease in receipts from ordinary passengers of £6,969." After the Chairman had further explained the report, he said . "It does not occur to me that there is anything else to which I need call your attention. I think we may be fairly satisfied that during a considerably depressed period, with an exceptional winter, we have been enabled not only to obtain a slight increase in our receipts, but have succeeded in doing so with a less train mileage and a decreased expenditure, whereby we are in a position to declare an additional quarter per cent dividend, and to increase our balance forward by the sum of £3,211 This is extremely satisfactory, and reflects the greatest credit on our officers and servants, who, from the highest to the lowest, have shown a zeal and energy in working your property which is most encouraging"

The motion was put for the adoption of the report, and carried

This was the quietest shareholders' meeting since 1874. However, one of the shareholders did ask how it was that, with the goods, minerals, and live stock, and with a new steamer afloat, the receipts for this half-year were less than they were in the same period of 1894. The Chairman said he had explained all that in his remarks.

Another shareholder said: "As no other shareholder gets up, I should like to offer our hearty congratulations on the satisfactory report which the directors have presented to the Company. Of course, gentlemen, the mere fact of an increase of $\frac{1}{4}$ per cent in the dividend is not, standing by itself, a very great thing I think on the whole that the report cannot be considered other than most satisfactory, and the directors and the officials are entitled to great credit for the manner in which they have managed the affairs of the Company during the past half-year. I do not know that I need occupy your time any further. I will merely say that we, on this side of the table, think that you have presented us with a good dividend."

Another said: "I think we ought not to separate without passing a vote of thanks to our chairman for the manner in which he has conducted the business of this meeting. The business-like way in which he has laid the accounts before us is very creditable, and I move that we give our best thanks to him."

Another said: "I have very great pleasure in seconding the vote. I like a short meeting. There is something business-like about it."

The Chairman replied · "I am very much obliged to you, gentlemen. I can only say we have done our best. We always do our best, and if you believe that we do our best when perhaps the dividend may be a little bit down, I shall be still more grateful."

This is the last half-yearly meeting concerning which I shall be in a position to know the inner workings of the management sufficiently well to enable me to criticise the remarks made at these meetings. I have observed ever since 1873 that the shareholders have tried hard to penetrate into the management, with a view of establishing some improved policy. They increased the general manager's salary in 1879, but still matters got worse, and in 1883 they made a change in their chairmanship, and appointed a managing director at a salary of £2,000 a year, thus establishing, as one shareholder remarked, "two Richmonds in the field." Notwithstanding all this, the mismanagement and dissatisfaction have continued up to this date. It was evident that at this half-yearly meeting the shareholders had got weary of expressing their dissatisfaction, and had decided to rest and be thankful for small mercies. However, one asked the following question · "How is it that with the increased goods, mineral, and live stock traffic, and with a new steamer afloat, that the receipts are less than in the same period of 1894?" The chairman's explanation of this could not be considered satisfactory. Another shareholder remarked that the mere fact of declaring a 3¾ per cent dividend was not, standing by itself, a very great thing, but, considering the surrounding circumstances, they would be satisfied.

From the chairman's concluding remarks, there was not much prospect before the shareholders for better dividends, as he did not appear to foresee any better result than a 3¾ per cent dividend, and he himself thought that that was, or ought to be, satisfactory for shareholders of the Lancashire and Yorkshire Railway Company, although it might be considered a 10 per cent line. He asked the shareholders to be more grateful towards him when the dividends were a little bit down, because, as he said, "We have done our best We always do our best."

The Lancashire and Yorkshire Railway runs through the best districts in the country for producing railway traffic. Therefore it was not altogether a question of the great cost of constructing the line, but was more a question of applying its advantages when opened for traffic, by giving facilities adapted for commercial enterprise and to the local requirements, and to the public generally. To have done this would have ensured good and satisfactory results; but, unfortunately, the management got into incompetent hands, and in 1871 they adopted a policy which assumed that the public were made for the railway, instead of the railway being made for the public. They even wasted money, and won a bad reputation, by trying to prevent the public from helping themselves; but in spite of all their generalship, other railway companies penetrated, and secured a large share of their increased and growing traffic.

The Company made three great mistakes in Yorkshire. The first was in not taking up the position, when they had the chance, of keeping the London and North-Western Railway Company on the west side of Huddersfield, in 1849. The second was in not keeping the Great Northern Railway Company on the south side of Pontefract when they had the chance, in 1863; and the third when they discontinued divisional management and adopted the policy of centralised management, in 1871. However, the mischief is done, and the first two are irrevocable. The latter might be improved by altered management; but I fear, even then, the 10 per cent dividend will not be realised, as predicted by the directors in 1871.

The following is a summary of dividends paid by the Lancashire and Yorkshire Railway Company, from the end of June, 1847, to the end of June, 1895 :—

Date.	Per Cent.	Capital.	Miles Open.	Date.	Per Cent.	Capital.	Miles Open.
June, 1847	7	£		June, 1872	7½	£	
December, 1847...	7	5,377,062		December, 1872..	9½	24,751,654	
June, 1848	6			June, 1873	7¼		
December, 1848...	5	5,730,044		December, 1873..	7	25,333,237	
June, 1849	4			June, 1874	6		430
December, 1849...	3	8,699,310		December, 1874..	6½	26,627,087	
June, 1850	2			June, 1875	6		437¼
December, 1850...	2	11,926,494	195⅛	December, 1875..	6	27,859,289	
June, 1851	2			June, 1876	5½		
December, 1851...	3	11,917,296		December, 1876..	6¼	28,964,904	441
June, 1852	3			June, 1877	5¾		
December, 1852...	3	11,809,360		December, 1877..	6½	30,105,253	450¾
June, 1853	3¼			June, 1878	4¾		
December, 1853...	3½	12,096,352		December, 1878.	6	30,998,131	457¼
June, 1854	3½			June, 1879	4		
December, 1854...	3½	12,301,856		December, 1879..	5¼	33,682,234	475¾
June, 1855	4			June, 1880	5		
December, 1855...	4	12,740,448	212⅝	December, 1880..	5¾	34,405,589	485½
June, 1856	4½			June, 1881	4¼		
December, 1856...	5	12,832,847		December, 1881..	5¾	35,619,874	493
June, 1857	5			June, 1882	4¾		
December, 1857...	4¼	13,593,608	213⅝	December, 1882..	5	37,302,643	497
June, 1858	3¾			June, 1883	4½		
December, 1858...	4	13,847,618		December, 1883..	4¾	38,667,091	496½
June, 1859	4½			June, 1884	4		
December, 1859...	5	18,471,494	362	December, 1884..	4½	40,145,112	496½
June, 1860	5½			June, 1885	4½		
December, 1860...	6	18,831,230		December, 1885..	3¼	41,221,611	496½
June, 1861	5½			June, 1886	3		
December, 1861...	5	19,272,705		December, 1886..	4	42,111,810	496½
June, 1862	3¾			June, 1887	3¾		
December, 1862...	4	19,790,778		December, 1887..	4¾	43,261,092	500¾
June, 1863	4¼			June, 1888	3¾		
December, 1863...	4¾	19,913,571		December, 1888.	4½	45,242,693	511
June, 1864	5¾			June, 1889	4¼		
December, 1864...	6	20,255,371		December, 1889..	4¾	46,035,876	529¼
June, 1865	5½			June, 1890	4		
December, 1865...	6¼	20,917,285	403	December, 1890..	4½	46,722,036	529¼
June, 1866	6¾			June, 1891	3½		
December, 1866...	6¾	22,001,104		December, 1891..	4¼	47,626,947	527
June, 1867	6½			June, 1892	3¼		
December, 1867...	6½	22,456,610		December, 1892..	4	48,145,064	527
June, 1868	6¾			June, 1893	3¼		
December, 1868...	6¾	22,853,038	411½	December, 1893..	3	48,661,531	527
June, 1869	6¾			June, 1894	3½		
December, 1869...	6¾	23,043,340	423	December, 1894..	4½	52,771,295	529¼
June, 1870	7			June, 1895	3¾	53,277,765	529¼
December, 1870...	7	23,518,683	428½				
June, 1871	7¾						
December, 1871...	8	24,092,512					

You will observe by the recorded list of past dividends paid to the shareholders, at the end of December, 1852, that a 3 per cent was paid, and the capital account shown then to be £11,809,360. The next 3 per cent dividend was paid at the end of June, 1886; capital account then shown to be £41,221,611. After the management had spent over twenty-nine millions of money, in thirty-four years, they found themselves again at a 3 per cent dividend, although, in the meantime, the general manager's salary had been substantially increased, and, in addition, a managing director appointed, at a salary of £2,000 a year. Notwithstanding this extra cost in the management, with the increased population and trade throughout the system, the dividends are still in an unsatisfactory state up to this date, the end of June, 1895, when a dividend was declared of $3\frac{3}{4}$ per cent; capital account shown in report, £53,277,765.

The Lancashire and Yorkshire Railway management have been asleep, whilst other railway competitive companies have been wide awake, watching their opportunity. Through the help of the disappointed public, who had been so long neglected in regard to the necessary railway facilities and to their grievances being so narrow-mindedly dealt with, which had the effect of retarding their various and important industries, the other companies succeeded in penetrating into the very midst of this Company's heavy paying traffic, leaving nothing for themselves but the crumbs that fell from their masters' table.

My observations throughout this book are verified from the returns of the earnings of the four companies concerned for the half-year ending December, 1896. These returns were copied from the newspaper reports.

Increased receipts for the half-year :—

London and North-Western Company £207,285
The Midland 168,929
Great Northern....... 91,537
Lancashire and Yorkshire. 70.825

It is still more observable, the increased receipts for Christmas week alone, for this year, 1896, over last year, 1895 :—

London and North-Western Company £26,511
The Midland 20,827
Great Northern 16,662
Lancashire and Yorkshire 5,203

Formerly the Lancashire and Yorkshire Company always showed the highest increased receipts of any other company at holiday times, particularly at Whitsuntide and Christmas week

I may also mention, in conclusion, another source of loss to the interests of the Company. This arises through the dissatisfaction prevailing amongst the Company's servants. The policy of management debars promotion in the service to those who have well earned and merited it. The remunerative positions are stored up for favoured friends. They are given, in some instances, to mere youths, who are not only young in experience in the Company's service, but in age. Although inexperienced, they are put into responsible positions, where practical qualified men ought to be placed, and over the heads of those who have entered the service of the Company with the view of gaining such positions as they arise.

CONCLUDING REMARKS.

1. Central management never did produce a well-matured scheme in any way likely to serve the public generally and be remunerative to the Company. Never-

theless, there were those in the ring of management who claimed the merit of feasible suggestions; at any rate, they claimed to have foreseen that which came to pass, so easy is it to be wise after the event. Is it not a curious fact that we have no record extant of any one of them whose prescience could discern the ultimate outcome of the railway system? The results of central management since 1872 verify this.

2. Few things would be more cognate to the scope and purpose of this book than a record of the vast growth of the population and staple industries, for the past fifty years, within the area through which the Lancashire and Yorkshire Railway trains run.

3. The proprietors of railways ought to have some surety of a reasonable dividend in recognition of their coming forward with millions of money, and risking it in construction and working, finding employment for hundreds of thousands of people. It also creates an amount of industry, providing employment greater than all the productive industries of the country, and, increasing year by year, constantly adds to the wealth of the nation

4. Concerning the vast magnitude and importance of the railway system, it is somewhat unaccountable that an historical record of some improved policy of management has not hitherto been published, especially when noting, for the past fifty years, the rise and fall of the various railway companies in England consequent upon the management. However, I have ventured to describe two methods of railway management which have come under my close and immediate observation during the past forty-nine years, on a line noted for its vastly-increasing population, its varied and numerous industries, having the best traffic-producing districts in the country, and covering an area of ground over which the Lancashire and Yorkshire Com-

pany have constructed close upon five hundred and thirty miles of railway. It will be observed that this book treats principally upon two separate policies of management, which have been well tested by this Company. Firstly, divisional management, which encouraged development, maintained efficiency and harmony, mixed with divisional rivalry in earning money at the least cost in working the traffic. This management resulted in the directors declaring a dividend of 9¼ per cent; the shares sold in the market at 166½. After the Company had risen to this high position, it baffles all comprehension why the directors could have been prevailed upon to change the existing policy of management, which had done so well, to that of centralisation, of which management they knew nothing. However, they said it was to be only an experiment. Centralised policy destroyed development, efficiency, energy, and enterprise with the divisional officers; caused continuous experimenting, thus adding to the working expenses and loss of traffic; and also placed every obstacle in the way of practical suggestions for earning money. This management in fourteen years' time resulted in breaking the back of one of the most prosperous railways in England, the directors having to declare a dividend of 3 per cent, whilst the shares in the market were sold below par. This was most disastrous and deplorable, especially in face of an increasing population, with its various industries, throughout the line. It will be observed this was worse even than what I predicted to the general manager in June, 1871. The Company seemed to be drifting to the position they were in fifty years ago—that was when the bailiffs took possession, and the staff were without wages for over a month. This definition of the two separate policies of management is clearly demonstrated by facts contained in this book, from 1847 up to the end of June, 1895.

I remember being approached by a gentleman, who expressed a desire to become a director of the Lancashire and Yorkshire Railway. At that time the balance of the directorate was greatly in favour of Lancashire, which was a disadvantage to Yorkshire. Had it been otherwise in 1863, the Great Northern Company would never have been on the north-west side of Pontefract only through the permission of the Lancashire and Yorkshire Company. I, therefore, with a view to strengthen the directorate in Yorkshire, brought to bear what influence I had upon the question, when his desire was gratified in 1875. I had hoped, knowing his business abilities, he would have been one to have tried to avert the gradual degradation of the Company's position.

I also remember, in 1879, receiving a letter from one of the directors, desiring me to call at his office on the first opportunity. I called the following day. He named a certain gentleman, and asked me if I thought him a suitable person to hold the position of railway director. I thought this was another chance to strengthen the directorate for Yorkshire; and from the conversation we had afterwards on the subject, he was appointed a director on Wednesday, 26th of March, 1879, and proved to be a very regular attender at the board meetings.

Owing to the shareholders being so dissatisfied with the management, it was decided to appoint a new chairman. A special general meeting of the proprietors was held at Manchester on the 23rd of March, 1883, for that purpose. I thought this was another opportunity to give Yorkshire a further lift up the ladder by choosing a Yorkshire director for the new chairman, and with that view I had interviews with many of the large shareholders in Yorkshire, who attended the special meeting with the intention of supporting his nomination. However, a Lancashire director, who had served on the

24

directorate a longer period, was appointed as new chairman and managing director, at a salary of £2,000 a year, and the Yorkshire director was appointed deputy-chairman.

I conclude this book, which contains many happy reminiscences of my having helped persons to improved situations, not only in England, but also others who have emigrated, and of having had the influence to help many more to occupy high positions during my railway career.

The following is a copy of my conditions, submitted to the general manager on my retirement —

"March 5th, 1895.

"J. H. Stafford, Esq., General Manager,

"Lancashire and Yorkshire Railway Company,

"Manchester

"Dear Sir,—This being my seventy-first birthday, I thought it an opportune time to reply to the question you put to me when at your office on Monday, the 18th of February, and in order to do so I am somewhat reluctant to make special mention of the services I have from time to time rendered to the Company.

"I have now served the Company faithfully for more than forty-eight years, over thirty-six of which I have held the position as district superintendent for Yorkshire Division, and during that time I have done a great deal of work, both day and night

"I have also attended superintendents' meetings, both in London and elsewhere, devising traffic arrangements with other companies' superintendents, and often attended the Board of Directors' meetings, up to June, 1871, when the policy of management was changed; and if it was then considered to be to the Company's advantage to continue me in so responsible a position, although with circumscribed powers of acting, the Company has received the benefit.

"In July, 1866, I received some injuries to my head and shock to the system, in a collision near to Crofton Station, and had to lay up for twenty days.

"In November, the same year, I had two ribs broken, and was otherwise severely shaken, in a collision near Horbury Station, and had to lay up for five weeks. I received no compensation for injuries for either of these accidents

"In July, 1868, I had again to lay up for three weeks, brought on with hard continuous working, not having sufficiently recovered from the severe shock received in the two named collisions

"From 1862 to 1866, in addition to my ordinary duties, I undertook to manage the Excursion Agency, which effected a saving of commission to the Company of close upon £3,000. I desire this, together with the injuries I received in the two collisions, to be taken into consideration on my retirement.

"In 1868 the general manager for the Great Northern Railway Company desired to give me an appointment on their line, and I should have accepted had not our directors pressed me not to leave them, and promised that eventually I should be made all right. With this understanding I remained with the Company; nevertheless, I am a poorer man to-day—owing to misfortune not within my own control—than when I first entered the Company's service.

"I was a shareholder in this Company in 1876, but eventually I had to dispose of my shares at a loss of over fifty pounds, to help me to pay off undertaken responsibilities. This absorbed all the money I had, and more, even to the confiscation of my life policy, through a dastardly fraud having been practised upon me by one whom I had ever considered a friend. It will take me some little time to make the necessary arrangements to

ensure a livelihood after I have left the service. Therefore I trust that, after devoting the best part of a lifetime
to the Company, you will kindly and favourably consider
my long services as the oldest officer of the Company,
and help me at a time of need with a special grant of one
year's salary and an annuity of one pound per week, as
my life cannot, in any case, be long prolonged, and to
continue my general free pass on the line.

"I will prepare to retire from the Company's service at
the end of June, 1895, and at the same time I shall
always be glad to render the Company every assistance in
my power, with the knowledge and experience gained
through a lifetime spent in official service.

"Yours obediently,
"THOMAS NORMINGTON."

On March 27th I had a reply to my letter of the 5th,
informing me that my letter had been laid before the
directors, and that, having regard to the somewhat
exceptional circumstances, they treated my application
specially, and would pay me six months' salary on my
retirement.

On April 2nd I replied to the letter of the 27th. I
said · "I duly received your reply to my letter of the 5th
of March, which had reference to my resignation; but
surely it would not have been considered that I could possibly accept it to be satisfactory to myself, especially when
I look back to other officers who have retired before me,
and whose services have been much more favourably
considered than even what I asked to be done for me,
although they had not served the Company so long as
myself—in the first case by twenty-four years, in the
second case by ten years. Even a station master, who
had not served the Company so long by ten years, was
paid one year's wages. After these precedents, I feel
fully justified in asking you and the directors to kindly

re-consider my moderate request. I think that it is neither yours nor the directors' desire to see an old officer of the Company, after devoting his energies during the best part of a long lifetime in enhancing the interests of the Company, that he should be left for the remainder of his lifetime to be knocking at the door of the union workhouse. However, to cast me into such a position, I fear my friends in Yorkshire will be asking what wrongs I have committed to justify my long— nearly forty-nine years—services, to be so unfairly dealt with. I am well aware that I shall receive some allowance from the superannuation fund, but remember I have made monthly payments into that fund from its commencement, in 1873. The others whom I have named had similar advantages, if they had chosen to do so   "Yours obediently,
                    "THOMAS NORMINGTON."

On April 4th I received a reply to mine of the 2nd inst , to say that the Company contributed large sums of money to the superannuation fund, and the directors strongly objected to any additional payment being made to me.

On June 10th I replied to the letter received on April 4th. I said : "In reply to yours, since that time I have written twice to the secretary of the Superannuation Fund, with the view of my case being considered specially by that committee, and to exercise the powers given to them in rules 4, 6, and 7, to allow me to make back years' contributions, a sufficient number to be added to my membership which would ensure my superannuation allowance being increased by £1 per week. I have received a reply to say that my desire cannot be entertained, although I had served the Company more than twenty-six years prior to the fund being established ; therefore circumstances force me again to appeal to the directors, through you, to kindly exercise on my behalf their powers, specified in section 34, to supplement my superannuation allowance by £1 per week, if even only for two years. I need not say that I feel somewhat degraded to think that my forty-nine years' services to the Company—thirty-six of which I occupied the position of district superintendent, and is not worthy of being appreciated, at any rate equally at least with a station master or goods inspector, whom I know had a grant of twelve months' wages on their retirement, although they also had not served the Company so long by ten years. I should be more satisfied if my services were even as favourably acknowledged as by granting to me twelve months' salary.

"I am very sorry indeed to be so much disappointed. I have always considered that I had a just claim upon the Company for the extra continuous hard work which devolved upon me, particularly from 1859 up to the change of management in 1871, owing to the superintendent's staff at that time being only the superintendent and the assistant, with one office clerk, to contend with the entire management of the Yorkshire Division ; in fact, I find from entries that it was day and night work for myself, including even Sundays. At that time the directors acknowledged I was underpaid for services rendered, and promised me if I would remain with them I should be eventually made all right. I undertook to do the Excursion Agency, in addition to my own duties, and saved the Company close upon £3,000, which would otherwise have had to be paid in agents' commission, these being the years when the dividends to the shareholders rose to $9\frac{1}{4}$ per cent Upon these and other grounds I justify my claim, which was prior to the establishment of the superannuation fund.

"Yours obediently,
"THOMAS NORMINGTON."

On June 13th I received a reply to mine of the 10th, as follows · "I regret to say I am unable to do more than has already been communicated to you."

On July 15th I wrote to acknowledge having received the grant of half-year's salary awarded to me by the directors in recognition of my forty-nine years' services to the Company, for which I thanked them. "Nevertheless, I am sure, if you were in my place, knowing that others who had retired, and not having served the Company as long, but still were more favourably considered, you would come to the same conclusion as myself, and say that you had not been fairly or justly dealt with. I have been asked by some of the old shareholders in Yorkshire as to the recognition the directors had made in my case, and on my telling them they became very sore, and purposed bringing the matter before the shareholders at the next half-yearly meeting, with the view of my long services as officer of the Company being more justly acknowledged. I have no desire for my railway career to terminate in such an unprecedented manner.

"I have therefore determined, with the view of maintaining my future pecuniary requirements, to try the shareholders to do me some justice in another way, by subscribing to a book I am about to write on my observations and recollections during my forty-nine years on the Lancashire and Yorkshire Railway. I presume you will raise no objection to the correspondence which has passed between myself and you in reference to the question of my retirement being inserted in my book.

"Yours obediently,

"Thomas Normington.

"J. H. Stafford, Esq., General Manager,
"Lancashire and Yorkshire Railway, Manchester."

On July the 16th I received a reply to mine of the 15th, telling me that the publishing of such a book as I named would not, he thought, be a profitable speculation.

It will be observed, from the above correspondence in reference to my retirement, the effort I made and the right I had previously earned to ensure a sufficient allowance during my lifetime to maintain the position I had held with the Company and the public for forty-nine years, thirty-six of which I held as district superintendent. Yet the moderate figures which I submitted were not half the amount that had been awarded to other superintendents who had retired before me. The directors attempted to cover their generosity and justice by falling back on the superannuation fund. I then appealed to the committee which controlled the superannuation fund to help me out of my difficulty, and I also failed there. I then turned again to the directors to justify my conditions, and considered I had a good and honest claim upon the Company for the twenty-seven years' services rendered prior to the establishment of the superannuation fund, seeing that the superintendent who retired in 1871 was allowed to retain his full salary up to the end of his life, although he had only served the Company twenty-five years. But still they held their determination not to do justice to an old officer. They carried out the narrow-minded policy of their management even unto myself.

After my retirement I considered it would not be advisable to give up altogether my active life. I therefore looked out for a place of residence in the country, with the view of curtailing my expenses, and to gain assistance in the several occupations; also to persevere in what had already been so beneficial to my health since 1868. After that date I distributed my annual leave of absence to an occasional day's shooting during the season, this arrangement being agreed to by the directors, through my medical adviser, and hope to continue my open-air exercise so long as I am able.

During that time I had many sporting dogs, but the one that died on Tuesday, the 15th of December, 1894, aged 13 years, was the best I ever had. I will give a few instances of his sagacity. He was a black, wavy-haired, large retriever, a good all-round one-gun sportsman's dog. We had travelled thousands of miles together to the various shooting grounds He never required looking after when travelling either at railway stations or elsewhere. The dog looked after his master, and was always there when wanted. He was eleven months old when sent to me on trial. The first day I had him out with the gun, I was crossing a fallow field, making my way to the railway station. The dog made a stop; I called him on, but he would not move from his position. I thought what a stupid dog I had got, and turned back to give him a good whipping. Just before I got to him, I was surprised to see a fine hare jump up some forty yards away I fired my gun and thought I had killed it, and told the dog to fetch it in. But before he got to the place the hare bolted with a broken leg. I sent him after it; he had a good chase over the next field, and both disappeared through the hedgerow. After waiting some fifteen minutes I walked towards the fence where I had seen them disappear, when I saw the dog coming across the next field with the hare in his mouth. He gave it up to me alive, giving me a winning look, showing the white corner of his eye, as much as to say, " Will this do for you ? " I then named him Jack the Boy, and decided he should be my dog at whatever price.

The following season I was out for a day's shooting with two friends in the neighbourhood of Ripon. We threw off to range a rough pasture field on the river side. My position was nearest the river. After going a short distance a cock pheasant got up nearest the far gun to my right. He fired both barrels, but missed the bird. The pheasant was making its way to cross the river to the covert behind us. Coming nearer the middle gun, he also fired, and appeared to have missed. The bird then came nearer to me in passing to the left. I fired a barrel and winged it, when it dropped amongst some high-standing reeds at the other side of the river. My friends remarked how unfortunate to lose the bird, there being no means whatever of our crossing the broad deep river. I said to my dog, "Jack," at the same time pointing towards where the bird dropped, "fetch it, old boy." Away he went across the river amongst the reeds; we all three stood, watching the result. To our surprise, we saw him come out of the reeds some five hundred yards away, swimming across the river with the bird in his mouth. He gave it up to me, alive and dry. My two friends, who were both old sportsmen, declared they never saw a bird so cleverly retrieved; and after the day's sport, they said that whenever I went again for a day's shooting I was not to forget to bring "Jack the Boy."

I well remember one December day being out for a day's shooting, and, of course, having "Jack the Boy" with me. It commenced to snow about midday, the snow continuing to fall steadily throughout the day. About two o'clock we squatted on the snow under a hedgerow to eat our lunch. Seeing that the snow was getting very deep on the ground, and that the branches of the trees, hedgerows, and the underwood in the coverts were all drooping with its weight, although I had made a poor bag, I determined to give it up, and on making my way to the railway station I had to cross a field along the side of a covert, when Jack suddenly stopped, and showed me the white of his eye, which I understood meant that game was scented. The weather being so severe, and darkness coming on, I thought it was not possible to see to shoot anything, and called him away. I had not gone very far when he stopped again. I said, "Go in, you old fool," and away he went. Shortly after I heard a pheasant rise amongst the snow - laden trees, and saw it skimming along under the drooping branches. I fired my gun, but could not tell whether I had hit the bird or not. After waiting some ten minutes, I whistled in my dog. Soon after I saw him some four hundred yards away in the next field, to my surprise, coming with the bird in his mouth. He gave it to me alive, with a broken wing, and from the appearance of the dog he had evidently had a hard chase. He was always strong on pheasants, and always seemed so proud when retrieving them. We have had many rough and enjoyable days together. We never feared rain, frost, cold, or snowy weather. We have often ranged about the fields, I with icicles hanging from my beard, and the black dog made white with frost and snow. He never killed or mangled his game, but retrieved them home alive when wounded. Besides his retrieving propensity, he seemed to have the qualities of a setter dog, as, when ranging a field, he would take his distance in the range, and stop at any game he scented squatting. The last time we were out together for a day's sport was on Saturday, December 22nd, 1894. We were ranging a beanfield for partridges. On my arriving at the top of the field I missed the dog, and asked the man I had with me where he had seen him last. Pointing to the place, he said it was where he had seen a pheasant get up. I turned and whistled him in. Not answering to the whistle, and knowing his weak condition, I thought something was wrong, and went back in search of him. On the side of the hedgerow there was a deep dyke covered over with brambles and deep grass. I saw his head in the distance, peeping through the rough grass which covered the top of the dyke. It was not possible for him to have got out without help. I went and sat down beside him, put down my gun, and said, "My poor old Jack, here we are—one, two, three—myself, my dog, and gun, all grown old together, and have never feared cold or stormy weather." Jack's feelings may be better imagined than described when he found himself being conveyed in a trap to the railway station. He lingered some two or three months, and after his death I felt as though I had lost a true and faithful friend, and a friend that had never deceived me.

INDEX.

JOHN HEYWOOD, Excelsior Printing and Bookbinding Works, Manchester

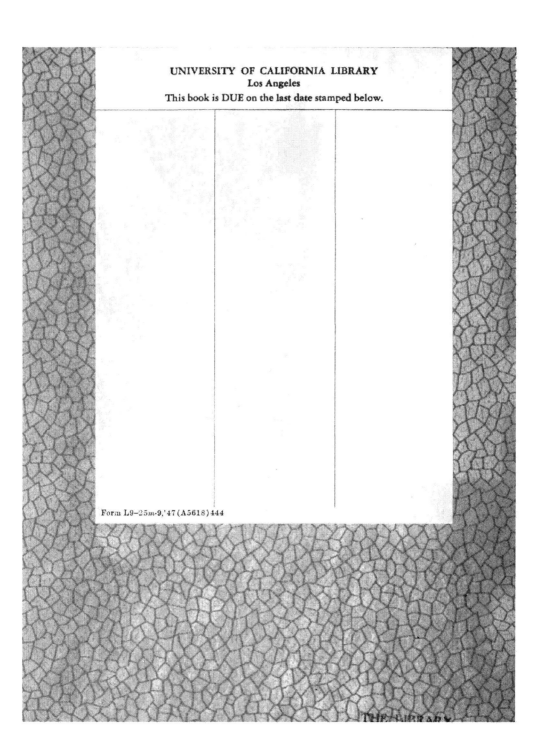

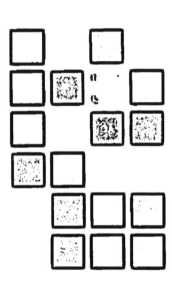